Politics in Western Europe

A Comparative Analysis

THIRD EDITION

Gordon Smith

HOLMES & MEIER PUBLISHERS, INC. • New York

Third edition first published in
the United States of America 1980 by
Holmes & Meier Publishers, Inc.
30 Irving Place
New York, N.Y. 10003

First edition published in the United States of America 1973 by
Holmes & Meier Publishers, Inc.

Library of Congress Cataloging in Publication Data
Smith, Gordon R
    Politics in Western Europe.

    Includes bibliographies and indexes.
    1. Europe – Politics and government. 2. Comparative
government. I. Title.
JN94.A5S63   1980   320.3'094   80-81211

ISBN 0-8419-0627-0
ISBN 0-8419-0628-9 (pbk.)

Manufactured in the United States of America.

Contents

Preface

In writing *Politics in Western Europe*, I have had two aims in mind. The first is to give a rounded account of European politics; frequently one finds the political affairs of the smaller countries are neglected in contrast with the generous coverage extended to, say, Britain and France. As a remedy, I have taken a wide variety of examples in the hope that the reader will gain an insight to the politics of several states. The second aim is to provide a link between the study of individual countries and the requirements of a more general comparative perspective; in this I have sought to show the similar patterns and trends, without at the same time glossing over the real differences in national and political institutions. If the book fulfils both these aims, then it should be of use to students specifically concerned with European Studies and to those reading Comparative Politics.

Throughout the book the emphasis is on making an across-the-board comparison, and in so doing it would not be feasible to give a detailed account of the political structures of the individual states. However, within each of the major themes I have tried to strike a balance between general interpretation and the provision of sufficient background information. So that the reader is able to have some of this in a compact form, there is a final section, 'The Nations of Western Europe', giving a short political profile of each country, a summary of recent elections and political developments, and suggested reading.

The underlying theme is that of 'political balance' as this is shown in the liberal democracies of Europe, in their societies and their political institutions. But it is just as relevant to examine the stresses to which liberal democracy is subject and the non-democratic forms which can ultimately result—for this reason I have also included an account of the recent West European dictatorships.

'Western Europe' in this book is simply Europe minus the Communist states; it is notoriously difficult to define and justify any particular 'area' to be taken as the springboard for comparison, and the motley of European states is no exception. It is possible to point to their common reliance on a market economy and to their shared historical experiences; yet both features apply to a number of non-European countries as well. However, for the states with which we are concerned there is an important additional factor which involves an element of self-selection. This is the momentum towards economic and political integration which, in varying degrees, affects them all. Ortega Y Gasset viewed the feeling for and the idea of 'nationality' as Europe's 'most characteristic' discovery. Yet at the present time a reverse process is under way—a movement beyond the nation-state as the means of political innovation; it is relevant therefore that the final chapter should be concerned with the problems and forms of European integration.

In taking a deliberately wide canvas for this comparative study, there are bound to be certain deficiencies, especially in interpreting the significance of one country's politics as part of a more general pattern; nevertheless the attempt is worth making, for it is in comparison that we can best appreciate the texture of one nation's politics. And apart from this, a comparative treatment can open up a stimulating discussion; in these respects I hope that my own assessment will be a contribution.

Since *Politics in Western Europe* was first published in 1972, the European scene has altered in various ways—most notably we can now refer to the Greek, Portuguese and Spanish dictatorships in the past tense. For this third edition an amount of the original material has been revised and up-dated, but the basic arguments still appear to be valid. I realise there is a case for making changes in the structure, and possibly to present some issues with greater attention to their subtle features. However, an extensive revision might also weaken the primary purpose of the book: to provide an introductory account of European politics.

G.S.
October 1979

1

Introduction—The Politics of Liberal Democracy

THE MAJOR concern of this book can be simply stated: it is with how the democracies of Western Europe handle their political affairs. And we can best begin by taking a general view of the hallmarks of these states; in effect, this means examining the significant features of *liberal* democracy. There would be little disagreement about the importance of the three aspects we shall deal with here, even if the value placed upon them varies from one interpreter to another. We can say that a typical liberal democracy provides three things:

> mechanisms of political choice;
> balanced political structures;
> a stable political system.

These three characteristics are, of course, related one with another, and the general reputation of stability which liberal democracies have can be seen as a product of the other two—that choice provides the opportunity for political balance, and that choice and balance together foster stable democracy by giving satisfactory channels through which demands on the political system can be made. Such a highly-compressed account, however, misses out the context in which choice, balance, and stability operate; we should look at each term in more detail.

The premium which liberal democracies put on freedom of choice is in its *origins* an economic freedom rather than a political one, that is to say, one bound up with the free operation of the market system. A growing market economy established several requirements: the ability for individuals to accumulate capital, the mobility of both capital and labour, the basic freedom of contract, and above all the unimpeded operation of market forces to provide the most favourable situation for the exercise of rational economic choice. Historically, economic liberalism was the precondition for political liberalism, and there is certainly a tight relationship between the development of capitalism and the rise of liberal democracy—as Macpherson points out: 'Liberal democracy is found only in countries whose economic system is wholly or predominantly that

1

of capitalist enterprise . . . It would indeed be surprising if this close cor-respondence between liberal democracy and capitalism were merely coin-cidental.'[1] The demand for political choice acted as an important supple-ment to the market economy, but it was not primarily a democratic de-mand, rather a way of securing the foundations of the whole system. Each with its own set of institutions, economic and political choice developed in tandem.

As long as the power to exercise political choice was restricted to the few, the institutions needed only to develop a rudimentary form, but in their modern and democratic expression they are well-defined and various: fully-representative institutions, unrestricted party formation, freely-contested elections, and the operation of a competitive party system. They all hang together: if any of them is entirely eliminated then the basis for exercising democratic choice vanishes. Underlying them all is the recognition of 'legitimate opposition'; this is the cardinal principle of a liberal democracy, and in its institutional form it acts as the summation of all the others. Dahl has described the institution of 'opposition' as, 'one of the greatest and most unexpected social discoveries' that man has ever stumbled upon.[2] It is no exaggeration to say that the entire political mechanism of the liberal democratic state revolves around this one basic 'axiom'. Not only is it fundamental to the other institutions of political choice, it is also the motor of peaceful government succession. The possibility of choosing and changing governments enables minorities to establish a stable relationship with political authority and power.

If these minorities are unable to win power for themselves, their rights as a minority are nevertheless entrenched in the political system by the various balances which operate. The idea of legitimate opposition is itself an integral part of balance, but it is supplemented by a whole group of checks. There is first the belief in 'limited' as opposed to absolute government—expressed another way it is the principle of *qualified* majority rule. The sum total of these balancing arrangements is seen by Vile to amount to, '. . . a frank acknowledgement of the role of government in society, linked with the determination to bring that government under control and to place limits on the exercise of its power'.[3] This is no less than the doctrine of constitutionalism, the mainspring of all devices which seek to combine effective government by the majority with a concern for individual and minority rights.

Just how much government intervention is compatible with the leading precepts of liberal democracy—justice, liberty, equality, and property rights—is problematic. The attempt to give them all a substantive content, that is, to create 'positive freedoms', must make for continuous and expan-ding government action, not least in ironing out the contradictions that any one of them involves with the others. Anyway, the balance provided by the strictly constitutional elements (principally those relating to the functioning of government) is only part of a wider social balance, with the political parties taking an intermediate position in linking the power of government to society.

The balance provided by a party system is said to ensure two things. Firstly, it acts as a counterpoise between the main social classes, and related to this it is a realistic expression of the plural interests in society; 'pluralism' is another way of indicating the possibilities of social balance. Essentially, the pluralist view holds that each individual is 'a universe of interests' and that no single one of them can claim his undivided loyalty. Liberal democratic society is portrayed as being composed of a host of competing and co-operating group interests, and regardless of the number of parties (as long as there is a plurality) the structuring of interests will ensure that they are adequately voiced both through the parties and at all levels of society.

This will seem an uncritical version of how liberal democracy works—almost saying that 'balance' exists by definition—yet there is no doubt that the models of choice and balance do work in some such fashion. However, a critical view will question the extent to which choice is allowed to operate and deny that, except occasionally, anything like an equal expression of divergent social interests is allowed. We can at least appreciate the theoretical justifications of liberal democracy, in its third leading characteristic, stability, and in the explanations given of this we can also see the justifications of inequality. The link between stability and the idea of balance is made explicit in a conclusion reached by Lipset: 'The available evidence suggests that the chances for stable democracy are enhanced to the extent that groups and individuals have a number of crosscutting, politically relevant affiliations.'[4] Any discussion of democratic stability, in seeking an explanation, necessarily brings to light other features as well.

Democratic 'stability' is a disarmingly deceptive term. There is a natural inclination to regard *government* stability as the central measure, to view recurring government 'crises' as evidence of a deep-seated malaise. But many countries—for instance, present-day Finland—are quite inured to frequent changes in government without showing other signs of breakdown. At the other extreme, stability may be equated with the sheer 'survival power' of the system; in this sense, the Third French Republic, racked with crisis as it was, has been the most stable democratic form since the Revolution. Should one identify stability with survival and simple longevity? The time-span must be a factor, since the undisputed models of European stable democracy—the majority of Scandinavian states, Britain, and Switzerland—owe their reputation in part to the continuity of their democratic traditions; stability in depth cannot be an overnight acquisition. But the difficulty in arriving at a common criterion is well illustrated by the case of Germany which on one set of conditions Lipset counts as an unstable democracy, whilst Eckstein described the same country as 'hyperstable'.[5] The different conclusion is related to the time factor: only since 1949 has Germany (its western part) proved to be a pillar of the liberal democratic virtues.

If it has to be conceded that general views of democratic stability are quite imprecise, then there is very little practical difficulty in assessing the situation of a particular country at a particular time. Yet the problem of accounting for stability is similarly beset by difficulties. There are numerous explanations put forward which we can group under three loose heads. There are the 'economic' explanations which show a connection between the level of economic development and democratic stability. Secondly, there are 'structural' accounts in which the emphasis is put on the compatibility of various social groupings. Thirdly, there are versions of stable democracy which concentrate on the values and beliefs of the mass of the people as well as those of key social élites.

The economic thesis is simply put by Lipset: 'The more well-to-do a nation, the greater the chances it will sustain democracy.' And in more detail, '. . . all the various aspects of economic development—industrialization, urbanization, wealth and education are so closely interrelated as to form one major factor which has the political correlate of democracy.'[6] It can easily be demonstrated that the various indices of economic well-being give the liberal democracies of Western Europe a much more favourable rating than, for instance, the three recent West European dictatorships.* This is indisputable, but it may not be a real explanation. Except by invoking 'special circumstances', the economic argument is not very helpful in explaining important lapses—such as Nazi Germany. This difficulty has led Eckstein to say that it is the timing and the rate of industrialization which helps to give the correlation between economic development and stable democracy. He points out that the high-scorers, '. . . are precisely those which developed industry most gradually, but still lead the field because of their early start . . . It becomes apparent that the level of economic development . . . matters only because the speed of economic development matters.'[7] Thus even if economic wealth is a good indicator, the reasons for stability may be found in the social effects of the *initial* changes; late or very rapid industrialization is likely to set up tensions of a structural kind. Such a formulation goes some way in explaining the weakness of the Weimar Republic; compared at least with some other European countries, Germany had industrialized both rapidly and late.

Structural explanations of stable democracy take a number of forms. The most general of them is expressed in the idea of 'mass society'. Theorists from de Tocqueville onwards have argued that the type of social structure which is inimical to stable democracy is one which is 'unstructured', where the masses stand in a direct relationship to the state. There are no adequate secondary organizations to cushion the mutual impact of

* Greece, Portugal, and Spain—see the Table of Socio-Economic Comparisons, p. 263.

élite and mass; the result is either an unstable hyper-democracy or a totalitarian system with the masses directly available for exploitation by the élites. This is given a modern rendering by Raymond Aron: 'A classless society leaves the mass of the population without any possible means of defence against the élite, . . . (and) would superimpose a unified élite upon an undifferentiated mass.'[8] The juxtaposition of 'mass' and 'élite' is integral to structural explanations of liberal democracy and provides the clue to its functioning: the recognition that élite leadership is fundamental. This is the first strand in what we can call a 'restrictive' view of democracy.[9]

Similar reservations are made by other writers. For Bendix, who applies his argument especially to Western Europe, the critical historical factor was the development of a dual concept of representation—plebiscitarian and functional. The former gave direct representation under a national government and the latter took account of the 'differential affiliation of individuals', in other words, of their unequal power position in society. 'The two ideas', says Bendix, 'reflect the hiatus between state and society in an age of equality . . . The system of representative institutions characteristic of the Western European tradition remains intact as long as this tension between the plebiscitarian idea and the idea of group representation endures, as long as the contradiction between abstract criteria of equality and the old as well as the new inequalities of the social condition is mitigated by ever new and ever partial compromises.'[10]

Bendix puts forward a theory of balanced inequalities, and in rather a different form this is also true of Eckstein whose explanation combines elements of structure and values. His standpoint is that, 'A government will tend to be stable if its authority pattern is congruent with other authority patterns in society of which it is a part.'[11] Since by their very nature governments must be commanding (if not authoritarian) in character, the theory of congruence requires that other parts of the political system should be so as well—especially the politically-relevant parts of society which 'impinge on government'. Thus in British stable democracy the cabinet system finds its congruent twin in the structure of the political parties: 'At no point in the segmentation of British society is there any abrupt and large change in authority patterns, and throughout one finds at least some imitation of government forms.' Eckstein contrasts the British situation with that of the Weimar Republic—in the latter, political life was democratic but social life was still authoritarian: 'Not only were society and polity to some degree incongruent; they existed in a unprecedented contradiction to one another.'[12] He concludes that the pattern of government authority should be a mixture of democratic norms and traditional–authoritarian elements, an amalgam which takes account of the undemocratic aspects of society. His finding is firmly in the restrictive vein: 'Governmental democracy will tend to be stable only if it is to a significant degree impure.'[13]

Not surprisingly, the third general version of stable democracy, based on people's values and beliefs, is equally restrictive. We can take the theory of the 'civic culture' as being representative of this type of explanation. Gabriel Almond and Sidney Verba contrast the 'classical' ideas of how a democracy should work with the reality. In its classic rendering, one supposed the ideal-typical citizen to participate fully in political life, basing his actions and his vote on sound judgement, the model 'rationally-active' citizen. However little that accords with what anyone really thought about the way democracy works is another matter,[14] but it is a sharp contrast indeed if one argues that there is, in fact, a useful role for political apathy in a liberal democracy—that a high voting turnout may be evidence of instability. A case in point which supports this view is the high participation at the Reichstag elections prior to the demise of the Weimar Republic, with mass support for the Nazi Party—what Kurt Schumacher, the German Social Democrat, once called 'the mobilization of human stupidity'.

The general theme advanced by Almond and Verba is unambiguous: 'There exists in Britain and the United States a pattern of political attitudes and an underlying set of social attitudes that is supportive of a stable democratic process.'[15] This particular mixture of attitudes, called the 'civic culture' does preserve the traits of the model, active citizen, but it combines them with other attitudes of passivity, uninvolvement, even a shade of deference. There is respect for government and a pride in political and other institutions together with a wide-spread trust in others and in public officials. There is also a high *potential* in the civic culture for the individual to become involved. But for stable democracy it is better if this remains a potentiality—the responsible citizen will normally consider 'other things' more important than politics. There is thus an active-passive balance which provides a good 'fit' with the needs of democratic government—government power tempered by a responsiveness to the needs of the people. A government has the authority to govern, but it must be ever-wary of the 'potentially-active citizen'. Typically, in such a stable democracy as Britain, there will be 'cycles of citizen involvement, élite response, and citizen withdrawal',[16] the attitudes of the political élites neatly complementing those of the ordinary citizen, and he, '. . . must turn power over to élites and let them rule.'[17]

The original survey conducted by Almond and Verba also included West Germany and Italy, and these lacked the attributes of the civic culture. The Italian political culture is portrayed as one of 'relatively unrelieved political alienation and of social isolation and distrust'.[18] With little in the way of national pride, citizen competence, or participation the average Italian could contribute little to stable democracy. The German citizen's view could be described as one of political detachment allied with confidence in government administration. Although the aloofness from politics was coupled with a high 'subject-competence', the individual satisfaction did not extend to a more general civic trust; the implication of the findings was that, though on some counts a stable democracy, West Germany lacked the reserves of commitment to weather a prolonged political crisis.

The general failing of the accounts we have given is that they frequently appear to idealize a given situation—the role of élites, power imbalances between one social group and another, widespread passivity. Alternatively, they may not amount to a causal explanation, but only provide an index in the way that economic wealth does. This objection applies to some cultural explanations of liberal democracy. Thus the theory of the 'civic culture' is entirely built up on contemporary survey material, and if, as is usually held to be the case, a country's political culture—the aggregate of knowledge, beliefs, values, and accepted behaviour in relation to politics—only changes very slowly over the years, then a current analysis is insufficient; it can only provide some scale of rating.

Brian Barry[19] points out that it is the *performance* of the democratic institutions over a period of time which gives rise to a type of political culture, simply that people who get reasonable treatment from the authorities are much more likely to develop a civic culture than those who do not; legitimacy depends on effectiveness. Barry's argument has other important implications which can be used to counter vague allusions to democratic 'consensus' and 'legitimacy'. Belief in the legitimacy of democratic government has to be sharpened to mean, 'legitimacy in the eyes of the appropriate people',[20] and this implies alternative sets of legitimacy depending on the situation. It leads to the question: which groups by the withdrawal of their support will endanger or even topple the system? The close association of legitimacy and support, with the latter ultimately dependent on the satisfaction of demands made on the political system, brings us to the brink of saying that system performance is the real determinant of stable democracy. As a consequence structural and value-related explanations take on a subordinate role, and, as Barry concludes: 'Values are at best the last link in the chain of causation before behaviour itself.'[21] One can make this point in a rather different way via the concept of political culture. The process of political socialization imparts the values and beliefs of the prevailing culture and in doing this it underpins the legitimacy of the political authorities and the ruling groups. Yet the socialization process also *generates a set of expectations* concerning how the political system *should* operate, and if these expectations are continually disappointed, then the whole edifice will become suspect; political socialization works more than one way.

The wide claims sometimes made for the liberal version of democracy go back to the optimism of the nineteenth century liberal ideal, especially as viewed by Isaiah Berlin, with its belief, '. . . in the unlimited power of education and the power of rational morality to overcome economic misery and inequality'.[22] But this optimism was later to be tempered with the realistic requirement of a 'democratic élitism', even if there was the concession that the élites should be 'open' and 'responsive'. The open question is whether this combination of idealism and realism, the liberal democratic method, shows a sufficient appreciation of the realities of social power, whether its reliance on political techniques and parliamentary majorities is adequate to bring about basic social change. Maurice Cornforth is representative of those who argue that the proponents of liberal democracy, '. . . deceive us about democracy . . . in their assumption that the "democratic institutional control of power" operates independently of classes, class interests and class struggles.' Furthermore: 'The causes of inequalities in property relations and class relations remain . . . only glossed over, but not alleviated, by the existence of certain "equalities" of political rights and "equality before the law".'[23]

Yet these criticisms do not gainsay the resilience of liberal democracy in Western Europe. Political choice and political balance may have worked in favour of the established class élites, but what of the social interests which were thereby deprived? European socialism in the nineteenth and early twentieth centuries rejected the values of the capitalist market economy and the terms of the new industrialism. Socialist parties first sought the legal and political rights of citizenship as the first step in transforming society, but once having chalked up these victories, they increasingly made use of the liberal political system as the means of satisfying their further economic and social demands; in so doing they also came to accept the essential tenets of the market system. Parliamentary socialism was destined to become a bulwark of the liberal democratic state and to become so without losing the support of its mass following.

This is a necessarily brief account of the features, assumptions, and explanations of liberal democracy. Yet all the topics touched on here return in one guise or another in the course of the following chapters. Their relevance will be evident in looking at the social basis of political loyalties, the nature of the political parties, and the forms and function of opposition. This also is true of the later chapters: the implications of constitutionalism, the relationship of parliaments to governments, the challenges made to the liberal democratic order. Taken together, a study of these facets of West European politics should lead to a view of democratic stability and the terms of its future development.

NOTES AND REFERENCES

1. C. B. Macpherson, *The Real World of Democracy*, Oxford University Press, 1966, p. 4.
2. R. A. Dahl (ed.), *Political Oppositions in Western Democracies*, New Haven: Yale University Press, 1966, p. xvii.
3. M. J. C. Vile, *Constitutionalism and the Separation of Powers*, Oxford University Press, 1967, p. 1.
4. S. M. Lipset, *Political Man*, Heinemann, 1960, pp. 88–9.

5. Lipset, op. cit., p. 49. H. Eckstein, 'A Theory of Stable Democracy', appearing as an appendix in his *Division and Cohesion in Democracy: A Study of Norway*, New Jersey: Princeton University Press, 1966, p. 271.
6. Lipset, op. cit., p. 50 and p. 58.
7. Eckstein, 'A Theory of Stable Democracy,' op. cit., p. 279.
8. R. Aron, 'Social Structure and the Ruling Class', in L. Coser (ed.), *Political Sociology, Selected Essays*, New York: Harper and Row, 1966, pp. 82, 91.
9. An 'impure' element is also introduced by the theory of 'consociational democracy', originally formulated by Arend Lijphart. The consociational model attempts to account for the phenomenon of the 'stable yet fragmented' democracies, primarily the smaller ones in Western Europe such as the Netherlands and Switzerland. The important modification of the pluralist version of democracy lies in the independent role ascribed to the political and social elites. Despite the existence of social cleavages—and to an extent overriding them—the elites seek to reach a harmonious accommodation with one another. Thus the inter-elite bargains are seen as a prerequisite for continuing democratic stability. See A. Lijphart (ed.), *Politics in Europe*, Prentice-Hall, 1969; also, K. McRae (ed.), *Consociational Democracy: Political Accommodation in Segmented Societies*, Toronto: McClelland and Stewart, 1974.
10. R. Bendix, *Nation-Building and Citizenship*, New York: Wiley, 1964, pp. 101–4.
11. Eckstein, op. cit., p. 234.
12. ibid., pp. 247 and 248.
13. ibid., p. 262.
14. It can be argued that a 'classical' theory of liberal democracy never really existed even in the nineteenth century. See Carole Pateman, *Participation and Democratic Theory*, Cambridge University Press, 1970.
15. G. Almond and S. Verba, *The Civic Culture: Political Attitudes and Democracy in Five Nations*, New Jersey: Princeton University Press, 1963, p. vii.
16. ibid., p. 484.
17. ibid., p. 478.
18. ibid., pp. 402–3.
19. B. Barry, *Sociologists, Economists and Democracy*, Collier-Macmillan, 1970, p. 51.
20. ibid., p. 67.
21. ibid., p. 96.
22. Isaiah Berlin, 'Political Ideas in the Twentieth Century', in R. C. Macridis (ed.), *Political Parties: Contemporary Trends and Ideas*, New York: Harper and Row, 1967, p. 209.
23. M. Cornforth, *The Open Philosophy and the Open Society*, Lawrence and Wishart, 1968, p. 271 and p. 285.

Additional References

G. Almond and S. Verba (eds.), *The Civic Culture Revisited*, Boston: Little, Brown, 1979.

P. Bachrach, *The Theory of Democratic Elitism*, University of London Press, 1969.

B. Barry, 'The Consociational Model and its Dangers', *European Journal of Political Research*, vol. 3/4, December 1975.

B. Barry, 'Political Accommodation and Consociational Democracy', *British Journal of Political Science*, October 1975.

R. Bendix (ed.), *State and Society*, Boston: Little, Brown, 1968.

S. I. Benn and R. S. Peters, *Social Principles and the Democratic State*, George Allen and Unwin, 1959.

P. Birnbaum, J. Lively, G. Parry (eds.), *Democracy, Consensus and Social Contract,* Sage Publications, 1978.

L. Bramson, *The Political Context of Sociology,* Princeton University Press, 1961.

I. Budge, *Agreement and the Stability of Democracy,* New York: Rand McNally, 1970.

M. Friedman, *Capitalism and Freedom,* University of Chicago Press, 1962.

O. M. Heisler (ed.), *Politics in Europe: Structures and Processes in Some Post-Industrial Societies,* New York: David McKay, 1974.

W. Kornhauser, *The Politics of Mass Society,* Routledge and Kegan Paul, 1960.

A. Lijphart, *Democracy in Plural Societies: A Comparative Exploration,* Yale University Press, 1977.

A. Lijphart, 'Consociational Democracy', in R. J. Jackson and M. B. Stein, *Issues in Comparative Politics: A Text with Readings,* Macmillan, 1971.

A. Lijphart, 'Typologies of Democratic Systems' in A. Lijphart (ed.), *Politics in Europe,* Englewood Cliffs, New Jersey: Prentice-Hall, 1969.

J. Lively, *Democracy,* Oxford: Blackwell, 1975.

C. B. Macpherson, *The Life and Times of Liberal Democracy,* Oxford University Press, 1977.

L. Mayer, *Politics in Industrial Societies,* New York: John Wiley, 1977.

D. Nicholls, *Three Varieties of Pluralism,* Macmillan, 1974.

D. Nicholls, *The Pluralist State,* Macmillan, 1975.

J. Obler (and others), *Decision-Making in Smaller Democracies: The Consociational 'Burden',* Sage, 1977.

G. Parry, *Political Elites,* George Allen and Unwin, 1969.

G. Sartori, *Democratic Theory,* New York: Praeger, 1965.

J. A. Schumpeter, *Capitalism, Socialism and Democracy,* George Allen and Unwin, (rev. ed.) 1966.

D. W. Urwin and K. A. Eliassen, 'In Search of a Continent: The Quest of Comparative European Politics', *European Journal of Political Research,* vol. 3, 1975, pp. 85–113 (Review Article).

2

Politics and Society

The Social Bases

PEOPLE VOTE, take active part, and otherwise relate to politics in a fairly predictable and consistent way. To a great extent we can, for instance, forecast likely voting behaviour given the knowledge of one or two key variables relating to a person's socio-economic circumstances. Of these, it is usual to regard the economic influences—and the class structure to which they are related—as easily the most important. Yet even if one agrees that this is the case, there are still a number of other influences which are all to some degree independent of a strict economic interpretation: the force of nationalism, the community of language, religious commitment, contrasts in rural and urban environment.[1] Any of these can result in the formation of enclaves of loyalty which have a political significance, that is, in 'sub-cultures' which resist a uniform structuring of national politics solely on economic lines. Such situations do not arise overnight; they are the product of particular types of historical development. But their 'historical' nature does not diminish their importance: often it is these non-economic alignments which provide the ingredients for head-on political conflict, rather than the muted contest of class politics, and even when these alignments are not paramount, they can still act to modify national politics in such a way that each country presents a different line-up of social forces—best seen in the nature of their party systems.

The countries of Western Europe are broadly similar in the stage of their economic development, and this similarity extends to the class structure based on a common experience of the market economy of capitalist systems. All the same, there are still wide differences in the level of economic wealth,* and political differences are evident too. Indeed, Europe displays a variety of political culture and 'styles'—even if the liberal democratic form of government is the norm; to explain the diversity we have to take account of the basic social features of each country—historically-conditioned factors—to understand why one country, Britain, presents a picture of a broadly homogeneous society,

* For various measures of economic development, see the table on p. 263 below.

whilst a second, Italy, is rent by political cleavage, and a third, the Netherlands, manages to contain a diversity of political allegiance within an overall consensus, for which 'consociational democracy' is one explanation.

The term 'homogeneous' in the sense we have used it here, needs some explanation; it does not mean that political loyalties are distributed randomly throughout the population regardless of socio-economic differences, but that there is only *one* major variable which has a political relevance. In a completely homogeneous society, real differences in wealth and social class are apparent, but the other influences we have mentioned are not politically operative. This may be because there is only one language, a single, and undisputed, religion, and because the society is completely urbanized. Alternatively, it may be that the 'other influences' are distributed equally throughout society regardless of social class, and possibly for this reason they fail to result in the throwing-up of live political issues.[2]

Some European countries are anything but homogeneous in their political make-up. Blondel uses the term 'sectionalism' to describe such situations where, 'the distribution of variables . . . depart(s) significantly from a normal distribution',[3] to give a cluster of social and cultural traits associated with the major variable—usually to be taken as the underlying class structure.* Thus a high degree of sectionalism occurs in those countries where class differences are compounded by other, apparently independent, social and cultural distinctions. In a sectional society, the economic issues need not appear to be the critical ones; the intensity of conflict may be shown in other ways. The peculiar sharpness of non-economic questions may arise, as Rose and Urwin have pointed out,[4] because the disputants put forward claims which are essentially 'non-bargainable'—the Pope is either infallible or he is not; against this, economic conflict is made up of a host of issues, all open to some compromise—accommodation in terms of 'more' or 'less' or resolution by economic growth and social mobility—so that decisive confrontation is continually postponed.

The force of sectionalism is that it can harden economic conflict to give two irreconcilable camps. Thus the issue of clericalism in Italy follows the left-right axis fairly closely. Anti-clericalism reinforces anti-capitalism, and the two issues become intertwined; the Catholic Church also becomes an object of attack because of its vast material wealth. Geographical factors add a further dimension to sectionalism: it is not just the disparities of wealth and their association with non-economic differences, but the occurrence of these in well-defined areas which make for the most implacable cleavages.[5] Any concentration of national minorities will help cement a sub-culture, and on an economic level, certain regions may become per-

* For a diagrammatic rendering of various models of 'homogeneous' and 'sectional' society, see 'Social Cleavages and Party Systems', pp. 33–6 below.

manently underprivileged, with rural poverty or declining industry; these may show political tendencies contrary to more fortunate parts of a country.

However, it would be wrong to describe a homogeneous society as of necessity 'conflict-free', or a sectional society as 'conflict-ridden'. In conditions of homogeneity, class differences will be the major determinant of political behaviour—the unresolved question here is whether this must mean an intensification of class conflict, and one which we shall have to consider. Likewise, a sectional society need not be one of continual conflict—especially where the sectionalism fails to generate one major line of cleavage. In the case of the Netherlands, the presence of two major Churches, Protestant and Catholic, together with a strong secular influence, combined to make economic issues less relevant: a supporter of the Catholic People's Party or of one of the Protestant parties might be rich or poor, farmer, businessman, or trade unionist. The phenomenon of the three 'pillars' of Dutch society, its *Verzuiling,* is an expression for the existence of at least three distinctive sub-cultures: Catholic, Protestant, and a 'general' latitudinarian one—the last of which itself subdivides into Liberals and Socialists on a political plane.* We may describe this as a vertical division of Dutch society; its effect is to cut across the horizontal divisions of the class structure, preventing the formation of 'armed camps' which one naturally associates with sectionalism. In a less pronounced fashion, any relatively homogeneous society will show a similar tendency: non-economic considerations act to blur the significance of the class structure without themselves coming to the forefront. And where any single commitment fails to be exclusive, people are subject to a number of cross-pressures which act against a single, major line of conflict becoming the sole preoccupation. It is the balance provided by an individual's competing loyalties that is seen as a precondition for stable democracy. To this extent, both the 'weak' sectional societies exemplified by the Netherlands† and a homogeneous society with a muted class polarization are capable of containing political differences.

No two European states follow the same political pattern; yet one can argue that there is an underlying similarity, a common trend for the non-economic influences to decline in political salience, leaving the economic issues, and related aspects of social class, exposed as the main determinant of political activity. We can best examine this contention by first reviewing the main roots of party politics today.

Language and National Minorities

The rather untidy patchwork of European states has one great merit: it

* For a listing of the individual parties, see the table, 'Party Systems in Western Europe', pp. 98–9.

† For a diagram illustrating the political structure of Dutch Society, see p. 34 below.

means that national boundaries generally run along language frontiers; the force of national aspirations in the past has resulted in a relatively large number of independent states, and removed one of the most fertile sources of political stress: the national minority. In this century, the three latecomers to national independence—Finland, Ireland, and Iceland—have substantially defined the European limits of national self-determination.

For most countries, the presence of linguistic minorities is no real problem. Thus in Finland the Swedish People's Party, representing the ten per cent of Swedish-speakers, is a gradually declining force. In Norway, the *Nynorsk* movement arose as a neo-Norwegian language form based on various dialects, an expression of 'cultural defence' against city influences and therefore a type of rural-urban conflict; but the only residual problem is how the two language variants can best be amalgamated. The German-Danish frontier gives rise to small linguistic minorities on both sides; the parties representing their interests are no longer significant, and their protection rests on an inter-state treaty. Similarly, a bitter, fifty-year dispute between Austria and Italy was resolved in 1971 by giving the German-speaking inhabitants of the South Tyrol (Alto Adige) a measure of cultural and political autonomy; the South Tyrol People's Party is now an integral part of the Italian party system.

There are, however, still a number of dissident minorities: the Basques in Spain, Bretons in France, Catholics in Northern Ireland, Scottish and Welsh Nationalists. The presence of a linguistic element is not a necessary feature, and the movements differ considerably in the extent of their demands and the means they are prepared to employ. Their activities may be felt as no more than pin-pricks to national unity, but their minority position makes it difficult for the minorities to work for a parliamentary majority or rely on conventional politics alone: there is the possibility of a swift progression from protest and disruption to violence and fervent terrorism. The Basque minority in Spain (only some five per cent of the total population) conforms exactly to the extremist model, and the transition to parliamentary democracy from dictatorship has not altered Basque claims nor has it led to a reliance on peaceful methods. A 'national minority' can represent the most intractable problem for any political system.

Two countries are notable exceptions to the rule of linguistic homogeneity, Switzerland and Belgium; the contrast between them is enlightening. The similarity is the presence of a very large language minority in both countries. The Flemish (Dutch-speaking) Belgians are in a majority with 55 per cent of the population, and in Switzerland German is the main language of 65 per cent. In both cases, French-speakers are in a large minority, with other very small minorities as well—German-speaking in Belgium, Italian and Romansch in Switzerland. That language differences alone do not lead to fundamental cleavage is amply demonstrated in Switzerland, where there have been no linguistic-cultural parties of any importance. Part of the answer may lie in the degree of decentralization provided by the federal structure*—though the significance of this has to be appreciated in terms of historical growth rather than as a ready-made formula. What it does mean is that issues of a cultural-linguistic nature are resolved at a point below the federal level. The relation of the language frontiers to the political boundaries of the cantons is of some importance: although the linguistic divisions are clearly defined, they tend to cut *across* many of the cantonal boundaries; it is the religious boundaries which follow more closely those of the cantons. Whichever language a person speaks, the really important loyalty is to the canton, and this loyalty is reinforced by the relative religious homogeneity within the canton. In a sense, the Swiss cantons are a parallel to the vertical 'pillars' of Dutch society.

The ingredients of the Belgian language issue are fairly simple, even if the political implications have become complex. Belgium is an overwhelmingly Catholic country, a unitary state, with a clear language frontier, little-changed since the Middle Ages, running east-west across the country with French-speaking Walloons to the south and the Flemish to the north. The position of Brussels has come to highlight the problems involved: historically it is a Flemish city, and well within the Flemish area, but the city itself is now largely French-speaking. For long, the French language was that of the dominant élite—economic, social, and governmental; in contrast the Flemings were the poor country cousins, with little to contribute to Belgian culture, and a language that was an amalgam of dialects. Above all, outside the large cities, Flanders was economically backward. Brussels became symbolic of Walloon and Francophone predominance.

What has changed in recent times is the economic fortunes of the two areas. Flemish nationalism was slow to develop; in the course of the First World War it took a 'disloyal' and separatist line, but since then most of the language demands have been met—in the fields of education, law, and administration. Yet the tensions between the two communities have persisted; the formal parity which was gradually achieved went along with the changing economic balance in favour of Flanders. Wallonian economic supremacy vanished as the older, heavy industries declined, and Flanders benefited from new industry and a progressive agriculture. The economic antagonism was well-shown in the course of a strike by Limburg (Flemish) coalminers in 1970, who alleged that the price of their coal (and therefore their wages) was being held down as a form of hidden subsidy to the uneconomic Wallonian steel industry around Liège. Thus it is the turn of the minority French-speaking population to be on the defen-

* See below, pp. 211–18.

sive, but French is still the dominant language, epitomized in the position of Brussels—now three-quarters French-speaking—a thorn in the side of Flemish aspirations.

There is a mutual suspicion: Wallonian economic weakness is accentuated by the minority position of the French speakers (40 per cent); with justification in the past, the Flemish felt the effects of cultural discrimination and now see their numerical supremacy and economic progress as means to redress the balance. In this, the Brussels-question is pivotal for both protagonists, with Flemish hopes to reassert its Flemish character and at the very least to halt the intrusion of the French language into the surrounding countryside. It took several years to brew up a satisfactory constitutional compromise, finally reached in July 1971. The terms of these proposals involved a large measure of regional decentralization—especially in cultural and economic affairs —with the ministers of the regional councils still responsible to the national parliament, and the councils made up of parliamentarians. At the same time, Brussels, a third 'region', had its city limits definitively fixed and was made permanently and officially bilingual, thus meeting minimum Flemish demands, but hardly satisfying the Francophones who have come to regard Brussels as 'naturally' French-speaking and the restrictions as artificial. Although the radical constitutional changes secured a large measure of inter-party agreement (Social-Christians, Socialists, and Liberals), the new formula still has to be proved in practice. The test of its acceptability is likely to be seen ultimately the fortunes of the linguistic parties. In the 1950s they counted for little in national politics. The Flemish *Volksunie* was the first to make an impact, and the French-speaking parties (*Rassemblemement Wallon* and the Brussels *Front des Francophones*) emerged later. In 1968 the total 'linguistic' vote was around 15 per cent; in November 1971 (after the constitutional compromise) it rose to well over 20 per cent. As a result, the problems of government facing the major parties were not eased at all. Furthermore the traditional parties—Social-Christians, Socialists, and Liberals—have all been deeply affected. They have had to concede the autonomy of their linguistic wings and can only preserve their unity as 'confederations' of regional parties.*

The upsurge of the language issue in Belgium, and the strains it has put upon the party system, may appear to be exceptional, but the real point may be that it is not language differences by themselves which lead to crisis, rather it is the economic and social discrimination that, wittingly or not, accompany them which leads to a fundamental cleavage. However, once the language differences become community symbols, they can take on a life of their own and lead to a peculiar intractability, and this the Belgian case well illustrates.

* For full details, see below pp. 269–71.

The 'community symbol' need not be based on language. As the distur-bances and political impasse in Northern Ireland amply demonstrate, both nationalism and religious differences can achieve a similar result. The permanent Protestant majority in Northern Ireland (approximately 65 per cent of the population) had resulted in the hegemony of the ruling Ulster Unionists for some fifty years, with no possibility of democratic erosion; indeed, this was the basis of the partition of Ireland. Yet behind the reality of Protestant dominance, there was the further reality of a social and economic discrimination, with a Roman Catholic underprivileged 'class'. Although the present crisis found its origins in the civil rights movement rather than as a religious issue, the latter soon became the operative sym-bol and the point of cleavage—the Catholic minority was also a social minority. But behind these two factors lies the third, that of Irish nationalism, and the escalation of violence since 1971 was a reassertion that ultimately there was a *colonial* problem to be solved, 'a war of in-dependence'—alternatively, a military action against 'lawless terrorists'. The painful search for a 'constitutional formula' to contain the various stresses has yet to be found; short of conceding to the Irish nationalist demands, solutions might take the direction of the Belgian reforms or even introduce elements of the Swiss collegial system of government.* Despite attempts at reform, the initial difficulty of finding a basic consen-sual element between the two communities remains the real stumbling-block.†

The Swiss situation, in contrast, is partly a result of constitutional arrangements and partly of the intermingling of the social factors, and both are the product of a long historical evolution; certainly it provides no ready-made answers. Even Switzerland has experienced its own minority problem in miniature. Beginning in 1962 there were demands for autonomy by the French-speaking minority in the Bernese Jura, and their demands eventually led to the creation in 1978 of a new canton from the existing German-dominated Canton of Bern. That case shows the ever-present potential of minority issues. Their importance may be exaggerated—apparent for both Welsh and Scottish nationalism—but very easily they can pose threats to the unity of the state.

Religion and Politics

Apart from the rather special case of Northern Ireland, most people would probably regard the religious factor in politics as of very small im-portance. It may then be surprising to learn that, 'Contrary to popular belief religion, not class, is the main social basis of parties in the west today.'[6] This does not mean, with rare exceptions, that political issues are

---

* See below, pp. 112–13, 309–11.
† See below, pp. 315–16.

seen primarily in religious terms or that religious disputes are the main content of politics, rather it is that a person's religious commitment is an important variable in deciding the direction of his political outlook and thus his voting loyalty. One can put this connection in a slightly different way: a religious standpoint merges with and corresponds to other social variables with the result that few issues are seen as purely religious or anti-clerical arguments. But by the same token very few issues are completely divorced from them either. If religion rather than social class forms the major basis of political parties, it is to be interpreted as a passive rather than an active force in the sense that religious persuasion, or lack of it, will be a good guide to party affiliation.

We can best relate our discussion to the three patterns of religious balance found in Western Europe: the mainly Roman Catholic countries, those with approximate Catholic and Protestant parity, and countries which are largely Prostestant. It is in the Roman Catholic countries that religion has the most direct political connection, and this for three reasons. The wide claims of Roman Catholicism, especially its strongly developed social doctrines, make the teachings of the Church of political relevance, so that it frequently finds itself drawn into the political arena. Secondly, its tight hierarchical structure forces it into a rigidity of attitude and thus to a ready identification with particular political lines. Thirdly, the links with Rome made it appear as an anti-national element serving ultramontane interests. These three factors can combine to give rise to strong anti-clerical sentiments, the more so when the Catholic Church in any country becomes firmly identified with particular socio-economic élites, and anti-clericalism becomes part and parcel of an attack on these élites.

In some countries, the position of the Catholic Church is so powerful that anti-clericalism scarcely arises. The nature of the regimes in Spain and Portugal was such that the Church became part of the ruling order, and an important source of legitimacy for the authoritarian rule.* Of the democratic states, the Republic of Ireland alone afforded the Catholic Church an almost unquestioned supremacy—a complete absence of anti-clericalism despite occasions when the Catholic hierarchy has actively intervened in politics; the small Irish Labour Party certainly could not afford the charge of being anti-clerical.

The more usual situation is for a sharp polarization between the Church and secular society. When this occurs, the response of the Church is to cast its net wide into the associational groupings of society, and numerous lay organizations affiliated to the Church are in evidence: trade unions, agricultural associations, women's and youth movements; these serve to underpin the summit of political Catholicism—the Christian Democratic party. The inevitable accompaniment is a similar set-up on the anti-clerical side; the product is a high degree of competitive associationalism

* See below, pp. 132–3.

which can affect the citizen at every point in his life; his later politics will be largely determined by his initial religious (or anti-clerical) contacts, and the linked associations with which he becomes involved will tend to confirm them. The classic case of social and political bifurcation was pre-war Austria. On the one side was ranged the strongly anti-clerical Socialist Party; this was, of course, class-based and largely urban, with its stronghold in Vienna, but the party by no means had a monopoly of the working-class vote. On the other side were the Christian-Socials, an out-and-out Catholic party, strongly backed by the clerical hierarchy. The Christian-Socials could gain a majority in what was virtually a two-party system because they could rely on the support of practising Catholics regardless of social class and were almost completely dominant in rural Austria. The heavy involvement of the clergy in right-wing politics was balanced on the other flank by the fervour of Socialist anti-clericalism and its 'Austro-Marxist' ideology. For their part, the Socialists were remarkable in achieving '. . . a degree of political organisation unequalled in free parties, through their system of cadres . . . they controlled the workers' leisure time by providing them with a full set of avocational organisations for everyone from cyclists to anti-alcoholics.'[7] The result was two hostile camps, and a '*lager*'-mentality to match which froze political attitudes and activity around the religious and anti-clerical polarization.*

France provides a useful contrast with Austria, since there has never been a strong and avowedly clerical party, and the Catholic Church has been simply identified with social conservatism. But religious conflict has run deep—with the village priest and the village schoolmaster the symbols of a mortal combat. The battles of the nineteenth century, culminating in the law of 1905 separating state and church have not been repeated since, but it is as well to remember that it never was a purely religious issue, since the Church was lined up with the anti-republican forces: to reject clerical power meant also to embrace the Republic and to 'accept' the Revolution. After 1905, the Catholic Church saw that it had to come to terms with history and the Republic—hence the specific rejection of right-wing Catholic extremism of the type represented by the *Action Française* between the wars; the last flicker of the old sentiments was fanned briefly into life in the support for the authoritan Vichy regime after the defeat in 1940.

It would be mistaken to conclude that religion is no longer relevant to politics in France. It is true that the post-war period has seen the failure of the progressive Catholic MRP and the lack of any impact of successors such as the Democratic Centre, but this shows rather the way in which religion is identified with conservatism. Nor are religious issues quite dead: 'On the surface, anti-clericalism does not appear to

---

* For a diagram of the pre-war Austrian situation, see below p. 34.

stir the population ... yet in 1959, State subsidies to Church schools roused more opposition than any other issue and millions of Frenchmen signed a petition against the bill which Parliament was discussing.[8] That was perhaps an echo from the past, but it underlines one continuing strand in French politics—that religious observance is still one of the best indicators of voting behaviour. Studies show that the Gaullists and their ally, the UDF, rely on the votes of practising Catholics (with a rural, age, and female bias), whilst the left is served by lapsed Catholics and agnostics, even though neither side makes 'religion' an issue: 'Class dominates, but religion remains a powerful factor.'[9]

At this point, we can pause to set out the terms of a two-step process by which religion comes to be sundered from politics. The first step involves the transfer from religion as a political issue to one where it is a passive determinant of voting behaviour. This appears to be the stage reached in France, as it is too in post-war Austria—where the Catholic Church has formally withdrawn from any political involvement. The second step occurs when voting behaviour no longer shows any marked correlation with religious ties or observance. This second step has not occurred in the Catholic countries. Indeed, Ireland can be regarded as in a pre-primary stage—religious values permeated state and society; only recently has the role of religion in public and private life been questioned seriously.

Italy is still in the primary phase: religion is involved as a part of the political scene in the sharp polarization between the values of the dominant Christian Democrats and the largest Communist Party in Western Europe. Whilst in other Catholic countries overt intervention by the clergy is not common, in Italy pulpit-politics is an everyday reality, and this is supplemented by the political utterances of the Vatican—with its own radio station and newspaper. The influence of the Church on social life is sanctioned by the Concordat of 1929, and in spite of its fascist connotations, all attempts to amend the treaty have been successfully resisted by the Vatican. More than in other countries, the network of church lay organizations serve to keep the Christian Democrats in power. In particular, Catholic Action, by other European standards a right-wing association, links the demands of the Church with a socially involved and politically active élite, and Catholic Action is a major staging-post by which this élite enters parliament and government.

The case of divorce-law reform illustrates the problem of church-state relations. Ninety-two years after it had become a live political issue, and after a five-year battle in the Italian Parliament, a bill incorporating a set of modest proposals eventually reached the statute book in 1970. On its way there, the Vatican showed unremitting hostility and used all its resources and influence to defeat the legislation, claiming that the proposals were in breach of the Concordat. Successive government crises in 1969 and 1970 were partly a result of this intervention, although defeat for the bill would certainly have rekindled active anti-clericalism as the issue of Vatican tax exemption on its vast investment income had done a few years previously. Even when the divorce law was passed, the matter was not allowed to rest; it could still be challenged by popular referendum. To initiate this, a petition signed by 500,000 electors, each attested by a notary, was required. This was a formidable task, but parish priests were willing to help, using the churches as registration centres, and enjoining their parishers to sign—for the glory of Jesus Christ and the Madonna. In the event, the petition was signed by well over a million voters, and the referendum on the repeal of the divorce law (eventually held in May 1974) resulted in a clear victory for the supporters of the divorce law (59 per cent were against repeal) and was consequently a severe defeat for the Catholic Church, signalling the decline of Christian Democratic hegemony.

A portrayal of religion and politics in Italy purely in these terms is possibly one-sided. Christian Democracy is not simply a monolithic church party, and many inside the party would welcome a complete autonomy. Nor is the Communist Party to be equated with anti-clericalism—the party was not in the forefront of the divorce law campaign, and it is anxious not to have its energies diverted into sterile anticlericalism; indeed, its spokesmen have declared that the party is no longer anti-clerical. One can appreciate their wisdom: as long as the party were regarded as militantly anti-church, it would be permanently cut off from any possibility of increasing voting support; additionally, with religion 'out of the way', the chances of reaching an 'understanding' with the Christian Democrats would be enhanced.* It is conceivable that the move to the second stage of passive vote determination could take place; this might still leave the Christian Democrats in a favourable position, since its vote is widely spread amongst all classes, with about one-quarter of the lowest income-groups, working class and peasantry, voting for the party.

The second pattern of religious balance, approximate Catholic and Protestant parity, occurs in West Germany, the Netherlands, and Switzerland. In these three, there is a peaceful coexistence of the two; no longer does a person's religion result in political or social discrimination, nevertheless, religion does have a salience for politics, and the two churches are still to an extent in competition with one another. In Switzerland, the relative religious homogeneity of the cantons and the cantonal competence for religious and cultural affairs serve to make religion a local affair. And although the Catholics are in a national minority, the weighting in the federal upper house, the Council of States, favours the small, and mainly Catholic, cantons; in the event, it is the language *and* religious minority which has control of the Council of States, so that the balance of interests is maintained. There has been no necessity to form a Christian Democratic party to link the two confessions, but the Catholic

* See below, pp. 144–5.

'Conservative Christian-Socials' have now opted to rally to this 'new' banner of Christian Democracy. The Catholic vote goes loyally to the Catholic Party, whilst Protestants vote Radical, for the Peasants' Party, or the small Evangelical Party. In general, with the absence of religious issues, party commitment is related to religious observance, but only for the Catholics does this link have a particular party significance.

The religious-political connection in the Netherlands is complex. Until the mid-1970s there were no less than three large confessional parties and a number of smaller ones; of them all, only the Catholic Radical Party could be described as 'on the left'. The Roman Catholics constitute a large minority of the Dutch population (around 40 per cent) and, like Switzerland, their vote went predominantly to the Catholic People's Party. But the Protestant vote was divided amongst a number of parties chiefly based on doctrinal differences; the two major ones, the Anti-Revolutionary Party and the Christian Historical Union reflected differences which hardened in the nineteenth century: voting for one of the religious parties involved identification with a defined religious viewpoint, not just a 'Christian' commitment. Until the 1960s the total 'religious' vote amounted to over a half of the whole—the highest proportion in any country. The most important result was that class differences were minimized. Thus, although over half of the Dutch Labour Party vote came from the lower income groups, the confessional parties were not far behind. There was also a strong tie between religious observance and voting, especially for the Catholics and the Calvinist Anti-Revolutionary Party.

We saw earlier that the 'pillars' of Dutch society represent a passive encapsulation of social attitudes rather than a source of active cleavage. The religious parties for long shared in coalition government, an active cooperation dating back to the last century when the Catholics and Protestants made common cause over the issue of denominational schools. Such issues became less relevant, but the passive religious connection to politics was maintained and translated into a political dominance for the religious parties. In the recent past there have been signs of a fundamental realignment of the party system in part caused by the erosion of the religious vote.* One reaction was the formation in 1976 of the Christian Democratic Appeal from the CHU, ARP, and Catholics—a firm indication of weakening religious influence.

The third country with a Catholic-Protestant balance, West Germany, has shown the most rapid change in the relation of politics to religion. This has been aided by the division of Germany in 1945; before then the Protestants were in a substantial majority, but the loss of the eastern territories and the creation of the German Democratic Republic affected Catholic numbers very little, since they are concentrated in the south and

* See below, pp. 157, 297–9.

west whilst the Protestants were weakened considerably. In the past, and with some reason, the Catholics thought of themselves as a beleaguered minority—especially at the time of Bismarck's *Kulturkampf*—and this for long hindered a wider social integration. The Catholic Centre Party, both in Imperial Germany and in the Weimar Republic, was mainly concerned to defend Catholic interests, and it retained a firm hold on the faithful, regardless of social class. The result was a so-called 'tower mentality' (after a pamphlet published in 1906, *'Wir müssen aus dem Turm heraus'*, a plea to end the isolation of German Catholicism) which persisted into the Nazi era. After 1945, a successful attempt was made to end this isolation. The new spirit of co-operation with the Protestant community, until then associated with the orthodox conservative parties, was helped by the common feeling of responsibility for the Nazi success, at least by default. A unique 'double-compromise' was forged between the two confessions and, because of church following, between the classes as well. In this new-style Christian Democracy, the support of the Catholic churchgoer could be guaranteed; this was less true for the Protestants until the decline of the small right-wing parties.

On a formal count, church membership in Germany is very high, and this can be gauged accurately by the fact that over 90 per cent of the working population pay the 'church tax'—10 per cent of a person's income tax liability collected by the state for distribution to the churches. To be set against this is the fact that only a tiny proportion of Protestants are regular churchgoers and only about one-third of all Catholics. Furthermore, the number of those 'contracting out' of the tax, deliberately leaving their church, has risen steeply in recent years. The connection between religious commitment and voting is still apparent, but there is now no barrier at all to a good Catholic voting Social Democrat, and anti-clericalism on the left is a thing of the past; where such issues still arise—for instance over church schools—they are 'cultural' matters and therefore remain at the Land level and do not become national issues.[10]

In these respects, West Germany appears to be on the point of entering the third stage of development—in its completed form the lack of any correlation between voting behaviour and religion. This stage is most nearly seen in Britain and Scandinavia, countries which are largely Protestant. The Protestant churches have never been so tightly knit socially nor so corporative in spirit that they have been able to override class differences for any length of time. Unlike Roman Catholicism, the 'national' nature of Protestantism has led to the ready identification of the state churches with ruling-class values; indeed, they have been the main-prop of establishment unity—to the extent that at one time the Church of England could be described as 'the Conservative Party at prayer'. By itself, Protestantism, especially with a state church, is more likely than Catholicism to expose a simple class polarization. One can argue that Britain has entered the third stage; this accords with the observation made by Butler and Stokes in their detailed study of British voting: 'The ties of religion and party in the modern electorate are distinctly a legacy of the past.' But the attenuation of these ties observable in Britain is of recent origin: 'It is hardly too strong to say that British politics ... were still rooted in religion in the Nineteenth Century';[11] the early years of this century saw bitter conflict over at least three religious issues (Ireland, Church Schools, Welsh Disestablishment). The erosion of the link between party and religion was greater for the young, but for the middle class, whether or not they actually went to church, the religious element was a way of identifying with the leading values of society. In *this* sense, the significance of religion in Britain, as part of a wider social order, was far from residual. But the direction of influence is reversed: religion no longer determined political loyalties, the political loyalty (of the middle class) was still supported by a religious value.

The waning of the political significance of religion—if Britain can be taken as a model—places strain on all conservative parties, as Lipset points out: '... conservative politicians know that they must find ways of securing considerable lower-class support. They cannot win without it. Conservative parties must attempt to reduce the saliency of class as the principal basis of party division by sponsoring non-class issues . . .',[12] and religion has given many of them a useful force to attract the necessary quota of the working-class or peasant vote. It need not, of course, be religion, and religion need be only one element in a wider value system which is used as an attraction.

This line of argument may go too far in stressing a relationship of religion to conservative politics. If 'Christian Democracy' is an attractive banner for conservative politicians to fly, it is also the case that these parties must be socially progressive, if they are to retain working-class support. And there is no necessary connection between religion and social conservatism. Christian Socialists were active in the West German CDU after the war, and, with their influence at work, one of the party's first post-war programmes (Ahlen 1947) was decidedly anti-capitalist in flavour. In Scandinavia, the most important religious party, the Norwegian Christian People's Party, shows that the identification of religion with the right-wing does not necessarily hold in all cases, since it is in the middle of the party spectrum: 'The religiously active are least extreme in their politics and tend to shun both Socialists and Conservatives.'[13] Thus the bias of religious voting, even where it persists, is not automatically to the right.

Whether or not other countries, and particularly the Catholic ones, follow the path of the Protestant countries, it is evident that even the passive relation of religion to voting is amenable to considerable erosion in the long term, and this goes along with a general decline in religiosity, if measured in terms of formal observance, as well as in the secular influence of the church authorities.

Rural and Urban Contrasts

As an overwhelmingly industrial society, Britain is not typical of Western Europe in the distribution of her population, especially in its high urban concentration, with almost three-fifths living in cities of over 100,000 people; nor in the tiny proportion of the work force engaged in agriculture.* Yet in all countries the direction of change is the same; in spite of the far higher proportion engaged in agriculture—in the southerly states, Spain, Italy, Greece, and Portugal up to 35 per cent—the trend is towards a European norm of about 10 per cent, as against below 3 per cent in Britain.

The general change can be illustrated by Denmark. In spite of her reliance on farming, the proportion employed in agriculture fell from almost 30 per cent in 1929 to below 10 per cent in the 1970s, and is still declining. At the same time, there has been a steady growth of the towns: around two-fifths of the Danes live in cities of over 100,000 people, and only a quarter live in 'rural' districts. Before examining the political implications of these movements, we should take a further example of structural change. France, outside Paris and the larger cities, is traditionally regarded as anchored in the small town and the peasant holding. But over the past two decades there has been a virtual 'flight from the land'. As recently as the mid-1950s, farmers and agricultural workers formed over a quarter of the working population, but by the late 1970s the proportion had plummeted to around ten per cent, more in line with the northerly states. Yet the speed at which the change occurred disguised considerable local variations: in the south and west of France employment in agriculture remained high, comparable to that of Greece and Spain. Pierre Avril commented: 'Could it be that there are two Frances, which coexist with some harmony, one attached to the past and the other in the throes of modernization?'[14]

We can take Avril's original question about France and make it of more general application to Western Europe. It is evident that the forces of social change and industrialization do cause considerable distortion and imbalance on a *regional* level; they are factors which overlay the pre-existing rural and urban contrasts. These contrasts are not simply occupational; they are made up of cultural differences, political outlook, and economic wealth. The effect of rapid economic change and demographic movement on existing differences is considerable; and the overall effect, in the course of years, is likely to lead to a national homogeneity, in other words, that the particularities of a specifically 'rural' outlook are likely to disappear in the development of urban

* For comparisons, see the table on p. 263.

society. In itself, of course, there is no one rural form, as we shall see the rural vote can cover the whole political spectrum, and 'political geography' is a crystallization of varied historical experiences. Particularly in rural areas, these can show a remarkable persistence.

Italy provides the leading example of extreme regional imbalance and with it a strikingly variegated political map. The sharpest contrast is between the comparatively rich and industrialized northern provinces, with a high rate of economic growth, and until recently the persistent stagnation of the largely agricultural south. The natural process of seepage of economic benefit has not percolated southwards; instead there has had to be a massive and continuing government intervention in the economy,* and, with a high natural increase in population, the main safety-valve has been emigration in large numbers—roughly half to the other EEC countries and Switzerland and the other half to the urban north of Italy.

The pattern, especially in agriculture, is more diverse than this simple north-south dichotomy indicates. The nature of landholding varies greatly from one region to another and with it so do political loyalties. The north-east is typified by the small, independent farmer, the so-called direct-cultivator, who in these 'white provinces' gives strong support to the Christian Democrats. Central Italy has a widespread system of share-cropping, the *mazzadria,* and the injustices of this type of tenant farming result in widespread support for the Communist Party—the 'red belt' in which Communist control over local government is usual. Finally, southern agriculture is dominated by large estates, the *latifondi,* with a system of day-labouring. The high rate of emigration has here hindered the emergence of a cohesive rural proletariat; political power is exercised by patronage, with the Christian Democrats naturally dominant—yet only nominally so, because there is wide scope for the influence of local notables. Thus the geographical distribution of landholding accounts for the local variations in party supremacy; and Dogan concluded: 'In short, the political struggle in an agricultural milieu reflect(s) the conflicts between the social classes.'[15]

Although this pattern of support has been partially hidden by the general advance of the Communist Party in the 1970s, it is not a transitory phenomenon—there are still similarities between the distribution of the left-wing vote now and over fifty years ago. Sartori saw this persistence as inexplicable on purely economic grounds: 'Regions with high income have either a low or a high communist turnout. At times a rapid increase in the standard of living breaks communist allegiance, but in other instances does not affect it in the least. Moreover, the voting behaviour of rural areas defies economic explanations.'[16] That led him to regard the critical variable as the degree of 'organisational incapsulation

---

* See below, pp. 234–5.

and cultural saturation' that the Communists (or for that matter the Christian Democrats) have been able to achieve. Why this incapsulation should have arisen in the first place can be related to historical factors: much of the 'red belt' was once under papal rule, and according to Dogan, 'Where the temporal power of the Church was strong in the past, contemporary parties with a Christian orientation are weak and vice versa.'[17]

All the major parties can secure an 'incapsulation' of voting loyalties in rural areas better than they can in industrial and urban ones. The small-town and country bias of Christian Democracy is still very marked, and whilst the Communist Party has been spectacularly successful over the past decade in capturing the government of several large cities, it has also been able to capitalize on the 'historical' agricultural and rural connections of the party in particular regions.[18]

We have to read such conclusions alongside the changing rural-urban balance in Italy. During the 1970s the farm population fell well below 20 per cent, and although employment in the agricultural sector is still far higher than the average for Western Europe, the contrast should be made with the 1930s when the share was over 50 per cent. Another decade of accelerating change would considerably alter the social basis of Italian politics. A greater urban concentration will lead to an increased fluidity of party-voter relationships as industrialization proceeds, and in consequence we should expect to see short-term fluctuations in the fortunes of the two major parties.

The phenomenon of the 'red peasant' in France is akin to that of the Communist rural vote in Italy. This particularly applies to the agricultural departments of the south and south-west, especially to the *Massif-Central*. One can rely on both economic and cultural explanations: Ehrmann summarized the economic situation in the 1960s: 'West of a line drawn from Marseilles to Le Havre, the average income is smaller by half than the income east of that line where eighty per cent of France's industrial activities are concentrated.'[19] In contrast to the Italian situation, the independent peasant farmer is often disposed to support the Communist Party: in doing so his vote is quite likely to be one of general protest against the state and government, any government, and far less one of positive commitment. Whilst there is no denying the relative poverty of large areas, the cumulative effects of regional economic policies are diminishing the gap; as the number of peasant farmers decreases, and the size of farmholding increases, so this 'protest' vote will decline. Whilst the largest advances of the left-wing parties since the 1960s have been in areas where they were previously weakest, their combined vote remains high and stable in the regional bastions of the south and west.[20] One has to take account of 'cultural' factors which have proved to be extraordinarily durable: 'The Revolution of 1789, by undertaking the partition of the large domains of the Church and nobility, transformed the peasants of some regions into allies of the Republic. The return of the Bourbon in 1815, with the support of the Church, renewed the question of land ownership. Thus the republicanism of many peasants was tinged with anticlericalism.'[21] The effect was to make large areas 'dechristianised' and to give a permanent left-inclination to the vote. The economic and cultural factors interlock.

Elsewhere in Europe the Italian and French forms of agrarian Communism are not in evidence, and the normal political expression of the rural vote is an identification with social conservatism and the established religion, and even where farming has declined in relative importance, these patterns have changed very little. To take one example, Bavaria for long had a tradition of rural backwardness—cattle-drawn ploughs were a common sight until the early 1950s. The political colouring was always deeply conservative outside the larger cities, and the Bavarian Christian-Social Union (the independent sister-party of the national CDU) is closely identified with the values of the Catholic Church. The rapid rise in the standard of living, the mechanization of farms, and the rationalization of previously scattered land-holdings (*Flurbereinigung*) have all altered rural political loyalties very little. The agricultural working-population has fallen from 30 to less than 15 per cent since 1950, but the CSU has also adapted itself to the fast changing occupational structure, and at the present time controls 60 per cent of the total Bavarian vote: traditional values have not been relinquished despite modernization.

The conservative nature of most rural politics is well-established, but in Scandinavia another direction has been taken; this is shown in the widespread occurrence of specifically 'agrarian' parties, neither sharing in the radicalism of the left nor the conservatism of the 'bourgeois' city parties; their place in the party spectrum is indicated by the general and recent change of name to 'Centre' parties. Their political importance is obvious, for they barred the way to cohesive non-socialist groupings, and frequently led to 'farmer-labour' (Red-Green) alliances. Their rise, as a Scandinavian phenomenon alone, requires explanation. Historically, the reason may be the relatively early political mobilization of the peasantry and an independence stemming from the general lack of feudal traditions in Scandinavia.

There is no doubt that rural-urban conflict is more embedded in the politics of this part of Europe and does much to account for the Scandinavian version of the multi-party system.* The origins of the conflict were as much cultural as they were economic; in Norway, it centred on the language-issue: the struggle to have the standard rural language accepted nationally, a form of cultural defence against the Danish-influenced language of the urban élites. Rokkan argues more generally, 'This conflict between rural claims and urban dominance goes far to explain the difference

* See the diagrams, p. 35 below.

between the Scandinavian multi-party system and the English two-party system. In Scandinavia there were few and only tenuous ties between the rural and urban élites; in Norway this chasm was even deeper than in Denmark or Sweden as a result of centuries of foreign domination channelled through the cities.' He sees the basic difference in English development in the fact that the rural-urban conflict was settled *before* lower-class mobilization got under way, whilst in Scandinavia, 'The two waves of mobilization came close on each other's heels and one set of issues had not come anywhere near settlement before the next forced itself on the body politic.'[22] The result was a persisting double basis of cleavage, essentially a three-cornered contest—the new working class, the urban bourgeoisie, and the agrarian interests.

How far this pattern will extend indefinitely in the future is another matter; with declining farm populations, a pure agrarian party is likely to become an anachronism, and this is partly conceded in the change of name to 'Centre'. Where such parties exist in other countries—the Netherlands and the Finnish Rural Party—they may be part of a more general protest movement, in both countries a reaction against the hegemony of the ruling parties. The Dutch Farmers' Party in 1966 actually gained respectable support in the three largest cities. The old-type rural-urban conflict is losing its basis—a substantial farm population; increasingly, issues are 'nationalized' in the context of urban society and although the outcroppings of older conflicts persist, they give way to the problems of regional imbalance. But this division is no longer a rural-urban split; it is a debate about the attraction of new industry and the rate of urbanization, problems which appear on a regional level but which have to be settled in a national context.*

Class and Politics

Close to the centre of the web of influences on political loyalty are the straight economic factors. These are readily given expression in terms of social class, a common recognition of social inequality which is ultimately based on *perceived* differences in economic wealth and the consequences which stem from them. The term 'class' by itself is an abstraction—necessarily so, for it depends on a more or less arbitrary grouping of socio-economic data. Only when social groups *form and act cohesively* as a reaction to these differences does it become a reality. The political party is one of the main expressions of this cohesion, and class politics are an integral part of European politics. What we have said so far, however, shows that the parties and their conflicts express much more besides class interests. Indeed, nowhere in Europe can party politics be read as a straightforward translation of class issues on to the political stage.

* See below, pp. 228–36.

The first comparison we can make is between the British situation and that in most of mainland Europe. Britain is a good starting-point because she is on most counts a completely urbanized society and so (arguably) a precursor of developments elsewhere. British society is also relatively homogeneous in the sense that (until the resurgence of the national issue in Wales and Scotland) there was a simple polarization around one variable, social class. The other sources of social cleavage we have discussed have been little in evidence or have dried up. If it is accepted, that besides class explanations of politics, as Pulzer wrote, 'all else is embellishment and detail',[23] then it does not follow that the conflict-base of the polarization is thereby sharpened. This was once well put by Finer: 'Class is important—indeed central—in British politics only because nothing else is.'[23] This idea of the *residual* nature of class politics has to be related to a number of other changes in society— any of which, as now seems to be the case for Britain, can generate new lines of cleavage—and to changes in the nature of social class itself. Hence, 'residual' does not just mean 'static' or even 'attenuated', nor, if social classes are not fixed entities, will it result in a final hardening of social cleavages as suggested by the Marxist argument.

There are special features in British politics and the inter-relation of these gives a particular form to their homogeneity. Of first importance has been the overriding nature of the system of social values. An indication of this dominance is seen in the nature of the Labour Party; unlike its counterparts in Europe it has never been an anti-clerical party, nor has it shared at all in the Marxist tradition; it has at no time been a 'Socialist' party, has never attacked the leading features of the political and social establishment, and has favoured limited reform. Yet so strong and pervasive are the leading values that Frank Parkin found it possible to regard even its modest challenge as deviant: 'Political deviance, examined from a societal level, is manifested not in working-class conservatism, but rather in electoral support for Socialism on the part of members of any social stratum. Social voting can be regarded as a symbolic act of deviance from the dominant values of British capitalist society.'[25]

This may overstate the case, but the formulation of working-class conservatism as an expression of dominant class values raises the question of how these came to be enshrined in British society. The answer lies partly in the comparatively smooth way in which the evolution took place from its pre-democratic position to the filling-out of liberal democracy: it was a unified ruling class which faced the claims of mass democracy; we have just seen that in Scandinavia this was not the case. The change can be expressed alternatively by saying the critical problems of political and social development were encountered one by one, and each resolved before a new one arose. This pattern made for a high continuity of leading values and of social élites; as Norman Birnbaum points out: 'British history is remarkable in the continuity of its élite structure—precisely through the changes which have seen the displacement of feudal nobility by landed gentry by aristocratic magnates by new capitalists ... A pronounced capacity to assimilate new groups with new modes of procuring wealth has frequently saved the old élites from superannuation.'[26]

The contrast with many other European states is obvious. The critical problems were often shelved or occurred simultaneously. We can see the nature of these problems and the way they can crowd in on one another in the case of Germany: 'The history of Germany in the nineteenth century might very well be written in terms of the interplay between the simultaneous problems of state and nation-building, and demands for participation and welfare. Demands for political participation, particularly on the part of the middle classes in the various German states, became assimilated into demands for national integration.'[27] And although the social élites long remained intact, the 'double-rupture' they suffered in the wake of defeat in the two world wars vanquished them and the values they represented. To a lesser extent, and with different degrees of emphasis, the same type of prolonged crisis has faced other countries; what Otto Kirchheimer referred to as the 'pristine beauty' of British development was largely exceptional.

Earlier we made the point that the conservative and bourgeois parties could not hope to achieve power in their own right as undiluted class parties; the necessary amount of cross-voting had to be secured by some other inducement—typically religion. The British Conservative Party did not have to induce support in this way, for it already stood as a succinct expression of social values, of which the established church was but one. The result can be shown in various forms, of which the most direct is to postulate two conditions to create a system of the British type:

> that there should be only *one* political expression of the bourgeoisie; if there is more than one major contender, then none of them can claim a monopoly of leading values;
> that given this unified political expression, then these values (especially those of a social nature) should not be challenged by the opposing class party.

In most of the European systems, only one of these conditions is met, or neither. Put briefly, working-class conservatism in Britain related very easily and in a number of ways to the dominant value system, and they almost always ran to the benefit of a single party.[28] The ease of identification in other countries is made possible by the overt religious tie; the mainstay of many Christian Democratic parties is the lower-class Catholic worker, but the cross-cutting of loyalties works two ways: the proportion of working-class voters is only assured if the religious pull is maintained, otherwise these parties veer to becoming minority class-parties. Pre-war Austria fulfilled the first of our conditions, but not the second; the increasing strength of the post-war Austrian Socialists may indicate that the Austrian People's Party (formerly Christian-Socials) is running into this difficulty.

The large bourgeois parties in West Germany and France may bear some resemblance to the British Conservative Party in that they fulfil the first condition in part, but neither can represent the 'unquestioned' values of society; the traumatic effect of the Nazi era prevents any party laying such a claim. In France, the RPR does extol Gaullism, yet this concept was hostile to parliamentary, if not to republican values. In these two countries, the double problem the bourgeois parties face in the future is the possibility of a declining religious attraction and the certainty of the erosion of the groups (rural and small-town) for which the appeal to religion can most effectively be made. An alternative format is provided in multiparty systems where more than one bourgeois party exists and each one has a limited success in attracting working-class support; the Netherlands is the best example, and to a limited extent it is also true in Scandinavian countries. In Denmark, Norway and Sweden there have been recent examples of 'bourgeois' coalitions ousting the dominant Social Democrats, but they all lacked cohesion and soon fell apart.

There may be a temptation to say that everyone is out of step but the British, since we have argued from the apparent 'modernity' of the British social structure—the urban society, its homogeneity leaving exposed the residual class issues. But it becomes clear that her modernity is of a very special kind—resting precisely on the non-modernity of the total value system—nor are other countries likely to evolve in this way; the relationship of British conservatism to central values was the result of a long historical process. Obviously, one can go too far in explaining differences solely in 'value' terms. From other points of view, the Conservative Party in Britain is no more than a highly-successful class party. Its class skew is evident, since it always secures 90 per cent of the upper-middle class vote and three-quarters of the 'solid' middle class. To this reliable base, it can add up to a third of the working-class vote, sometimes appreciably more. Yet the same order of effect is reached in other countries, singly in some, by an aggregation of the bourgeois parties in others.

We should also appreciate the rather different perspectives of the Socialist parties; the main difference is in their specific class-appeal, and this they have been able to maintain in spite of the counter-attractions of religion along with a generally rising standard of living which, for individuals at least, has the ring of upward social mobility: 'With the exception of Holland and West Germany, the leftist parties secure about two-thirds or more of the working class vote, a much higher percentage than during the depression of the 1930s.' Lipset adds: 'A look at the political history of Europe indicates that no mass lower-class-based party, with the single exception of the German Communists, has ever disappeared, or significantly declined through losing the bulk of its votes to a party on its right.'[29] Since this was written, the leeway of Social Democracy in West

Germany has been made up, and the same is largely true for the Dutch Labour Party.

This stability on the left combined with increasing working-class support has not been the result of unadulterated insistence on class issues. In the past this appeal was combined with an open anti-clericalism or a defence of parliamentary institutions, but these are no longer the rallying calls they once were. Depending on its local support, the party does anyway speak in rather different voice to tenant farmers, smallholders, car-workers, or government employees, but these are mainly tactical ploys. The really important change has been the attempt to increase the potential of voting support.

This drive to go beyond the traditional limits of left-wing support, beyond the working class, is fraught with consequences. It is a basic change, and it is no longer sufficient to make a static juxtaposition of 'class' and 'party'; neither can be regarded as fixed entities. We shall take up the discussion of this in the following chapter, so that here a brief illustration of party change will suffice. At the turn of the century, the German Social Democrats formed the largest and the most orthodox of European Socialist parties. Its strict class emphasis gained it only a minority of votes—the 'one-third barrier'. This restriction, and the superficially Marxist programme that went with it, persisted after 1945. Faced by defeats at successive elections and the undeniable affluence, dubbed the 'economic miracle', the pressure for fundamental party reform proved irresistible. The turning-point came with the 1959 Godesberg Conference of the party. A new party programme was penned; almost overnight, the SPD became a 'People's Party'—calling to all, irrespective of class, indeed specifically denying that it was a class party. In place of Marxist doctrine, it put a broad humanitarian idealism, and turned its back firmly on any anti-clerical sentiment. The 1959 reforms paid off: at the three elections prior to the new programme, the party averaged 30 per cent of the vote; but subsequently support rose sharply—the SPD became the largest party with 45 per cent in 1972. Nor was the response based on a heightened class awareness; elections were fought largely on the issue of economic stability, 'law and order', and in 1972 on Brandt's Ostpolitik. This sketch is open to other interpretations—one can argue that the party would have gained increased support *whatever* it did. It is probably more convincing to see the change resulting from a changing class awareness, and, appreciating this, the Social Democratic Party, particularly its leaders, attempted to redefine the content of Socialism.

Social Cleavages and Party Systems

Some of the relevant issues regarding social cleavage and consensus which we have discussed in this chapter can usefully be summarized in diagram form. This can also be related to the prevalent types of party system, though the models set out below are not intended exactly to correspond with particular systems. The most useful distinction to be made is between 'homogeneous' and 'sectional' societies in the sense used by Blondel and defined on p. 12 above. However, it is apparent that there are both different types as well as degrees of homogeneity and sectionality; the diagrams show the main variations. The main direction of party formation is along the major source(s) of social cleavage, indicated by a continuous line. The discontinuous lines represent weak, alternative lines of polarization, and may or may not lead to party formation along them. If they do not, the discontinuous line may represent strong consensual elements which unite the whole society or sections of it. The lettering, A–E, has been used so that the diagrams are left with general application; illustrative party formations are in brackets.

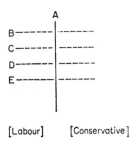

homogeneous society

One major source of social cleavage (A). The discontinuous lines, B–E, represent cross-cutting affiliations which modify the effect of the prime division (e.g. A = socio-economic class). Party formation takes place either side of the 'A' line to give a stable two-party system with limited polarization. The degree of polarization depends on the number of society-wide unifying factors.

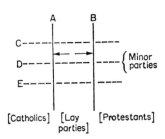

mixed homogeneous—sectional society

'A' and 'B' are two major sources of cleavage. They do not reinforce one another (hence the diverging arrows) and there are three major sources of party formation. The potential fragmentation of the system is prevented by numerous cross-cutting affiliations (C–E) which may act as minor sources of party formation. The result may be a stable multi-party system. The vertical 'pillarization' of Dutch Society is directly applicable here.

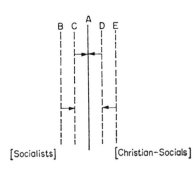

sectional society (1)

Only one major source of social cleavage, but the other politically-significant variables are not randomly distributed throughout the population. They therefore tend to confirm and reinforce the prime division (hence converging arrows). The result is an unstable two-party situation (e.g. pre-war Austria).

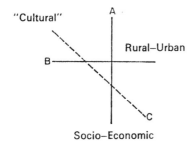

sectional society (2a)

Two major lines of cleavage running athwart one another. A limited multi-party system results; this will be stable if minor cleavages cut across two or more quadrants. This type is applicable to Scandinavian systems with the rural-urban cultural cleavage persisting alongside the socio-economic one.

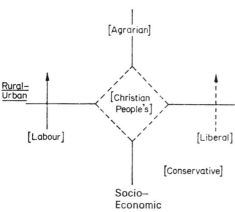

sectional society (2b)

The Norwegian party system illustrates the practical application of the general 'Scandinavian' type. The five parties shown share 75 per cer cent of the vote; four of these make an appeal across at least one line of cleavage—e.g. Labour to small farmers and fishing communities. The Agrarians are now the Centre Party.

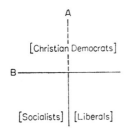

sectional society (2c)

The four quadrants of type (2a) may not be of equal significance, i.e. the effect of one of the prime divisions is nullified or overridden for certain sections of society. The T-shaped variation is of practical significance: socio-economic class only partially operative ('A' partly discontinuous, whilst a clerical/anti-clerical division, 'B', persists throughout.)

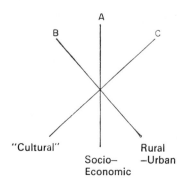

sectional society (3)

Several cleavages are apparent and they do not stand in a close relationship with one another. If these are all very strong, then the party-situation will be one of numerous 'armed camps' and likely to fragment. If they are weak, the result will be a moderately unstable multi-party system. This third major type of sectional society corresponds to Duverger's portrayal of the Fourth French Republic in his *Political Parties;* however, the various 'segments' in the diagram do not show the full range of party possibilities. *Three* major cleavages, in permutation, give *eight* party directions.

Thus Lipset* shows the overlapping of cleavages in French politics giving a party configuration related to three competing traditions, and applying to the Fourth Republic:

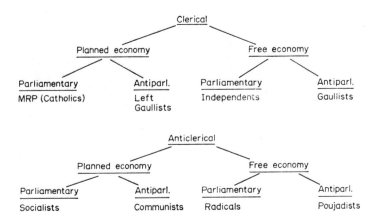

All except the Left Gaullists represent independent parties. The planned economy/free economy axis corresponds to a left/right division. The parliamentary/anti-parliamentary division is an amalgam of historical factors and social class influences.

* S. M. Lipset, *The First New Nation,* Heinemann, 1964, p. 297.

NOTES AND REFERENCES

1. These four categories are indicated by S. M. Lipset and S. Rokkan (eds.), *Party Systems and Voter Alignments: Cross-national Perspectives,* Collier-Macmillan, 1967, p. 14. They give four critical lines of cleavage: workers—employers and owners; churches—government; primary— secondary economy; subject—dominant culture.
2. There is difficulty in determining which variables are independent and which are related to other structural conditions. For the 'age' factor: 'We must not ask how old

an elector is but when it was that he was young.' D. Butler and D. Stokes, *Political Change in Britain*, Macmillan, 1969, p. 59. Of course, the *effects* of age-sex differences can be momentous. See M. Dogan in *Party Systems and Voter Alignments*, pp. 159–67. The excess of women over men voters, notably in West Germany and Italy, runs to the benefit of Christian Democracy. A German Social Democrat once complained, 'The woman's vote has ruined the party.'

3. J. Blondel, *An Introduction to Comparative Government*, Weidenfeld and Nicolson, 1969, p. 53. He illustrates the term 'sectionalism': 'A country will therefore be sectional if Roman Catholics, for instance, are not spread evenly ("normally") among the various classes, but clustered mainly among workers or in some areas. The same would be true of races or any other social variable.' The way in which the word 'homogeneous' is used in the text also follows Blondel's formulation.

4. R. Rose and D. Urwin, 'What are the Parties based on?', *New Society*, 7th May 1970, pp. 774–6.

5. Blondel regards the regional aspect as most important: 'Sectionalism related to geography has more profound political effects than any other form of sectionalism.' op. cit., p. 55.

6. R. Rose and D. Urwin, 'Social Cohesion, Political Parties and Strains in Regimes' in M. Dogan and R. Rose (eds.), *European Politics: A Reader*, Macmillan, 1971, p. 220.

7. F. C. Engelmann, 'Austria: The Pooling of Opposition., in R. A. Dahl (ed.), *Political Oppositions in Western Democracies*, New Haven: Yale University Press, 1966, pp. 263–4.

8. J. Blondel and E. D. Godfrey, *The Government of France*, Methuen, 1968, pp. 23–4.

9. V. Wright, 'The French General Election of March 1978: *La Divine Surprise*', in *Conflict and Consensus in France*, Frank Cass, 1979, p. 39.

10. Dissension over abortion law reform revived some old feelings. A law brought in by the Socialist/Liberal coalition was subsequently ruled invalid by the Constitutional Court in 1975. Interestingly, however, the chief target for attack by reformers was the Court itself—it had undermined the will of the political majority.

11. Butler and Stokes, op. cit., p. 129 and p. 124

12. S. M. Lipset, *Revolution and Counterrevolution: Change and Persistence in Social Structures*, Heinemann, 1969, p. 164.

13. S. Rokkan, 'Norway: Geography, Religion and Social Class', in *Party Systems and Voter Alignments*, p. 422.

14. P. Avril, op. cit., p. 229.

15. M. Dogan, 'Political Cleavage and Social Stratification in France and Italy' in *Party Systems and Voter Alignments* op. cit., p. 149.

16. G. Sartori, 'European Political Parties: The Case of Polarised Pluralism', in R. A. Dahl and D. E. Neubauer (eds.), *Readings in Modern Political Analysis*, Prentice-Hall, 1968, p. 122.

17. M. Dogan in *Party Systems and Voter Alignments*, p. 184.

18. See S. Tarrow, *Peasant Communism in Southern Italy*, Yale University Press, 1967, and P. Allum, 'Italy' in S. Henig (ed.), *Political Parties in the European Community*, Allen and Unwin, 1979.

19. H. W. Ehrmann, *Politics in France*, Boston: Little, Brown, 1968, p. 25.

20. For an analysis of the regional distribution of left-wing support, see J. Frears, 'The French National Assembly Elections of March 1978', *Government and Opposition*, Summer 1978.

21. M. Dogan in *Party Systems and Voter Alignments*, p. 183. For a study of 'historical persistence', see L. Wylie, *Village in Vaucluse*, New York: Harvard University Press, 1964.

22. S. Rokkan, 'Norway: Numerical Democracy and Corporate Pluralism', in

Political Oppositions in Western Democracies, p. 79.
23. P. G. J. Pulzer, *Political Representation and Elections in Britain*, George Allen and Unwin, 1967, p. 98.
24. S. E. Finer, *Comparative Government*, Allen Lane, 1970, p. 142.
25. F. Parkin, 'Working Class Conservatives: A Theory of Political Deviance', *British Journal of Sociology*, (18), 1967, pp. 278–90.
26. N. Birnbaum, *The Crisis of Industrial Society*, Oxford University Press, 1970, p. 17.
27. G. A. Almond and G. B. Powell, *Comparative Politics: A Developmental Approach*, Boston: Little, Brown, 1966, p. 318.
28. See, for instance, R. T. McKenzie and A. Silver, *Angels in Marble*, Heinemann, 1968, and E. A. Nordlinger, *The Working Class Tories*, MacGibbon and Kee, 1967.
29. S. M. Lipset, 'The Changing Class Structure and Contemporary European Politics' in *Revolution and Counterrevolution*, pp. 223–4.

Additional References

E. Allardt and Y. Littunen (eds.), *Cleavages, Ideologies and Party Systems*, Helsinki: The Westermarck Society, 1964.
M. Anderson, 'The Renaissance of Territorial Minorities in Western Europe', *West European Politics*, vol. 1/2, May 1978.
M. S. Archer and S. Giner (eds.), *Contemporary Europe: Class, Status and Power*, Weidenfeld and Nicolson, 1971.
S. H. Barnes, M. Kaase et al., *Political Action in Five Western Democracies*, Sage Publications, 1979.
S. Berger, *Peasants against Politics*, Harvard University Press, 1972.
I. Crewe (ed.), *Elites in Western Democracy*, Croom Helm, 1974.
C. Crough and A. Pizzorno, *The Resurgence of Class Conflict in Western Europe since 1968*, (2 volumes), Macmillan, 1978.
H. Daalder, 'Parties, Elites and Political Developments in Western Europe', in J. LaPalombara and M. Weiner (eds.), *Political Parties and Political Development*, Princeton University Press, 1966.
R. A. Dahl and E. R. Tufte, *Size and Democracy*, Oxford University Press, 1974.
R. Dahrendorf, *Class and Class Conflict in Industrial Society*, Routledge, rev. ed. 1972.
S. H. Franklin, *The European Peasantry*, Methuen, 1969.
A. Giddens, *The Class Structure of Advanced Societies*, Hutchinson, 1973.
S. Giner and M. S. Archer, *Contemporary Europe: Social Structures and Cultural Patterns*, Routledge and Kegan Paul, 1978.
S. R. Graubard (ed.), *A New Europe?*, Boston: Houghton Mifflin, 1964.
R. Irving, *Christian Democracy in France*, Allen and Unwin, 1973.
M. S. Lewis-Beck, 'Explaining Peasant Conservatism: The West European Case', *British Journal of Political Science*, vol. 7/4, October 1977.
D. Martin, 'The Religious Condition of Europe' in Giner and Archer, op. cit.
D. Martin, *A General Theory of Secularization*, Oxford: Blackwell, 1978.
K. D. McRae (ed.), *Consociational Democracy: Political Accommodation in Segmented Societies*, Toronto: McClelland and Stewart, 1974.
W. Miller and G. Raab, 'The Religious Alignment at English Elections between 1918 and 1970', *Political Studies*, June 1977.
F. Parkin, *Class Inequality and Political Order*, MacGibbon and Kee, 1971.
F. Parkin, *Marxism and Class Theory: A Bourgeois Critique*, Tavistock Publications, 1979.

N. Poulantzas, *Political Power and Social Classes*, New Left Books, 1973.

S. Rokkan, *Citizens, Elections, Parties*, Scandinavian University Books, 1970.

S. Rokkan, *'Lire et Ecrire* and "Peasants into Frenchmen": Two Major Studies of the Geography of Modernisation', *European Journal of Political Research*, vol. 6/3, September 1978.

S. Rokkan, 'The Growth and Structuring of Mass Politics in Western Europe', *Scandinavian Political Studies*, Yearbook 5, Oslo: University Bookstore.

R. Rose (ed.), *Electoral Behavior: A Comparative Handbook*, Collier-Macmillan, 1974.

S. Rothman, *European Society and Politics*, Indianapolis: Bobs Merrill, 1970.

S. Tarrow, *Peasant Communism in Southern Italy*, Yale University Press, 1967.

P. Thorburn, 'Political Generations: The Case of Class and Party in Britain', *European Journal of Political Research*, June 1977.

J. Vaizey, *Education*, Macmillan (Studies in Contemporary Europe), 1971.

J. H. Whyte, 'The Catholic Factor in the Societies of Democratic States, *American Behavioral Scientist*, vol. 17/6, 1974.

See also the references on page 64 below.

3

Pluralist Politics: Parties and Interests

Parties: Steadfast and Changing

Of all the expressions of liberal democracy, it is the political party which is the summation of pluralist traditions. It is not only that the parties enshrine the competitive spirit; they also show a remarkable continuity and resilience. And the fact that they arose when they did, and how they did, has had consequences for the remote future. To this extent, the parties are factors in their own right, a part of social reality, to which other social forces have to adjust.

Once established, parties develop their own traditions. These may become permanent symbols of what a party 'stands for' in its own eyes or those of the electorate. Parties also build up a permanent organization, and within it a means of leadership selection, which from the viewpoint of party officials and the leadership groups is too valuable an investment to be readily jettisoned. Alongside its symbols and organization, the party fosters a voter-tradition; party support is hardly ever ephemeral, its core element is firmly rooted in certain sectors of the population, and voting patterns are transferred intact from one generation to another. The sum total of these traditions and vested interests imparts an inertia to the established parties which is difficult to break.

European parties encompass a variety of historical traditions, a number of characteristic 'streams', all readily identifiable in the wide spread of a multi-party system, but in others jostling or simply coexisting within a few major parties. Michael Smart's analysis of parliamentary representation in Western Europe since 1946* isolates a number of these streams and shows, by aggregating the experience of the various countries, how they have ebbed and flowed over a fairly long period. Naturally by weighting results in favour of the more populous states, the pattern is often influenced by changes in these, but the features of this total European movement are usually applicable to the smaller countries as well. Although certain years show a changing 'centre of gravity', it is impossible to pin-point

* See below, pp. 318–26.

any one of them as marking a decisive watershed, after which a new and permanent trend becomes apparent—unless one holds that Gaullism represents a new and persistent phenomenon in French politics. For the major streams, relative decline at certain periods has usually been followed by recovery.

It is this constancy of the political streams, and in turn the tenacity of the individual parties, which is a hallmark of the European party systems. It is an integral part of the balance obtained in Western democracies, and as such requires explanation. This accords with the conclusion reached by Rose and Urwin in a study of a number of party systems: 'The electoral strength of most parties in Western nations since the war had changed very little from election to election ... or within the lifespan of a generation ... A first priority of social scientists is to explain the *absence* of change in a far from static period in political history.'[1]

The hold of party inertia can be broken. Severe discontinuities in the political system can destroy long-established parties or weaken them past recovery. Thus 1945 marked a definite new era for some countries, particularly Germany and Italy; yet it is also true that for most other West European countries the former party patterns quickly reasserted themselves—the party system towards the *end* of the Fourth French Republic was essentially similar to that of the Third, and this was true for the smaller European states whether they had escaped German occupation or not. The rise of new social forces is also a factor making for long-term change, but these may be slow-moving and for long contained within the existing party system. This was not so in the late nineteenth and early twentieth centuries since existing systems were then in a state of initial flux. Brand-new parties frequently jump into the limelight but their ability to make a lasting impact depends on the ability of the older ones to meet their challenge; these have to adapt to changing social conditions by making gradual changes in their appeal, but even if they fail to respond, a loyal section of the electorate will keep them going for many years.

Patterns of the present-day can usually be traced back to the nineteenth century, and particularly to the initial growth of party systems on a restricted franchise; the original basis of party cleavage could be summed up as conservative-traditional versus liberal-progressive, with little attention paid to the non-enfranchised majority of the population. Yet within this restricted fold various polarities existed: bourgeois-nobility, rural-urban, clerical-anticlerical. The precise pattern for any country depended on the extent and social distribution of these cleavages and remained at least until the mass of the people gained the vote. Even afterwards, the grip of the older parties was sufficient to ensure that the advent of peasant and working-class politics was only an amendment to the party system, not its total restructuring.

The rapid extension of the franchise in the late nineteenth and early twentieth centuries and the equally rapid rise of Social Democracy at the same time posed severe problems for the established parties. Part of the challenge was organizational, a move from the old-type 'parties of notables' and 'individual representation' towards new, mass parties. Inevitably, the Social Democratic parties led the field. Their aim of achieving Socialism by means of the democratic parliamentary institutions required a mass organization to deliver the working-class vote and the creation of manifold links between party and member: the party acted as the focus of working-class loyalty and aspiration. The speed with which they advanced put great pressure on the other parties. One of the first expressions of Social Democracy, and for long the most powerful, was the German movement, originating in 1863 with Ferdinand Lassalle's *Allgemeiner Deutscher Arbeiterverein,* and by the turn of the century almost all West European countries had a well-organized working-class party. Thus the Finnish Social Democrats, one of the youngest of the Scandinavian parties, quickly built up a mass membership—a ratio of one member to every three voters by 1907—and in 1916 it actually held an absolute majority in parliament with 47 per cent of the popular vote.

So quickly and naturally did Social Democracy become an integral part of the political scene, that the question originally posed by Werner Sombart in 1906, 'Why is there no Socialism in the United States?', may seem to be a purely American problem rather than a European one; yet it can be argued that it is the particular European circumstances which have to be explained. A necessary condition for Social Democracy was the rapid industrial and urban growth in the nineteenth century; a contributory one may well have been what Leon Epstein terms a 'residual feudal sense of class identification' which made the working class in Europe especially responsive to a class appeal. But were these two factors sufficient in themselves? Epstein argues that the critical condition lies in the *timing* of the working-class entry into politics, and for strong Socialist parties to develop it was necessary that, 'The suffrage on which parties are based came when large numbers of urban industrial workers were already present.'[2] In this way, the class-situation, and the sense of identity which went with it, quickly determined the nature of working-class politics once the vote was won.

All of these conditions contrasted with the situation in the United States—most importantly, the sequence of timing was reversed. Even if one allows for the greater carry-over of older class values in Europe, or points to the greater social mobility in the United States, as Sombart did, it is clear that these have long since ceased to be differentiating factors. Class-*related* politics are important in the United States as they are in Europe, but the continued absence of class-*based* parties in the one and their presence in the other, underlines the particular way in which European politics has developed and the inertia of political traditions which the parties crystallize.

Faced with this challenge from the organized working class—and largely a unified one until Communism offered a more militant alternative from 1919 onwards—the bourgeois parties had a number of choices, as well as a number of restrictions. Their earlier establishment had already given a permanent expression to some cleavages in society; these could not simply be eradicated in the face of the Social Democratic threat, and the problem of securing a mass vote could not easily be overcome. Britain was largely exceptional in both respects: the party system had avoided fragmentation before the arrival of the mass vote, and the two parties, Conservatives and Liberals, continued their ruling position for some time by attracting a large part of the newly enfranchised electorate. The more normal picture was of four or even more parties (orthodox conservative, one or two varieties of liberals, agrarian and religious parties) ante-dating Social Democracy and often by their nature unsuited to make a wider appeal. They either waned rapidly, as did the Liberals in Belgium and Italy once the franchise was extended, or they carved out a fairly modest place for themselves with a sure, if restricted, clientele.

However, some were well-suited to make an appeal to the working class. We saw earlier that religion offers a means of securing a class-compromise, protecting the existing social order and securing a proportion of the mass vote. Such a development came fairly early in the Low Countries. The Social-Christians in preponderantly Roman Catholic Belgium have been the leading government party since 1884. Their victory over the anti-clerical Liberals in the long drawn-out battle over church-state relations from the 1840s onwards (centering on the schools issue) led them in the end to become defenders of the constitutional order, with the approval and advice from Pope Leo XII at the end of the century: 'In the present state of modern society, the system of freedom is favourable to the Church. Belgian Catholics must not only refrain from attacking, they must also defend the Constitution.'[3] Belgian Catholicism thus avoided becoming identified with conservative reaction. The mass-based party, underpinned by Church lay organizations, conservative yet fully constitutional and socially enlightened, gave a strong alternative to Belgian Socialism. It was a powerful formula which others later were to emulate.

It was not immediately applicable to other countries. In Germany, the Catholics were just a strong minority, most concerned to defend Catholic interests in a hostile environment. Indeed, the success of the Catholic Centre Party in permanently harnessing a fifth of the vote meant that there was little chance of creating a large, moderate conservative party unless religious differences were settled first. In Italy, the force of anticlericalism and the dominance of the Liberals until the First World War worked fatefully in another direction. Because of the struggles of the Vatican with the Italian state, a papal edict prevented Italian Catholics from taking any part in politics. These restrictions were only lifted gradually, and it was not until 1919 that Don Luigi Sturzo received permission to form a Catholic

People's Party; this had a radical programme of social and land reform. With the collapse of the Liberal Party, whose hold on Italian politics was made possible by Catholic 'self-denial' and the limited franchise (even after the 1913 reform less than 25 per cent of males had the vote), the Catholic People's Party stood a chance of taking the place of the Liberal Party. However, its appearance was belated and gave insufficient time to remould Italian politics before Mussolini's successful bid for power.

The weakness of the Liberal parties in Germany and Italy was evident elsewhere, and always became drastic when the vote widened. The Swiss Radicals together with the Old Liberals still share a quarter of the total vote, the last stronghold of European liberalism, but the Radicals experienced a rapid decline after 1919. Even without the mass vote, Liberalism suffered notoriously from a lack of cohesion, as it did in Britain. In the Netherlands after 1885 there were always two, sometimes three, Liberal parties. The same was the case in Germany: the Liberals first split in 1861, and (with new party labels) this dualism continued afresh in the Weimar Republic, and in Germany, as elsewhere, quite disparate social forces were behind the liberal banner, ranging from constitutional-radicals to power-hungry nationalists, the front-runners for heavy industry.[4] It was rarely a united class-interest, and not one which for long could attract a large part of the working-class vote.

The fact that Liberalism tended to have a narrow class appeal, and that the religious parties were often handicapped by religious differences or their association with reactionary forces, meant that the challenge of Social Democracy was usually met on a piecemeal basis: a bourgeois coalition, failing that, even the conditional acceptance of a minority position. The working-alliance of the non-Socialist parties in the Netherlands proved quite equal to the task; the various religious parties were able to make an inter-class appeal, and these with the help of the Liberals made the Dutch Socialists an isolated and minority party. In Scandinavia, the bourgeois parties have been in a minority position, but the Social Democrats, in falling short of an absolute majority, have had to rely on some other party to maintain it in power. Here we have the Scandinavian phenomenon of the 'Red-Green' alliance, and with variations this was the pivot of Scandinavian politics dating from the 1930s which only in recent years has broken apart. The 'Green' or Agrarian parties had an important bridging function in these countries, containing Social Democracy and at the same time preventing the formation of a homogeneous non-socialist block. The fragmentation of the bourgeois parties did not have dire effects, for not only were the Social Democrats contained by the need for coalition, or at least voting support, they were also amongst the first of the European Socialist parties to move from a radical to a moderate reformist programme.

We can draw together the threads of this discussion of party development by examining the later consequences for three countries which initially failed to create a mass and unified party of the moderate right—Italy, West Germany, and France. The intermediate consequence was a right-wing political radicalization, but the later development has been a consolidation of the moderate right. Post 1945, the Belgian prototype of Christian Democracy was a model for the class-compromise reached in Italy and West Germany. As the pre-war situation in Austria showed, however, the mere existence of a 'Christian' party could just as easily exacerbate class conflict unless the churches are prepared to play a passive role in political affairs. This orientation is implied in Fogarty's definition of Christian Democracy as, '. . . a movement of those who aim to solve—with the aid of Christian principles and "democratic" techniques—that range of temporal problems which the Church has repeatedly and solemnly declared to lie within the "supreme" competence of lay society, and outside direct ecclesiastical control.'[5] If the clerical hierarchies are prepared to accept this self-denying ordinance, then the Church acts to provide a loose framework of commitment, and within it there is wide scope for political compromise. This formula has worked in the case of Germany, and with more hesitation in Italy—the clergy and the Vatican have somewhat regretfully allowed the Christian Democratic politicians to make the running. In Austria, the refurbished People's Party (previously the Christian-Socials) cut its clerical connections and was declared not to be a 'successor party', and though 'linked to a great and proud tradition' was 'young' even 'revolutionary' after 1945.[6]

The success of Christian Democracy did not extend to France, and some of the instability of the post-war years can be ascribed to the failure of the MRP (*Mouvement Républicain Populaire*). Born in the spirit of the Resistance in 1944, the MRP was the political expression of radical Catholicism. The new party shouldered the full responsibility of government throughout the Fourth Republic, but the party, with its radical outlook, failed to win the confidence of the Catholic voter. After the first flush of post-war success, it rapidly dwindled to become another small party of the centre. Its support sank from over five and a half million in 1946 to two million by the end of the Fourth Republic. Its failure was due in part to the essentially conservative nature of French Catholicism; moreover, it never seemed to fit into the French party system: 'The other parties never understood or accepted the MRP. By the end of the Fourth Republic they had forced it into a position on the Right that they could understand but that it had never wanted.'[7] Efforts in the Fifth Republic to create a more widely based Democratic Centre were not successful either in providing an alternative to Gaullism or to help give a broad alignment of the centre-left.

The evolution of the French moderate and mass right-wing party came from another source, from Gaullism, and without an overt religious appeal. We have seen earlier that the UDR relied heavily on the devout churchgoer, but in the first place this is a conservative vote. A delayed effect of de Gaulle's personal appeal was the creation of a party independent of its founder, though still embodying some of his values. From the start, with the Rally of the French People (RPF) and later in the successors (the UNR and the UDR) the 'party' was little more than a supporters' club for de Gaulle—a necessary evil for him, since parties always tended to play the parliamentary game. Yet the electoral following that grew up round him in the first decade of the Fifth Republic was not dissipated when he left the stage. The UDR became a self-confident governing force, most nearly resembling an 'orthodox' conservative party in the British mould. In doubling its vote from four to nine and a half million between 1958 and 1968, the UDR won a significantly lower percentage of working-class voters than did Christian Democratic parties of other countries.

The end-result was often the same: the political balance was maintained by the ability of the moderate right to find a unified expression, at least in all the major West European countries. The formula adopted had to secure the bulk of the middle-class vote along with a good slice of the lower income groups, peasant or industrial worker. With the Social Democratic Parties still anchored in their apparently favourable class position, Christian Democracy operated a successful flanking movement. The boot was thus on the other foot: the initial momentum of the class-based parties gave way to the inter-class alternative, a mass party with a greater voting potential. Otto Kirchheimer[8] coined the term 'catch-all' parties to describe those which were based on broad popular support, not primarily on a class-appeal, and the catch-all parties with a right-inclination evoked a similar response on the left—we have seen in the previous chapter how this worked out for the German Social Democrats. And in West Germany, in spite of the similarity of the CDU and SPD party programmes, the mainstay of party support continues to be a particular class interest: whilst the SPD attracts 'employees', especially those in trade unions, the CDU is strong amongst the self-employed, professional groups, and the farming population. The CDU's 'Christian' emphasis is an additional factor—offset by the SPD's appeal for younger voters.[9] But in Germany as elsewhere the margins of support are open to accretion or erosion. Some factors point in favour of the left-inclined parties: the effects of industrial growth and a declining rural vote, together with the weakening hold of religion; others point in a different direction: the creation of new occupations and the decline of traditional industries, allied to the greater sense of social mobility which a rising standard of living brings.

The implications of the catch-all party for the nature of 'political opposition' we shall take up later,* and concentrate here on the class-basis of political loyalty. It is evident that the dispute over the 'middle ground' does not automatically run to the benefit of parties with a left or a right orienta-

* See below, pp. 83–7.

tion, since the political middle covers a complex of social change. There may be a temptation to see this as a generalized form of 'middle-class politics', as Kirchheimer did: '. . . a substantial new middle class of skilled workers, the middle ranks of white-collar people, and civil servants. . . . One may justifiably say that diminished social polarization and diminished political polarization are going hand in hand.'[10] Yet the absence of extreme polarization does not make class politics for that reason redundant, nor should one be dazzled by the changing occupational structure or by greater affluence. What we earlier termed the 'residual' aspect of class politics still has to be taken into account, and voting along class lines is still filling its potential. The paradox which Erik Allardt noted for Scandinavia is of wider import: 'All evidence indicates that social class explains more of the variation in voting behaviour and particularly more of the working class voting than some decades ago. This has occurred simultaneously with the disappearance of traditional class barriers. As equality has increased, the working class voters have been more apt to vote for the workers' parties than before.' That view was echoed by Butler and Stokes for Britain: 'The intensity of the class tie may have declined at the same time as its extent became more universal.'[11]

Such a predisposition need not be translated to voting support, particularly not to consistent support. The weak polarization, the competitive tactics of the catch-all parties, do not result in strong commitment. One result is a greater *volatility* on the part of the voters, and there is some evidence of this happening in countries where there are only two major parties in competition, such as in Britain.[12] Parties may be forced to re-emphasize their class differences in order to counteract the lack of commitment. How parties vary in their reading of the situation is shown by the Norwegian Labour Party and the Swedish Social Democrats. In Norway, where according to Rokkan, 'The crucial battles are currently fought over the votes of the rising middle class', the Labour Party deliberately scaled down its class and ideological appeal. The contrast with Sweden is indicative of a quite different reading of the electoral situation; the Swedish Social Democrats made a broad, but recognizably a *class* appeal. They '. . . recognised the risks of a "soft" strategy early in the fifties and soon found a powerful alternative: break down the old status divisions between manual workers and salaried employees and establish a *joint platform* for the defence of their interests against their employers.'[13]

More than strategic differences are implied here; the two approaches reveal contrasting ideas about the direction of social change. Whilst both are concerned with a reinterpretation of socio-economic class in the context of the changes affecting European society, the one views 'economic interest' increasingly as a sum of individual or multi-group aspirations, and the other is a reassertion of collective action. The difficulty is that the economic dimension of social stratification has various ingredients: it is not only the relative distribution of income, or the source of differences in wealth, but the occupational hierarchy which results as well. Any or all of these provide a sufficient basis for modern class politics. In recent years, the emphasis has been away from the 'injustices' of the first two of these, towards a preoccupation on the part of political leaders with the aspirations of new and enlarging occupational groups. Often these are lumped together as a 'new middle class' (equally, a 'new working class'), even if from other points of view there is little evidence of greater social mobility, equality in the distribution of income, or of changes in the ownership of the source of wealth.

The increase in white-collar employment supports arguments in a superficial way for the redundancy of class politics, and the parties of the left and right are seen to compete on equal terms for this important vote. On the left, the change in emphasis has been away from an egalitarian socialism towards a meritocratic version,[14] since this gives full expression to the rising aspirations of the occupationally mobile. As a result, there is a comparative neglect of the class differences which would lead naturally to egalitarian solutions—large disparities in the ownership of wealth and in consequent life-chances. And these differences have a habit of persisting in European countries, whether or not Social Democratic governments have been in power: 'After thirty-five years of socialist rule in Sweden, income differentials between working-class and middle-class occupational groups are no narrower than in Western societies ruled by *bourgeois* governments.'[15] This finding, of course, has to be modified to the extent that the highly developed system of social services in Sweden achieves a net redistributive effect. Sweden is without doubt the leading case by which developments in other countries can be judged, and Lipset points out for the same country that in spite of the efforts of the Social Democratic government in '. . . providing free access to universities together with state bursaries, the proportion of working class children taking advantage of such opportunities has hardly risen. Few commodities are distributed as unequally in Europe as high school and university education.' And these 'commodities' are basic to later chances in life. The widespread persistence of the disparities is evident from an OECD report of 1971: 'Students from the lower strata of society represent at best 26 per cent and in many countries only 10 per cent—or even less—of university enrolments although these classes constitute up to 50 per cent of the population.'[16]*

One can read the persistence of class differences, and their acceptance by Social Democratic parties, in various ways. Firstly, one can say that even when parties of the left maintain a radical egalitarian programme, the attempt to implement this within the existing structure of society is bound to fail. As a second argument, it can be held that the change in Social Democracy from its egalitarian past to its present-day acceptance of

* See also the comparisons on p. 263 below.

meritocratic inequality has been no more than a reflection of the changing aspirations of its supporters—though the objection to this view is not lightly to be dismissed: that there was no evidence of a decline in support *before* reformism got under way. The third possibility is to attribute the changing nature of Social Democracy to its increasingly middle-class leadership. This is the view that Parkin takes: that there is a two-stage process away from radical Socialism; the first is the initial acceptance of the constraints imposed by liberal democracy. 'Once the party has accepted the rules of the parliamentary game the way is open for the second phase of deradicalization—that brought about by the influx of "moderate" middle-class leaders and cadres. The process thus becomes a cumulative one. The greater the inflow of bourgeois recruits, the less militant the party becomes, so making it even more attractive to those who favour the interpretation of equality along meritocratic and welfare lines.'[17] This process, as Parkin points out, is distinct from the embourgeoisement of *working*-class leaders as a cause of 'moderation' put forward by Michels; the leaders are middle class before they assume office. All the same, it is questionable whether a politician's middle-class background inevitably makes him a 'moderate'—the history of socialist movements is studded with figures who overcame this apparent handicap.

Our analysis has concentrated exclusively on the relationship of Social Democracy to social class, and the changing nature of these parties should not obscure the fact that the terms on which the 'moderate and mass' bourgeois parties are able to compete have involved a parallel set of concessions, but with a difference: they operate from a position of harmony with the prevailing socio-economic system, and the political framework in which the decisions are made is one suited to preserve the status quo. Whatever the precise causes for the redefinition of Social Democracy (and for that matter the parties of the extreme left*), for the bourgeois parties it is much easier to point to a simple strategical consideration: to secure a make-weight from the lower income-groups. The more general, and as-yet unanswered, problem is to explain the high level of working-class integration, given the inequalities of a market-based society.

The Representation of Group Interests

Alongside the political parties, the power of organized interests is a second pronounced feature of liberal democracies. They are seen to be an essential complement to the decision-making process, providing a kind of balance to the system, working on the parties, the public, and at the governmental level. But the balance is never guaranteed; organized interests are in direct competition with the parties for the ear of government,

* See below, pp. 142–6.

and their influence over the parties may be so great that the latter may be reduced to a subordinate role. At various times, either a complementary or a competitive role has been taken by the main pillars of social interest: a vocal farm population, the trade unions, the Churches, the commercial and industrial interests, the small shopkeeper, and the professional organizations. Yet these are only the heavyweight members of the interest world; around them cluster a host of special interests, some defending the socio-economic position of their members, others advancing a particular cause.

This view of organized interests stresses their autonomous position and their *associational* character. An immediate contrast is apparent with traditional societies and totalitarian states; in both of these, for widely different reasons, interests are almost entirely furthered in an *institutional* setting, that is, their expression is entirely dependent on the official struc-ture of authority; in the first, they will be a natural extension of the traditional hierarchy of power, and in the totalitarian society, in so far as they are recognized as legitimate expressions at all, the leading interests will be incorporated as a part of state activity. It would be incorrect, however, to make too sharp a distinction between pluralist and other types of society; particularly within the state-machine of all liberal democracies, it is obvious that the interests of the armed forces and of the bureaucracy are expressed in an institutional rather than an associative manner. One can also show a similarity of another kind: to the extent that democratic governments rely on direct consultation with leading interests and even make this a *formal* aspect of the deliberative process, then a reversion to an institutional type is possible. The direct links forged between the government bureaucracy and organized interests is one obvious result of increasing state involvement in economic and social regulation, and Henry Ehrmann poses the question whether the 'subsystem autonomy' of pluralist society is not moving to a condition of neo-feudalism.[18] And when Almond and Powell argue that, 'A high incidence of direct in-stitutional interest-group articulation is particularly indicative of poor boundary maintenance',[19] neo-feudalism can be seen as a drastic re-drawing of the boundary lines between the political and the governmental processes—for 'corporatism' is an alternative expression.

Alongside this general view of a trend which could be applicable to Western Europe, we can distinguish several national variations, individual styles, which both confirm and modify the broad tendency. There are three main variables which, according to Eckstein, can account for national differences; the content of government policy, the structure of government decision-making, and the prevailing norms and attitudes within a society. The first of these, government policy, viewed as a wide commitment to social and economic development, does not differ that much from one country or one major party to another in Western Europe. Though the means and the emphasis vary, policies are directed to economic growth, regional development, social security, educational and social advance; the same *type* of government intervention is required, irrespective of differences, say, about the distribution of wealth and income. To this extent we should expect common interest group patterns to emerge.

It is otherwise with the second and third variables. The way in which government decisions are reached involves both the formal rule-making apparatus and the actual distribution of power. How interests will operate will depend on such factors as the decentralization of power and on the precise form taken by legislative-executive relations. Within these provisions, the party system will at least provide some indication of the distribution of power. Where one party is dominant for long periods, the structuring of interests will differ significantly from situations of multi-party government or where there is a fairly regular alternation. The power position of the bureaucracy is also important; partly this will depend on the formal power arrangements and the operation of the party system, but it will also be a consequence of the social composition of the state service—in what sense it is a 'representative' bureaucracy.*

The third variable, what may be termed the relevant features of a political culture, will help to establish the feasible, and acceptable, ways of promoting sectional interests, and even what kind of interest is to be allowed as 'legitimate'. Variations here may follow the lines suggested in the particular balance of 'participant', 'subject', and 'parochial' behaviour which is established in a society. Also relevant is the degree of consensus and cleavage on basic issues—a degree of mutual trust will allow organized interests considerable leeway in their dealings with parties and governments. Finally, the presence of strong subcultures will result in a fragmentation of interests which in a homogeneous society are given a unified expression.

We can illustrate the outcome of these influences by showing the marked differences in the style of interest representation which results, and take the examples of Sweden, West Germany, France, and Italy as representative of the others in Western Europe. One could put forward the Anglo-American system as a reference point, except that no single model emerges: in spite of the fact that they are both 'associational societies' and rank as 'civic cultures', with the ready articulation of specialized group interests, there are distinctive aspects in both. For instance, Almond notes that there is more flexibility, a 'greater substitutability of function' in the American system generally, in contrast with Britain, which shows 'a more centralised, predictable role structure'.[20] The British system is also more centralized than the American. The operation of the separation of powers at a national level in the United States spreads decision-making and allows interest groups alternative points of leverage, enabling them to 'play off'

---

* See below, 'Administrative Élites', pp. 184–91.

one point of power against another; the idea of the 'veto group' which emerges in this situation underlines the negative effect which strong interests can exert on public policy. The federal structure enhances the decentralization, and the overall result is to give multiple lines of access and alternative strategies to which the loose nature of the party system gives maximum scope.

Almost all of this picture contrasts with Britain; the decision-making process is highly centralized, in the government and in the parties. There is a natural gravitation of interests towards the central government—the ministers and the permanent executive. The parliamentary parties are often of marginal importance, especially in the making of *detailed* decisions, and the sheer amount of this activity is a responsibility which the parties and public are happy enough in practice to leave to the minister and his officials. This evidence of civic 'trust' results in decisions, and often key ones, being made by relatively few people, and the whole process tends to be little publicized, less-openly contentious, with the leading interests mostly identifiable as part of the political establishment. The 'trust' has a parallel in the high degree of subject-competence on the part of the individual: he does not feel that he will be unfairly dealt with by the authorities. In both countries, the ease with which 'attitude' or 'cause' groups are formed, their strictly constitutional nature underlining the confidence of their members in the system, shows the stable nature of associational societies. This is not a feature that is necessarily permanent, and the lack of stability in others is expressed by the withdrawal to a state of passivity, or with the sudden resort to violence of the 'anomic' group.

Of all European states, Sweden appears to have carried furthest the integration of interest representation with public life. Heckscher admits that organized interests, '. . . exercise a power almost equal to that of parliament and definitely superior to that of the parliamentary parties.'[21] Yet this superiority is not based on pressure group domination; it is rather that the interest-permeation is spread in such a way that political leadership is not sacrificed in the cross-fire of competing interests. It is a balanced political system, based on a homogeneous political culture, and in Castles' view, '. . . out of which, to some degree, has appeared a consensus about the roles of the state, party and interest organisation.'[22]

In this situation, no segment of the population feels that it is less-well represented than the others, and in spite of the ubiquity of group interests, the primacy of political leadership is not questioned. To explain this, one has to appreciate the highly public nature of interest representation which enables it to be accepted as a full complement of political representation by supplying a functional dimension. The important consequence is that interest groups operate as an integral part of the political scene; their activities are widely reported, their leaders in the public eye, and their members are well informed about the aims and tactics of their organization. This openness extends to the relationship of interests to the Riksdag and the government—as we shall see later;* the process of legislation is itself geared to a wide consultation with affected interests rather than to the fulfilment of party programmes.

The upshot is that organized groups can be said to be an essential part of the constitutional structure, spanning the 'input' and 'conversion' aspects of the political system to a greater extent than, say, in Britain. One can go even further and postulate a group dominance of political and social life: 'The total result is the formation of an almost exclusive system of groups ... and it is difficult to gain access to public decision-makers without working through one of these existing groups.'[23] These established groups which largely pre-empt the field are naturally strongest in economic affairs, with the two most powerful, the Swedish Trade Union Confederation (LO) and the Employers' Confederation (SAF) head and shoulders above the others. On the trade union side, there are separate organizations for white-collar workers, professional, and government employees. Though relatively small in comparison with the total labour force, these latter bodies are militant and well organized, quite on a par with the manual workers. Since 1966, all government employees have had the right to strike, and this led to an unprecedented situation early in 1971 when the Confederation of Professional Associations (SACO) and the National Federation of Government Employees (SR) called out their members in support of a claim to restore their differentials in comparison with the pay of manual workers. As a result of the strike in which key workers were called out in various sectors, industrial and social life was disrupted. The strike, '... closed down criminal courts, dislocated the national welfare services, stopped construction projects, deprived commuters of transportation to work and forced industry to lay off thousands of workers.'[24] After several weeks, the government was eventually provoked into calling a lock-out of public employees. This would have led to the farcical spectacle of 'locking out' some 3,000 of the country's 5,000 army officers! Only the passing of emergency legislation to give a cooling-off period prevented this development.

Dubbed as a 'luxury strike' of university graduates, the dispute is indicative of the tensions which beset a highly structured associational society, and one also has to take into account the no-less important interests in other areas besides that of employer-employee relationships—the farmers' unions, the co-operative movement, and the various religious bodies. Although Swedish political life is typified as 'the politics of compromise', this is by no means an easy-going relationship, rather a hard-fought battle—according to accepted rules. The tendency to a 'nationalization' of group interests, a neofeudalism, in which certain interests enjoy a paramountcy in public life and a special relationship with

* See below, p. 166.

the government, is evident in Sweden as elsewhere; the real core of the compromise is to preserve political institutions which are not overwhelmed by group pressures.

The Swedish system has evolved over a long period, and we can take the rather rapid changes that have occurred in Germany as a contrast, starting from a quite different basis and yet giving an equal impression of cohesion. The situation now ruling is quite unlike the circumstances prevailing in the Weimar Republic, of which Merkl writes, 'The major and minor interest groups from the trade unions to the farm, business and professional organisations of all kinds were divided along numerous lines according to class prejudices, ideological convictions and political preferences which added up to "an infinitely differentiated labyrinth" and contributed considerably to political chaos.'[25] The reshaping of these interests along simplified lines, to which the Nazi policy of *Gleichschaltung* doubtless contributed, was a feature of the period after 1945. Instrumental to the simplification were the political parties and the stable voting attachments they secured; in particular, the conglomerate nature of the CDU served to unite a diversity of interests under one roof, and under Adenauer's leadership the party developed a system of some ingenuity in channelling various economic and social demands. Outside of this largely governmental framework, and to some extent acting as a balance, came the formation of a powerful, unified trade union movement. Its unification depended on the severance of all political ties; this political neutrality probably helped organized labour to achieve a greater integration with the political system than would have been the case had it developed as a form of industrial opposition in the era of CDU dominance.

One should not be completely carried away by the new look of group activity in the post-war period; there are important aspects of historical continuity as well. Associations of economic interest in Germany have always occupied a privileged position in public life at all levels, and have had a public regulative function. Lewis Edinger points out that the local trade associations, '. . . have their roots in the corporate guilds of the Middle Ages. . . . These are non-autonomous institutions of public law which exercise compulsory jurisdiction over their members and are supposed to link all major sectors of the economy to the political system.'[26] These various trade and occupational associations operate from a local level upwards and are in a strategic position to act as mediators between the public authorities and their specialized membership—at the local municipal level, within the Länder, and in negotiation with the federal government.

A further dimension to the official and public nature of interest group activity lies in the structure of government itself: the individual Länder can be regarded as public-interest pressure groups as well as government structures. Each state government represents the particular socio-economic interests of its area in relation to the dispensations of the federal government, especially regarding the relative financial commitments of the two. We shall look later at the working of German federalism,* but we can note that the articulation of area interests is an important function and that these reach a focal point in the federal upper house, the Bundesrat, where all the state governments are directly represented. This idea of a public interest pressure group extends to lower levels of government as well—to the municipalities.[27]

Edinger rather forbiddingly describes the West German situation as reflecting 'the highly formalised patterns of polyarchic elitism and mass passivity'.[28] One can see evidence of formalization in the special position which interest groups have in many sectors of public life; the term 'mass passivity' has to be treated with some caution: it does correspond to the idea of 'detachment' as a feature of the German political culture, with group leadership showing a high level of professional competence, independent of the membership they represent—but the 'mass passivity' is not a sign of discontent or alienation.

In the economic sphere, these representative élites tend to balance one another's power, and in this sense they are 'polyarchic'. Their most complete expression can be seen in a number of important national organizations, the large and inclusive 'summit' organizations or *Spitzenverbände*. These harden into half a dozen or so key groups which are all-important for the economic life of the nation. On the employers' side there are various 'roof' organizations: the Federation of German Employers' Associations (BDA) contains several hundred individual employers' associations; the Federation of German Industry (BDI) unites about forty national industrial organizations, themselves structured on a federal basis; a third 'roof' organization brings into one fold the local and district chambers of industry and commerce—and membership of these is compulsory for all enterprises. Obviously there is a considerable overlap in membership, a criss-crossing at various levels of regional and particular industrial and commercial interests.

A parallel summit is reached by the trade union movement. Most of the trade unions are members of the German Trades Union Federation (DGB), with small, but powerful, separate organizations for civil servants and for the majority of white collar workers. The placid appearance of German industrial relations since the war is partly attributable to the highly rationalized union structure—the DGB has only sixteen constituent unions, organized on broad industrial lines and on a federal basis as well. Of equal significance has been the integration of the trade union movement with the general industrial set-up. Imperfect as the principle of 'co-determination' (*Mitbestimmungsrecht)* is generally admitted to have been in practice and only of partial application anyway, it does give expression to the corporate sentiments which have persisted for a very

* See below, pp. 214–16.

long time and which have made easier the handling of disputes—especially in the 'labour courts' for handling these. The absence of industrial conflict is only imperfectly explained by the continuing prosperity; the other relevant factors are the élitist, and unquestioned, authority of the professional leadership of the unions—a 'passivity' on the shop-floor—and the incorporation of the unions into a nation-wide, 'public' network of interests.

To the economic groupings have to be added the Protestant and Catholic Churches and, until the recent past, the various 'refugee' pressure groups. These, together with the economic interest groups (including those of the farmers), find it profitable to work at all levels of public life. It is in Bonn, however, that they find it most important to be represented. Direct negotiation with government departments and ministers is important, but there is no tradition of bureaucratic subservience to private interests. Almost as much is to be gained by having some influence in the Bundestag, especially as the work of the specialized and numerous Bundestag committees involves conducting inquiries and hearing interested parties. The 'corporate' leanings of German industrial society are such that there is an orderly gravitation of organized interests towards the decision-making centres. The official voice of the interests harmonizes quite naturally with the main 'arenas' of legislation—the federal government departments, the Bundesrat, and the Bundestag.

Now whether or not we wish to conclude that the pattern of West German interest representation represents a 'neofeudalism', it is quite clear that its basis is different from that existing in Sweden; in Germany, one might argue, it is their 'official' status which is all-important, whilst in Sweden it is their sheer power which has carved out for them a secure 'political' position. Turning to France, we can examine how far either of these standpoints could be held to be true of the Fifth Republic. It is evident that in both the Third and Fourth Republics, the power of group interests was largely political. Whilst in Sweden this power has not undermined the parliamentary system, but rather dovetailed with it, in France the cross-pressures of group interests did undermine political leadership. Williams and Harrison portray the situation: 'Under the Fourth Republic the summit of party ambition was to win a share of power rather than to exercise it outright. One way to achieve this was to outbid one's rivals for the support of a clientele—Gaullists against Conservatives against MRP over the Catholic schools, Communists against Socialists against Radicals on behalf of secular education—and each against all for the favours of home-distillers, ex-servicemen, peasants or small shop-keepers.'[29] And for a while these last were to show, in Poujadism, that they could find their own political expression if the established parties failed to deliver the goods. Group interests were by no means victorious, but their effect was to defeat government policies and make stable government impossible. In this sense, they were politically predominant.

Powerful as many of the lobbies were in the past—for instance, the colonial and arms lobbies in the Third Republic—those relying on a degree of mass membership have usually lacked stable support and are usually prone to doctrinal and other feuds. Nor, in a country of individualists, is it possible to rely on a high membership. This kind of associational weakness contrasts with West Germany and Sweden. Trade union membership, at around 15 per cent of the employed population, is far lower than for comparable countries, and it is split amongst four affiliations; the Christian trade unions are the main challengers to the *Confédération Générale du Travail,* still largely under Communist influence and with less than a third of the membership it had shortly after 1945. The same kind of organizational weakness besets other groups which rely on a mass membership. Ehrmann estimated that not more than 25 per cent of all farmers belong to one or other of the agricultural interest groups, and these are very numerous: '. . . the diversity of interests, the individualism and occasionally the sectarianism of their constituents explain the existence of close to five hundred rural defence organizations on the national level alone.'[30] Even the main agricultural confederation (FNSEA) faces competition from at least three other organizations, and internally has to cope with its own dissidents—not least the 'Young Farmers' who form a separate, activist wing. And even with the plethora of organized channels available, this does not prevent the sporadic outbursts of violence, direct action, on the part of discontented farmers. More cohesive, and for that matter more effective, are the industrial and employers' associations, and the very largest firms, successors to the former industrial dynasties, can take up their cause direct with the government. Even within the industrial associations there are wide differences of viewpoint—the politics of national and regional economic development, the contrasting outlook of small and large firms; and the young turks are as prominent in industry as they are in agriculture. It is a babel of interests—labour, agricultural, and industrial—which competes for the ear of government, never a united voice.

Whilst it can be agreed that the total effect of interest representation on the Fourth Republic was destructive, seen another way the parliamentary system had a value: 'The Fourth Republic Assembly acted more than was appreciated as both a shock absorber and a channel of communication between governors and governed.'[31] Both these functions dried up in the aridity of Fifth Republic parliaments. Instead, there was a natural, explicit switch of attention on the part of the interest groups from the Assembly to government—to where the decisions were made, within the executive. But the transfer of effort did not give the interest groups a greater leverage than before, although judging by the numbers they could at least expect to be consulted: 'On a national level alone, there exist now no less than five hundred "Councils", twelve hundred "Committees", and three thousand "Commissions", all bringing together group representatives and members of the bureaucracy.'[32] This proliferation of consultation does not at all mean that the interests hold sway; neither the government nor its bureaucracy is subject to an adverse vote, and given the fundamental disunity of the individual interests, it is not difficult to rule through division. Furthermore, the guiding principle of the Fifth Republic has all along been to tame the power of the political intermediaries—the interest groups as well as the parties. With the failure of the parties in the Assembly to regain their former position, the onus is firmly with the groups to secure an articulation and an aggregation of interests, but it is doubtful if they are always fit to this task.

Yet the whole drift of modern French politics has been towards a 'non-political' form of representation rather than a parliamentary one. As long ago as 1952 it could be said by a leading Fourth Republic politician: 'The remedies are neither on the Left or on the Right. They have no parliamentary label. They are technical steps, which must be taken in an atmosphere of political armistice.'[33] It can be argued that the power given to the executive in the Fifth Republic rationalized and made explicit a process of decision-making that was well under way in the Fourth—especially in the field of economic planning.* The French 'Plan' was never a parliamentary exercise, but a series of 'technical steps' requiring intensive preparation and co-ordination on the part of the bureaucracy in consultation with a variety of national and regional interests. In all of the seven economic Plans, spanning the years 1947–80, the Assembly has been a bystander, not even debating some of the earlier Plans.[34]

The Plan is symptomatic of the downgrading of parliamentary institutions, alongside the shackles imposed by the constitution. To convert this to 'democratic planning' by allowing for a wide functional consultation stumbles on the power position of the higher bureaucracy; and the evocative term 'technocracy' endows the state-machine with a political purpose. As long as this retains its cohesion and is looked upon favourably by the government of the day, then the 'political' and even the 'official' status of group interests is kept in a subordinate position.

Though the term 'neo-feudalism' might still be applied, the French way of accommodating interests accords neither with the German nor the Swedish. We can introduce the fourth national style, the Italian, to show yet another variation. Indeed, this form contrasts with the other three in that it shows traits of a much older kind of politics in which 'pluralism' has not yet eroded traditional relationships, in a sense still 'feudal'. The ingredients are various, but related: the dominant position of the Christian Democrats, the place of the Roman Catholic Church as the strongest of all group interests, the weakness of the Italian bureaucracy; the conjunction of these three elements gives a special pattern. Alternatively, one can portray the

---

* For a more detailed account, see below, pp. 232–3.

divisive effect of the sub-cultures: the deep cleavage between the Church and the anti-clerical forces, with the summits of political confrontation in Christian Democracy and Communism; the other split, just as dramatic, between north and south—industrially, economically, and socially.

Least of all is Italy an associational society. The segmentation of Italian society is one aspect, the other has been the hegemony of Christian Democracy over government since the war—if one adds to this the equally long period of authoritarian rule previously, then most interest groups have grown up in the context of a government that is regarded as permanently in power. This permanence makes the relationship of party and bureaucracy of special importance. Joseph LaPalombara advances two concepts, the *'parentela'* and the *'clientela'*, which help considerably in appreciating the articulation of interest groups to the political structure. What is more, both are terms which express the persistence of older traditions in Italian society.

The *parentela* relationship is almost in the way of being a kinship tie: 'In the traditional South, whence most of Italy's bureaucrats are recruited, ties of *Parentela* are particularly strong, implying the kinds of rights and obligations that are generally associated with pre-industrial societies.'[35] It is natural that these rights and obligations are accorded to the hegemonic Christian Democracy and to the interests which it represents: 'The bureaucrats and functionaries tend to obey the minister and the party in power, and . . . ignore those parties and those associations that are not instruments of or representatives of the parties in power.'[36] This pervasive outlook is supplemented by the *clientela* relationship; this involves regarding certain interest groups as, '. . . the natural expression and representative of a given social sector which, in turn, constitutes the natural target or reference point for the activity of the administrative agency.' And this 'naturalness' is a survival from an earlier form of society whose influence still runs deep: 'The contemporary feudal power in Italy is represented by the industrialist class, and particularly by monopoly capitalism . . . contemporary dominant groups have succeeded in having medieval corporative values widely accepted by vast sectors of Italian society.'[37]

What emerges is a triple alliance of party, interests, and bureaucracy. Christian Democracy itself is a conglomerate of interests, and on this it depends for its voting power. Ranged behind the party are the Catholic Church, large sections of the farming community, and industrial interests. Chief of the flanking organizations in each field are Catholic Action, the Association of Direct Cultivators, and the Confederation of Italian Industry (*Confindustria*). The first two of these are an integral part of Christian Democracy, whilst *Confindustria,* no longer the important financial backer it was in the early post-war years, preserves a more independent stance—particularly objecting to any 'opening to the left' undertaken by the Christian Democrats. It differs as well in that unlike the mass membership of the farming associations and the lay organizations of the Church, it is not in a position to 'deliver the vote'. Both Catholic Action, with its related bodies, and the Direct Cultivators provide a voting loyalty, and they also manage to place a large number of their members in the Italian Parliament; the parliamentary party of the Christian Democrats is composed of an alliance of interests, and the party must act as broker to various factions, all of which are in a privileged position in Italian society.

The power of Italian industry is primarily exercised through the large firms acting individually, rather than by means of the interest associations: '*Confidustria* has a reputation for power which is highly exaggerated. It, as well as the trade associations, is used by the large firms for certain purposes, such as providing a means for the large ones to keep the small ones in line. ... The real power lies in the large firms themselves.'[38] Alongside the dozen or so very large concerns, there are the two giant state combines, the IRI (Industrial Reconstruction Institute) and the ENI (National Hydrocarbons Trust). These are not nationalized concerns in the strict sense, but mixed enterprises, subject only to overall political control. By the mid-fifties the IRI had become, '. . . a bewildering maze of more than a thousand interrelated companies',[39] especially strong in shipbuilding and banking, and inheriting many of its interests from the fascist period. The ENI is concentrated in the energy-producing industry, particularly oil, chemicals, mining, and natural gas—with control too of a leading Milan newspaper. How is one to sum up the total effect of this massive state intervention in almost every field of the economy? It has not led to any substantial weakening of the private sector; rather it has served to blur the division between state and private interest, placing public employees in close relation to a variety of commercial pressures. These state concerns also give a power of influence and appointment to the ruling party; a colonization of government-controlled organizations.

Facing this 'contemporary feudal power', the trade union movement has been unable to present a united front. Four major confederations are concerned: the Communist and Socialist CGIL, the Social Democratic UIL, the Catholic CISL, and the right-wing CISNAL. Attempts to maintain a unified movement broke down in 1948 when the Catholic and Socialist factions split away from the Communist-led CGIL, and for long the labour movement was in danger of being subordinated to the political parties. Efforts to heal the schism have been made in recent years, and political differences in leadership have not prevented tactical alliances. Because the unions are financially weak, the main tactic is the big, brief strike—often directed to broad social objectives, such as improved health services, housing and pensions. This extra-parliamentary leverage has now become an accepted part of the Italian political scene, and an effective one in wringing concessions from the government.

On almost every count, the structure of Italian interest representation differs substantially from the other countries we have considered; and it is evident that any one label such as 'neo-feudalism' is inadequate to take account of the national differences and the nuances involved in the complex of party, government, and interest relations. But the general drift is the same in most countries: an elevation of interest representation to the detriment of the political parties and the parliamentary system, and an increasingly close connection between powerful interests and the government bureaucracy, in various ways and guises an institutionalization of pressure group activity.

Attempts to 'house train' these forces by linking them to parliamentary institutions have not been especially successful, nor is a political assembly likely to concede much power to an 'economic and social council'. Leaving aside the rather irrelevant 'functional' composition of the Irish Senate, most councils—as in Belgium, Italy, and Luxembourg—have consultative functions: legislative input but no real rule-making powers. The French Social and Economic Council has stronger traditions, inherited from the Fourth Republic, but de Gaulle's attempt to replace the existing Senate by a revamped version of the Council was defeated in the 1969 referendum. The French council encourages group participation (trade unions, public bodies, private industry), especially with the infrastructure of regional planning and the formulation of the periodic general Plans. The Dutch Social and Economic Council (equal proportions of trade union, industrial, and government representatives) is more powerful. Although decisions require a two-thirds majority (and are subject to a cabinet veto), the advice tendered by the council is difficult for the government to ignore. Yet as Stephen Holt comments: 'It is the unique structure of Dutch society which gives the council its power, *not* its institutional framework.'[40]

The case of the Netherlands shows that the success of schemes incorporating group interests into the decision-making process depends largely on the nature of political and social traditions. Thus the Austrian system of five separate 'chambers' representing various facets of economic life is highly successful in securing wide consultation and agreed policies, but it could scarcely be imitated. Moreover, countries such as Sweden—a society of advanced 'associational' character—have no formal method of functional representation, whilst Western Germany makes use of a flexible device of 'concerted action'. An argument against any general extension of formal representation is that organized interests are influential enough already—further 'assimilation' to the political process could endanger party and political leadership. In this connection it will be of interest to see how the Economic and Social Council of the European Community ultimately develops in relation to the European Parliament once the latter, directly-elected, seeks to increase its own authority.

Beyond the formal institutions built up around organized interests, there are other, more general tendencies apparent, especially those associated with the idea of 'corporatism'. This term has been used to describe a new relationship of the state with the economic sector which some feel not only threatens to by-pass the established forms of representative democracy but also to weaken the basic pluralist model of West European society. Free from any association with the fascist 'corporate state', the corporate model points to an increasingly close 'partnership' between the leading economic interests and the state. The economic imperatives, it is argued, have drawn the modern state into a whole range of commitments and responsibilities, and whilst the framework of the market system is retained, in fact the process of decision-making depends on the cooperation, even interlocking, of the state's administrative apparatus with the private sector. This picture can be overdrawn, but it is apparent that the label of 'state corporatism' does highlight a significant shift from the conventional account of liberal democratic politics.[41]

NOTES AND REFERENCES

1. R. Rose and D. W. Urwin, 'Persistence and Change in Western Party Systems since 1945', in *Political Studies*, September 1970, vo. 18, pp. 287–319.
2. L. D. Epstein, 'Political Parties in Western Democratic Systems', in R. C. Macridis (ed.), *Political Parties: Contemporary Trends and Ideas*, New York: Harper and Row, 1967, p. 144.
3. V. Lorwin, 'Belgium: Religion, Class and Language in National Politics', in R. A. Dahl (ed.), *Political Oppositions in Western Democracies*, New Haven: Yale University Press, 1966, p. 156.
4. The split personality of German liberalism was evident even in the Frankfurt Assembly of 1848; a liberal deputy took this view: 'The path of power is the only one which can satisfy and satiate our urge for liberty. For this urge does not primarily aspire to liberty; to a greater degree it lusts for power which so far has been denied to it.' See H. Kohn, *The Mind of Germany: The Education of a Nation*, Macmillan, 1961, p. 141.
5. M. P. Fogarty, *Christian Democracy in Western Europe*, Routledge and Kegan Paul, 1957, p. 6.
6. H. Hürten, *Christliche Parteien in Europa*, Osnabrück: A. Fromm, 1964, p. 146.
7. M. Steed, 'France', in S. Henig and J. Pinder (eds.), *European Political Parties*, George Allen and Unwin/PEP, 1969, p. 119.
8. O. Kirchheimer, 'The Transformation of the Western European Party Systems', in J. LaPalombara and M. Weiner (eds.), *Political Parties and Political Development*, New Jersey: Princeton University Press, 1956, pp. 177–200.
9. For a recent analysis, see K. von Beyme and M. Kaase (eds.), *Elections and Parties: Socio-Political Change and Participation in the West German Federal Election of 1976*, Sage Publications, 1978.
10. O. Kirchheimer, 'The Waning of Opposition', in R. C. Macridis and B. E. Brown (eds.), *Comparative Politics*, Homewood, Illinois: The Dorsey Press, 1964, p. 287.
11. E. Allardt quoted by S. M. Lipset in 'The Modernisation of Contemporary European Politics', *Revolution and Counterrevolution*, Heinemann, 1969, p. 222. Also, D. Butler and D. Stokes, *Political Change in Britain*, Macmillan, 1969, p. 116.
12. For the increasing volatility of the British electorate, see W. Miller, B. Särlvik, and J. Alt, 'Partisan Dealignment in Britain, 1969–1974', in *British Journal of Political Science*, April 1977. More generally: A. Zuckerman and M. Lichbach, 'Stability and Change in European Electorates', *World Politics*, October 1977.

13. S. Rokkan, 'Geography, Religion, and Social Class: Crosscutting Cleavages in Norwegian Politics', in S. M. Lipset and S. Rokkan (eds.), *Party Systems and Voter Alignments: Cross-National Perspectives,* Collier-Macmillan, 1967, pp. 434–5.

14. See F. Parkin, *Class, Inequality and Political Order: Social Stratification in Capitalist and Communist Societies,* MacGibbon & Kee, 1971, pp. 122–8.

15. ibid., p. 121. For a positive assessment, however, see F. Castles, 'Scandinavian Social Democracy: Achievements and Problems', *West European Politics,* February 1978, and his book: *The Social Democratic Image of Society,* Routledge, 1978.

16. S. M. Lipset, *Revolution and Counterrevolution,* p. 243, and the *OECD Observer,* no. 50, February 1971, p. 13.

17. Parkin, op. cit., p. 132.

18. H. W. Ehrmann, 'Interest Groups and the Bureaucracy in Western Democracies', in M. Dogan and R. Rose (eds.), *European Politics,* Collier-Macmillan, 1971, p. 350.

19. G. A. Almond and G. B. Powell, *Comparative Politics: A Developmental Approach,* Boston: Little Brown, 1966, p. 91.

20. G. A. Almond, 'Comparative Political Systems', in Macridis and Brown (eds.), op. cit., p. 57.

21. G. Heckscher, 'Sweden', in H. W. Ehrmann (ed.), *Interest Groups on Four Continents,* University of Pittsburgh Press, 1958, p. 170.

22. F. G. Castles, *Pressure Groups and Political Culture,* Routledge, 1967, p. 62.

23. J. B. Board, *The Government and Politics of Sweden,* Boston: Houghton Mifflin, 1970, p. 64.

24. *The Times,* 10th March 1971.

25. P. Merkl, 'The Structure of Interests and Adenauer's Survival as Chancellor', in *European Politics,* p. 371.

26. L. J. Edinger, *Politics in Germany,* Boston: Little, Brown, 1969, p. 207. The German system of representation is akin to the Austrian where the 'corporate' idea is even more strongly marked. The Austrian 'Chamber' system provides separate and *statutory* representation for the major interests, especially Commerce, Agriculture, and Labour.

27. See W. Hofman, 'The Public Interest Pressure Group: The Case of the Deutsche Städtetag', in *Public Administration,* Autumn 1967, pp. 245–59.

28. Edinger, op. cit., p. 198.

29. P. H. Williams and M. Harrison, *Politics and Society in de Gaulle's Republic,* Longman, 1971, p. 144.

30. H. W. Ehrmann, *Politics in France,* Boston: Little, Brown, 1968, p.176.

31. Williams and Harrison, op. cit., p. 163.

32. Ehrmann, op. cit., p. 184.

33. Antoine Pinay, quoted by Castles, op. cit., p. 56.

34. See D. M. Green, 'The Seventh Plan—The Demise of French Planning?', *West European Politics,* February 1978.

35. J. LaPalombara, *Interest Groups in Italian Politics,* Princeton University Press, 1964, p. 306.

36. ibid., pp. 312–13.

37. ibid., pp. 260, 262.

38. N. Kogan, The Government of Italy, Thomas Crowell, 1962, p. 65.

39. J. C. Adams and P. Barile, *The Government of Republican Italy,* Boston: Houghton Mifflin, 1966, pp. 193–200.

40. S. Holt, *Six European States,* Hamish Hamilton, 1970, p. 363.

41. For an introduction to the idea of 'Corporatism' and a review of the literature, see A. Cawson, 'Pluralism, Corporatism and the Role of the State', *Government and Opposition,* vol. 13/2, Spring 1978.

Additional References

J. Blondel, *Political Parties: A Genuine Case for Discontent?*, Wildwood House, 1978.

J. Blondel, 'Mass Parties and Industrialised Societies', in J. Blondel (ed.), *Comparative Government: A Reader*, Macmillan, 1968.

B. E. Brown, *The European Left Confronts Modernity*, Cyrco Press, Eurospan, 1977.

F. Castles, *The Social Democratic Image of Society*, Routledge, 1978.

L. Derfler, *Socialism since Marx: A Century of the European Left*, Macmillan, 1973.

M. Duverger, *Political Parties: Their Organization and Activity in the Modern State*, Methuen, 1964.

L. Epstein, *Political Parties in Western Democracies*, Pall Mall Press, 1967.

A. J. Heidenheimer (ed.), *Comparative Political Finance*, D. C. Heath, 1970.

S. Henig (ed.), *Political Parties in the European Community*, Allen and Unwin, 1979.

R. Irving, *The Christian Democratic Parties of Western Europe*, Allen and Unwin, 1979.

R. Irving, *Christian Democracy in France*, Allen and Unwin, 1973.

T. Judt (ed.), 'Socialists and Socialism in the 20th Century' *Journal of Contemporary History*, (whole issue), June 1976.

Z. Layton-Henry, *Conservative Politics in Western Europe*, Sage, forthcoming.

M. Kolinsky and W. Paterson (eds.), *Social and Political Movements in Western Europe*, Croom Helm, 1976.

J. LaPalombara and M. Weiner (eds.), *Political Parties and Political Development*, Princeton University Press, 1966.

G. Lichtheim, *A Short History of Socialism*, Weidenfeld and Nicolson, 1970.

V. R. Lorwin, 'Working Class Politics in Western Europe', in Macridis and Brown, op. cit.

M. Lyon, 'Christian Democratic Parties and Politics', in G. Byrne and K. Pedersen (eds.), *Politics in Western European Democracies*, New York: Wiley, 1971.

J. Madeley, 'Scandinavian Christian Democracy: Throwback or Portent?' *European Journal of Political Research*, vol. 5/3, September 1977.

S. Neumann (ed.), *Modern Political Parties*, University of Chicago Press, 1967.

W. Paterson and I. Campbell, *Social Democracy in Post-War Europe*, Macmillan, 1974.

W. Paterson and A. Thomas, (eds.), *Social Democratic Parties in Western Europe*, Croom Helm, 1977.

G. Pridham, *Christian Democracy in Western Germany*, Croom Helm, 1977.

R. A. Webster *Christian Democracy in Italy, 1860–1960*, Hollis and Carter, 1961.

See also, additional references for Chapters 4 and 6.

G. Almond, 'A Comparative Study of Interest Groups and the Political Process', in H. Eckstein and D. Apter, *Comparative Politics*, New York: The Free Press, 1963.

G. Braunthal, *The Federation of German Industry in Politics*, Cornell University Press, 1965.

B. E. Brown, *Pressure Group Politics in the Fifth Republic*, in Macridis and Brown, op. cit.

G. Causer, 'Private Capital and the State in Western Europe', in S. Giner and M. Archer (eds.), *Contemporary Europe: Social Structures and Cultural Patterns* Routledge, 1978.

F. Castles, 'The Political Functions of Organised Groups: The Swedish Case', *Political Studies*, vol. 21/1, March 1973.

T. Clarke and L. Clements (eds.), *Trade Unions under Capitalism*, Harvester Press, 1978.

Government and Opposition, 'Trade Unions and Politics in Western Europe', (whole issue), 13/4, Autumn 1978.

J. Hayward, *Private Interest and Public Policy. The Experience of the French Economic and Social Council*, Longman, 1966.

J. Hayward and R. Berki (eds.), *State and Society in Contemporary Europe*, Martin Robertson, 1979.

J. Hayward (ed.), 'Trade Union Politics in Western Europe', *West European Politics*, 3/1, January 1980.

Industrial and Labor Relations Review, 'European Labor and Politics: A Symposium', October 1974/January 1975 (both whole issues).

G. Ionescu, *Centripetal Politics: Government and the New Centres of Power*, Hart-Davies, 1975.

W. Kendall, *The Labour Movement in Europe*, Allen Lane, 1975.

R. Kimber and J. Richardson (eds.), *Pressure Groups in Britain*, Dent, 1974.

T. C. May, *Trade Unions and Pressure Group Politics*, Saxon House, 1975.

J. Richardson and A. Jordan, *Governing under Pressure*, Martin Robertson, 1979.

P. C. Schmitter and G. Lehmbruch (eds.), *Trends Towards Corporatist Intermediation*, Sage, 1979.

A. Shonfield, *Modern Capitalism*, Oxford University Press, 1968.

R. Taylor, *The Fifth Estate: Britain's Unions in the Seventies*, Routledge, 1978.

D. Truman, *The Government Process*, New York: A. Knopf, 1956.

R. Vernon (ed.), *Big Business and the State: Changing Relations in Western Europe*, Macmillan, 1974.

G. Wootton, *Pressure Politics in Contemporary Britain*, Lexington Books, 1978.

4

Party Systems

Determining Features

OUR EXAMINATION of the social basis of politics in Western Europe pointed to a few, key social variables which—in particular combinations—shaped the nature of party politics for individual countries. We should round out this picture by considering what other factors are relevant in accounting for a characteristic type of party system. The various explanations can be grouped under two broad headings: for convenience we can label them the 'social forces' and the 'constitutional factors'. In the main, the account we have given so far has been one concerned with the underlying social features of a society—the class structure flanked by others of a cultural and geographical nature. The alternative view, and the one we shall look at in detail here, is that the party system is also the product of a number of provisions made generally to ensure the running of the state, or more particularly aimed at the working of the political parties, summed up as a 'constitutional' view. Both types of explanation are concerned with why a party system remains as it is or gives way to another type.

The constitutional determinants are often regarded as of marginal importance by those who seek a complete 'social' explanation of politics, and, in Lipset's words, who '. . . tend to see party cleavages as reflections of an underlying structure, and hence . . . frown on efforts to present the enacted rules of the game as key causal elements of a social structure.'[1] But the framework within which parties grow up and continue to operate cannot be discounted entirely: the form of government, the legal constraints on the parties, the electoral system; these will all affect the expression which parties can give to the social forces they represent.

We can illustrate the effect the form of government may have on the party system by comparing the United States with Western Europe, since the particular combination of a presidential system with federalism in the USA has no counterpart in the mainly unitary and parliamentary European systems. The American structure of government results in a uniquely ambivalent two-party system. On the one hand, it is a strict two-party situation in that third parties are always unsuccessful on a national level, and this is so despite the numerous issues which would make for a multi-party system in other countries. Against that, it is a two-party system in name only, given the almost total autonomy of the state parties and of the representatives in Congress. In this respect, it can be seen that the separation of powers and the federal structure act as powerful agents of dispersion. At the same time, the presidential system, ensuring that the 'winner takes all', enforces a minimum of cohesion at the national level —contesting parties must aim at gaining half the national vote. The European situation is different in almost all respects: the great majority are unitary states with a parliamentary system of government, and national politics predominate. In West Germany and Austria, the nature of the federal system is quite secondary to the national parties.[2] Only in Switzerland does the federal form ante-date the modern parties, but the Swiss multi-party system functions without a separation of powers and without a directly-elected president.

The parliamentary system, which is general throughout Western Europe, means that there is no effective separation of assembly and executive;[*] it is true that this does not have any common numerical effect on the party systems—a usual minimum of three parties to eleven currently in the Netherlands—but within the assemblies there is a high degree of party unity and discipline. The fragmentation, where it occurs, arises at an *earlier* stage, for cross-voting on the part of deputies is regarded as a highly-deviant act by their parliamentary parties. Contrast this with congressional behaviour in the United States where the two-party label hardly conceals the ability of representatives to vote entirely according to the issues at stake. It is reasonable to conclude that the European parties are forced into a similar mould by the common fact of government responsibility to the assembly, with all that this entails, and that this similarity transcends variations in the number of parties.

Only France closely resembles the United States in the matter of presidential election and his subsequent governing position, so that it is possible to gauge the influence of this Fifth Republic innovation on the party system. Whilst the French variant of the presidential system has as yet had no decisive effect on the party system, popular voting at the three presidential elections—each time with a run-off—has polarized issues around two candidates. At first the Gaullists were dominant, but with the election of Giscard d'Estaing in 1974, the mantle has passed more generally to the parties 'of the majority'. There is a premium on retaining this cohesion for future presidential contests. On the left, the melting-pot process has been similarly arrested, despite efforts to forge left-wing unity—the 'Federation of the Left' from 1964–68, and the common cause made by Communists and Socialists in the 1970s, especially their almost successful bid for the presidency in 1974.[†] But the

* See below, pp. 109–11.
† See below, p. 278.

two parties remain basically in a jealously competitive position towards one another as well, just as the Gaullist RPR resents its displacement from the presidency. The party system has been unwillingly pressed into a two-bloc mould, each bloc itself composed of antagonistic elements. Even though the presidential system has encouraged two 'broad tendencies' in French politics, the transfer from tendency to cohesive system faces the barrier of *existing* party structures, the 'inertia' of political parties mentioned earlier: they are factors in their own right, modifying the impact of social and constitutional forces.

The fundamental arrangements of government appear to modify the expression of social differences which the political parties voice. In a similar way, provisions aimed specifically at the parties act as a constraint on the nature of the parties and the numbers competing. Two illustrations from West Germany help to make this point. The first is the provision of the Basic Law (Article 21) that parties must be 'democratic', leaving those open to prohibition which, '. . . by reason of their aims or the behaviour of their adherents, seek to impair or destroy the free democratic order or to endanger the existence of the Federal Republic.' The use of this article on two occasions, against the Communist Party and the extreme right, was of limited effect—the parties concerned only had a minute support anyway—but the potential of such limitations is vast.

The second West German innovation has less obvious but still profound implications for the party system. This is the provision for the state-financing of the political parties which has now reached considerable proportions. The measure was aimed at reducing the dependence of parties on the traditional pay-masters of politics, especially industrial interests, and by this means increase their democratic potential. The amounts received may not be critical for the future existence of the larger parties, but it could be a factor sufficient to alter the relationship of party to supporter; a party may become less interested in building up or retaining a large membership for active help or paying dues, instead paid officials and agencies could replace voluntary help. Thus whilst parties may become less susceptible to financial blandishments, they may also show an increased bureaucratization and state-dependence, and with such a secure financial base, they may become less competitive. On the other hand, as the size of the subsidy depends on the share of the national vote, an additional spur to success is present. Moreover, since even those parties which fail to gain Bundestag representation also receive a share from the kitty, small and new parties have a continuing incentive to fight elections.[3]

Such examples as these show clearly that the impact of 'the enacted rules of the game' can affect the nature of party competition at all points. Overriding all the others, at least as a focal point for discussion, are the 'rules' of the electoral system. There is a wide divergence of viewpoint, ranging from those who trace a direct line from the type of voting arrangements used through to the number of parties represented and thence to the stability of government, even to the stability of the political system itself, and at the opposite extreme, others who are inclined to reverse the causal sequence and argue that the nature of the ongoing party system maintains a particular type of electoral system in being.

The fundamental distinction is between those countries which adhere to the principle of proportional representation and those which operate on the majority principle. The idea of proportionality is that all shades of political opinion should be represented in a popular assembly in direct correspondence to their weighting in the political community; it is a principle of representation, not one of government. Majority systems, although conceding the claim for 'one man, one vote', in effect favour the needs of government over the exact representation of opinion; in theory at least, by sacrificing exact representation, a majority system will contain political opinion within a few political parties, and these will 'govern' as well as 'represent'. The implicit extension of the argument is that since such parties are necessarily government-oriented, the 'needs of government'—presumably stable government—are likely to be better met than where representation is the sole consideration.

These are matters to which we shall want to return after examining the various types of European electoral system. Although the *principle* of proportional representation is quite explicit, how this is arrived at in practice leads to a large number of possible systems, all having particular features or bias. Apart from the previous Portuguese use of the 'block vote', only two countries operate a majority system: Britain and France. The British system of 'first-past-the-post' in single-member constituencies, can result in two kinds of bias; firstly, within each constituency, the minority—or even a majority—fails to win any party representation; secondly, if the constituencies throughout the country are similar in their social make-up, then this homogeneity will always work to the advantage of one party—indeed, at an unlikely extreme, and as did occur in Portugal with the help of multi-member constituencies, it could be the only party represented at a national level. The fact that this does not happen in British circumstances depends partly on constituency size and partly on the uneven spread of political loyalties. The relatively large size of the House of Commons (635 members) reduces one bias, and the pattern of industry, and with it the distribution of socio-economic variables, lessens the other. As a result, the British system is generally representative over a period of time; had it not been so, then the strength of disaffection shown in non-parliamentary ways would probably have forced a radical change in the system. As it is, however, some political parties are permanently under-represented or gain no seats at all. This applies to smaller parties whose support is fairly evenly spread geographically: the Liberal Party gained over 18 per cent of the vote in October 1974, but actually received less than 2 per cent of the total seats. Other parties with a pronounced local appeal may have the chance to fare better: the Scottish and Welsh National parties. These two were conspicuously unsuccessful until 1974, but then helped to fragment the British party system. The Irish Nationalists also flourished at Westminster before Irish independence was gained and unsettled the 'two-party' format until the First World War.

The French variation of the majority system, second ballot in single-member constituencies, is fundamentally different in its effects. Whilst the British system operates to give a fairly representative assembly over a period of years, at least to the major parties, the second ballot may not even do this. The mechanics of the second ballot give any party, with an absolute majority of votes at the first ballot, a constituency seat as out-right winner. At the second ballot, held a week later, the first-past-the-post principle operates, and the party with the most votes gains the seat. Unless the party is very strong locally, it will have to fight the second ballot, and this implies considerable horse-trading amongst the parties at a national level in order to secure favourable electoral pacts in time for the second ballot. In this situation, a party must win allies or suffer heavy dis-crimination; parties near the centre may have some benefit, but the Com-munist Party has usually been the chief loser: in 1958 the party was awarded less than 2 per cent of the assembly seats with almost 20 per cent of the votes cast. Although conceivably this arrangement could meet the 'needs of government', the representative principle goes by the board, and since there is no necessary discrimination against smaller parties, the process of government formation may be no easier than where the propor-tional principle is observed; the most that can be said is that it makes for a sophisticated electorate. With declining Gaullist dominance, the distor-tions of the second ballot have become less marked, and the isolation of the Communists has ended, but the ingrained tendency of French parties in power to 'make' elections is never far from the surface.

Some variation of the proportional principle is used in all other West European states which rely on democratic elections.[4] In general, most of the systems have been employed for a considerable time, and with the exception of West Germany and Ireland, there has been no strong move to adopt majority systems; in the Republic of Ireland a proposal to do so was defeated by referendum in 1968. Normally the electoral system will suit the parties in power, since presumably it helped them to get there, and changes in the system, usually on par with a constitutional amendment, will require a large measure of inter-party agreement; if changes are mooted, some parties will naturally suspect the motives of the others, thus making a fundamental revision quite unlikely.

The practical application of proportional representation varies accor-ding to two rather conflicting criteria. The first is to ensure that party representation in the assembly reflects their performance at an election; the second consideration is to provide voters with some choice as between can-didates, not merely between parties. If only the first condition is met, the result is a pure 'party list' system; this means that the party will have a complete say in the order of preference for its candidates, and by placing favoured ones high on the list their subsequent election will be assured—in effect, the equivalent of the 'safe seat' in the British House of Commons. The majority system can be adapted to give a measure of choice between candidates of the same party by the institution of the 'primary' election, and in rare cases in the United States, the 'open primary'—open to all registered electors, regardless of their party affiliation. However, the use of the party list system can be adapted to the same end, giving voters a choice between parties and candidates on the same occasion. The extent of this choice varies considerably. Thus the Belgian system allows a vote either for the party's list (and therefore its order) or for one particular candidate of that party; once the party's total allocation of seats has been calculated, it is then possible to work out who its successful candidates will be according to those who voted for the party list and those who have expressed their own preference. Variations on this theme are general in Scandinavia, the Netherlands, Italy, Luxembourg, and Switzerland. In some, a large degree of choice is provided, including the possibility of combining the candidates from more than one party list. The element of personal choice, to which party list systems have to be adapted, is the leading characteristic of the Single Transferable Vote as used in the Republic of Ireland and Malta. This system, besides ensuring that no votes are 'wasted'—that is, cast in excess of what a candidate needs to ensure election in a multi-member constituency—ensures also that voters' preferences always remain 'personal': the transferred vote is never to a 'party' but to a 'candidate', whilst under party list systems this distinction cannot be maintained.

A further difference between types of proportional representation arises from the size of the constituencies. Unlike majority systems where the representation is likely to be improved as the number of constituencies is increased, the reverse applies for proportionality: only in a large multi-member constituency will it be possible to share out seats at all accurately, and only if the whole nation is treated as a single constituency for this purpose will distortions be minimized—as is the case in the Netherlands. Yet this 'remoteness' of the deputy from his electorate is perhaps also undesirable; consequently, an alternative is to have sub-national constituencies and hold back a 'remainder' of seats to secure an overall (national) proportional effect after constituency allocations have been made.

By various such devices, proportional systems can provide for voter choice, constituency-effect, and accurate representation. Their strict proportionality can also be modified by simply stipulating a cut-off below which very small parties gain no representation. In Denmark, it is as low as 2 per cent, in West Germany 5 per cent. This form of doctoring of the system is easy to institute since almost all the established parties will stand to gain in seats if some are excluded. West Germany's electoral system is a good example of adaptation: although the overall effect is strictly proportional, half of the Bundestag members are elected by relative majorities in single-member constituencies. The voter has two votes, one for a constituency candidate and the other for a party list. The party's total Bundestag representation is decided by the list vote; from that total is then deducted the number of constituency seats (if any) it has already won. The only tangible difference is that some of a party's Bundestag membership will have won a seat in their own right and the others will be there thanks to their high position on the party list.

From these rather straightforward considerations, we can turn to some of the wider implications of electoral systems for party systems and for government. The observation made by Duverger is central to the discussion: 'An almost complete correlation is observable between the simple-majority, single-ballot system and the two-party system.'[5] The *implication* of Duverger's finding, and one which is frequently voiced, is that there is a similar relationship between proportional voting and multi-party systems. Whilst it is admitted that two-party systems frequently go together with simple majority voting, there is no question of this being a necessary consequence, and Duverger's formulation breaks down where there are strong *regional* loyalties—as Colin Leys remarked for British politics in the early part of the century: 'It took more than the electoral system to get rid of the Irish.'[6]

The strong association between proportional voting and numerous parties appears justified if one takes into account the numbers represented in the assemblies of Western Europe—on average six. But many are very small indeed, and if these are excluded—say, those with less than 10 per cent—then no assembly has more than four parties which can be called substantial. It is around the nature and relative size of these that a system develops its special characteristics. Further, with the possible exception of the Netherlands and recently in Denmark, no indefinite proliferation is involved; systems appear to reach a natural maximum number, beyond which new parties either fail to make an impression or they replace declining ones.

But it is also true that the number of parties represented can be very low under a proportional system. Malta has only two parties, and these shared over 99 per cent of the poll in 1976 with almost 95 per cent of the electorate voting, and Austria has been hovering on the brink of a two-party system for years. There has been a progressive decline in West Germany from eleven parties in 1949 to three at present, though the introduction of the 'five-per-cent clause' has helped this process. France has operated numerous electoral systems in the present century, but the number of parties has remained a quite independent factor. This is not to argue that electoral systems are without effect. It is reasonable to suppose that a majority system makes it more difficult for new parties to make an initial impact (although the regional aspect should not be forgotten) and that it also leads to a more rapid extinction of declining parties. The converse is that proportional systems enable new parties to gain a foothold and rescue others that would otherwise disappear. We can show how both of these effects have worked under proportional representation.

The classic example of proportional voting helping a new party is that of the National Socialists in the Weimar Republic. At three successive elections in the 1920s, the National Socialists had a minute, and declining, support—finally under 3 per cent. Only in 1930 did the Nazi appeal broaden, with a significant share of 18 per cent.The argument to be favoured here is that the Nazis had a small but vociferous representation right through the 'lean' years, a base on which they were quickly able to build once the economic storm broke. The stronger argument that proportional representation had a *direct* causal influence on the growth of the Nazi Party is rejected by Georges Lavau who finds a close parallel in the rapid growth of the Labour vote in Britain between 1910 and 1929—but in the context of a 'hostile' simple majority system. He asks, if the rise of the Labour Party was a normal evolution, why should the Nazi movement be regarded as abnormal? 'Past and present experience, alas, shows sufficiently that fascism is a development just as "normal" as democracy ... One can ask oneself whether a simple plurality system would not have brought about a much more rapid rise of the National Socialists.'[7] Lavau goes even further and rejects the 'foothold' argument as well: 'It is frequently asserted, with regard to the Nazi Party, that in a majority system a party which has hardly 7 per cent of the votes (as was the case in 1924) would have been swept away at the following election. The example of the Labour Party does not prove this.'[8] Against this interpretation one can say that the context of the two parties was different; in Britain the Liberal Party was falling apart, and inevitably a new party was given maximum scope, whilst the Nazi Party, in the mid-twenties, had no such benefit; to this extent, the fact that it could retain a small group in the Reichstag until the situation was favourable is directly attributable to the system of voting.

The second example demonstrates the 'rescue' effect of proportional representation. Prior to 1894, Belgium had a two-party system with simple-majority voting: a Catholic party and the anti-clerical Liberals. Thereafter, the Socialists gained representation with the extension of the franchise, and there was a catastrophic fall in the number of Liberal seats. Unwilling to be left alone with the Socialists, the Catholic majority introduced proportional voting in 1900, and this quickly helped to restore Liberal fortunes—a threefold increase in Liberal seats. As a result, a genuine three-party system was preserved throughout the inter-war period. Such rescue operations may only lead to an attenuated prolongation of a spent political force—European assemblies are dotted with these survivals: the Old Liberals in Switzerland, the Swedish People's Party in

Finland, the Republicans in Italy. However, the period of survival may allow a rejuvenation to take place. The decline of the Belgian Liberals set in once more after 1945, but shedding its anti-clericalism, the party was able to make a straight bid for the middle-class vote, and by stressing national unity it gained on the other parties until beset by its own linguistic factions. This may be an exceptional case, but the principle could apply to any other party in the doldrums; Communist parties in several countries, such as Sweden, can seek to make a renewed appeal with more success than would be possible in Britain.

Another, and related consequence of an electoral system is sometimes said to be the resulting stability of government. The argument is that a two-party system, with simple-majority voting, leads to greater government stability. Of course, 'stability of government' is only one of a number of criteria to judge the viability of a party system. It is probably the most favoured index of government performance, since it is the least impressionistic, and it stands in the middle of two extreme criteria: the quality and quantity of government decision-making and the ability of the political system to survive intact. The implication is that 'stable government' is both a measure of the acceptability of government decision-making and of the chances that the system will not break down.

However, the problem of using 'stability' as an index of system performance is closely akin to the general one we came across in the first chapter, that of stability as a feature of liberal democracy. One may first query whether government stability, in the sense of duration of government by the same party or parties in office, is necessarily desirable. The apparent breakdown of civilian government in Northern Ireland followed on some fifty years of unquestioned rule by the Unionist Party—in fact can be held to be a direct consequence of that hegemony. Only if at the same time government decision-making is acceptable (presumably to be judged by the absence of extra-parliamentary disaffection), can one use government duration as an adequate guide. One may say that the Fifth Republic in its first ten years showed great government durability: one president, two prime ministers, and only one party effectively in power—despite the numerous changes in government composition at ministerial level. Yet this stability was a prelude to the rising of May 1968 which showed a significant discontent in French society.

Duration of government does vary considerably, but there is no tight connection between this and the number of parties, so that even if it is conceded, as Blondel delicately words it, 'that countries which have the majority systems are more likely to be two-party systems and countries which experience proportional representation are more likely not to have two-party systems',[9] it still does not make the electoral system a direct causal influence on government durability.* He shows elsewhere[10] that for

---

* This can also be considered in relation to assembly functions, see below, pp. 153–9.

a given post-war period, British governments averaged 3.3 years, precisely the same figure as for Germany and Norway, as against five years for Sweden. And whilst Austrian governments averaged 2.3 years with only three parties, the Netherlands with twelve or more maintained an average of 2.2. At the bottom of the table come Finland (1.0), Italy (0.9), and France (0.7). Yet this numerical similarity hides a wealth of difference. Finnish society is undeniably stable, yet Finland has averaged a government a year for the past sixty years. Christian Democratic governments in Italy have been very short-lived, but the size of that party has not meant that any one government crisis has rocked the system. Only in France (since the period Blondel examined covers the Fourth Republic) was life of government correlated with deeper political instability.

It is rather a different question to speculate on whether the 'quality' of government is likely to be better with a two-party system. Although this system gives a ready-made 'alternative government', the other possibility—of coalition government—is not simply a 'less eligible' alternative. It can be argued that the dualism inherent in the British 'classic' type of two-party system, with the ever-alternating ins and outs of office, is more suited to some historical periods and to some political cultures than to others. The Swiss pattern of government, though unlike all others in its arrangements, gives the essence of alternative possibilities. Much depends on how the function of opposition is evaued, and it is one perspective of party competition we take up shortly in looking at 'patterns of opposition'.

The whole debate on the relative effects of constitutional and social forces can hardly be conclusive. Even though electoral systems may affect the number of parties and that in turn may affect the *way* in which decisions are made, there is no necessary consequence for the viability of the party system. One qualification to the power of constitutional factors is that they cannot simply be accepted as 'given'; their origins and the fact that they are retained in a certain form, have to be related to the social context in which they operate. In this sense, it is the social situation (and with it the party system) which maintains an electoral system—not the other way round. The party system is the important resultant: the means by which a reconciliation is sought, and dominance expressed.

System Trends

A classification that goes beyond a simple numerical ordering is needed if we wish to generalize about European party systems. The significant variables are:

the relative size of the major parties;
the deployment of all the constituent parties in respect of socially relevant issues.

The first expresses a simple power position: What numerical combination can supply a governing majority? The second takes into account the feasibility of such combinations according to the social basis of party support and the actual relations between the parties. A combination of these two features gives three typical forms of party system: imbalance, diffusion, and balance.[11]

It is not difficult to show the numerical aspect of imbalance, since it occurs when one party, or a closely-related group of parties, is in a commanding position for considerable periods; the gap between it and the second party is large, and this will mean that, exceptional combinations apart, the dominant party is indispensable to government formation; a feature of such dominance is that it is unlikely to be eroded from one election to another.

Apart from Britain and Ireland it has not been normal for one party to enjoy a large majority in the assembly for long periods, although the Norwegian Labour Party had a majority in the Storting until the 1960s and the Austrian Socialists were similarly placed in the 1970s. However, there are a number of sporadic examples.[12] Indispensability for the formation of government and a leading place within it may be a better guide to a modified form of dominance. Several parties have been dominant in this sense in the period after 1945. It applied to the West German CDU until the end of the Adenauer era, to the Italian Christian Democrats for the whole of the post-war era until the present time, and to the Swedish Social Democrats from the 1930s until 1976. The Gaullists in France enjoyed a similar position from 1958 until the election of a non-Gaullist president in 1974. We can add the Irish Fianna Fail as well as the Social-Christians in both Belgium and Luxembourg, since they have been in office for a large part of the post-war period. The Luxembourg case is a limiting one *numerically* because the Christian-Socials rarely had a large lead over its rivals. But until 1974 it had been the senior party in every government since 1919, and the *feasibility* of the alternative Socialist-Liberal alliance was low. The Socialists and Liberals thus neatly alternated as junior coalition partners from 1947 until 1974 when they ousted the Christian-Socials. In 1979, however, the latter won back their governing position.

A diffused party system requires a relatively large number of parties, none with a decisive superiority and several having a comparable share of the vote. Just as important: the parties show no sign of a clear or pronounced polarization; they represent rather the different facets of an overall social cohesion. The party system in the Netherlands best exemplifies this category: at the present time eleven parties are represented, the two leading parties have only about a third of the vote each, and the range of coalition possibilities is fairly wide. Several countries are in this position. It was a typical feature of the French Fourth Republic, and Belgium, Denmark, Finland, and Switzerland all now fulfil most of the requirements for diffusion. Inevitably, there is a tendency to regard a diffused system as also having the characteristic features of an unstable multi-party system, but governmental instability is not a necessary outcome. In the Netherlands, for example, the initial formation of governments is very difficult, but over a very long period the average life of governments has been about two years. Similarly, the increasing diffusion which has become apparent in Belgium since the 1960s has forced the traditional parties of government to cooperate with one another—if they do not hang together in face of the linguistic issue, they may hang separately!

In the conditions of a balanced system the major requirement is that there should be a single clear line of polarization. It is natural in this situation to think that there should be only two parties, but there could equally be two 'clusters' of parties. 'Balance' requires that neither pole should be predominant, and if there is a numerical balance between the two parties or clusters, then the basis for a simple alternation of government is present. In practice that alternation may not occur for long periods, but even if it does not, both contestants must act with the eventuality in mind—typically the case for Britain, although she was affected by a temporary diffusion of the party system in the 1970s. With a fully balanced system we should expect the two major parties to obtain about 90 per cent of the vote. That pattern is true for both Austria and West Germany. Although in Germany's case the medium of a small third party has been operative in securing a shift in government power, the essentials of a balanced system are present. The less pronounced form of the 'balanced cluster' is evident elsewhere, notably in Scandinavia and the Fifth French Republic.

This typology of party systems—imbalance, diffusion and balance —has the merit that all West European countries can be fitted reasonably into one category or another. But we need to bear in mind that they do not occupy static positions; most systems have shown signs of change in recent years, and it is worthwhile examining those cases where there appears to be a developmental sequence. There are certainly grounds for believing that some party systems have shown a move away from long-term dominance, although it is not possible to show that either the balanced or the diffused form is becoming the typical one for Western Europe.

In the case of diffused systems, it can be argued that where they have been based on historically defined 'cross-cutting social cleavages', the emergence of a more 'homogeneous' society should make the old lines of party cleavage redundant. A conclusion would be that that homogeneity should leave social-class differences as the main *residual* factor: the decline of sectionalism opens the way for 'balanced' systems showing only a moderate degree of polarization. But it is also evident that West European party systems have also acquired new sources of diffusion in recent times: *historical* sectionalism has undoubtedly declined, yet multi-party systems are still the flourishing norm. The only reasonable explanation appears to be that our more homegeneous forms of society can support various political expressions and that those 'expressions'—typically seen in ecological movements—neither enforce a new sectionalism nor offer a determined and sustained challenge to the existing political order and the stability of government.

Rather different considerations apply to imbalanced systems and their decline. One can argue that an imbalanced system results from a relative lack of cohesion in another part of the political spectrum. Where social class has been the main motor in the development of a party system, then any imbalance will have been caused through either the bourgeois or the socialist parties having failed to attain adequate or unified expression. Thus fragmentation or inadequacy on the left or on the right makes for a pronounced 'lag'—the lag is shown by a numerical inferiority and implicitly by the weak development of a party, in its structure and ideology. There is no need to assume that some kind of social parity must obtain—party imbalance might be prolonged indefinitely if the social and political lags are entrenched.

Let us take an example of a country where the conditions of an orderly developmental sequence can be clearly discerned. Western Germany in the post-war period fits a three-stage model: from initial diffusion, through temporary imbalance, reaching a current state of balance. The first stage, seemingly a throwback to the Weimar Republic, showed the two major parties, CDU and SPD, able only to muster about 60 per cent of the vote between them. That phase passed quickly with elimination of the smaller parties and the rise of the CDU from 1953 as the dominating force. We have seen that the CDU was one of the new-type parties, bourgeois yet with a general 'Christian' appeal, and we have also noted the later response of the SPD: its large numerical lag facilitated a fundamental change in the party's orientation. The end of CDU dominance came with the formation of a 'grand coalition' with the SPD in 1966, and a balanced system resulted in 1969—the CDU was forced into opposition and the SPD became the major governing party.

France—spanning the Fourth and Fifth Republics—has shown a somewhat similar evolution to balanced polarization. The hopeless diffusion which typified the Fourth Republic was quickly replaced in the Fifth Republic from 1958 by Gaullist dominance. The emergence of a mass—and moderate—bourgeois party was a new event in France, as it had been in Germany, and for a while the spectacular rise of the Gaullist party meant that the lag in development appeared on the left. The dominance of the UNR (later UDR) waned especially after de Gaulle's departure in 1969, but the cohesion of the bourgeois alliance—the Gaullists with the Independent Republicans (later the UDF)—was maintained. In its turn the French left—chiefly the Communists* and

* See pp. 145–6 below, for an assessment of the Communist Party.

Socialists—made a sustained effort to form a united front which came near to winning the presidential election of 1974. The two-bloc system which emerged—aided by the pressures of the presidential contest itself—takes the form of a 'balanced cluster', and although the French left is still denied governing power the feasibility of supplanting the 'parties of the majority' remains high.

The dominance of the Christian Democrats in Italy has been of a different order from that which existed in Germany or France. The religious vote going to the DC for long prevented a simple class polarization and also made the party less 'bourgeois' in orientation—and therefore more able to take up a 'centre' position, with straddling alliances of a centre-left nature. Nonetheless, the steady growth in the Communist vote has placed the PCI in a competitive position with the Christian Democrats. DC dominance is now 'residual': after the 1976 election the party had to form a minority government—relying on the PCI to keep it in office, a disguised form of 'grand coalition'.

The largest disparities in voting support between the first and second parties—a prima facie indication of imbalance—have been evident in Scandinavia: Denmark, Norway and Sweden. There is a long tradition of the imbalance favouring the left and concomitantly a considerable fragmentation of the bourgeois vote. Commencing in the 1930s, the Social Democratic parties were in an overtowering position in all three countries for decades at a time, but that era has now passed. For several years the Danish Social Democrats, although still by far the largest party, have more often than not had to resort to minority government. Their position has been helped perhaps by the dazzling diffusion of the party system which first came about in 1973 when the number of parties in the Folketing jumped suddenly from five to ten—in 1977 the *second largest* party had only 14.6 per cent of the vote, whilst the Social Democrats won 37 per cent. In a sense, therefore, it is a case of 'dominance by default'.

The Norwegian situation has also become more complex in the 1970s. The Norwegian Labour Party lost its overall majority in the Storting in the early 1960s and suffered seriously from internal party dissension over the question of European Community membership, especially in the wake of the 1972 referendum. As the Storting is elected for a fixed term (thus avoiding frequent elections) the stability of government has not been affected by Labour's decline. The outcome, in fact, has been a situation of 'permanent' and stable minority rule by the Labour Party, with a continuing ability to govern thanks to the weakness of the four main bourgeois parties.

In Sweden there is also a large disparity between the Social Democrat vote and that of the second party and a similar fragmentation affecting opposing parties. The Swedish Social Democrats have been dominant for a long period, in government from 1932 until 1976, although rarely having an absolute majority. Usually the party was in alliance with the Agrarians (later Centre), the 'Red-Green' alignment, although in latter years the support of the diminutive Communist Party took its place. Throughout the 1970s there was a gradual decline in support for the Social Democrats culminating in the 'historic' change of 1976 when a coalition of bourgeois parties (Centre, Liberals and Conservatives) was formed, a shift confirmed by the 1979 election.

In some respects the development of Scandinavian party systems shows the loss of dominance bringing about a more balanced form, although the Danish case shows that the result may be increased diffusion, and there are other countries where diffusion has become progressive as well. In the Netherlands, the existence of several religious parties made it impossible for the party system to develop a balanced form: the ability of the religious parties to appeal across the lines of social class worked to the detriment of the Dutch Labour Party. However, the decline in the religious vote over the past twenty years has meant that the party system has remained anything but static. One result was the 'defensive' fusion of the three major religious parties to form the Christian Democratic Appeal (CDA). That simplification on the other hand has been offset by the rise of new progressive parties such as the Democrats '66 and the Radical Catholic Party. Their formation strengthened the chance of an alternative to the old-style hegemony of coalitions based on the traditional religious parties. Moreover, the gradual improvement of the Labour Party in recent years—it became the largest party in 1977 with a third of the vote—offers the possibility of a balanced cluster emerging: the CDA allied to the Liberals on the one side and some smaller parties forming a progressive bloc with Labour on the other. However, that presentation depends on the role taken by the CDA: there is strong resistance in the party against being permanently shut off from a centre-left alignment.

We have already looked at the reasons for the growing diffusion of Belgian politics; until the late 1950s there was a fairly balanced four-party system, with the leading parties, Social-Christians and Socialists, sharing 80 per cent of the vote. The active resurgence of the language issue in the late 1950s changed the pattern completely. The renewed success of the Liberals (Party of Liberty and Progress) occurred at roughly the same time as the rise of the specifically linguistic parties: the Flemish *Volksunie*, the Wallon *Rassemblement*, and the Brussels *Front des Francophones*. By the 1970s their combined vote reached over 20 per cent, sufficient with the Liberal revival to set the two major parties in disarray. The linguistic issue was also one they had to contain within their own parties as well, so that the tensions were powerful: the party system appeared to be on the brink of fragmentation. Yet the success, admittedly long drawn-out, in reaching a linguistic compromise has resulted in the minor parties being willing to participate in government.

At least the basic stability of the political system has been maintained and a limit may now have been reached in the process of diffusion.

Such examples of developing diffusion have to be set against others where change is less apparent. Finland's party system is very static: the four largest parties share 80 per cent of the vote, and only rarely does any one reach a quarter of the total. The parties do show a clear spread on the 'left-right' axis and there is the basis for a balanced cluster. Two factors work against a clear polarization however. One is the strategic position occupied by the Centre Party, which is the linch-pin for most coalitions, and the party shows a preference for centre-left groupings, reminiscent of the red-green formation. The second factor relates to Finland's international position: the country is best served by broad coalitions—not excluding the Communist SKDL. These two factors favour coalitions of four or five parties, although the resulting governments are usually unstable. The balanced cluster evident in the *distribution* of Finnish parties does not show itself at the level of government coalition, nor perhaps would it be desirable if it did.

In the case of Switzerland the position is so static that we can say a form of 'institutionalized' diffusion has taken hold. The federal structure and the collegial system of government make it almost impossible to visualize *any* change. The 'government club' of the four major parties precludes any mechanism of development—beyond increasing the size of the club. The three largest parties, Radicals, Socialists, and Christian Democrats (Catholics), each with 20 to 25 per cent of the vote, have an equal and permanent share in government—two seats each, with the remaining one going to the smaller People's Party, a ratio which has remained constant since 1959.* Dissatisfaction with this hegemonic 'system' has, as in the Netherlands, led to the formation of protest parties: the *Landesring*, and the 'National Campaign against Foreign Domination of People and Homeland'. The latter movement was a reaction against the high level of migrant workers in Switzerland, and much of its impetus was gained from a referendum held in 1970 to cut immigration sharply, a proposal resisted by all the established parties. Protests of that nature are not insignificant, but they are unlikely to threaten government cohesion: a new party which really did become a force to be reckoned with would simply be offered a seat on the Federal Council, and its acceptance would entail a pledge of the party's future cooperative behaviour.

Given the instances of continuing or increased diffusion, there is clearly no inevitable trend towards balanced systems.† But we have seen that the picture for imbalanced systems is rather different, and there are other

---

* For an account of how the ratio is determined see, C. Hughes, *The Parliament of Switzerland*, Hansard Society, 1962, pp. 69–83, and below pp. 112–13 and 309–11.
† For the overall balance on a *European* level, see the diagram pp. 322–3 below.

examples of decline. Even though the Fianna Fail in Ireland is the largest party, it was suddenly ousted by an alliance of the two smaller ones in 1973, Fine Gael and the Labour Party, a change with similarities to the switch in Luxembourg. Even though Fianna Fail was returned in triumph in 1977 there is always the chance of the two other parties mounting a further successful challenge. A similar decline can be noted for the Independence Party in Iceland which was in power almost continuously after Iceland gained full statehood in 1944 until the 1970s. In the past ten years, however, the Independence Party has been in opposition on two occasions, and the gradual rise of the left-wing vote has removed the lop-sided look of the party system.

There is no doubt that 'founding' parties can create an initial imbalance in a party system which may persist for many years. The Icelandic Independence Party and the Fianna Fail in Ireland are good examples. More generally, a 'founding' party may enjoy a favoured position where a strong discontinuity occurs in the political system: the Christian Democrats in Italy after fascism, the CDU in post-war Germany, the Gaullists at the beginning of the Fifth Republic. A current example is that of New Democracy in Greece which, since the downfall of the military dictatorship in 1974, has taken an apparently unassailable position. It is not a necessary development: neither in Portugal nor in Spain can any one party exercise undisputed power—indeed in both those countries the initial condition of the party system is unambiguously diffused.

Neat patterns of development are not to be expected. The model of West German evolution, leading to a balanced system, is found in only a few countries, such as Austria, and other balanced ones—with Britain as the major example—have had difficulty in maintaining their two-party characteristics. Nor on the other hand should we expect the influence of new social forces to change party systems overnight or beyond recognition. Even though one or other of the older parties may go into decline for a while, its existence need not be jeopardized and it may obstruct changes for a long time. Furthermore, the party itself may belatedly adapt to changing social circumstances in order to preserve its position.

If existing political parties do have a power of 'obstruction', then trends in party systems will be neither uniform nor of sudden occurrence. Negatively at least, a political party has to be treated as an independent variable, to be taken into the reckoning along with the 'constitutional' and 'social force' influences. The persistence of the parties can also be applied to their parent *systems* as well. A two-party system has its own inertia—as the behaviour of the major parties in Britain showed during the 1970s—and the 'habits' of a multi-party system become similarly ingrained. The dictates of the established party system determine the tactics followed by the parties: how questions of coalition are viewed, how the issues are put by the parties to the electorate.

Usually the electorate will respond in terms which reinforce the existing parties and the system, a process of mutual conditioning. Just how parties and systems vary with regard to the key question of alliance and coalition, a critical difference in the operation of party systems, we can appreciate by sketching the different ways in which the idea of 'democratic opposition' can be handled.

Patterns of Opposition

The common faith in the necessity of allowing organized opposition, as the means of preserving political choice in the liberal democracies, obscures important differences both in the value which parties place upon it and in the way which opposition is expressed. Dahl's account of the dimensions involved,[13] which we shall follow here, shows how various factors interact to determine the strategies adopted in their quest for power—and this quest is the reality behind any opposition. One of the factors concerns the ultimate aims or 'goals' of the parties. But how these goals are pursued will depend on the more general characteristics of the system—the 'distinctiveness' that an opposition acquires in a particular party system. In Dahl's formulation, the three factors are:

the nature of the site for 'decisive encounters';
the degree of competition which a system is able to maintain;
the cohesion of opposition.

These shape the character of a system, and together with the goals of the competing parties they will determine how the political struggle is waged.

We can illustrate these terms by the case of Britain. The site for decisive encounters is normally the general election, and the system is highly competitive—in the nature of a zero-sum game: victory for one party means the total exclusion from power for the other. The opposition is also highly cohesive, for not only is it for all practical purposes located within one party, party discipline ensures as well that for most important issues the party will speak with one voice. It need hardly be said that these three features of the British system stand very much together—if elections were not decisive, then the nature of inter-party competition would change, and in turn party cohesion could be undermined. But much would depend on *why* elections became indecisive, whether it came about because of inter-party agreement or because (as was true of the 1970s) there was an increase in the number of parties.

In a formal sense, the assemblies of parliamentary democracies are regarded as the important site—ideally, with the fate of governments and legislation depending on a strongly contested assembly vote. The real situation is much more complex, for the assembly is only one of *five* possible arenas or sites. As is the case for Britain, a decisive election result may largely reduce the importance of the decision-making powers of the assembly in practice. Yet even if the election is indecisive, this does not necessarily make the assembly stronger, for the real power may rest with the subsequent coalition which is formed. Beyond this, power may be effectively dispersed to the permanent bureaucracy and in its relations with the governing parties, and finally to the relations of government with the organized interests of society at large.

Certainly, although a country's politics may be focused on just one site, the others will never be irrelevant. No parties in a competitive system can regard the outcome of elections as only marginally important, but they may well be inconclusive. The process of coalition-building becomes a factor in its own right, and even if account is taken of how the various parties fared at the preceding elections, the eventual coalition is not just dependent on electoral success. The way in which coalitions are formed becomes an important factor, and therefore interparty negotiations can be prolonged—as in Finland, the Netherlands, and Italy; further, inter-election changes in government can come about without any direct reference to the preceding election. Where one party has an absolute majority, as until 1973 in France, the result is a foregone conclusion once the election is over. But it is comparatively rare for any party to be in this position,* and even when it is, the addition of one or more coalition partners is frequently preferred. The usual situation is for a number of permutations to be examined, with critical issues emerging concerning coalition policy, the ratio of portfolios, and party control over particular ministries.

It may be that even the formation of a coalition is not conclusive—where, for this instance, decision-making is moving out of the hands of the parties into government agencies. Sheer instability of government may be one cause; sustained direction of policy becomes impossible, and by default the bureaucracy becomes involved in policy-making at a high level. This possibility is inherent in all forms of party government, however. We have earlier seen how this may work in a position of one-party dominance, as the *clientela* relationship has developed in Italy. Later, we shall look more generally at the power of administrative élites.† The final arena is the totality of the relationships which a government develops with organized interests, and the various 'styles' of interest group representation which we have already considered have a definite connection with the locus of decision-making in a political system.

Sweden provides an example of how the arena for decision-making may become diffused. The long-term dominance of the Social Democrats did make elections conclusive in some respects. However, the Swedish system places an emphasis on the assembly for real deliberation. The op-

---

* For examples of absolute majorities, see below, p. 95 (footnote 12).

† See below, pp. 184–91.

position is by no means helpless; it can maintain itself indefinitely by organizing, mediating, and leading the various interest groups; the parties in opposition, until 1976 the never-never alternative government, worked effectively in the Riksdag and operated on the government direct. The long years of opposition for the bourgeois parties was not the wilderness it would be in Britain. This diffusion is also maintained in Switzerland, for neither the election nor the coalition is decisive, and the Federal Assembly, though it does not exact the full 'responsibility' of government, retains a share in decision-making. The diffusion is made all the more marked by the constant potential of the referendum as a feedback device.* Finally, in the twenty-year 'permanent' coalition in Austria after the war, the elections only decided the ratio of ministerial portfolios between the two parties—the decision to prolong the coalition was made by the parties prior to the elections; the elections were then of marginal importance only, and the popular vote only related to the 'Proporz' system: the exact sharing of all government appointments according to party strength.

The competitiveness of a party system can be related to this issue of determining site. Thus, where what we can call 'primary' sites (elections and assemblies) are conclusive, there is likely to be a high degree of system competitiveness, and this will decline to the extent that 'secondary' sites (coalition, bureaucracy, and interests) become important. Although without exception elections are hard-fought, this struggle is often a prelude to concentration on the secondary sites. Persistent association with either the primary or secondary sites, though these are not sharp alternatives, contributes to the distinctiveness of an opposition. The third factor, the cohesion of opposition, also imparts a particular character to a system, but it is a product of various short- and long-term influences. Cohesion in the short-run depends on party morale: the strength of an opposition is to be judged in part on how quickly short-run upsets can be absorbed without a fundamental weakening of opposition. This reflects on the morale of the individual parties; in a multi-party system, any one party bears less brunt of the reverses in electoral and other fortunes, and in this sense they are more resilient than the opposition in a two-party system. However, the cohesion of the opposition as a whole is always more difficult to maintain where several parties are involved; a single party in opposition has the problem of its inner-party tensions to resolve, hence the much more critical question of party leadership in a two-party system, but once these are settled, then the united opposition presents a formidable challenge to government.

Whilst the factors we have considered so far are general to all the parties in a particular system, the distinctiveness of an opposition and the strategies it employs will also be determined by the goals which the parties pursue, and these are defined by each party for itself. Dahl lists the types

* See below, pp. 118–21.

of goal in ascending order of fundamental change: the personnel of government, specific government policies, the political structure, the socio-economic structure. A party limited to changing the personnel of government will emphasize the new leadership it can supply, but once in office at least, it will minimize policy changes and will be mainly concerned with succouring special interests. Most European parties have the second type of goal: specific policy changes *in addition to* changes in personnel—each level of goal subsumes those in the preceding categories. There is a tradition of issuing detailed, and binding, policy documents; in this sense they are 'programmatic'. The emphasis in a two-party system on personnel changes is not so relevant for others because it is impossible to foresee the actual make-up of government; furthermore, the 'binding' policies turn out to be bargaining-counters in the realities of multi-party coalition.

Social Democratic parties have wider goals; at least in the past these have included the making of basic changes in the socio-economic structure of society. But for them the goal-ordering is not cumulative—they miss out on the third level—a fundamental re-ordering of the political structure as well. It is precisely this goal which typifies an 'extremist' party.* In the case of right-wing extremism, the scrapping of the present political order may be the summit of ambition; once a new political edifice has been erected, the socio-economic order can be left intact. Only on the extreme left are all four levels of change considered integral to a party's aims. Indeed, the Communist criticism of Social Democracy has always been that its socio-economic aims are unattainable without at the same time working for the destruction of the existing political system—since this is a bastion of social and economic inequality.

In large measure, the cohesion of the West European party systems results from the similar types of goal which the individual parties are willing to pursue, and the common commitment to maintain the political fabric of liberal democracy intact. And even if a party is quite free to define or redefine its own goals, it is continually subject to the pressures of the system, to the 'parliamentary embrace'. The more a party subscribes to the dictates of the party game, so its goals become displaced and effectively come to resemble those of its competitors—a tendency long ago noted by Sorel, and finding a contemporary echo in the reaction of an 'extra-parliamentary' opposition.

The difficulty of throwing up and maintaining fundamental alternatives has led to the view that there is a secular decline in the quality of opposition in parliamentary systems. Otto Kirchheimer[14] saw this 'waning of opposition' as a general development affecting the 'opposition in principle' of ideologically based parties as well as those functioning in the British sense of 'Opposition' with the total emphasis on *alternative* government (which

* See below, pp. 139–46.

in fact requires important continuities in policies to minimize the disruption of party alternation). As we saw in the preceding chapter, this view of the decline of opposition is connected to the change from sectional to 'catch-all' parties. With this similarity, it becomes increasingly difficult for an opposition party to 'identify' itself and provide a credible alternative. The only way for a party to survive is to become a governing party, in coalition with the others. That at least seemed to be the trend: a choice between a Swiss-type coalition and permanent, basically sterile, opposition.

Such a view is essentially a rendering of the 'end of ideology' seen in party terms: a series of catch-all parties, all operating near the centre of the spectrum, equally desperate to participate in government, and their consequent strategy contingent on the behaviour of all the others, with the whole system mainly responsive to the balance of group pressures. Against this deterministic view have to be set a number of qualifications. Firstly, it is not at all the case that 'Opposition' in the sense of alternative government has become less viable—the German Social Democrats did at last come to power, the bourgeois parties in Norway and Denmark were able to form governments on their own account, the twenty-year Austrian coalition did in the end break down. A second objection is that parties do manage to 'breathe' for an extraordinary length of time in opposition, and the strength of the European party traditions is such that, as Kirchheimer himself recognized, they are unlikely to become mere brokerage parties; the competing versions of Liberalism, Christian Democracy, and Social Democracy should not be dismissed as simply attenuations of a past age: they still provide a standpoint from which current policies can be judged.

A final objection lies in the imponderable nature of social evolution. Our analysis earlier pointed to class issues as the chief residual factor in politics. Even in settled states, this cleavage provides the basis for a limited polarization, evident in balanced systems. Nor, of course, should the potential of 'opposition in principle' be underestimated; weakened now, these party traditions are available should the limited polarization of class become more pronounced. All of these qualifications make forecasts based on an apparent 'waning' of opposition of limited value. And even a stable parliamentary system may fail to reflect the force of outside challenges: a party system cannot be judged solely on its success in harnessing electoral forces. As a conclusion to this discussion, we can examine the conditions under which parliamentary systems succeed or fail.

Breakdown of Parliamentary Systems

Putting the question, 'Why do systems fail?', may not seem particularly relevant to most West European states, but parliamentary government does fail on occasion, and for a variety of reasons. We can express this another way by saying that a successful parliamentary democracy has to fulfil the following four functions:

1. Supply governments with an assembly majority, and provide for smooth government succession.
2. Governments must be able to make an acceptable minimum of authoritative decisions within the context of assembly participation.
3. The important parties, in government and opposition, must subscribe to certain ground-rules and develop some cohesion one with another.
4. Together the parliamentary parties must provide a means of integration for all significant sectors of society.

A syndrome of system failure, incorporating all these elements, is one where unstable and ineffective government is chained to an assembly in which the parties are at one another's throats, whilst outside, hostile forces are gathering to put an end to the parliamentary morass. Rarely will all these symptoms appear at once, but none is quite independent of the others. The survival power of apparently shaky parliamentary democracies depends on at least *one* of the conditions being met. Unstable government is tolerable as long as some important decisions are being made, and even when these are not forthcoming, the cohesion, possibly the inertia, of the party system may prolong its life. And if the largest parties can function together to provide workable government, then the fact that sections of the population are quite alienated from the parliamentary regime can be ignored for some time. The stability of any European system can be judged against this check-list, and weaknesses will be seen normally to be restricted to one head.

Actual breakdown in recent years has occurred only in France (1958) and in Greece (1967), so in order to bring out all features clearly we have to refer to the pre-war position as well—notably the collapse of the Weimar and the first Austrian republics. The case of Greece we examine in detail later*; it is important because it shows that even if the parliamentary system is functioning—supplying governments and policy output within a cohesive assembly structure—the fact that an important social group (the army) found the results unpalatable was quite sufficient to topple Greek democracy. Our concern in this section is with those cases where a significant part of the collapse took place *within* the parliamentary framework.

Obviously any complete examination of the Weimar Republic would have to take into account a wide range of socio-economic factors, and we

---

* See below, pp. 136–8.

shall look at the role of fascism and the military in other contexts. The economic predicament and the unresolved social situation following the collapse of the Imperial order unleashed forces which the Reichstag was hardly equipped to contain; nevertheless, the party system which resulted can be said to be an accurate reflection of the currents at work in German society. This analysis concentrates only on the *parliamentary* features of instability and collapse.

On a parliamentary level, the growing and finally insuperable problem was the inability to provide a stable government combination—and near the end *any* combination at all. Normal if fairly short-lived coalitions were the rule until 1930, relying on Reichstag majorities to put measures through. From 1930 onwards it became necessary for governments to rely on the sweeping presidential decree powers, and once this path was taken, the Reichstag had effectively abrogated its authority. Resort to elections to end the parliamentary stalemate was no help either; at successive elections from 1930 onwards, swelling numbers voted for the

	Alignments and Coalitions					
	'Left' parties	Weimar	'Great'	Right-Centre	National Opposition	Anti-System
1919	45	76	81	54	10	8
1920	42	44	58	57	15	20
1924–a	34	40	49	56	26	20
1924–b	35	46	56	60	24	12
1928	41	37	55	53	17	13
1930	38	40	45	43	25	31
1932–a	36	35	36	26	43	52
1932–b	37	33	35	29	42	50
1933	31	30	32	26	52	56

Notes to table. The figures in each column refer to the percentage of votes gained at each Reichstag election by the parties making up a particular grouping, whether the grouping was formally in existence or not. Thus the 'National Opposition' was only formed in the last years of the Republic, but the constituent parties were contesting elections much earlier.

'Left' parties were the Communist Party, the Independent Social Democrats, and the Social Democrats. They were *never* in alliance, and anyway never had a majority.

The 'Weimar Coalition' parties were the Social Democrats, the German Democratic Party and the Catholic Centre.

The 'Great Coalition' included the Weimar parties above and Stresemann's German People's Party.

'Right-Centre' coalitions included various combinations from the radical German Democrats to the right-wing German National People's Party—plus some very small 'conservative' parties.

'National Opposition' includes German National People's Party and National Socialists.

'Anti-System' aggregates National Socialists and Communists (and Independent Socialists until 1920).

National Socialists who promised to end the unedifying regime of the parties. Paradoxically, by 1933 it was possible to produce a Reichstag majority, but it was a majority for the extremist combination that was to put an end to the Republic.

In all this, the root cause did not rest in an undue proliferation of the parties—though there were usually around twelve represented—but in the peculiarly diffuse expression which they gave to the party system at a critical period, and this was the prior condition to breakdown. At the outset of its short life the parliamentary system provided a number of possible government combinations. The table on page 89 shows clearly the different phases by totting up the relative strength of the various coalition possibilities as a result of each election.

The overall trend from left of centre in 1919, through centre and centre-right majorities, to a final right-extremist supremacy, is readily apparent. But the three critical elections from 1930 to 1932, especially the one in 1930, show an utter dispersion of the system with no conceivable coalition grouping able to supply a governing majority. The hollowing-out of the democratic centre proceeded apace from 1932 onwards, but it was the initial indeterminateness of the position in 1930 which encouraged the ultimate polarization.

With the parties of the extreme left and right committed to the destruction of the parliamentary system, there was little chance of supplying the cohesion which seemed possible in the middle years of the Republic; nor were the parties on the left capable of working together—they were at daggers-drawn from the very beginning, and even if they had managed a common front, numerically they were always in a subordinate position. Loyalty to the Republic was also questionable on the moderate right— only the three 'Weimar' parties, who were responsible for the constitution, were deeply committed, and even here the Catholic Centre at times played an ambivalent role. In spite of all this, up to 1930 governments achieved a reasonable policy output, especially in the field of foreign relations under Stresemann's guidance. But of the requirements we set out for successful parliamentary democracy, in the end not one was met.

The background to the Weimar Republic was one of incessant government upheaval—twenty-one governments from 1919 to 1933. And the Fourth French Republic also became renowned for government instability—no less than twenty-five in the comparable time-span, 1946 until 1958. Yet the problems facing France after 1945 were not of the same order as those facing Germany in 1919. The essential form of government was not seriously in question, there were not the destabilizing influences of wartime defeat—this shock had already been absorbed by the Vichy government—and the economic problems of postwar France, though immense, were no greater than she experienced after the First World War. It can be argued that political extremism, hence lack of cohesion of the parliamentary parties, was in a large measure responsible for the eventual failure. The 'anti-system' parties: Communists, Gaullists, and Poujadists—as far as these last are to be counted—had in common at least a suspicion of the parliamentary system. But, granted they had the power of disruption, were they powerful enough to destroy? And were their actions always negative?

Undoubtedly, the greatest Communist threat came after the party left the post-war tripartite government, which included the Catholic MRP and the Socialists. Immediately the country was plunged into a series of challenging strikes, but with gradual economic recovery this impetus was spent, and it was shown in the declining electoral fortunes of the Communists, partly as a result of the voting system. Whilst the Communist Party at first had 183 deputies in an Assembly of 635, they dropped to 100 between 1951 and 1956. On two counts, size of representation and industrial challenge, the Communist Party was a greater threat to the Republic at the beginning than at the end. Although the party's assembly vote made government formation and survival that much more difficult, its negative role should not be overestimated, as Macridis points out: 'Ample illustration was given of the party's willingness to co-operate. They helped elect Socialist Le Troquer to the presidency of the National Assembly in 1954, 1956 and 1957; they voted for the investiture of Mendès-France and Guy Mollet; and on two occasions the "conscience" of the party was sacrificed . . . in 1956 the Communist Party voted for the credits to continue the war in Algeria and to give the government extraordinary powers to fight the rebellion.'[15] Finally, and at the end, it was one of the parties most concerned to rally to the parliamentary republic. Certainly, the pro-system parties feared the power of the Communists; it is less certain that the party was ever in a position to do very much—for most of the time it was 'excluded', on the defensive, and 'manipulated' by the deliberate effects of the 1951 voting law.

Were the threats from the political right of greater moment? At its inception in 1947, de Gaulle's Rally of the French People looked capable of taking the country by storm, and its behaviour was often reminiscent of a fledgling fascist movement. Yet by the time the RPF was able to contest the first available national elections in 1951, its attraction had declined. It did then become the largest parliamentary group with 120 seats, but by 1956 this had become a tattered remnant of twenty-two deputies, and long before then it had disintegrated as a parliamentary force—and was disowned by de Gaulle. The fact that many Gaullist deputies were inclined to co-operate with the governing parties, voting for personnel of government and their measures, led to de Gaulle's disenchantment. One cannot discount entirely the evidence of co-operation both from the left and the right, and this fact together with the numerical decline of Gaullists and Communists in the assembly in the 1950s shows that the grounds for parliamentary failure must be sought elsewhere.

It can hardly be laid at the door of the Poujadists either. In 1956, M.

Poujade and his followers positively leapt into the parliamentary arena with two and a half million votes and 52 seats. The phenomenon of Poujadism was the almost inarticulate howl of the small-shopkeepers' anti-tax lobby, and as to its views of wider national import: 'It had not the slightest idea as to what to do with its group in the Assembly, and, as the absurdity of Pierre Poujade's political views became apparent, it broke up.'[16] Difficult as government formation and survival was throughout the Fourth Republic,[17] the anti-system parties of whatever colouring never rose in aggregate much above a third of the whole, and with a peak in 1951 long before the critical period. Moreover, except by accident, the extremists could not act in a united fashion.

The weakness of the Fourth Republic lay just as much in the parties which were committed to its survival. Essentially, they came to be divided amongst themselves, and their lack of cohesion proved fatal. Socialists, Radicals, MRP, and Conservatives, were the buttress of democratic government, but by no means a unified bloc, rather 'an aggregation sundered by France's historical cleavages'.[18] The divisions ran deep: church-state relations, the economic role of the state, European unity, the future of the colonial empire. Any or all of these issues could quickly destroy the fragile consensus of a government majority. To this picture one has to add the 'deputy-centred' nature of the parties, a characteristic the Fourth Republic inherited from the Third. What this meant in practice was that deputies saw their loyalties as much in terms of their special interests and those of their constitutents as with the government in power. Deputies retained the strong base of local connections in spite of efforts to extend party control via the list system of proportional representation introduced in 1946. Instability of government, an average life of seven months, is the key index of failure; behind it lay the failure of policy output.

The failure was perhaps relative; on the credit side there lay the progress towards European unity, the rapprochement with Germany, economic recovery, and some essential steps in decolonization. Progress was often made behind the Assembly's back; French planning went on its way unhindered. Increasingly, however, all governments became deadlocked by the cross-pressures at work in the Assembly. The inability to resolve urgent issues, the failure to make decisions in spite of the widespread demand that they should be made, is summed up in the characteristic term 'immobilisme'. And the tactics of government—such as 'the majority for the occasion' employed by Mendès-France, a constant redeployment of voting alliance—were in the end of no avail. The 'occasion' of the festering Algerian problem was to prove greater than the resources of the system.* Faced with this episode, the Fourth Republic may have been 'unlucky', just as the Third Republic was 'lucky' to have

---

* For the role of the military in this, see below, p. 196.

survived so long. The immediate cause of the Republic ending its own life, preferring 'the lesser evil' of de Gaulle, was the gathering of hostile forces outside the Assembly, the threat of armed insurrection in Algeria and even in mainland France. But the final threat from without was just the last stage in a long process, preceded by the failure of the political parties and a growing public indifference to the fate of the party republic. It was perhaps ironic that M. Pflimlin, the last prime minister prior to de Gaulle, should have enjoyed the largest vote of confidence ever accorded to a Fourth Republic politician—just before throwing in the towel!

Once again, we see the complete 'syndrome of failure' in evidence, as it was for the Weimar Republic. The third example, the pre-war Austrian Republic, differs in two important respects: the absence of extremist parties and of any party proliferation. The electorate had a clear choice between the two major parties, the Christian-Socials and the Socialists. We have already seen* that this polarization was not based on an underlying consensus, that the cleavages in Austrian society followed the same route: the Catholic Church, rural society, and the middle classes ranged on one side, and a largely anti-clerical urban proletariat on the other. There were two antagonistic 'armed-camps', but the gulf between them was deep rather than wide. The Socialists would have no truck with the tiny Communist Party, and for their part the majority of Christian-Socials did not favour the extremism of the Austrian Nazis or that of the local product, the Heimwehr—a cross between a political party and a para-military force. At what was to prove to be the last election, held in 1930, the Nazi Party and the Communists won no seats at all, the Heimwehr was reduced to a rump, and for the first time the Socialists emerged as the strongest party. Compared with many other states of that time and later, the results might have appeared to confirm the strength of parliamentary democracy.

The Christian-Socials remained in power with the support of the remaining Heimwehr and a small peasants' party, the Landbund. This gave the government a miniscule majority, and in any system a voting-stalemate is likely to occur in such circumstances. But a complete parliamentary impasse will only result if there is a total lack of cohesion between the parties. The impasse was quickly reached in Austria, and Chancellor Dollfuss used it as a pretext for dissolving the assembly in March 1933; this action marked the end of parliamentary democracy. The personal leanings of Dollfuss towards some kind of corporate state should not obscure his other preoccupations: the growing threat of German fascism as well as his virulent, yet on the whole representative, hatred for the Socialists. To a later suggestion that he should reconvene the assembly and seek a reconciliation with the leader of the Socialists, he exclaimed: 'I sit again in a Parliament with Otto Bauer? Never, never!'[19]

---

* See above, pp. 18–19.

That was the extent of the antagonism between two comparatively moderate parties, and only when the external situation had further deteriorated was there a belated attempt at co-operation. In a sense, the Austrian case is a simplified version of the French experience—without the extremist parties in the assembly, and only two divergent forces in place of the cross-pressures of the French moderate parties. Both showed a failure of the parliamentary system before outside forces effectively intervened.

Rarely does extremism make an early and sufficient impact to destroy a system quite by its own efforts. And various warning-lights are available: government stability and the ability to make key decisions are two critical areas where indications are apparent, but countries differ in the degrees of tolerance allowable: the French Third Republic showed remarkable powers of survival, Finland has contentedly carried on for years with short-lived governments—a situation that could prove intolerable in Britain after three or four doses. Countries differ as well in the type of relationship which the parties build up one with another and with society at large. The cohesion between the parties necessarily rests on some common view of the parliamentary system: the idea that it is 'representative' works two ways: on the one side, it aims to reflect the interests of all important social groups, but the other side of 'representation' is that the parliamentary process should act as an efficient method of canalizing demands made on the individual parties. Thus an assembly with a strong parliamentary tradition, as in Britain, functions both to voice social demands *and* to provide the parties with some insulation from those pressures. It is the ability to balance the two which results in a cohesive system. Fundamentally, this is an élitist view of the political process, but it may be unwise to assume that *parliamentary* democracy works in any other way.

NOTES AND REFERENCES

1. S. M. Lipset, 'Party Systems and the Representation of Social Groups', in R. A. Dahl and D. E. Neubauer (eds.), *Readings in Modern Political Analysis,* Prentice-Hall, 1968, p. 94. Lipset adds, 'Electoral laws determine the nature of the *party system* as much as any other structure available.'
2. German federalism may have helped to produce a 'quasi-party' the Christian-Social Union in Bavaria. In the Bundestag the CDU-CSU form an *Arbeitsgemeinschaft,* a working partnership. The chief power of the CSU is to block any CDU chancellor-candidate it does not approve; the CSU leader, Franz-Josef Strauss, is able to present himself as 'kingmaker'. In 1979 the CSU was even able to force the CDU to adopt Strauss as the joint CDU–CSU chancellor candidate for the 1980 federal election.
3. Any party winning 0·5 per cent of the national vote is entitled to a state subsidy; a party with as little as 2 per cent will net well over £100,000. A similar arrangement also applies for parties contesting *Land* elections. See K. Sontheimer, 'The Funding of Political Parties in West Germany', *The Political Quarterly,* July–September 1974. A

ruling of the Constitutional Court in April 1976 extended the right of state-subsidy to independent, non-party candidates.

4. For a tabular summary of European electoral systems, see S. Henig and J. Pinder (eds.), *European Political Parties*, George Allen and Unwin, Political and Economic Planning, 1969, p. 514. Also, Enid Lakeman, *How Democracies Vote,* Faber and Faber, 1970, discusses the effects of proportional representation in the European states, pp. 169–214.

5. M. Duverger, *Political Parties*, Methuen, 1954, p. 217.

6. C. Leys, 'Electoral Systems and Party Systems: The Duverger Doctrine', in J. Blondel (ed.), *Comparative Government: A Reader,* Macmillan, 1969, p. 140.

7. G. Lavau, *Partis Politiques et Réalités Sociales*, Paris: A. Colin, 1953, pp. 33–4.

8. ibid, p. 53.

9. J. Blondel, op. cit., p. 201.

10. J. Blondel, 'Party Systems and Patterns of Government in Western Democracies', *Canadian Journal of Political Science*, June 1968, pp. 180–203. For a more recent study of the problems of measuring government 'stability', see D. Sanders and V. Herman, 'The Stability and Survival of Governments in Western Democracies', *Acta Politica*, 1977, vol. 3, pp. 346–77.

11. The classification can be extended to include a further category of 'fragmented' party systems. The possibility is not discussed in this section since it is not immediately relevant in Western Europe, although the idea of fragmentation is basic to the subsequent discussion on the 'Breakdown of Parliamentary systems', pages 87–94 below. For a discussion of an inclusive typology applicable to Western Europe, see G. Smith, 'Western European Party Systems: On the Trail of a Typology', *West European Politics*, 2/1, January 1979.

12. The following are examples of absolute majorities in the post-war period, elections and assemblies:
Austria: in 1966 (Austrian People's Party 48.4%, but an absolute majority of seats); in 1971, 1975 and 1979 the Socialists won over 50% of the vote.
Belgium: in 1950 (Social-Christians 47.6%, with an absolute majority of seats).
France: in 1968 (the UDR with an absolute majority of seats).
Germany: in 1957 (CDU-CSU 50.2%).
Greece: in 1974 (New Democracy 54.4%); in 1977 a majority of seats.
Italy: in 1948 (Christian Democrats 48.4%, but with an absolute majority of seats).
Ireland: Fianna Fail had a majority of seats at four elections from 1957 onwards, but with less tham 50% of the vote; in 1977 50.6%.
Norway: The Norwegian Labour Party had a narrow majority in the Storting from 1945 until 1961.
Sweden: in 1968 (Social Democrats 50.1%).

13. The discussion following is based on Dahl's typology, 'Patterns of Opposition' in R. A. Dahl (ed.), *Political Oppositions in Western Democracies*, New Haven: Yale University Press, 1966, pp. 332–47.

14. O. Kirchheimer, 'The Waning of Opposition', in R. C. Macridis and B. E. Brown (eds.), *Comparative Politics*, Ill., The Dorsey Press, 1964, pp. 280–91.

15. R. C. Macridis, 'The Immobility of the French Communist Party', in R. C. Macridis (ed.), *Political Parties: Contemporary Trends and Ideas*, New York: Harper and Row, 1967, p. 193.

16. M. Steed in *European Political Parties*, p. 106.

17. The difficulties of initial government formation for the 'constitutionalist' majority were also numerical problems, as shown by S. E. Finer, *Comparative Government*, Allen Lane, 1970, pp. 293–5.

18. ibid., p. 294.

19. A. Sturmthal, *The Tragedy of European Labour*, Gollancz, 1944, p. 175.

Additional References

M. Balinski and H. P. Young, 'Stability, Coalitions of Schisms in Proportional Representative Systems', *American Political Science Review*, vol. 72/3.

H. Berrington, 'Towards a Multi-Party Britain?', *West European Politics*, 2/1, January 1979.

F. Burin and K. Shell (eds.), *Politics, Law and Social Change. Essays of Otto Kirchheimer*, Columbia University Press, 1969.

K. H. Cerny (ed.), *Scandinavia at the Polls: Recent Political Trends in Denmark, Norway and Sweden*, Washington: American Enterprise Institute, 1977.

S. Finer (ed.), *Adversary Politics and Electoral Reform*, Anthony Wigram, 1975.

G. Hand, J. Georgel, C. Sasse (eds.), *European Electoral Systems Handbook*, Butterworth, 1979.

Hansard Society, *Commission on Electoral Reform*, June 1976.

F. A. Hermens, 'Electoral Systems and Political Systems', *Parliamentary Affairs*, Winter 1976.

F. A. Hermens, 'The Dynamics of Proportional Representation', in H. Eckstein and D. Apter, *Comparative Politics*, New York: The Free Press, 1963.

G. Ionescu and I. de Madariaga, *Opposition: Past and Present of a Political Institution*, C. A. Watts, 1968.

E. Lakeman, *How Democracies Vote*, Faber and Faber, 1970.

E. Lakeman, *Nine Democracies: Electoral Systems in the Countries of the EEC*, Arthur McDougall Fund, 1975.

A. Lijphart and R. W. Gibberd, 'Thresholds and Payoffs in List Systems of Proportional Representation', *European Journal of Political Research*, 5/3, September 1977.

I. McLean, *Elections*, Longman, 1976.

W. Miller, B. Särlvik and J. Alt, 'Partisan Dealignment in Britain, 1964–1974', *British Journal of Political Science*, April 1977.

W. Miller, *Electoral Dynamics*, Macmillan, 1978.

A. Milnor, *Elections and Political Stability*, Boston: Little, Brown, 1969.

D. Rae, *The Political Consequences of Electoral Laws*, Yale University Press, 1967.

R. Rose (ed.), *Electoral Behavior: A Comparative Handbook*, op. cit.

R. Rose and D. Urwin, 'Persistence and Change in Party Systems', *Political Studies*, 18/3, September 1970.

G. Sartori, *Parties and Party Systems: A Theoretical Framework*, New York: Harper and Row, 1977.

G. Sartori, 'European Political Parties: The Case of Polarized Pluralism', in R. Dahl and D. Neubauer (eds.), *Readings in Modern Political Analysis*, op. cit.

L. Sigelmann and S. Yough, 'Left-Right Polarization in National Party Systems', *Comparative Political Studies*, October 1978.

M. Taylor and V. Herman, 'Party Systems and Government Stability', *American Political Science Review*, (65), March 1971.

J. Thomas, *The Decline of Ideology in Western Political Parties*, Sage, 1975.

S. Wolinetz, 'The Transformation of Western European Party Systems Revisited', *West European Politics*, 2/1, January 1979.

A. Zuckerman and M. Lichbach, 'Stability and Change in European Electorates', *World Politics*, October 1977.

BREAKDOWN OF PARLIAMENTARY SYSTEMS

F. L. Carsten, *Fascist Movements in Austria: From Schönerer to Hitler*, Sage Publications, 1977.

T. Eschenburg and others, *The Road to Dictatorship, 1918–1933*, Wolff, 1964.

F. Fellner and J. Rath, 'Austria', in P. F. Sugar (ed.), *Native Fascism in the Successor States: 1918–1945*, Oxford: The European Bibliographical Centre, 1971.

D. MacRae, *Parliament, Parties and Society in France, 1946–1958*, Macmillan, 1968.

N. Leithes. *On the Game of Politics in France*, Stanford: Oxford, 1959.

S. M. Lipset, *Political Man*, Heinemann, 1963.

R. Manvell and H. Fraenkel, *The Hundred Days to Hitler*, Dent, 1974.

K. J. Newman, *European Democracy between the Wars*, Allen and Unwin, 1970.

A. J. Nicholls, *Weimar and the Rise of Hitler*, Macmillan, 1968.

A. J. Nicholls and E. Matthias (eds.), *German Democracy and the Triumph of Hitler*, Allen and Unwin, 1971.

G. B. Powell, *Social Fragmentation and Political Hostility: An Austrian Case Study*, Stanford University Press, 1970.

P. M. Williams, *Crisis and Compromise: Politics in the Fourth Republic*, Longmans, 1964.

PARTY SYSTEMS IN WESTERN EUROPE

	Communist & Allies	Independent Socialist	Social Democrats	Liberal-Radical
Austria	(Communist)		Socialist	
Belgium	Communist		Socialist	
Denmark	Communist	Socialist People's Left Socialists	Social Democrats	Radical-Liberal
Finland	SKDL		Social Democrats	Liberal-People's
France	Communist		Socialist	Left-Wing Radicals
Germany	(DKP)		Social Democrats	Free Democrats
Greece	Communists-Exterior	Communists-Interior	PASOK	
Iceland	People's Alliance	Liberal Left	Social Democrats	
Ireland			Labour	Fine Gael
Italy	Communist	Democratic Proletarian	Socialist	Republican Radical
Luxembourg	Communist		Socialists Social Democrats	Democrats
Netherlands	Communist	Pacifist-Socialist	Labour Democrats '70	Democrats '66 Radicals
Norway	(Communist)	Socialist-People's	Labour	(New People's)
Portugal	Communist		Socialist	
Spain	Communist		Socialist	Democratic Coalition
Sweden	Communist-Left		Social Democrats	
Switzerland	Party of Labour		Social Democrats	
United Kingdom			Labour	Liberal

Centre	Christian	Liberal-Conservative	Conservative	Right-Wing	Ethnic/Regional
	People's	Freedom			
	Social-Christian	Liberty and Progress			FDF, Rass-emblement, Volksunie, VB
Centre-Democrats	Christian-People's	Venstre	Conservative	Progress	
Centre	Christian Union		National Unity	Rural	Swedish People's
		UDF RPR			
	CDU		CSU	(NPD)	
Democratic Centre		New Liberals	New Democracy	National Rally	
Progressive			Independence		
			Fianna Fail		
	Christian Democracy	PSDI Liberal		MSI	South Tyrol People's
	Christian-Social				
Farmers'	CDA Calvinists State Reform	Liberals			
Centre	Christian People's	Liberals	Conservative	(Progress)	
	CDC	PSD			
Democratic Centre				National Union	Catalan Cons. Basques (PNV and HB)
Centre	(Christian)	Liberals	Conservative		
Swiss People's	Christian-Democrats Evangelical	Old Liberals Radical-Democrats	Landesring Republican	National Campaign	
			Conservative	(National Front)	Scottish-National Welsh-National Ulster-Unionists

Parties not represented in recent elections shown in brackets. See notes overleaf.

Notes

The table of 'Party Systems in Western Europe' shows the spread of parties on a broad 'right' and 'left' axis. Those placed in brackets are not currently (mid 1979) represented in their national parliaments. The ten 'streams' used for the classification include almost all of the major European political traditions. (In most but not all cases the streams correspond to those used by Michael Smart in 'Parliamentary Representation in Western Europe', p. 318 below.) Only a few countries actually come near to being represented in all the streams—notably Denmark. Whilst the ordering of most party groups is reasonably unambiguous, there are exceptions. The positioning of a 'Liberal' party—whether it is liberal-conservative or liberal-radical is best gauged from the nature of alliances and coalitions which it enters—thus both the West German FDP and the British Liberal Party count as 'liberal-radical' on this score: the FDP's coalition with the SPD since 1969 and the Liberal Party's 'pact' with the Labour Government from 1977 until 1978. The 'Independent Socialist' stream may contain parties which in some ways are more radical than the 'Communist' one—as is the case for the Democratic Proletarians in Italy. There are some difficulties in allocating 'Social Democrats'—the party label may be misleading as with the PSDI in Italy and the Portuguese PSD. Both are more right-wing than their titles suggest; to count them as 'liberal conservative' is only one of the possibilities.

Some parties are difficult to classify at all since they enshrine special national peculiarities. That is evident in the case of the Irish Fianna Fail and Fine Gael. The same is true for France, especially for the Gaullist RPR, in some ways a conservative party yet also with a *travailliste* following. It is also difficult to disentangle the RPR from the UDF on a conventional left-right ordering. There is a general difficulty existing for most 'Christian' parties, for they have a wider appeal than implied by their insertion between 'Centre' and 'Liberal-Conservative', and there is wide individual variation. Parties classified as 'Right-wing' may be neo-fascist as with the Italian MSI, but may be more Poujadist and 'protest' in character as with the Danish Progress Party. The Ethnic and Regional stream has no fixed political direction. The Basque HB is extreme left, whilst the Belgian *Vlaamsche Blok* is well to the right—as is the case for the Ulster Unionists.

For details of individual parties listed in the table and their representation at recent elections, see the 'National Profiles', pp. 267–317.

5
Constitutional Balance

European Constitutionalism

FROM THE focus in the preceding chapters on the basic social forces and their expression in the political parties, we can turn to the more formal institutional context in which they operate. Really, this aspect all hinges on the exercise of government power, and on the control of that power; behind both stands the liberal democratic doctrine of constitutionalism. Partly the term implies 'limited' as opposed to 'absolute' government, but more than this is involved. It has also been called 'a practical limitation of democracy',[1] and this is surely the point: that it limits the *public* power, as well as that of government. The two elements of constitutionalism are well brought out in the term 'liberal democracy', and in Macpherson's formulation that such states became liberal first and democratic later.[2] Their liberal institutions at first guarding against the threat of absolutist rule were later to serve a more general purpose of 'modifying' democracy.

Constitutional government in Western Europe arose as the product of two different sets of historical forces. The first was the sustained struggle to bring absolute government under *legal* control; the second was to bring it under *popular* control. The former resulted in governments which were bound by the supremacy of law and which at the same time were subjected to numerous institutional checks to give 'balanced' systems of power—of these the pure theory of the separation of powers is an extreme example. In general, one can say that the legal and institutional controls were the contribution arising from the political struggles of the rising bourgeoisie. The later, popular impact on the development of constitutionalism was of a quite different order; it was a claim for the political representation for the whole of the people, not for institutional balance; it was a demand for a government responsible to the people, not primarily for a limited one. Yet the popular governments which emerged, representative and responsible as they became, were in fact grafted on to the prior conceptions of balanced and limited government.

One can read this development in two ways. One can portray it as a harmonious continuity. In practice this was often the case, for the demand for popular participation was satisfied by having a greater voice in the working system; there seemed to be no need to create a new one. And in this respect we should take into account the real gains which were made in securing individual and corporate freedom; all classes stood to benefit from the extension of civil rights. Why should not the same system secure equality in other directions as well?

The alternative reading shows the tensions and possible contradictions involved. Here we can best refer back to the concept of a dual system of representation put forward by Bendix.* The duality is expressed in the direct plebiscitarian principle existing alongside a group representation based on 'the differential affiliation of individuals'; the one corresponds to the idea of popular control and a national citizenry, the other to a balance of forces, in society and in government. Bendix sees this tension as a source of continual compromise, and from that point of view providing a dynamic for political development. A rather different conclusion is that the 'differential affiliation' gives such a sharp imbalance of power in practice that there is a blatant contradiction between formal popular participation and the actual direction of government decision-making, that the power of economic wealth makes for gross inequalities in the effects of affiliation.

The disparate strands which together make up modern European constitutionalism perhaps give it a rather fragmented aspect, but it is a single, unified idea as well. This unity can best be expressed by pointing to the high *normative* quality of the individual constitutions:[3] it is the constitution itself which is said to speak with authority, irrespective of the nature of particular powerholders. The authority of the constitution, as a higher form of law, can be traced to the special place which the legal profession came to occupy in these societies and to the central part it took in the early development of constitutional government. But the regard for abstract, legal principles is also symptomatic of the trends in Western society over a long period, portrayed by Max Weber as a move to societies based on the exercise of 'legal-rational' authority; both 'legality' and 'rationality' are fundamental to all normative constitutions.[4]

However, if we ask what it is that gives these constitutions such a sanction in the West European states, we are finally referred back to the social context, to the political culture of a country. It is the prevailing consensus of attitudes and beliefs which sustain constitutional government, provide the necessary support, and give a sense of legitimate authority. For the narrow confines of written constitutions and constitutional law, one has to substitute whatever is to be regarded as 'acceptable' behaviour on the part of the political authorities—and those who challenge them. This question of acceptability is taken up by Sartori in what he calls the 'role theory approach': 'What is the impact, or the role, of a constitution vis-à-vis the role-taking of the power holders? That is, does it help to enforce, and if so what extent, a desired "role performance" upon the persons in office?'[5]

From the idea of the constitution enforcing particular roles, one can

* See p. 5, above.

turn to its 'symbolic capability' as part of the wider capability of the political system taken as a whole.[6] The symbolic appeal lies partly in the history which the constitution enshrines and also because it can act as 'a showcase of the norms and symbols of a given society'.[7] We can see this to good effect in the constitution of the Fifth French Republic. In its preamble and first five articles, most of the national symbols are displayed. Besides defining France as an 'indivisible, secular, democratic and social Republic', attention is drawn to the Declaration of 1789, the tricolour, the Marseillaise, the Republican motto of 'Liberty, Equality and Fraternity'. In 1958, the political authorities had to draw heavily on these symbols to strengthen the claims of the new order; of itself, the constitution was just one more in a long line, and lacked the legitimacy which time alone could give it.

Because of its long duration, and perhaps just because it is unwritten and quite flexible, the British constitution is a powerful admixture of normative and purely symbolic elements. The once-powerful institutions of state which have since become 'dignified façades', and which in Bagehot's view concealed the real working of the system, have not just become of nominal importance; they have been promoted to high symbolism—the sovereignty of Parliament, the role of the monarchy. The 'efficient secret' of the British constitution lies partly in the facility with which the empty shell of political institutions can be retained as symbols whilst they are robbed of substantive power.

Not all constitutions can claim historical sanction or act as a showcase for national symbols. For instance, the founding of the German Federal Republic in 1949 came at a time of sharp discontinuity, and almost every historical tradition was unavailable. The one acceptable symbol was that of a unified German nation, and this was given due expression in the preamble to the Basic Law: 'The entire German people is called upon to achieve by free self-determination the unity and freedom of Germany,' And to that end the whole constitution was made provisional, pending reunification. Such a constitution as the West German has to be regarded, initially at least, in mainly instrumental terms for achieving an acceptable distribution of power. This does not necessarily make it less effective; in Germany, legal norms are powerful, and the recurrent failure of the political system helped to make the sanction of the 'Basic Law' the major determinant.

How should we sum up the doctrine of constitutionalism so far? We have seen that it is concerned to limit the power of government and to contain the 'arbitrary' effect of popular will. We can add that, in theory at least, the doctrine does not limit the development of state or society to any particular direction—simply expressed, it is only concerned with 'how' things are done, rather than with 'what' is done, that ultimately it is a set of procedural devices. But no constitution can be ideologically 'neutral'; indeed, its whole genesis and operation will voice prevailing beliefs even if these are not made explicit.[8] That the liberal democratic constitutions can avoid an explicit statement of ideology is made possible because the nature of the procedural arrangements arrived at provides precisely the wide ambit demanded by a pluralist society, serving to perpetuate an existing power balance. The symbolism and the formal arrangements add up to an ideology which helps to give 'an idealized description of the way in which the system actually works'.[9] How far this idealization merely conceals the real adjustment of social forces, and how far it disguises the true nature of political power, is the more elusive problem. Thus a Marxist would argue that any constitutional limitation of powers is, in effect, a 'bourgeois device' for trammelling the working class, and dismiss constitutionalism as the generic term for such schemes.

At least we should be on guard against regarding constitutionalism as existing apart from the society in which it operates. Whatever interpretation is put on its basic nature, three characteristics stand out: it seeks to place limits on the power of governments and of the public; it is one of the means by which power in society is legitimized; it is an expression of the integral power balance in society.

The Distribution of Power

The individual hallmark of a constitution lies in the specific provisions made to secure a dispersion of government power. In liberal democracies, these provisions vary considerably in their scope and stringency. In the United States, there is a strict divorce of the executive from the legislature, together with a federal system, and these are backed by an inflexible constitution and the wide sweep of judicial review. The West European pattern differs fundamentally in actually merging legislative and executive powers in important respects, although the degree of emphasis laid on any one technique of power distribution varies considerably. We shall look at these in detail in following sections;* here, we should examine the more general question of the efficacy of constitutions in securing a power dispersion, whilst bearing in mind that the constitutionalist prescription of controlling power by ensuring its dispersion is only one of possible approaches.

The normative quality of a constitution is an essential feature if power is to be dispersed significantly. To appreciate the full flavour of this, the predominantly normative type of constitution in Western Europe can be contrasted with situations where this does not apply. One possibility is the purely 'semantic' constitution; this is not simply a linguistic exercise having no connection with reality, rather it merely formalizes and rationalizes the actual power distribution within a state. We have to go outside Western Europe for an extant example, and the German Democratic Republic provides an illustration: Article 48 of the 1968 con-

---

* For a broad comparison of constitutional provisions, see the table on p. 265 below.

stitution gives the single-chamber Volkskammer full sovereign powers. Article 1, however, bases the leadership of the socialist state on 'the working-class and the Marxist-Leninist Party'. Since the 'sovereign' Volkskammer almost always accepts this leadership unanimously, one can argue either that complete harmony prevails or that it is just a rubber-stamp. In fact, there is no contradiction between what the constitution says and what actually happens. We can say that the whole document is semantic, and that the only relevant condition is Article 1. Given the fact of leadership by the Marxist-Leninist Party, the constitution is unnecessary, for the form of leadership is a permanent feature of the state and is sufficient to determine, except in detail, its entire functioning. Thus the value of such a constitution is mainly symbolic, but it also pays homage to the power of legal forms.

The nature of West European society has precluded this type of development, but it has not prevented the emergence of constitutional forms which can be labelled as 'nominal'. This description applies to those constitutions which, although setting definite standards, remain largely inoperative, are irrelevant to the real exercise of power, and can be altered at the whim of government. The former Portuguese constitution fits into this category. Although the constitution framed in 1933 was deliberately authoritarian in tone, there was a provision for a National Assembly. Elections to this body took place regularly, but the reality of power was shown by Salazar's continuous rule until his incapacity in 1968. Of itself, this continuity in office does not prove nominality, but the only legal political organization was Salazar's National Union, and it always won all the seats at elections. Alongside the prime minister, there was also a president elected at first by direct (if limited) suffrage. Shocked by the size of the opposition vote in the 1958 presidential election, Salazar declared: 'This is the last time a constitutional coup d'état is possible.' The 'threat' amounted to 23 per cent of the vote, and the offending clause in the constitution was amended by the National Assembly to allow only for indirect election.

The nominality of a constitution is a question of degree. Opposition candidates in Salazar's Portugal were permitted to contest assembly elections—parties were illegal in opposition, but permitted to function for the immediate election period. The last election held in October 1969 under the more liberal regime of Salazar's successor, Dr Marcello Caetano, still did not result in a single opposition candidate being returned; a wave of arrests followed, and the power of the secret police appeared to be undiminished. An impartial report concluded that, 'in spite of the opposition having been granted unprecedented rights' the elections were not free.[10] The dividing line between what is nominal and what is normative can therefore only be decided by particular cases, of which the conduct of elections is a critical test for a liberal democracy. The Greek constitution, approved by popular referendum in September 1968 and, according to one commentator, 'in itself a thoroughly democratic conception',[11] perhaps attracted such a large measure of support—ninety per cent in favour with voting compulsory—because of its promises. But the constitution remained nominal because the ruling military junta found it quite inexpedient to allow free elections or the restoration of civil liberties.

Such examples of constitutions which for one reason or another lack a normative impulse, make it clear that the distribution of power is unlikely to spring from the constitution itself, but to be part of a deeper social balance, of which the law and the constitution form a part. It implies a willingness of important groups in society, not just the government, to accept certain restrictions. A particular concern in this respect has been for the protection of individual liberties and the containment of arbitrary decisions; de Tocqueville's fear of 'democratic despotism', the tyranny of the majority, refers to both, and the two precepts can be illustrated in their European context. Many states seek to protect individual liberties by an extensive Bill of Rights in the constitution. Italy, West Germany, Switzerland, and the Irish Republic do so, whilst the Austrian constitution incorporates many of the laws of the Habsburg Empire; the current Danish constitution (1953) provides such guarantees. On the other hand, France, Belgium, and the Netherlands, together with the majority of the Nordic states, make no specific provision. A typical and extensive listing of such rights is given in the West German Basic Law, Articles 1–19.[12] Quite reasonably, such countries as Germany, with recent experience of oppression, have been most concerned to build constitutional safeguards; they provide some protection against an over-zealous servant of state, if not against the rulers themselves. These rights are regarded as fundamental to the liberal democratic creed; where they are not separately listed, they have long become a part of the law of the land—the battles have been fought and won in courts and parliaments. This is true in the case of Sweden, yet the proposed amendments to the constitution in the 1960s included a bill of rights; it is doubtful whether much would be gained by such a supplement.

Constitutional provisions can become nominal in other ways as well, by being beyond the inclination or even the power of governments to enforce. The Portuguese 'revolutionary' constitution of 1976 is replete with socialist ideals, but subsequent political development has made whole sections apparently irrelevant. The Irish constitution has a special chapter, 'Directive Principles of Social Policy', but Article 45 declares that they 'shall not be cognisable by any court'. A typical clause says that the ownership and control of the community's resources should be distributed 'amongst private individuals and the various classes as best to subserve the common good'. In a similar vein, the Italian constitution in Article 4 establishes 'the right to work', and Article 32 states that 'The Republic protects the health of the individual ... and guarantees free medical treatment to the poor.' The most that we can be sure of is that the hearts of those who framed the constitution were in the right place.

That a constitution simply cannot give blanket guarantees is shown by Article 13 of the West German Basic Law. This says that 'The home is inviolable', but its categorical assurance is heavily modified in the next two sub-sections: besides the power of judges or 'other legally prescribed bodies' to permit entry, the home is violable 'to avert a common danger' or an 'imminent danger to public security', to counter terrorism or even to alleviate the housing shortage, to combat the danger of epidemics and to protect endangered juveniles. It is very little special protection that the German citizen obtains from this clause.

The real protection lies in the adjudication of the courts and the curtailing of executive discretionary power. This is summed up in 'the rule of law', but this effect can hardly be established by constitutional edict; it is the product of a long process of 'structural differentiation', resulting in a degree of freedom for the courts from political interference. Besides obvious regard for the verdict of the courts, their freedom is shown in matters of personnel appointment, security of tenure, and of preferment. Taken as whole, the courts in Western Europe have gained independence in these areas—there is an effective dispersion of power.

In most European countries, the status of a judge is more that of a civil servant than in Britain, and often, as in West Germany, that means being trained as a career judge under state supervision. In practice, it makes little difference to the subsequent independence of the judiciary, and the judges are pretty well irremovable—thus in Finland when civil servants lost security of tenure by a law of 1926, judges were specifically excepted. One device used to insulate the judiciary from political pressure is to have an independent judicial council, with complete supervisory and appointive powers. This innovation in the French Fourth Republic was made against strong opposition from the Ministry of Justice, and the High Council of the Judiciary that was set up—consisting of professional judges and of jurists selected by the National Assembly—quickly showed itself to be independent of the government; in spite of efforts by the Ministry of Justice to sabotage its work, the Council finally came to control the career structure of French judges. This is the type of in-fighting that has to be expected, for the habits of patronage and active intervention die hard. Italy is similar in having made constitutional provision for the autonomous organization of the judiciary. In West Germany, on a federal level, judges are well-protected by the constitution; possibly initial appointment, since judges are civil servants, may appear to be more under the influence of the political authorities, and that could apply in the courts of the Länder. However, dismissal is only possible 'under authority of judicial decision', and the federal judges can only be dismissed by a decision of the Constitutional Court. Similar protection is granted in other countries. In both Italy and West Germany at least, the problem has sometimes been too great a security of tenure; the courts in both countries were for long peppered with judges who had over-loyally interpreted the will of the totalitarian parties.

In this way we can see that the root of the problem is perhaps not the constitutional position ascribed to the judiciary, nor the conditions of service or civil service status, but the question of whether the judiciary can develop a corporate 'professional unity' independent of the executive. In Britain, the professional ethic emanates from the legal profession itself, with High Court judges recruited from active members of the Bar. But this can hardly serve as a general model—the French Council of State is an integral part of government administration; yet it has not prevented a professional unity from emerging within this body, as part of the élitist *'grands corps'*. One simple device which helps ensure its independence and cohesion is to make promotion strictly according to seniority.

The importance of such professional independence, however it originates, shows that the real dispersion of power is likely to operate at a deeper level than the constitutional provisions. This is what Vile has in mind when he refers to the 'internal rules' which develop alongside formal rules and status, and what he says of the Lord Chancellor in Britain has a much wider application: 'This man, when acting as a judge, is expected to show impartiality and that expectation is enforced by the attitudes of the members of the legal profession, who would quickly denounce any attempt to use the office for purely party ends.'[13] The idea of internal rules is evidence of the deeper cross-currents at work in a constitutional system. It provides a clue to the reality of judicial independence, and to the dispersion of power more generally. The longer such internal checks have been left to develop, the more effective they are likely to prove. But as Loewenstein points out there is a price to pay: the professional ethic carries with it élitist implications—'Basically the independence of the judiciary resolves itself into the sociological dilemma of a judicial caste.'[14]

So far, we have concentrated on giving a more or less 'legal' account of constitutionalism; this is but one aspect of the doctrine. A normative constitution also gives some definition of how government power is to be exercised—the definition alone acts as a counterweight to political authority. Although lip-service may be paid to unabridged sovereignty—the ruler, people, or parliament—the plural nature of authority is never far from the surface. The usual formula is to ascribe sovereignty to the people, as expressed in representative institutions, but in a federal system this is quickly dispersed, as in Switzerland: 'The Cantons are sovereign in so far as their sovereignty is not limited by the Federal constitution' (Article 3), and later in Article 71, 'Without prejudice to the rights of the people and cantons, the supreme power in the Confederation is exercised by the Federal Assembly.' In other ways, parallel types of power dispersion are typical for all liberal democracies.

Whilst traditional accounts of, say, the separation of powers were couched in terms of institutions which, like early versions of the atomic particle, were considered as homogeneous entities, constitution framers were well aware that this was not the whole story. Nevertheless, the balancing of various *total* institutional structures was seen as the best, practical means of securing a dispersion of power; the more subtle, internal checks could only develop within a functioning institutional framework. With that in mind, the four broad areas of power distribution can be summarized as:

1. Assembly-Executive relations.
2. Constitutional jurisdiction.
3. The devices of direct democracy.
4. Federal structures.

As will become apparent, there is a considerable variation from one country to another, in the use made of each 'area' and the actual application. Switzerland, West Germany, and Austria as federal states show a wide spread, whilst the European monarchies have a narrow concentration. We can take each of the first three areas in turn as the basis of comparison, leaving the question of federalism until we examine the various aspects of the territorial dispersion of power.*

Assembly-Executive Relations

At the heart of the liberal democratic order is the relationship which has evolved between assemblies and their executives; historically, it has been the struggle between these two which in the end provided the essential constitutional structure, around this the other institutions are grouped in a supportive manner. The power balance which resulted gave two common qualities: a strong executive and a substantial degree of unification between executive and legislature. We can say that a unified system is one in which:

the executive is not separately elected (or if in part it does come to office by other means, then this only involves a formal exercise of power); the executive is responsible to the legislature.

Both of these conditions need amplification. In the case of 'election', this can literally be so as in West Germany, where the members of the Bundestag vote for the chancellor, or effectively so, as in Britain, where the prime minister is the leader of the majority party in normal circumstances. The second condition, involving executive responsibility to the legislature, can be expressed the other way round—that an executive, if it is to stay in office, must have control over the decisions of the legislature. The executive is responsible to the assembly, but the price is to accept executive leadership—via the party system.

* See below, pp. 211–18.

These conditions, whatever the variations in detail, are the essentials of parliamentary democracy. There are two other possibilities. The first is a presidential system, involving direct election of the chief executive and some form of separation of powers. In this case, neither of our two conditions is met. The other possibility is 'convention' government; in this situation both conditions are fulfilled, with the important difference from the parliamentary system that the government is never in a position to control the decisions of the assembly. Parliamentary and presidential systems are normally sharply distinguished; the chief exception is the hybrid type of the Fifth French Republic which we examine shortly. Parliamentary systems can always slide towards the other possibility, to 'government by assembly', whenever governments are unable to control the parties for any length of time.

Needless to say, the conditions we have outlined for a unified system require realistic amendment to take account of the overriding importance of the political parties; parliamentary democracy has long since become party democracy, and party democracy makes for some additional features in unified systems:

that the government should be in the hands of the majority party (or with a coalition having that majority);
that an assembly itself does not decide; it only mirrors the decisions made by the electorate on the one hand, and by the party (or coalition) in power on the other.

This is an 'ideal-type' version. As de Gaulle said of the party system of the Fourth Republic, the 'mirror' may be cracked, and if it is, then there results a virtual autonomy to the assembly parties from *all* other institutions, government and electorate. Rather than party democracy, it means a 'democracy of the parties'.

The normal European form is a unified system based on executive responsibility to the assembly. The West German system can be taken as the model: 'The Federal Chancellor is elected, without debate, by the Bundestag on the proposal of the Federal President. The person obtaining the votes of the majority of the members of the Bundestag is elected. . . .' (Article 63). The second principle, that of responsibility to the assembly, is expressed in West Germany by the formula of 'constructive no-confidence': 'The Bundestag can express its lack of confidence in the Federal Chancellor *only* by electing a successor by the majority of its members' (Article 67). It must be said that this idea of constructive no-confidence, aimed at eliminating purely negative actions on the part of assembly parties, is peculiar to West Germany, but in one way or another all the European assemblies manage to enforce responsibility with the ultimate sanction of a vote hostile to the government—except, as we shall see, in Switzerland.

In Italy, although the initial appointment of the head of government is actually made by the president, both he and his ministers must subsequently obtain votes of confidence from both houses of the Italian parliament. In most other countries, as in Britain, responsibility is to one house only, and practice varies as to whether an initial positive vote is required. In theory, the first test of confidence comes for a British government on the division following the Queen's speech—which led to the fall of the Baldwin government in 1924—but normally (until 1974)[15] it is the election returns which are decisive before Parliamant ever meets. Whatever the variations in detail, unified systems ultimately require the executive power to be sustained by an assembly majority.

In this context, the two important anomalies are France and Switzerland, and the unification which we have outlined is for both seriously incomplete. Before we assess the extent of their departure from the prevailing pattern, we should first deal with those countries where the exceptions are of marginal importance. Thus the European monarchies—Britain, the Netherlands, Belgium, Luxembourg, Norway, Sweden, and Denmark—all reserve only symbolic and representational functions to the monarch, though in almost every case one can speculate on other roles in the event of a great constitutional crisis. In Greece, where the monarchy for long took a more political role, the decision of King Constantine to accept the colonel's coup in 1967 as constituting a legal government, gave the military vital early support. The restored monarchy in Spain may similarly find itself caught by such cross-pressures. In Belgium, a commission was set up by the government at the time of King Leopold's abdication crisis. One of the chief charges against the king was that he had refused to allow the Belgian cabinet to continue as a government in exile when Belgium fell in 1940. The commission recommended, in effect, a purely representative monarchy, and the occasions when any monarch can take an active political part have become progressively fewer. In Sweden, a constitutional change has been implemented by which the monarch is reduced to a figurehead, and the power to nominate a new prime minister in the event of a government crisis now belongs to the speaker of the Riksdag.

Of the European republics, the presidents in West Germany, Austria, Iceland, Ireland, and Italy all have very limited powers which hardly affect the working of the parliamentary system. After the disastrous experience in the Weimar Republic, where the president was elected by popular vote and had strong appointive and reserve powers, the Bonn Republic opted for a simple figurehead, chosen by a federal assembly of the Bundestag together with representatives from the Land assemblies. Similarly, the Italian president is elected by parliament frequently resulting in a huge number of ballots before one candidate is ultimately successful, a process quite out of proportion to the president's modest powers. He has some power of veto, but his chief practical importance is to act as a mediator in the difficult task of forming new coalitions. He most nearly resembles the president of the French Third and Fourth Republics, and in France before the advent of de Gaulle the president was always regarded as an assembly nominee and a quite minor figure—'I always vote for the stupidest', Clemenceau once remarked. But even where the president is directly elected, this is no guarantee of special power; the presidents in Iceland, Ireland, and Austria have little power in spite of their popular origin.

The Finnish president is a partial exception. He is elected by a special electoral college, in turn popularly constituted, and enjoys prestige and power quite independent of the Finnish parliament. Even before the war, Finnish presidents had become national figures, a position which has both political and constitutional grounds. The congenital instability of Finnish government—on average a new ministry every year since 1919—has given the president an amount of power by default, for he has a free hand in selecting the numerous caretaker administrations. Presidents have usually been political figures in their own right before coming to office; once elected, he becomes non-partisan, but the constitution gives him considerable powers, especially 'to determine the relations of Finland with foreign powers' (Article 33); the president also has a suspensory veto over legislation, and on the fifty occasions this has been used since 1919, only four times—with an intervening election—has the veto been overridden by parliament. Finland therefore represents a mixed parliamentary-presidential system; only a marked decrease in international tension or an unusual increase in government stability would diminish his political functions.

The other two countries to depart from strict unification, Switzerland and France, do so in different ways. Whilst the French system is a parliamentary-presidential hybrid, the Swiss position does not result from any presidential element, but from one important variation in parliamentary practice. Unlike any of the other states, the government, the Federal Council, is not responsible to either house of the Federal Assembly in the sense that it can be dismissed by a vote of no-confidence. Both the Federal Assembly (the Council of States and the National Council) as well as the Federal Council have the same *fixed* period of life—four years. Their conterminality has been described by Hughes as 'a stroke of constitutional genius';[16] its genius, if that is the right word, guarantees government stability, without at the same time having to resort to a different channel of executive selection which a presidential system requires. In constituting the Federal Council by election from the Federal Assembly, an essential ingredient of the parliamentary system is maintained.

The resulting government stability is further enhanced by the collegial system of government. In effect, this is government by permanent coalition, without any one person or party being able to take a commanding position. As the excluded minor parties claim, it is government by a cartel, but unlike an economic cartel, it is never worth the while of any member party to leave it, since the result would be a permanent exclusion from government. There are manifest reasons for the Swiss system: the need to preserve national unity, the counter-balance provided by the cantonal structure, the belief that 'real' democracy resides more in the rights of the people, using direct methods, rather than in the idea that parliamentary opposition is the necessary corollary of parliamentary government. The conditions underlying the Swiss system are unlikely to be met elsewhere; thus the semi-permanent coalition in Austria after the war was a move towards collegial government, but the balance of the party system allowed the possibility of one party being able to rule on its own account, as has been the case since 1966.

The constitution of the Fifth French Republic was an attempt to overcome the parliamentary weaknesses which had bedevilled the Third and Fourth Republics. Both the previous editions were in the parliamentary mainstream, even at times verging on 'government by assembly', with a largely powerless president and a government unconditionally bound to parliament. The avowed aim of those who framed the constitution was to achieve a 'genuine' and 'responsible' parliamentary system, whilst taking into account the special problems of France, in particular the nature of the party system. It appeared insufficient to rely on simple devices to shore up government power and stability vis-à-vis the assembly; this had to some extent already been tried in the Fourth Republic without success. The solution was to incorporate both parliamentary and presidential elements: a government still in the last resort responsible to the assembly, and a president armed with strong powers who was quite immune to parliamentary pressures.

They succeeded in creating a constitutional structure which, although in a formal sense retaining many parliamentary features, became increasingly presidential in tone—a not unexpected development since de Gaulle dominated the political scene. The change in the mode of presidential election made by referendum in 1962, from electoral college to direct popular vote, merely confirmed the developments which had taken place since 1958. It is true that the constitution speaks of the president as a kind of passive arbitrator who 'endeavours to ensure respect for the Constitution' and who provides for 'the regular functioning of the public authorities and the continuity of the state' (Article 5). But unlike other European presidents he is not very easily kept aloof from the process of government, for his powers are not just 'reserve' or 'emergency'; the truth is that the constitution gave him ample leeway to become the effective head of government as well as head of state. Thus the constitution gives him the right to appoint the prime minister—not merely to nominate him—and as events were to show in 1968, he could practically dismiss him as well. Even though Pompidou, at that time prime minister, submitted his own resignation, he had apparently incurred de Gaullle's displeasure. The constitution also gives the president the chairmanship of the Council of

Ministers; this was a formality in the Fourth Republic, in the Fifth it made the prime minister a subordinate of the president in the cabinet.

He also became a powerful force against the assembly, since the right of dissolution is his, and there are no reciprocal controls; the power of the assembly, such as it is, could only be used against the government, the president remains immune. Add to this his power to use the referendum, to negotiate with foreign powers, his completely unrestricted right to declare an emergency—with a blank cheque as to what he does and for how long the emergency is to last—and the total sum of his powers appears formidable, all on a seven-year term of office.

There is no real comparison here with the presidency in the United States, for the French president controls the life of the assembly, and 'his' government controls its work. Nor in the absence of effective counter controls can it be in Michel Debré's disingenuous phrase 'a responsible parliamentarianism'. If it is neither, can it be more than transitional, and in what sense is it to be regarded as constitutional? The answer to the first part of the question is speculative. The serious power imbalance of government and assembly is inherently unstable—masked by the correspondence between the Gaullist parliamentary majority (with its allies) and the similar complexion of government. But separate election of assembly and president does not give an automatic correspondence—as the experience of the United States shows, where the president's term of office is linked much more closely to congressional elections.

Could the system survive for long with an active president faced by a hostile assembly? The only constitutional solution would be some kind of presidential 'retreat'. For instance, it could become conventionally necessary for an incoming prime minister first to seek assembly approval (which, in fact, Debré did do as the first prime minister of the Fifth Republic). The parties could also 'recapture' the president: future presidents could be by origin both parliamentary and party men—not the case with either de Gaulle or Pompidou. On some such basis a president could assume a more 'acceptable' role. President Pompidou was less inclined than his predecessor to use the full armoury of presidential powers, and Giscard d'Estaing (elected in 1974) is a parliamentary figure. Yet it is the balance of political forces (confirmed by the defeat of the left in 1978) which allows the system to be constitutional. It is still a precarious balance.

In all the systems we have looked at, the key aspect is the nature of assembly-government relations, and we shall examine these in more detail in Chapter 7. At this point, we can turn turn to the supportive institutions: constitutional jurisdiction and direct democracy.

Constitutional Jurisdiction

This term refers to power of ordinary or special courts to give an authoritative interpretation of the constitution which is binding on all the parties concerned. To avoid a treatment which might become involved, we can summarize this power of judicial review as applying to:

1. Conflicts between the state and individuals (or groups) in relation to their basic rights under the constitution;
2. Ruling on the constitutionality of laws;
3. Deciding on inter-organ conflicts concerning areas of constitutional competence.

In the United States, the home of judicial review, the Supreme Court exercises its powers under all three heads. In Europe, the two extremes are best represented by Britain and West Germany. We can also distinguish between those states where there is no special provision for review outside of the ordinary courts, and those where a special constitutional court exists apart from the normal court system. Those countries which have a special review body are: West Germany, Italy, Austria, and France. The remainder rely on the normal courts, and as is to be expected, their jurisdiction is much more limited. Particularly in Britain, the absence of a codified constitution would make judicial review in the full sense (1–3, above) a highly political and uncertain weapon; for this reason, the doctrine of the supremacy of Parliament means that the courts are limited to ascertaining the will of Parliament and to determining whether particular acts of the executive are ultra vires.

The really effective contribution of British courts has been under the first head only—in protecting individual liberties within the framework of common and statute law. This limited function of the judiciary is typical of the West European countries. Traditionally, there is a preference for relying on political means to settle disputes of constitutionality and competence—and the ability to do this is an index of the strength of their political systems. The experience of France and West Germany shows that the securing of individual liberties need not be left to the ordinary courts. It has often seemed odd to outside observers that the French Council of State, which stands at the apex of the administrative hierarchy, should be the final court in cases involving the citizen in dispute with the public authorities. Partly this is to be explained on a 'pure' separation of powers argument—that the ordinary courts should have no jurisdiction in cases involving the public service. Once this view is accepted, then the rational development is to have a separate body of administrative law, administrative courts, and finally 'administrative justice'—an abomination for those brought up in the tradition of Dicey. Yet the fact remains that the Council of State does act as an independent review body; in this, and in other aspects of its work, one simply has to accept the fact of its independence from government: 'As a court the Council is completely independent, in fact probably freer from pressure than the ordinary judiciary where advancement is not necessarily based on seniority.'[17]

The constitutional court in West Germany is easily the most powerful review body in Western Europe. As far as the protection of individual rights is concerned, and numerically this forms the great bulk of the court's work, there is the important innovation of granting direct access for public complaints, besides giving rulings which are incidental to cases coming through the normal courts. The court has a punitive power as well: individuals and group can be deprived of some of their constitutional protection if they breach the constitution in specified ways—we have seen how this can be used in relation to the political parties. The very detailed listing of basic rights in the West German constitution means that the court can be involved in a number of ways—and legislation can be quashed if these rights appear to be infringed. The protection of basic rights has a special significance in relation to the power of the executive, and we look again at this problem in the context of the control of the executive power.*

The second area of judicial review, that of ruling on the constitutionality of laws, can only be fully implemented where a special court is provided—Austria, West Germany, and Italy. In France, there exists the equivalent of the Constitutional Council, the prime function of which is to watch over legislation. In the main, the other states are unwilling to allow the challenge to extend beyond the bounds of the national parliament, and where they do, it is to allow for some form of popular decision.† There are no problems of interpreting competence in Britain, given the flexibility of the constitution and the supremacy of Parliament. For states with a written constitution the position is not so clear-cut. In Norway, there is some tradition that the courts are able to to rule on the constitutionality of laws. In others, such as Sweden and Finland, formal machinery exists in the parliaments to advise governments on the constitutionality of proposed legislation. Where a clear constitutional amendment is envisaged, then special assembly majorities are needed to pass the legislation, an intervening general election, a referendum, or some combination of these. As we shall see, in Switzerland the possibility of challenging legislation by referendum is of particular importance as the Federal Tribunal has no power to rule on federal legislation, although it does have this power with regard to the cantons.

The importance of the Constitutional Council in the Fifth Republic arises from the partial separation of executive from assembly, and from the rather complex division of legislative authority between the two‡—analogous to the division of competence in a federal state; it rules on whether the correct legislative procedure has been adopted according to the various types of law specified in the constitution. More realistically,

---

* See below, pp. 197–202.
† For the interesting Luxembourg variation, see below, p. 295.
‡ See below, pp. 164–5.

it can be regarded as one more control device to be used by the government against the assembly.

Inherent in any such judicial procedure there is a political element at
work. The Italian constitutional court, since its inception in 1956, has
been much concerned in judging the validity of laws passed in the fascist
era and still on the statute book. The West German court has had to concern
itself with highly-charged political matters—for instance, whether the
European Defence Community commitment was constitutionally valid
and later in ruling on the validity of the Basic Treaty between East and West
Germany. In the United States, there is an inherent tendency to seek a
judicialization of political decision-making, and the dangers of the overt
politicization of the Supreme Court were only overcome after the 1937
crisis. In the Euopean countries, this extreme position has not yet had to be
faced.

There is a wide range of judicial activity concerned with the question of
the validity of legislation: from a constitutional court whose decision on
voiding legislation may make it the centre of political controversy, to the
behind-the-scenes activity of, say, the French Council of State acting in its
role of expert adviser to the government. It is this body (not the
Constitutional Council) which at the drafting stage of both ordinary and
delegated legislation vets the government proposals, and its advice
becomes virtually binding on governments. Ministers will not want to see
their laws or decrees voided at a later date by the Council of State acting
as an administrative court of appeal. It was the Council of State which in
1962 had the temerity to rule invalid the special military tribunal set up by
de Gaulle, using his emergency powers, to try the army leaders of the
Algerian revolt. The verdict of the Council of State was as binding as that
of the most powerful constitutional court.

The third area of judicial review, ruling on inter-organ conflicts, is best
applied to the special problems of federal states. The territorial division of
competence, since it cuts across almost every field of government
and legislative activity, has to allow for some formal process of
adjudication—otherwise there would be a rapid accretion of powers in
one direction or another, probably to the centre. The constitutional courts
of West Germany, Austria, Switzerland, and Italy are all concerned to
achieve a central-local balance. For Italy, this function involves securing
the position of the regional governments. Of the federal states, the Swiss
Federal Tribunal and the West German court, have helped to resist cen-
tralizing pressures, with the former only having the power to rule on competence, not on actual legislation. The Austrian court does not appear to
have acted as the champion of states' rights, rather the reverse, that the
needs of the central government should be paramount. Inter-organ disputes in unitary states mainly involve assembly-executive relations, and
any attempt to judicialize these is simply an admission that the political
system is not viable. In unified systems, it will not be the case that two dis-

tinct sets of personnel become involved. As a result, disputes can be settled 'internally' in the context of the party system. Thus the *political* aspects of inter-organ control are more important than the legal ones in unified and non-federal systems.

On the general question of whether judicial review is a significant aspect of the dispersion of power, an unqualified agreement is only possible in the first area, that of individual rights. For the other two areas, organ competence and constitutionality of laws, it is apparent that there are a number of diverse approaches. As far as legislation is concerned, it is probably wiser to relate the problem of 'constitutionality' to the *whole* legislative process, rather than to the narrow basis of judicial review; this then becomes essentially a political problem in a similar fashion to that of the competence of the various organs of state. Only in a federal system, where the political authorities are explicitly divided, is a straight political resolution usually unworkable. And if the territorial dispersion of power in Europe becomes much more marked than it is at present, say by a greater emphasis on regional government, the need for a 'third party' judicial balance will become apparent.

Direct Democracy

Until the spate of referenda held in Ireland, Denmark, Norway and Britain on the question of their membership of the European Community,[18] it could be said that direct methods were only of marginal importance for the countries of Western Europe. Certainly, the climate of opinion is changing in favour of a greater popular share in decision-making. Yet generally the parties view direct intervention in the decisions of government as hostile to the representative system to which they are bound. Issues which appear to be tailor-made for a referendum are also capable of splitting parties down the middle and of raising the political temperature considerably. Far better to resolve the issue by inter-party agreement than to pass the hot potato to the electorate. The Norwegian experience confirms the pessimistic view, foe subsequent to the 1972 EEC referendum the party system was threatened with a fundamental change.*

Nevertheless, there is widespread provision for some form of popular voice. West Germany, exceptionally, has no use for direct methods at a national level (the issues of the recognition of the German Democratic Republic and acceptance of the Oder-Neisse line would have been relevant opportunities). Often, as in Austria, Finland, and Iceland the direct vote is mainly restricted to the election of the president. In Ireland, the president is also popularly elected, and all constitutional changes are subject to referendum approval. In 1968 a proposal to institute a relative

* See pp. 300–1 below.

majority system of voting was defeated, although the measure was favoured by the largest party. In Scandinavia, the consultative referendum is much preferred to the binding form, since by 'consultation' the supremacy of the legislature is retained. The Scandinavian referendum is used for issues which may or may not be of a basic constitutional nature. Thus in the inter-war years Norway had two referenda on the question of prohibition, and in Sweden the referendum has been used by the government to give the electorate a choice between alternative pensions plans. In 1955 the Sweden electorate voted overwhelmingly against changing the rule of driving on the left of the road, but it was only a consultative referendum; some years later, without further recourse to the electorate, the change was made just the same.

It is true to say that for most countries the use of direct methods in practice is quite sporadic. The 1974 Italian referendum on the challenge to the divorce laws was the first since the constitution came into force in 1948, yet the constitution made ample provision for its use. Similarly, the referendum has only been used once in post-war Austria, despite its availability under the constitution. The result of that one referendum, held in November 1978, was a setback for the government, for the vote went against its nuclear energy policy. Specifically the question involved the commissioning of Austria's first nuclear plant, already built at huge cost, and 50.5 per cent of those voting were hostile.

Belgium provides an example of how the decision made by referendum can exacerbate matters. The issue before the electorate in 1950 was whether King Leopold III should return to the throne. The question split the nation in two, and although a majority voted for his return, this was a minority in two important areas, Wallonia and Brussels. Since the vote was in his favour, the king attempted to resume his reign, but this action was greeted by widespread strikes and some bloodshed, and he was forced to abdicate.

The opposing views on the value of the referendum are summed up in the contrasting experiences of France and Switzerland, the only two countries where it has played a central part in the political process. Its use in France has a long and vexed history: the referendum can even be regarded as an anti-democratic technique, the power of a dictator to manipulate the popular will and always to obtain the answer he requires, as Napoleon III was able to do. In the Third and Fourth Republics, the parties made no use of the referendum, except in 1945 and 1946 to gain acceptance for a new constitution. The results were hardly satisfactory. In 1945, the draft constitution was rejected, and in the following year it was approved, but this did not build up a new consensus: the electorate was split three ways: nine million in favour, eight million against, and a further eight million abstaining.

In de Gaulle's hands, under Article 11 of the 1958 constitution, the referendum became a weapon to be used against the parties in the assembly, part of his 'dialogue with the nation'. Each successive referendum was aimed to create a strong presidential system identified with his person—just as much personal votes of confidence as a means of settling the issue at hand. The approval of the 1958 constitution, the Algerian issue twice, in 1961 and 1962, and the method of presidential election in 1962, all of these consultations resulted in large, favourable majorities.* His one defeat, in 1969, highlights some of the objections. The issue facing the electorate was formally about proposals to reorganize the Senate and to reform local government, but it was also an issue of confidence in de Gaulle. The terms of the referendum required one answer to at least two distinct questions; it was a complex document of 68 articles requiring the amendment of 19 articles of the constitution. The bemused voters could work up no enthusiasm, and the defeat of the referendum bill led to the departure of de Gaulle.

The referendum on the changed method of electing the president shows particular unconstitutional features. The proposal for direct election was clealy a constitutional change, and under Article 89 required the prior approval of the National Assembly. This provision de Gaulle blithely ignored, the Constitutional Council declared itself powerless to intervene, and of course the favourable result made the action retrospectively constitutional. Napoleon III had also obtained such retrospective popular sanction for his overthrow of the Second Republic.

The contrasting feature in the Swiss use of the referendum lies in its completely depersonalized nature; it is a weapon for the electorate. Swiss voters have two important powers: to challenge federal laws, and to propose and vote upon constitutional changes. There is an absence of power, at a federal level, to promote legislation; this is not such a serious restriction since the the very detailed constitution is open to the type of amendment which in other countries would be the province of ordinary law-making. The constant use made by the electorate of 'challenge' and 'constitutional initiative' shows that the referendum need not be a destabilizing influence, and in fact it is well-integrated with the rest of the political system. The issues raised can be handled by the political parties, and the nature of Swiss government ensures that the challenges made never become a question of 'confidence', since the federal government cannot 'fall'; this may well be the reason why direct democracy does not easily combine with normal party government—frequent resort to referendum would hinder coalition and party unity. Even in Switzerland, the Federal Council over the years has developed techniques for avoiding popular challenge to its legislation.

The only country to follow Switzerland to some extent has been Denmark where, as a result of the 1953 constitution, the upper house was abolished and a popular check introduced instead. Constitutional changes

---

* For details of results, see p. 276 below.

require a positive vote with at least 40 per cent of the *electorate*. Perhaps more far-reaching is the provision that one third of the assembly can demand a referendum on a bill—and this will result in its defeat if it is rejected by a majority of voters (and 30 per cent of the electorate). Thus a government with a narrow assembly majority will find it difficult to pass controversial legislation.

The limited British experience of the referendum shows how public opinion may differ from established party lines. The 1975 referendum (67.2 per cent in favour of European Community membership) demonstrated a consensus despite party rhetoric. The 1979 referenda on the proposed Scottish and Welsh assemblies exposed the hollowness of 'nationalist' party claims: far from the required 40 per cent of the *electorate* in favour, in Scotland it reached only 32.5 per cent and in Wales a mere 11.8 per cent of those entitled to vote.

A modest, yet important, argument for the referendum is made by Christopher Hughes: 'It is the "people" who decide. It is this which gives the device and educational quality unparalleled by any other political institution, and which gives it a moral value which is first and last the referendum's main justification.'[19] In this way, it can be a valuable supplement to party politics, but not of great importance in the distribution of power. One can also say that it has the healthy effect of cutting through the muzzle of other political institutions. The so-called Schwarzenbach Initiative is a good example from Switzerland. This aimed to amend the constitution and drastically reduce the number of foreigners living and working in Switzerland—these, largely Italian, account for a third of the total labour force. The initiative was opposed by the entire political establishment: the major parties, trade unions, churches, industry, and by the Federal Council. In the event, the proposal was narrowly rejected in 1970, but illiberal as the initiative was the size of the vote showed that this viewpoint was widely held. Perhaps the function of political establishments is to *prevent* such issues coming to the fore. And isolated examples of the value of the referendum, such as the decisions on whether to enter the European Community, cannot hide its basically negative nature nor the fact, as Blondel remarks, that it is inadequate as a channel for policies, as opposed to particular issues.[20] More convincing solutions are found in the ramifications of the representative system.

Constitutional Dynamics

The ways of securing a distribution of power which we have just examined can only provide a partial explanation of the tensions and balances that are integral to the idea of constitutionalism. Some of these techniques are only of very partial application, and even where, as for instance with judicial review in relation to individual rights, the function is of general application, there is a passive aspect; of course, judicial power is itself politically passive. Once a constitutional order has been settled, it is the relationship between the executive and assembly which becomes the critical and active factor. The balance and tension which operates here is of a special kind in unified systems. Although the basic, and formal, order may remain unchanged, there is also a dynamic balance which results from what can be termed the sub-constitutional factors—a shorthand expression for which is the party system.

The special nature of 'party democracy' in unified systems lies in the way that the parliamentary system provides a framework for the parties to effect a synthesis of electoral will and government power. In linking the social forces with the power of state, we can see that the party system operates at the crossover point where the input and output functions of the political system merge. In this respect unified structures provide a *single* focus for this activity, whilst any system operating a separation of powers results in two, probably static, bases of authority; a unified system apparently offers a more open-ended process of constitutional development. That does not make the European version of party democracy necessarily more successful. The onus on the party system to achieve a purely 'legislative' integration may prove to be too great. However, to the extent that an integration is achieved, it is the party system rather than the individual parties which acts as the independent variable; at least in Western Europe, the individual parties no longer provide a dynamic of their own—only in their interaction do they promote constitutional development.

The party system is not the only active constitutional ingredient. The idea that there are a number of internal checks and rules obviously has a wide application. There can never be a one-to-one correspondence of function and institution and certainly not one which remains constant over time. Within all general political institutions there is a continuous process of hiving-off and increased specialization—in effect a growing 'structural differentiation' to which we earlier referred, and this is a leading trait in the development of advanced societies.[21] This process and the operation of the party system combine with the more static elements of the constitutional structure to give the 'recognisable continuity' which Vile regards as inherent in the idea of constitutionalism. These constraints which act as an ever-present modification of political action are not just legal checks but '. . . a set of given historical and sociological facts. In the last analysis there exist no parliamentary constitutions, only parliamentary structures.'[22]

Yet in turn these structures depend for their efficacy on an underlying social consensus; if this is not present, constitutional government must continually be subject to question. And the consensus is not simply one to be equated with a parliamentary working majority. The breakdown of 'constitutional' government in Northern Ireland is relevant evidence. The study made of political attitudes in Northern Ireland by Richard Rose[23] revealed that no single group of attitudes towards the regime found the support of more than a quarter of the population, and this was true for the Protestant majority as it was for the Catholic minority. In that situation, the dominance of the Ulster Unionists only succeeded in masking the unresolved problems as long as the status quo could be maintained; once it was disrupted, the constitutional framework became irrelevant.

In later chapters we shall examine the structure of assemblies and governments, and their interaction, to appreciate how the parliamentary balance works in practice, but before doing so it is appropriate to take account of those states and movements which reject the constitutional order of liberal democracy.

NOTES AND REFERENCES

1. H. V. Wiseman, *Political Systems: Some Sociological Approaches*, Routledge, 1966, p. 66. 'In Western democracies . . . constitutionalism accepts a certain ambiguity and falling-short of "ideal" standards . . . as being "mature".'
2. C. B. Macpherson, *The Real World of Democracy*, Clarendon Press, 1966, p. 10. 'It is not simply that democracy came later . . . It was something the competitive society logically needed.'
3. See Karl Loewenstein, *Political Power and the Governmental Process*, The University of Chicago Press, 1965, pp. 147–53. His threefold classification of constitutions as 'normative', 'nominal', or 'semantic' is of more use than traditional ways—'rigid' or 'flexible'.
4. See R. Bendix, *Max Weber: An Intellectual Portrait*, Methuen, 1966, pp. 417–23.
5. G. Sartori, 'Constitutionalism: A Preliminary Discussion', *American Political Science Review*. December 1962, pp. 853–64.
6. On 'capabilities', see G. A. Almond and G. B. Powell, *Comparative Politics*, Boston: Little, Brown, 1966, pp. 190–212.
7. P. H. Merkl, *Modern Comparative Politics*, New York: Holt, Rinehart and Winston, 1970, p. 426.
8. See K. Loewenstein, op. cit., pp. 123–47.
9. R. A. Dahl, *Modern Political Analysis*, Englewood Cliffs, New Jersey: Prentice-Hall, 1963, p. 20.
10. A report of the Council of Europe Consultative Assembly, April 1970.
11. E. Wall, *Europe: Unification and Law*, Penguin Books, 1969, p. 169.
12. The West German Basic Law in Articles 1 to 19 provides for the basic freedoms: of speech, assembly, association, religious faith, choice of trade or profession, petition, movement, and of asylum. It also gives security to the home, family, and person as well as granting equality before the law, secrecy of the mail, protection of property (or just compensation)—protection of inheritance rights, security of citizenship. In Article 21 the free formation of political parties is guaranteed—as long as they respect the democratic order. The Constitutional Court has a final jurisdiction in all these matters.
13. M. J. C. Vile, *Constitutionalism and the Separation of Powers*, Oxford University Press, 1967, p. 324. He adds, 'There is no separation of powers here, for the "internal" restraints upon the Lord Chancellor are dependent upon his position in a profession the vast majority of the members of which operate *outside* the government machine.'

14. K. Loewenstein, 'The "Living" Constitution: Shadow and Substance', in J. Blondel (ed.), *Comparative Politics: A Reader,* Macmillan, 1969, p. 156. The presence of an independent judicial 'caste' leaves open the question of a common *class* recruitment.

15. The first election in February 1974 was indecisive, since neither Labour nor the Conservatives had an overall majority. The second (October) election gave Labour an initial majority, but subsequently, by 1976, it was in a minority position and finally succumbed to a no-confidence vote in March 1979—the first such defeat since that of the Labour minority government in 1924.

16. C. Hughes, *The Federal Constitution of Switzerland,* Oxford University Press, 1954, p. 108.

17. C. E. Freedemann, *The Conseil d'Etat in Modern France,* New York: Columbia University Press, 1961, p. 58.

18. The results of the referenda on EEC membership were as follows:
Ireland (June 1972) 80.0% in favour (71.0% voting).
Norway (September 1972) 53.5% against (77.6% voting).
Denmark (October 1972) 63.7% in favour (90.1% voting).
Britain (June 1975) 67.2% in favour (63.2% voting).

19. C. Hughes, op. cit., p. 102.

20. J. Blondel, op. cit., p. 471.

21. See G. A. Almond and G. B. Powell, *Comparative Politics: A Developmental Approach,* Boston: Little, Brown, 1966, pp. 306–10.

22. M. J. C. Vile, op. cit., p. 262, quoting the *Bulletin du Club Jean Moulin.*

23. R. Rose, *Governing Without Consensus: An Irish Perspective,* Faber and Faber, 1971. The conclusions Rose draws are based on survey material made in 1968 immediately prior to the onset of the present crisis.

Additional References

W. G. Andrews, *Constitutions and Constitutionalism,* Princeton: Van Nostrand, 1961.

P. Blair, Law and Politics in Germany, *Political Studies,* September 1978.

D. Butler and U. Kitzinger, *The 1975 Referendum,* Macmillan, 1977.

D. Butler and A. Ranney (eds.), *Referendums. A Comparative Study,* Washington: American Enterprise Institute, 1978.

T. Cole, 'Three Constitutional Courts: A Comparison', in H. Eckstein and D. E. Apter (eds.), *Comparative Politics,* New York: The Free Press, 1963.

S. A. de Smith, *Constitutional and Administrative Law,* Penguin Books, 1974.

I. D. Duchacek, *Constitutions and Politics,* Boston: Little, Brown, 1970.

I. D. Duchacek, 'National Constitutions: A Functional Approach', *Comparative Politics,* vol. 1, October 1968, pp. 91–102.

H. W. Ehrmann, 'Direct Democracy in France', in R. C. Macridis (ed.), *Political Parties,* New York: Harper and Row, 1967.

European Journal of Political Research, The Referendum in Western Europe (whole issue), 4/1976.

C. J. Friedrich, *Constitutional Government and Democracy,* Ginn and Company, 1950.

P. Goodhart, *Referendum,* Tom Stacey, 1971.

D. P. Kommers, *Judicial Politics in West Germany,* Sage Publications, 1976.

K. B. Libbey, 'Initiatives, Referenda and Socialism in Switzerland', *Government and Opposition,* vol. 5, no. 3, Summer 1970, pp. 307–26.

O. Hood Phillips, *Reform of the Constitution,* Chatto and Windus, 1970.

O. Massing, 'The Federal Constitutional Court as an Instrument of Social Control', in K. von Beyme (ed.), *German Political Studies Yearbook,* Number 1, Sage Publications, 1974.

G. Smith, 'The Referendum and Political Change', *Government and Opposition*, vol. 10/3, Summer 1975.

H. J. Spiro, *Government by Constitution*, New York: Random House, 1959.

C. F. Strong, *Modern Constitutions*, Sidgwick and Jackson, 1963.

D. V. Verney, *The Analysis of Political Systems*, Routledge and Kegan Paul, 1959.

K. C. Wheare, *Modern Constitutions*, Oxford University Press, 1966.

L. Wolf-Phillips, *Comparative Constitutions*, Macmillan, 1972.

A. J. Zürcher (ed.), *Constitutions and Constitutional Trends since World War II*, New York University Press, 1955.

6

Non-Democratic Variants

The Fascist Alternative

SET AGAINST the doctrine of constitutionalism, and the institutions and behaviour it implies, are the various forms of dictatorial rule. The chief of these, fascism, is paradoxically one of Western Europe's contributions to the twentieth century. It is the sharpest contrast to liberal democracy because it goes beyond simply arbitrary or despotic rule and adds the pretensions of a unified movement and a particular philosophy of state power to what would otherwise be a straightforward dictatorship. The classic form of 'revolution from above' as Barrington Moore has described fascism, may now seem to be a part of the history of the inter-war years, with little direct relevance to politics for most of present-day Europe. Yet, apart from the fact that it is the perfect antithesis to constitutionalism, an appreciation of fascism helps to an understanding of contemporary dictatorship; it is also necessary to assess the possibility of its active resurgence in Western Europe.

The 'pure' form of fascism has three attributes which have to be added to its principally *class* character:

1. A mass-appeal.
2. A revolutionary ideology.
3. An apparatus with which to create a *totalitarian society*:[1] the leader, the party, techniques of social control.

It is obvious that in all three respects fascism differs markedly from conventional, right-wing authoritarianism. Thus a run-of-the-mill dictatorship can get by with a minimum ballast of ideology, little popular appeal, and an economy of repression—a break-even point may actually be reached where the measures of a police-state appear to rest fairly lightly on the general population. Even so, despite the contrasts in impact and form, it can be argued that fascism and dictatorship have the same kind of effect on society, halting certain social changes, fostering others, to the benefit of particular élites and classes.

Mussolini's Italy and National Socialist Germany are usually regarded as the exemplary cases of fascism, perhaps the only authentic ones. Granted that the social conditions in the two countries were quite dissimilar (Germany already a largely industrialized state and Italy still

126

having the bulk of its population working on the land), in both, the three attributes of fascism were present as strands of a unified movement. Most readily appreciated are the techniques of totalitarian control; the 'total' control of society which resulted in both countries has to be seen as integral to the ideological basis of a fascist movement. Fascism, as an extreme opponent of both socialism and communism, must necessarily deny their basic premise of class conflict in society. Since the existing class structure has to be regarded as fundamentally in harmony, the fascist view is to reproduce the existing social order under a new guise. The idea of a 'corporate state', alternatively of a *Volksgemeinschaft*, fulfils these requirements. Class conflict is made redundant by definition, and organizations and parties which reflect a divisive, even a pluralist view of society are abolished or absorbed into an all-embracing national movement.

This view of society has to be enforced by a whole host of controls to ensure that corporative unity is maintained, ranging from police powers to social welfare measures. Put more starkly, the control involves three totalities: total terror, total regimentation, and total control of opinion.[2] The control apparatus can be identified with the political party, and this seeks to enhance national unity as embodied in the power of the state. It is then a short step to the glorification of this power as personalized in the party leader. The leader-figure represents the polar opposite of liberal democratic values: not only is his charismatic role sharply opposed to the exercise of rational authority, the *Führerprinzip* which he incorporates is unashamedly arbitrary.[3]

There is also the mass-appeal of the fascist movement. We have said that the fascist ideology is revolutionary, and this gives it a wide following; mass support is attracted because fundamental changes are promised. There is, first, a sweeping *political* revolution: as promised, all the institutional trappings of the liberal democratic state are abolished, and they include the political parties, the standardbearers of pluralist politics; at the very least, as with the churches, they will be kept on a short rein.[4] At the same time, fascism also promises a *socioeconomic* revolution— implicit in the idea of 'National Socialism'—but this revolution either fails to take place, or else takes a direction different from that which most supporters expect.

Despite the promises of the fascist leaders, wide differences in wealth and social prestige persist, and the economic basis of society remains unaltered. There are, however, fundamental social effects; chiefly, it is not a change in the relationship of person to person, nor of class to class, but in the relationship of the individual to the state. Shorn of the insulation given by pluralist organization, social life is dominated by state activity. And it is the new state bureaucracy—widely conceived to include the state party as well—which adds a new dimension to social class. Thus the old social order is supplemented by a new state élite; the masses are then in a doubly subservient position: the state machine must reinforce the class division, since the official ideology cannot admit that the basis of class conflict is present. Ultimately, popular support will wane, but that is incidental to later development; it is the promise of the socio-economic transformation of society which gives fascism its initial mass base.[5]

The appeal of fascism is greatest in periods of extreme social dislocation: to those who are uprooted, to those who see their position in society threatened. This is especially the case when a society is in the throes of modernization. Thus Organski sees a critical precondition for fascism in the changing nature of the rural-urban balance, a measure of which is the relative importance of the industrial and agricultural sectors.[6] He finds that a zone of instability lies in the area where non-agricultural employment is rising to 40 per cent and persists until it reaches 55 per cent; beyond this point, a society will have become substantially modernized. On this criterion, fascism is not a feature of advanced industrial societies, or if it is, then quite different conditions are relevant.

In the conditions of fundamental social change associated with modernization, it is not the changing balance of occupations which is in itself important, but the consequent social upheaval. The social context of fascism involves a triple line of conflict: the rural-urban one, the contest between élites, that is, between traditional and modernizing ones, and the underlying pattern of class conflict on which these other two are superimposed. From one point of view, fascism can be seen as an attempt to slow the pace of industrialization, or at least to stem its consequences and shift the costs; from another, it is a failure to 'tame' the traditional élites associated with the predominance of agriculture.[7] A successful fascist movement secures an alliance between new and old élites—as a reaction to the growing demands and successes of the urban proletariat; the 'mass entry' into politics of this new force is in the first instance a political threat which presages economic and social threats to follow.

For a variety of reasons, this pattern of conflict was avoided or mitigated in a number of countries. Changes were often gradual, and the rural-urban tensions were handled by the new economic élites on their own terms. Just why some societies managed to avoid a critical impasse and others stumbled from one crisis to another, is a question we cannot pursue here.[8] It is sufficient to point out the varieties of development that are possible in the type of social situation that leads to dictatorship or fascism. Where the old social and economic élites are still in control of the economy and of the state machine, a simple takeover is possible via the intervention of the armed forces. That was true for Portugal in the 1920s, where the old élites were still fully in command, and the dictatorship, set in train by the military, operated at an early stage of modernization. Where political mobilization has proceeded further—as was the case of republican Spain in the 1930s—the net result may be the same, but a political battle, involving the masses, has to be fought as well; hence one saw a pseudo-fascist movement (the Falange) being used as well as armed force, first to gain some popular sanction and later as an agent of political demobilization, but Franco's Spain never had to go very far in the direction of a fully fascist state.

In Italy, the homeland of fascism, all the apparatus was fully employed—the mass appeal, the revolutionary ideology,[9] the totalitarian order—and, as in Spain, the fascist movement faced a well-organized working class which first had to be demobilized. But once this was accomplished, the trappings of fascism as part of a new social order began to wear thin, and the Italian dictatorship, apart from the figure of Mussolini, showed little fundamental difference from the more conventional forms. According to Woolf, the final decade, '. . . saw an accentuation of factions within the party, while the centrifugal forces of an undisciplined, municipalistic-minded society reasserted themselves. Italian fascism was increasingly a dictatorship and ruled in a void by a particularly impressionable dictator.'[10]

The quality of German fascism was essentially different from the other three cases we have mentioned: at least on an *economic* level, Germany had already become a modern, industrial state; the agricultural population had already fallen below 25 per cent in the 1920s. Further, with the complete collapse of the Imperial order, *political* control of the new Weimar Republic was firmly in the hands of the mass parties. The social dislocation was not primarily a consequence of urban-rural changes, but of the economic disruption of defeat, inflation, and the slump. That this should have led to fascism arose in part from the continuing *social* power of the old élites; the democracy of the Weimar Republic scarcely altered their power position—most notably, and strategically, in the German officer corps and in the political and social connections of the German High Command.* This social élite was hardly an overpowering political force in its own right, but the values it represented were still dominant for large sections of German society, particularly the farming community and the Protestant middle class.

It was Hitler's political finesse to be able to play on the fears of the social élite, together with those who still accepted this élite leadership and value system, but at the same time to make a genuinely mass appeal, measured in millions. To achieve this wide alliance was only possible if the revolutionary ideology of fascism was given full expression. The political revolution then took the normal course: the destruction of liberal democracy and the demobilization of the masses. What was different from other dictatorships was that there also occurred a social revolution. It was certainly not the special form of 'socialism' promised, nor was the distribution of economic power significantly altered. What it did involve was the destruction of the influence and power of the old social élites—of

---

* See below, pp. 191–7.

which the eventual 'liquidation' of the military élite was the most striking. In this respect, German fascism was quite different from other dictatorships. Following the German collapse in war, and with the destruction of the fascist élite, a temporary *social* vacuum appeared in German society; put another way, the impact of German fascism had been to complete the modernization of German society.

In all the four states we have considered liberal democratic systems were supplanted by dictatorial regimes, and although each antidemocratic intervention took place in societies at different levels of social, economic, and political development, together their experience can be seen as part of a continuum. In one sense, the effect of the intervention was to secure the position of dominant élites and classes, if only temporarily; in another sense, the effect was to pave the way to a more modern form of society—and this is irrespective of whether the dictatorial power-holders came from the old or the new élites, or, as in the case of Germany and Italy, from neither.

This line of argument accords with Organski's conclusions. He writes: 'Fascism is part of the process of transition from a limited participation to a mass system, and fascism is a last-ditch stand by the élites, both modern and traditional, to prevent the expansion of the system over which they exercise hegemony. The attempt always fails and in some ways the fascist system merely postpones some of the effects it seeks to prevent.'[11] In assessing whether 'the attempt always fails', we should look at dictatorship as it has been practised in Western Europe in the recent past, which necessarily involves a more descriptive account than has been the case with other topics.

Three European Dictatorships

Besides their evident proclivity for non-democratic government, it is clear that Portugal, Spain, and Greece are hardly representative of the European mainstream on a socio-economic level either.* All three are still substantially rural and generally have a lower standard of living than the other countries. Along with economic and social backwardness, they have shared a prolonged experience of the police-state, and they were alike too in the kind of support which maintained their regimes in being: privileged social élites backed by the armed forces. All three however faced an identical problem: how to come to terms with changing European circumstances, for they could not remain immune to pressures to liberalize political life. But how could they guard against the threats to their privileged position in the process of liberalization?

In this perspective the aims of the rulers in Portugal and Spain differed substantially from those of the Greek military. The Greek colonels entered politics in 1967 with the apparently limited brief of forestalling an alleged

---

* See the table on p. 263, for the main socio-economic comparisons.

left-wing plot and thus make Greece safe for democracy. The Portuguese and Spanish takeovers occurred much earlier when liberal democracy everywhere was reeling under the impact of fascism, and their rulers never accepted democratic norms as desirable. All three regimes resulted from army intervention to bring down a legitimate government; in Spain and Portugal this meant the overthrow of existing republican governments; the Greek military and usurpers managed to preserve a legitimate façade—'invited' to form a government by King Constantine after they had effectively achieved power on their own account. The Portuguese coup, a fairly bloodless one, was led by General Gomes da Costa in 1926; in contrast, the Spanish Civil War, starting with a military revolt led by the chief of the Army General Staff, General Franco, was bitter and prolonged and lasted for almost three years, from 1936 until 1939. In all three countries, the military was representative of a social élite, and in Portugal and Greece the general populace took no part at all.

The Portuguese dictatorship proved to be one of the most stable in modern history—an uninterrupted span of almost fifty years, so that 'Pre-Salazar' is almost an effort of historical reconstruction. The Portuguese system could be characterized as one with minimal dictatorship combined with maximum sanctions. But its longevity was not just due to the efficiency of the secret police, and Salazar did not simply 'happen'; one also has to appreciate the 'national' justification for Portuguese dictatorship. The immediate cause of Salazar's rise to power was that the military government was incapable of solving the underlying economic and financial problems. As a univeristy professor of finance, Salazar was first made Minister of Finance, and by 1932 he eventually emerged as president of the council of ministers—and the author of a new constitution.

Although Salazar came to the aid of the military in its postcoup embarrassment, his real importance was to act on behalf of all those groups which despised the former republic. Their distaste was for democracy in general; the popular left did not figure in this at all, instead it was the rife corruption in the dominant Democratic Party which was the object of attack. The hatred for this 'demo-liberalism'—which persisted throughout was shared by both intellectual and class élites. Their common expression was found in the Portuguese 'integralist' movement—a loose appellation which included monarchists and those who were intellectually akin to the *Action Française* in France. H. Martins has pointed out that the intellectual side of the movement was not reminiscent of a *'lumpen-intelligenz'*, but was made up largely of the sons of well-to-do families. These integralists and the related Christian Academic Centre, active in the universities showed, '. . . the structural importance of academic peer groups in the behaviour of the Portuguese elite. The basic leadership of the Integralismo was constituted on this basis.'[12] It managed to sustain its identity until the end, when the old order was swamped by the revolution of 1974. Moreover, the 'Christian Democratic' element was then one of the chief casualties, for it was too readily identifiable with the old regime. During the dictatorship, the common recruitment of personnel to the intellectual movement was supplemented by a similar link to leading positions in government and society. It particularly applied to Salazar's successor, Dr. Marcello Caetano, and the network reached out from the political élite to the hierarchy of the Portuguese Church and to the military High Command. Thus the Portuguese establishment was unified in its origins and subscribed to a common set of values which were given permanent expression in Salazar's 'New State' constitution of 1933: a state based on authoritarian, corporate, and nationalist principles.

The whole spirit of the new state was, and remained, élitist. Despite a parliamentary façade, the franchise was very restricted and the results of elections were not left to chance. The Portuguese dictatorship was at least consistent in that it never sought a mass appeal: indeed, Salazar deliberately played on his academic remoteness, a figure either to be respected or feared. Power rested with the tight-knit alliance of the military and the government. The presidency was reserved for a personage from the armed forces, and all the paramilitary formations, including the secret police, were headed by army officers. Their hold on power meant that a new form of government could only emerge with army consent—as the eventual toppling of Caetano was to show.

Both the civilian élites and the army command shared the same vision of Portugal which came to its most bizarre expression in their attitude towards Portuguese overseas possessions. Whilst one after another of the European powers had accepted the change in world realities, Portugal clung to past glories and to a belief in her 'manifest destiny'. At huge cost in money and manpower Portuguese direct rule was perpetuated. After his accession in 1968, Caetano attempted a cautious liberalization at home and some autonomy for the colonies. But all dictatorships face their most severe test when they seek to modify their own powers, for popular expectations outrun the willingness of the regime to make concessions. Portugal was no exception, and the new mood of impatience was especially evident in the junior ranks of the officer corps. Their discontents linked up in 1974 with the growing political demands from the civilian population.*

What Portugal had in common with Spain, and there were major differences between the two dictatorships, was the power of the Roman Catholic Church, a factor in political life not to be ignored. The religious element is underlined by Hugh Trevor-Roper when he makes the basic distinction between 'dynamic fascism', the classic and revolutionary variety, and what he terms 'clerical conservatism': '. . . the direct heir of the aristocratic conservatism over which the liberal bourgeoisie triumphed in the second half of the nineteenth century.'[13] Clerical conservatism is not one which is simply church-oriented, but rather an alliance of interests

---

* See also, pp. 197, 302–4.

in which the attitude of the Church to popular democracy, and particularly towards socialism, made it the bastion of anti-democratic forces. This did not mean that the clerical hierarchy would underwrite any kind of authoritarian order. We can note too that in the case of Portugal, the fascist model was specifically rejected by Salazar because it implied giving supreme power to the state, whereas his belief, as well as that of his followers, was that the state power ultimately existed to uphold the position of the Roman Catholic Church in Portuguese society.

Neither in Portugal nor Spain was the Church willing to stand for the same kind of secular order as it did in the earlier years, and from being a leading backer of both regimes, at least in Spain it became a cautious, sometimes outspoken, reforming influence. Thus the Spanish hierarchy came out strongly against a proposed trade union law in 1970, aimed at perpetuating the state-controlled trade unions, the *sindicatos*, the bishops demanding instead that there should be free and representative trade unions. And in 1971, the Justice and Peace Commission of the Roman Catholic Church openly attacked the existing system: 'A fight against the present Spanish social structure is necessary because men cannot be asked to behave with justice if at the same time they are obliged to live under the inhuman weight of an unjust system.'[14] This attack brought a sharp warning from Franco himself, but it did not at all deter the progressive wing of the clergy which also demanded a complete separation of church and state.

A rather different part was played in both countries by the lay order of *Opus Dei* which can be loosely described as the Catholic answer to freemasonry; its membership and operation is semi-secret and naturally a subject of controversy. The members of *Opus Dei* represented a social élite and occupied numerous command positions in Spanish society: the universities, economic life, administration, and government. Their apparent brief was to aim at worldly success in this way to further the interests of the Church. During the 1960s, the adherents of the movement became prominent in Spanish government, but their presence neither represented a source of opposition to the dictatorship nor, as government ministers, could they simply be identified with the regime; in effect, they formed a new class of technocrats. Their apolitical stance enabled them to act as a counterweight to the old-guard of military power, and with the crumbling of the dictatorships these technocrats supplied an important element of continuity. They also constituted the core of the 'Christian Democratic' formations which, whatever particular party label was adopted, represented the only viable alternative to the challenge mounted by socialists and communists.

Superficially, Spain always appeared to be a closer approximation to the idea of fascism than Portugal, but of the two, the Portuguese movement represented a more coherent intellectual tradition. Franco, on the other hand, was quite content to take on a pseudo-fascist camouflage for as long as it suited him, but for long Francosim was, 'a vintage model of the conservative-nationalist dictatorship',[15] papering over the deep divisions which still persist in Spanish society. At the time of the Civil War, the Falange movement provided a suitable cloak for Franco, but it was always quite peripheral to his power base, which was the army. Nor was the Falange itself rooted in popular support. The founder of the home-grown variety of fascism, the son of General Primo de Rivera, who had been dictator in the 1920s, was cast in the aristocratic mould. In the elections of 1936, just prior to the Civil War, the Falange fared very badly, and with the onset of fighting, its leadership was decimated by imprisonment and execution; the Falange rump was glad enough to accept Franco's leadership, and only as Franco's forces prevailed did the various fascist organizations coalesce and become a mass movement as well.[16] But once Franco was securely in power and all the paraphernalia of party uniforms and personal adulation had served their purpose in ensuring mass support, the Falange and its leadership was allowed to deteriorate into 'a mere freemasonry of job-hunters',[17] and kept firmly away from any position of real power. If we recall the traits of a true fascist movement: its totalitarian nature, revolutionary spirit, and mass following, it is obvious that the *Movimento Nacional*, no longer graced even by its Falange title, was a non-starter.

To start with, Franco had charismatic pretensions, but in latter years he achieved something of Salazar's remoteness. Whilst the Falange rusted away, and the National Movement remained little more than a name, the government worked smoothly to modernize the Spanish economy. This was the contribution of the technocratic element, almost completely isolated from political or popular pressure. As in Portugal, no risks were taken. Popular representation in the assembly, the Cortes, was kept to a sixth of the total seats, with the vote mainly restricted to the heads of families; the remaining representatives were directly or indirectly appointed by the government. Franco ruled for life, 'Caudillo of Spain, by the Grace of God', and was the front-runner for the army and the established social interests. The tricky question of securing a successor to Franco was resolved by opting in advance for the restoration of the monarchy, and the accession of Don Juan Carlos of Bourbon upon Franco's death in 1975 offered the chance of a smooth transition back to the democratic fold.

That did appear to be an optimistic view. If Spain was undergoing a period of evolution, then as Novais argued the evolution represented 'the disintegration of Francoism',[18] and in the course of that disintegration it was to be expected that all the suppressed conflicts in Spanish society would once more burst into life: economic and social conflict, anti-clericalism, republicanism, and the claims of national minorities. These were after all major fault-lines inherited from the 1930s, and could a more liberal regime expect to contain them successfully?

Francoism had the effect of shoring up a pre-republican social élite which remained '. . . identical with that of the nineteenth century. All political and economic power resides in the army, the Church and the 125 families of the conservative right which monopolize banks and industry.'[19] It was not to be expected that the Franco regime had at all changed the structure of that domination. Economic conflict was for long decently hidden by the imposed corporate unity of 'vertical syndicalism', with the state, workers and employers nominally serving as equal partners. But in the latter years of the dictatorship the formation of semi-clandestine organizations of 'Workers' Commissions' was a portent of the activity which could follow in the post-Franco situation. A constitutional monarch might be caught between the still-entrenched military and social élites and a wave of industrial unrest which would certainly become politically oriented.

To the fundamental economic and social cleavages, we have to add the potentially fragmenting effects of regional loyalties and national minorities. Francoism, plus Castilian hegemony, had exacerbated those discontents, chiefly expressed by the Catalans and the Basques. The latter, because of its unique language basis, certainly represents the more intractable problem. The Basque liberation movement, far from being crushed by Franco, showed a resurgence in the 1960s and was therefore bound to present a challenge to a more liberal regime. Even so, the separatism of the Basques is a minority claim, and the general determination to preserve a unified Spanish state remains uppermost.

Faced with the various lines of battle, the course of liberalization followed after Franco's death under the constitutional monarchy was remarkable both for its speed and its radical nature. Elections were held in 1977 with the Communist Party able to participate, a situation quite unthinkable even a few years earlier, and a fully parliamentary constitution was ratified by referendum in 1978.[20] Moreover, the claims of the Catalans for their own regional government were largely satisfied. The 'disintegration' of Francoism did not bring with it the social chaos which had been widely predicted. Yet the military élite remained unscathed, the inequalities of the dictatorship's brand of 'neo-capitalism' still persist, and we should not forget that Francoism had a large middle-class following. Much of the credit for preventing the head-on conflict belonged to the restored monarchy, since the king managed to avoid becoming identified with any of the protagonists. An imponderable factor was the beneficial effect of the general economic advance over the past decades which may have blurred the old lines of conflict. At all events, none of the major social interests was prepared to run the risk of total confrontation as long as the new parliamentary system could supply workable government. Thus the Spanish experience of dictatorship, like the Portuguese, at least accords with the idea of European fascism as an episode in modernization rather than a recurring sickness.

Whilst the Portuguese and Spanish dictatorships acquired a certain patina of respectability in the course of the years, the Greek experiment in military rule appeared as a grand anachronism in the general European development. The 1967 coup was a throwback to the origins of right-wing dictatorship in Greece during the 1920s and 1930s. A less plausible account, but accepted by some at the time, was that the Greek military stood for a genuinely modernizing influence—a parallel to military intervention in some developing countries. What one does have to appreciate is that there is a long history of military involvement in Greek politics and that, on occasion, it has come to represent an autonomous social force. Between the wars there were numerous military coups; the final result was the relatively stable, and in origins constitutional, dictatorship of General Metaxas from 1936 to 1940 under the aegis of King George II. And alone of the West European states in recent times, Greece has experienced a prolonged bout of civil war, from 1944 until 1949; engaged in this struggle, the Greek National Army saw itself as the country's saviour from communism.

The military was able to define its own position in Greek society. Moreover, there was a lack of unity in the traditional élites and in particular no overwhelming loyalty amongst them for the Greek monarchy. In this century there has always been a strong element of pro-republican, yet conservative, sentiment in the armed forces. The fact that the crown failed to act as a unifying force for social conservatism led the army to seek its own definition of the national interest. In this, lacking an immediate social reference group, 'The new military rulers ... have capitalized upon the peculiar, maddening connection—in fact interchangeability between religion (i.e. the Greek Church) and nationalism. They have made the perpetuation of this link the basis of their claim to political authority.'[21] This trait was not new: the earlier military regime of Metaxas had shown 'a combination of national socialism and religious fanaticism'. The Greek Army thus formed a peculiarly independent élite, one which has always been in direct competition with the political parties—and in pre-war Greece at least, the highly fragmented and personalized nature of these earned them little respect. After the civil war, in the 1950s, the military was content to take a subordinate part in constitutional politics, chiefly within the 'Greek Rally'. Aided by the complete rout of the left, possibly also by manipulation of the vote, stable conservative governments led by the National Radicals were the rule.

In 1963 there came about a decisive shift in Greek politics. Whereas in 1960, 'Altogether some nine parties clustered around the centre ... their one unifying desire was to break the power of the Prime Minister and the National Radicals',[22] by 1963 a radical transformation of the party system had got under way. It was a simplification towards a three-party system in which the new, and left-inclined, Centre Union under Georgios Papendreou emerged as the strongest party, and this party with the United

Democratic Left (EDA) easily outnumbered the conservative National Radicals. Naturally the Communist Party had for long been illegal, so that the United Democratic Left, with up to 15 per cent of the vote, was a cover serving to unite communist and other left-wing forces. The EDA then also held the balance in the assembly, and not wishing to provoke the extreme right, the possibility of a Centre Union—EDA coalition was not taken up by the Centre Union. Further elections in 1964 actually gave the Centre Union an absolute majority of votes—53 per cent. For the first time in Greek politics it seemed as if democratic, majority-party government had arrived. Nor was it simply a question of changing numerical balance; the Centre Union was prepared to give voice to pent-up social demands. As Andreas Papendreou put it, 'The Centre Union was no longer simply the party of political democracy. It was becoming the basic force for national change.'[23]

Yet within three years the democratic state was overthrown. To explain this peculiar twist in political development, it is not necessary to go much further than an appreciation of the gulf between the majority of the electorate and the traditional élites, particularly the military. The gulf was personified in the divergent attitudes taken towards Georgios Papendreou. The extreme right viewed his Centre Union with utmost suspicion, and the suspicion multiplied in the case of his son, Andreas Papendreou; the particular and general causes of the military takeover crystallized around the younger Papendreou. The general suspicion was of left-wing infiltration; the particular crisis centred on his alleged involvement with the extreme left and a military conspiracy, ASPIDE, the 'shield', an alleged plot aimed at spreading socialist ideas in the army, even the overthrow of the constitution. How much of the charge was a fabrication is perhaps irrelevant; it anyway accorded with Centre Union thinking about the Greek Army —Papendreou senior announced in 1965 the planned removal of officers whose loyalty to the democratic government was suspect.

At that point, the role of the monarchy in precipitating the crisis was decisive. Papendreou senior's attempt to strengthen his position as prime minister by taking over the defence ministry himself met with the blank refusal of the king. Getting rid of Papendreou—who also presented a list of officers to be dismissed—was one thing, finding a successor who could enjoy the confidence of parliament—a constitutional requirement—was another. An alternative coalition of dissident Centre Unionists was drummed up, but the net effect of the king's heavy involvement was once more to fragment the party system, and there followed a series of unstable and minority governments. The only way out of the impasse was to have fresh elections—but with overwhelming victory for the Centre Union and the EDA as the likely result. Having disposed of Papendreou once, neither the king nor the army could relish the prospect of having him back; their position would have become untenable in the face of a democratic mandate; elections were to be held in May 1967.

The army struck on 21 April 1967: the initial ambivalence of the king towards the coup gave the military a valuable breathing-space. A few months later King Constantine was implicated in a loyalist counter-coup and was forced into exile. The military junta was not too concerned about this loss of legitimizing support and set about creating a new political system. The military leaders donned civilian clothes, and George Papadopoulos as prime minister emerged as undisputed ruler. The army believed it had a political mission, to eradicate the existing political establishment (especially the parties) and to regenerate the constitutional order. A new constitution was approved by referendum in 1968, but in practice repression and arbitrary arrest continued unabated—democracy under martial law.

What the experience of the Greek dictatorship shows, in common with most military regimes, is the difficulty of extricating the army from politics once it has become deeply involved. The Greek colonels mistrusted the parties and politicians and were loathe to forfeit their own hold on power. Such a stalemate can persist indefinitely, but in Greece two developments brought about a rapid crisis for the dictatorship. The first factor was the estrangement of Papadopoulos from his fellow officers. Increasingly, he sought personal power; a republic was declared in June 1973, and Papadopoulos had himself elected as the first president (and only candidate). He proceeded to build up an all-civilian government, and the suspicion that the 'revolution' had become debased led to an army coup in November 1973; Papadopoulos was in a weak position for he lacked any sympathy from the population and had destroyed the democratic institutions. The coup briefly brought Major-General Demetrios Ioannidis to power, but in reality the military rule was living on borrowed time, for the stalwarts of 1967 had even less idea than Papadopoulos of using political power. The sudden confrontation with Turkey over Cyprus in the summer of 1974 proved to be the second factor leading to a complete debacle for the regime: Greece was quite unable to match Turkish strength and prevent the partition of the island. Without military credibility and without popular legitimacy, the dictatorship caved in ignominiously. Ioannidis had the sense to call in the 'despised politicians', and the former prime minister, Constantine Karamanlis, came back from exile to lead the return to democratic government in July 1974. A bloodless liberation had been effected.

The collapse of the dictatorship in Greece does not necessarily mean the end of the army's role in politics, but its self-confidence has been shattered. Whether or not the army proves to have been sufficiently purged, the decisive part will be played by the revived political parties. With the establishment of a republic (decided by referendum in December 1974) the onus has been put on the party leaders to fashion a consensus for Greek society. The stability of civilian government since the collapse of the dictatorship points to a permanent resolution.

Extremism Today

In the previous sections we have been concerned with extremism at the government level as an alternative to constitutional democracy; the other perspective is that of extremism as a minority and oppositional movement. By 'extremism', whether of the right or the left, we mean that the goals of the party or movement include as a *minimum* a radical change in the political structure, and possibly radical changes in the economic and social basis of society as well.* In post-war Western Europe it is apparent that such challenges to liberal democracy have not originated from within the party system. The electorate has largely failed to express extremist sympathies, and the political parties have faithfully reflected this moderation. Major threats have come from outside the established political structure on occasion, but there is also the possibly to be considered that the system *as a whole* can lurch towards illiberal solutions, irrespective of the nature of the individual parties.

1. Right-wing extremism. Outside of Italy, extremist right-wing parties are virtually non-existent as political forces in Western Europe; the most that can be said is that they are perhaps in a state of suspended animation, awaiting the spark or catastrophe to bring them into the political reckoning. The appeals which they can make are diverse: to nationalism, race, militarism, simple anti-communism, and anti-democratic sentiments generally.[24] These seeds can germinate individually, but they are more likely to appear in combination; it is difficult, in fact, to assess whether such a fascist-type syndrome is made up of genuinely independent factors. One facet tends to entail the others: a rabid nationalism is normally both expansionist and implicitly militaristic; it is also bitterly mistrustful of 'anti-national' elements in society: racial minorities and international communism; and liberal democracy is seen to be infected by them, so a resort to non-democratic means is the only way to make the country secure. To take an illustrative example, Finland in the 1920s and 1930s had its full share of right-wing extremism. The most important faction was the 'Lapua Movement'; this enshrined the ideal of a 'Greater Finland', at its most ambitious stretching to the Urals; it was also violently anti-communist—obviously an 'anti-national' movement in view of the proximity of the Soviet Union—and its efforts led to the legal suppression of the Communist Party. Members of the Finnish General Staff were heavily implicated and underwrote the programme of violence, which included the aim of completely disrupting parliamentary government. Apart from the Movement's bitter hatred of anything Russian, it only lacked a suitable national minority to persecute; this did not prevent it adopting 'a fully fledged programme of anti-semitism, peculiarly absurd in Finland,

---

* For the various levels of party goals, see above, pp. 85–6.

where Jews are numbered in hundreds and are an utterly insignificant group'.[25] Thus the complete set of attributes was present.

Whatever the activating reason for such extremism, its full flowering probably requires all these issues to become part of the party's appeal, but they may not be central to the support which such a party obtains; the underlying reason is more likely to be the economic and social threats which middle-class groups see to their status and class position. The continued failure of right-wing movements in recent years cannot be dismissed as fortuitous, so that these threats to the middle class have presumably been absent.

West Germany provides a leading example because the essential bases of extremist appeal are undeniably present, and yet right-wing parties have failed to make any ground. The fundamental 'national' issue is the continuing division of Germany and the loss of the eastern territories to Poland and the Soviet Union. And this is not an academic debate: large sections of the electorate either originate from the 'lost provinces' or East Germany, or have close relatives who still live in the German Democratic Republic. There are other issues available: the question of 'national subordination' to NATO, in particular the ban on German nuclear weapons, and also the growing economic and political impact of EEC membership. And if anti-semitism is really no longer practical politics, there is a substitute for the Jews in the very large immigrant labour force upon which the German economy has grown dependent. Yet not one of these has provide the basis for a right-wing revival. Of the extremist parties, only the German National Democratic Party (NPD) has ever seemed likely to gain Bundestag representation. Never overtly undemocratic in its aims or behaviour, since this would invite the attention of the Constitutional Court, the NPD arose in 1964 as the most important of a plethora of fringe groups. The party's string of successes in Land elections reached a high point of 10 per cent in Baden-Württemberg in 1968, an area hardly associated with right-wing radicalism. However, the party failed to gain the requisite 5 per cent of the national vote at the 1969 federal election (4.3 per cent, a total of about 1½ millions). Thereafter, the decline of the NPD was rapid, and at subsequent elections (1972, 1976) the party secured less than one per cent of the federal vote.

Whether the NPD, or an equivalent, will eventually be more successful, depends not so much on the 'national' appeals by themselves, but on the underlying social and economic situation. Thus the first step towards a rapprochement with Poland made by the Social Democratic government from 1969 onwards gave little impetus to the far right; a sudden economic reverse would be more likely to do so. For instance, the early post-war 'Refugee Party' (BHE) made an appeal to those expelled from the eastern territories and to those 'deprived of their rights'; after some initial success, this party declined as the initially-rootless supporters became integrated in West German society and its prospering economy.

However, the continuing absence of a strong right-wing party does not deter some observers from perceiving dangerous tendencies in Western Germany. They can point to the host of tiny right-wing organizations and their activities.[26] Alternatively, they may argue that 'extremist' sentiments are still maintained *within* the electorate, even though voting behaviour is uniformly moderate. Yet—as the memories of National Socialism recede—it is increasingly difficult to give such renderings a plausibility.

If this is the picture of muted right-wing extremism in Germany, we should hardly expect other West European states to offer more, for their 'national' problems are fewer. Only in Italy does ultra right play any part. The *Movimento Sociale Italiano* (MSI) is the chief expression of neo-fascism, with fluctuating fortunes over the years. The party was much stronger in the 1950s than the 1960s, but rose to almost nine per cent of the national vote in 1972 (falling to 5.8 per cent in 1979). In some areas—Rome and Sicily—the party is considerably stronger than it is in northern Italy.

How is one to interpret the survival of neo-Fascism in Italy? On one rendering the MSI expresses a hankering for the past, a party of the ageing 'little shots' of Mussolini's Italy; the leader of the MSI, Giorgio Almirante, was once a member of Mussolini's government. Kogan argues that the problem is more deeprooted: 'It is the Fascist mentality that pervades sectors of the population who do not vote for the party which is the principal danger. It is mentality of subservience to autocracy'.[27] The MSI also depends on the social roots of neo-fascism. Its base-point is in the 'old guard' of Italian society, and their interests have been threatened by the economic and social pressures of modernization. For whatever reason, a chord is struck with a part of the electorate; the neo-fascists are quick to exploit political and social grievances, to seek a confrontation with the extreme left, and to bring the republican order into disrepute. As a result, political violence and intimidation have been practised by various extreme-right groups, extending even to planned coups in the armed forces. Often the neo-fascists have been given protection by sympathisers within the administration.

Fears of the extreme left prompt a search for an authoritarian solution, and Christian Democracy may appear inadequate to ward off the Communist threat. The DC, in order to control a governing majority, first had to open the door to the moderate left in the 1960s, and after the 1976 election was forced to rely on the tacit support of the PCI to remain in office. That strategy, if pursued in the future, could make the MSI a beneficiary, a haven for the disaffected. Even so, only the combined strength of the political extremes would pose a threat to the liberal-democratic order.

Successful parties of the far right are notably absent in all the smaller states. Belgium has a live national issue, and although the Flemish language movement was associated in the past with political extremism, this is hardly the case today. The sharpening of the national question in Northern Ireland has led to a greater reliance on extreme methods but without any clear political direction, rather a political incoherence. The British attempt in 1973 to introduce a 'power sharing' executive aided the rise of the ultra-loyalist Vanguard Movement which ultimately captured the party machine of the Ulster Unionists and the party's voting support. The Unionists were once the natural allies of the Conservatives at Westminster, but the 'new' party is firmly associated with the 'loyalist' cause and is therefore inevitably associated with those factions bent on upholding Protestant dominance at all costs.*

Taking Western Europe as a whole, the extreme right is electorally very weak. That weakness applies to the countries which have just emerged from dictatorship—Greece, Portugal, and Spain—as well as to the old-established liberal democracies. The National Front in Britain is more successful on the streets than at the polls, and in the Netherlands the government experienced no problems in banning an extremist, anti-immigrant party. Disaffection is more likely to take the form of an incoherent Poujadism: anti-tax, less government, as with the Progress Party in Denmark. It is too early to judge whether such movements can also forge a coherent political doctrine and, if so, whether their 'anti-statist' outlook would then necessarily merit an 'extremist' label.

2. *The 'Eurocommunist' Phenomenon*. The relation of the far right to the far left may be through the heightened consciousness which one successful movement arouses in its polar opposite. Yet the weakness of right-wing extremism is not at all balanced by a waning on the left, not at least if we count the Communist parties of Western Europe as being in any way 'extreme' in character.† The relevant parties in France, Italy and—of a rather different order—in Finland and Iceland, show that the left can rely on a consistent mass following in competition with the *proven* moderation of social democratic alternatives.

However, the idea of 'Eurocommunism' which gained currency in the mid-1970s pointed to a new and moderate course for the Communist parties of Western Europe. The description drew attention to a number of related features: a belief that the transition to socialism could be effected by peaceful rather than revolutionary means, the relinquishment of the claim to be the sole, authoritative voice of the working class, disavowing the basic dogma that the building of socialism required the imposition of a 'dictatorship of the proletariat'—a euphemism for the dictatorship of the Communist Party. These admissions were reinforced by a loosening of party ties with the Soviet Union: no longer was her

* See 'Northern Ireland' pp. 315–16 below.
† For the fluctuating fortunes of Western European Communism see 'Parliamentary Representation in Western Europe since 1946', pp. 318–26, below.

leadership or interpretation of 'proletarian internationalism' decisive for the policies adopted by any of the West European Communist parties.

Several important consequences result. One is that a Communist party becomes free to interpret *national* conditions and priorities in its own way. Another is that there is no barrier to the party joining in normal governing coalitions, both from its own point of view and that of its possible partners. Their compatibility stems from the less dogmatic position of Eurocommunism and also from the implied principle of 'reversibility': the willingness to admit that the party's policies, once adopted, could subsequently be countermanded by the electorate and by a change of government. In effect, the Eurocommunist parties have therefore moved to a fully *parliamentary* position, an acceptance of the tenets of liberal democratic politics.

These considerations all cast doubt on whether the Communist parties of Western Europe can still be regarded as 'extremist'. Whilst their ultimate goals continue to require a radical transformation of society, the means to those ends no longer present a challenge to the existing order. Nonetheless, the umbrella description of 'Eurocommunism' is open to criticism on a number of counts. Firstly, it misleadingly gives the impression of a unified movement, whereas it was, and is, a piecemeal adaptation to changing circumstances. Nor could there have been a single impulse, for as Joseph Starobin put it, there was 'no historically evolved fraternity of parties' but rather 'a collection of forces whose estrangement from one another has been concealed by a common ideology'.[28] In the wake of destalinization in the 1950s even this sense of common ideology was lost.

The 'Eurocommunist' label is also deceptive if it is implied that the changes took place almost simultaneously. In fact, the process was quite uneven in application. The 'polycentrism' advocated by Togliatti in the 1950s showed that the PCI was far in advance of the French Communist Party which well into the 1970s continued to adhere to a strict 'Moscow line'. The earliest signs of a real transformation actually occurred in a number of Scandinavian countries. A prime example is the Finnish SKDL (Democratic Union of the Finnish People) which since its formation in 1945 has claimed to be a party of general left unity. The Communists are only one element in the party which has avoided becoming a mere 'front' organization or too close an identity with the interests of the Soviet Union. The SKDL consistently wins up to a fifth of the vote, and on various occasions in the 1960s and 1970s has participated in coalition government without jeopardizing the parliamentary system. Similarly, the Icelandic Communist Party (People's Alliance) is, relatively speaking, a 'mass' party (with 22.9 per cent of the vote in 1978), and it has also joined in coalitions, most recently after the 1978 election. Willingness to support parliamentary government is shown too by the Swedish Communists: in the early 1970s after the Social

Democrats had lost their absolute majority, the Communists—themselves with a tiny share of the vote—helped to keep the minority Social Democratic government in power.

The position in Spain and Portugal is more difficult to assess in the course of transition from dictatorship. Whilst the Spanish Communists enthusiastically embraced 'Eurocommunism' and actively cooperated with the Centre-Democrat minority government, the Portuguese Communists are still the most intransigent; their leader, Alvaro Cunhal declared in 1975 that there was no place in Portugal for 'Western-style democracy'.

Those examples exhaust the Communist potential of the smaller countries. In some, their sheer unimportance enabled them to maintain a rigid orthodoxy—as in Denmark, Luxembourg and the Netherlands—but, hesitatingly, they have moved with the general tide. The Belgian Communists managed to halt a long-term decline by taking up the Wallonist cause, but for other countries—notably Austria, Britain and West Germany—the Communists are unable even to reach the starting-post; whether they count as 'extremist' or not is scarcely worth the argument.

The real crux of communist development concerns Italy and France, for the sheer size of the Communist vote in these two states puts them in a qualitatively different situation: the outlook and strategy of the *other* parties is decisively influenced by the Communist presence. Yet like the smaller editions in other countries, they were also faced by the challenge of a necessary evolution if they were not to be condemned to a static and sterile oppositional role.

The situation of the Italian Communists has always appeared the more hopeful, and this view was confirmed by the party's electoral breakthrough in 1976. The PCI has been notable for its independent thought, especially associated with the writings of its early leader, Antonio Gramsci,[29] as well as its weaker 'international' commitment. The party's fluidity in the post-war period owes much to the impetus given by Togliatti, both in his positive attitude towards inter-party cooperation and, later, from 1956, through his advocacy of polycentrism—the view that each country had to consider national circumstances in moving towards socialism. The national orientation of the PCI—being 'of' Italian society, not merely 'in' it—enabled the party to work within the existing political and social framework without becoming simply reformist. The position taken was that the party should avoid an isolationist mentality or an attitude of confrontation and instead assume an active leadership role in the renewal of Italian society: by alliance, permeation, and strategic compromise, summed up in the concept of 'structural reform'.

That the Italian party could not afford to insist indefinitely even on its 'hegemonic' claim to leadership was made increasingly clear in view of the strategy pursued by the Christian Democrats, especially once the

DC embarked on its 'opening to the left' in the early 1960s—an appeal to the parties of the non-communist left. The success of this strategy split the Socialists and threatened to leave the Communists in helpless isolation. It was partly to counter this threat that the PCI formulated its 'historic compromise' in the early 1970s, an olive-branch proffered to Christian Democracy. The point of the compromise was to allow the PCI not just to participate in government but to allow it to influence positively the future evolution of Italian society. Moreover, the alternative, albeit fairly remote, of a united left-wing government was actually the less eligible one, for that would increase the danger of a critical confrontation: a bare 'majority' was not enough—the transformation of Italian society had to be based on a substantial, even overwhelming, consensus. Thus as early as 1972 Enrico Berlinguer, leader of the PCI, put two conditions for participation in a DC-led government: to counter the threat of reaction and to implement a genuinely popular programme. Berlinguer concluded: 'The nature of the Italian crisis is such that these two conditions tend today to coincide.'[30]

The post-war history of the Italian Communists shows that the party has been anxious to collaborate: whilst it has always resented the political power of the Catholic Church, the party is also prepared to compromise—as was shown in the early post-war coalition when it accepted the continuance of the Concordat with the Vatican. In France, by contrast, the basis for such a dialogue between the left and right does not exist. The French Communist Party was always more 'Stalinist' in outlook and less willing to promote an independent 'national' line. Doctrinal disputes led in the late 1960s to the expulsion of two leading veterans, Roger Garaudy and Charles Tillon, who both favoured a 'revisionist' course. Nonetheless, the PCF has consistently sought to promote left-wing unity, if possible under its own leadership. An electoral alliance with the non-communist left (the FGDS) broke up in the holocaust of the 1968 election defeat, but by 1973 more substantial progress had been made, thanks largely to the emergence after 1971 of a surprisingly successful re-formed Socialist Party under the leadership of François Mitterrand. The central feature of the alliance with the Socialist Party was not just an electoral pact for the 1973 election but a joint *programme* as well, with a commitment to form a coalition. The alliance was continued for the 1974 presidential election, with Mitterrand as the joint candidate. But the very success of the new Socialist Party was also a threat to the PCF, for the two parties must compete substantially for the same vote. Their mutual jealousy became apparent in the 1978 election when, although the electoral alliance held, the joint programme was in tatters. Moreover, the Socialist Party emerged as the stronger of the two in 1978: it was no longer in the interests of the PCF to forge a unity which could work to its own disadvantage.

Doubtless, the French Communist Party has undergone a basic

change of outlook, however unwillingly. Thus in 1971 the party's secretary-general, George Marchais, declared that the PCF, 'While remaining faithful to its principles, rejects all dogmatism and routine ... which means to respond to the new demands with new ideas and new forms of action'.[31] Old-style Communism has died in France as elsewhere, and the party has long since lost any revolutionary fervour, as was convincingly shown by its reaction to the 'events' of the May 1968 rising in France.[32]

The loss of zeal for the revolutionary path to power is the best indication of the validity of the 'Eurocommunist' concept and the inapplicability of 'extremism'. That mantle has been donned by a section of the ultra-left which, although not an electoral threat does pose problems. Especially in Italy the advent of political terrorism as a reaction to PCI policies puts a constraint on the party's reformist strategy. But the degree of violence does not correlate at all with the strength or outlook of a Communist party—as the example of the Baader-Meinhof Group in West Germany showed—nor need 'terrorism' have any particular association with the conventional 'left-right' dimension of politics at all.

Once on the reformist road of Eurocommunism—avowedly only as to the means and not the ends—the Communist parties in Western Europe feel the pressure to make compromises. The alternative to cooperation is to wait upon the 'final' capitalist crisis, almost a Micawberlike-stance of 'waiting for something to turn up'.

3. *Extremism of the Middle.* The third type of threat to liberal democracy is said to emanate from the established parties of the system; what we may dub 'creeping fascism'. The implication is that it is not these constitutional power holders who are under attack, but that they themselves change to a more authoritarian bent. The suspension of liberal democracy and its guarantees is easily accomplished in time of war; the argument is that tensions of a similar order, prolonged economic crisis or social upheaval, can have the same effect. And the root cause is seen in the nature of the socio-economic system. Thus Ralph Miliband argues: 'The point is not that "bourgeois democracy" is imminently likely to move towards old-style fascism. It is rather that advanced capitalist societies are subject to strains more acute than for a long time past, and that their inability to resolve these strains makes their evolution towards more or less pronounced forms of conservative authoritarianism more rather than less likely.[33]

This view would see the very success of the established parties in monopolizing the electoral field as acting to squeeze out minority dissent. This dissent, perhaps manifesting itself as a form of 'extra-parliamentary opposition', then brings a predictable reaction from the ruling parties concerned to maintain the status quo. Precisely in the name of democracy: 'The State must arm itself with more extensive and more efficient means of repression, seek to define more stringently the area of "legitimate" dissent and opposition, and strike fear in those who seek to go beyond it.[34] The degree of stability of a liberal democracy is then no measure of its democratic content.

This view is open to criticism on a number of counts. After all, it has been the West European *illiberal* dictatorships which have crumbled in the past few years. There is also little *evidence* of an authoritarian direction taken by the liberal democracies in Western Europe; the gulf separating them from illiberalism is still enormous: political opposition, trade union activity, legal and civil rights, do not yet show the impress of authoritarian government. Whilst the British Industrial Relations Act of 1971 did appear to some to have been a move in this direction, to others it only sought to bring the situation in that country nearer to what has long been normal practice elsewhere. Whilst the Communist Party was banned in West Germany for several years, its successor has not been harassed in this way.[35] And although the uprising in France in May 1968 rocked French society to its core, the chief result was an electoral victory for the VUDR, not a massive retaliation. The extent of industrial strife in Italy is acknowledged, yet there has been no move to a confrontation on the part of the government. But of course, even if one is prepared to accept these judgements, it need not alter the underlying fact of crisis, that an authoritarian trend *in the future* is 'more rather than less likely'.

A second ground for querying the analysis lies in the nature of the party competition itself. The implication of a 'lurch' of the whole system is that inter-party competition fails to provide any compensatory balance. This is particularly true in situations of one-party dominance, but much less so where opposing parties are able to proffer real, if limited, alternatives. The earlier argument in this book was that, if anything, the trend is towards the evolution of balanced or diffused systems rather than ones of dominance.* In itself, this trend does not prevent authoritarian government from emerging, but the reversal of repressive policies is made that much more feasible.

A third counter-argument, whilst accepting the close connection between liberal democracy and capitalism (as a matter of fact as well as of origin), holds that the future performance of liberal democratic institutions is not for this reason predetermined; borrowing Marxist terminology, there can be an 'autonomy of the superstructure'. If this is true, then the character of the political institutions is of relevance for the future of these societies, and they can favourably affect the way in which particular crises are handled.

Finally, we can note that the vulnerability of liberal democracy to the seizure of power, as a question of pure technique, is neither less nor more difficult than it has ever been. As we have seen in the case of the three European dictatorships, the normal route to an authoritarian govern-

* See above, pp. 75–83.

ment is by way of the intervention of the armed forces. But for the other countries in Western Europe it now appears that they show a high level of integration with the rest of society:* their social recruitment accords with the rest of the political system and they lack specific isolative features. Moreover, against the technical feasibility of a coup, there has to be set the political maturity of the population; disaffection of the military would have to be accompanied by widespread civilian apathy—neither apathy nor immaturity are characteristics of these advanced states.

None of these arguments are in themselves conclusive; they rely heavily on the quality of the institutional arrangements which liberal democracy provides, and now that we have examined in the course of the last two chapters the constitutional framework of liberal democracy and the type of challenge it faces, we can look in more detail at some of these institutional arrangements: the parliamentary assembly and the organization of executive power.

NOTES AND REFERENCES

1. See C. J. Friedrich and Z. K. Brzezinski, *Totalitarian Dictatorship and Autocracy*, Harvard University Press, 1965. Their syndrome of totalitarianism consists of: an official ideology, a single mass party with an undisputed leader, a 'terroristic police', a monopoly of communications, a weapons monopoly, and central control of the entire economy. See also, N. Kogan, 'Fascism as a Political System' in S. J. Woolf (ed.), *The Nature of Fascism*, Weidenfeld and Nicolson, 1968.
2. J. H. Kautsky, *Communism and the Politics of Development*, New York: Wiley, 1968.
3. The arbitrary nature of German fascism was well-caught by Hans Frank, Nazi legal expert: 'Formerly, we were in the habit of saying, "This is right or wrong"; today, we must put the question accordingly: "What would the Führer say?" ' That was, indeed, the question!
4. The process of *Gleichschaltung*, the 'synchronisation' of all secondary organisations, brings the individual at every turn into a direct relationship with the state, precluding any intellectually-watertight compartments: 'The distinguishing feature of every totalitarian concept lies precisely in the establishment of a rigorous interdependence of all questions, with the result that an attitude to one necessarily involves an attitude to all others.' M. Duverger, *Political Parties*, Methuen, 1954, p. 233.
5. Initial mass appeal is critical, a phase in political mobilization: seventeen million votes for the NSDAP in 1933. The fascist bands in Italy had 100,000 members at the beginning of 1921 and 300,000 by the end of the year. An apex of 'popular' power in both countries, followed by the second phase of 'demobilization'—harmless parades, strict vertical controls.
6. A. F. K. Organski, 'Fascism and Modernisation', in S. J. Woolf (ed.), *The Nature of Fascism*, p. 25.
7. See Barrington Moore, *Social Origins of Dictatorship and Democracy*, Penguin Books, 1967. Moore says, 'The taming of the agrarian sector has been a decisive feature of the whole historical process . . . getting rid of agriculture as a major *social* activity is one prerequisite for successful democracy,' p. 429 (italics added).

* See below, 'Politics and the Military', pp. 191–7.

8. For different viewpoints on the critical reasons why some countries avoided the non-democratic route see, Barrington Moore, op. cit.; A. F. K. Organski, *The Stages of Political Development*, New York: A. Knopf, 1965; S. M. Lipset, *Political Man*, Heinemann, 1960; H. Daalder, 'Parties, Elites and Political Developments in Western Europe', in J. LaPalombara and M. Wiener, *Political Parties and Political Development*, Princeton University Press, 1969.

9. The weak ideological basis of Italian fascism was admitted by Mussolini in 1921: 'If Fascism does not wish to die or worse still, to commit suicide, it must now provide itself with a doctrine. . . . I do wish that during the two months which are to elapse before our National Assembly meets, the philosophy of Fascism could be created.' Quoted by Barrington Moore, op. cit., p. 451. For the convolutions, 1919–1922, see E. Nolte, *Three Faces of Fascism*, New York: The New American Library, 1969.

10. S. J. Woolf in S. J. Woolf (ed.), *European Fascism*, Weidenfeld and Nicolson, 1968, pp. 58–9.

11. Organski, op. cit., p. 41.

12. H. Martins, 'Portugal' in *European Fascism*, p. 306.

13. H. R. Trevor-Roper, 'The Phenomenon of Fascism', in *European Fascism*, p. 25.

14. *The Times*, 20th December 1971.

15. G. Ionescu and I. de Madariaga, *Opposition: Past and Present of a Political Institution*, C. A. Watts, 1968, p. 149.

16. De Rivera resisted alliance with conservative forces or the army. See F. L. Carsten, *The Rise of Fascism*, Methuen, 1967, p. 201. After amalgamation, the movement became the 'Falange-JONS'; the JONS itself was the product of various mergers combining National Syndicalists and para-military groups.

17. H. R. Trevor-Roper in *European Fascism*, p. 35.

18. J. A. Novais, 'Dictatorships of Spain and Portugal' in J. Calmann (ed.), *A Handbook of Western Europe*, Blond, 1968, p. 311.

19. Novais, op. cit., p. 313.

20. See P. Preston, 'The Spanish Constitutional Referendum of 1978', *West European Politics*, 2/2, May 1979.

21. 'Thucydides', 'Greek Politics: Myth and Reality', *Political Quarterly*, October–December 1970, p. 461.

22. J. P. C. Carey and A. G. Carey, *The Web of Modern Greek Politics*, New York: Columbia University Press, 1968, p. 164.

23. C. Tsoucalas, *The Greek Tragedy*, Penguin Books, 1969, p. 197.

24. C. Seton-Watson, 'Fascism in Contemporary Europe', in *European Fascism*, p. 342.

25. A. F. Upton, 'Finland' in *European Fascism*, p. 204.

26. For a brief but well-documented account of extreme right activities in the Federal Republic, see E. Kolinsky, 'Nazi Shadows are Lengthening over Germany', *Patterns of Prejudice*, November–December 1978.

27. N. Kogan, *The Government of Italy*, New York: Thomas Crowell, 1962, p. 44.

28. J. R. Starobin, 'Communism in Western Europe', in *A Handbook of Western Europe*, p. 299.

29. As an introduction to Gramsci's thought, see J. Joll, *Gramsci*, Fontana Books, 1977.

30. *The Times*, 14th March 1972.

31. Quoted in *The Guardian*, 25th August 1971.

32. See, B. E. Brown, *Protest in Paris: Anatomy of a Revolt*, New Jersey: General Learning Press, 1974.

33. R. Miliband, *The State in Capitalist Society*, Weidenfeld and Nicolson, 1969, p. 268.

34. ibid., p. 272.

35. The question of 'tolerance' in West Germany *is* a contentious issue. See K. Dyson, 'Left-Wing Political Extremism and the Problem of Tolerance in Western Germany', *Government and Opposition*, 10/2, Summer 1975.

Additional References

K. D. Bracher, *The German Dictatorship*, Weidenfeld and Nicolson, 1971.

M. Broszat, *Anatomy of the SS State*, Collins, 1968.

R. A. Brady, *The Spirit and Structure of German Fascism*, Gollancz, 1937.

A. Bullock, *Hitler: A Study in Tyranny*, Penguin Books, 1964.

G. Carocci, *Italian Fascism*, Penguin Books, 1974.

F. L. Carsten, *The Rise of Fascism*, Methuen, 1967.

A. Cassels, *Fascist Italy*, Routledge and Kegan Paul, 1969.

C. Delzell (ed.), *Mediterranean Fascism, 1919–1945*, Macmillan, 1972.

D. Eisenberg, *The Reemergence of Fascism*, MacGibbon and Kee, 1967.

P. Hayes, *Fascism*, Allen and Unwin, 1973.

Journal of Contemporary History, (various contributors), 'International Fascism, 1920–1945', January 1966.

Journal of Contemporary History, (various contributors), 'Theories of Fascism', October 1976.

I. Kirkpatrick, *Mussolini: Study of a Demagogue*, Odhams, 1964.

F. Neumann, *Behemoth: The Structure and Practice of National Socialism*, F. Cass, 1967.

N. Poulantzas, *The Crisis of the Dictatorships: Portugal, Spain, Greece*, New Left Books, 1976.

H. Rogger and E. Weber, *The European Right*, University of California Press, 1965.

D. Schoenbaum, *Hitler's Social Revolution: Class and Status in Nazi Germany*, Weidenfeld and Nicolson, 1967.

M. Steed, 'The National Front Vote', *Parliamentary Affairs*, Summer 1978.

T. A. Tilton, *Nazism, Neo-Nazism, and the Peasantry*, Indianapolis University Press, 1975.

M. Walker, *The National Front*, Fontana, 1978.

E. Weber, *Varieties of Fascism*, Princeton, New Jersey: Van Nostrand, 1964.

E. Wiskemann, *Europe of the Dictators*, 1919–1945, Collins, 1966.

E. Wiskemann, *Fascism in Italy*, Macmillan 1969.

R. S. Wistrich (ed.), 'Theories of Fascism', *Journal of Contemporary History*, October 1976.

D. Blackmer and S. Tarrow (eds.), *Communism in Italy and France*, Princeton University Press, 1975.

S. Carrillo, *'Eurocommunism' and the State*, Laurence and Wishart, 1977.

D. Cohn-Bendit, *Obsolete Communism: The Left-Wing Alternative*, André Deutsch, 1968.

M. Einaudi and others, *Communism in Western Europe*, Ithaca: Cornell University Press, 1951.

R. Garaudy, *The Turning-Point of Socialism* Fontana Books, 1970.

R. Godson and S. Haseler, *Eurocommunism: Implications For East and West*, Macmillan, 1978.

W. Griffith (ed.), *Communism in Europe*, Pergamon, 1966/7 (2 vols.).

G. Hermet, *The Communists in Spain*, Saxon House, 1974.

R. Johnson, *The French Communist Party versus Students (May–June 1968)*, Yale University Press, 1972.

W. Laquer and L. Labedz (eds.), *Polycentrism*, New York: Praeger, 1962.

G. Lichtheim, *Marxism in Modern France*, Columbia University Press, 1966.

J. Lodge (ed.), *Terrorism in Western Europe: Challenges to the Legitimacy of the State*, Martin Robertson, forthcoming.

A. Marsh, 'Explorations in Unorthodox Political Behaviour', *European Journal of Political Research*, June 1974.

N. McInnes, *The Communist Parties of Western Europe*, RIIA/Oxford University Press, 1975.

A. Ranney and G. Sartori (eds.), *Eurocommunism: The Italian Case*, Washington: American Enterprise Institute, 1978.

R. Tannahill, *The Communist Parties of Western Europe*, Westport, Conn.: The Greenwood Press, 1978.

R. L. Tokes (ed.), *Eurocommunism and Detente*, Martin Robertson, 1979.

A. F. Upton (ed.), *The Communist Parties of Scandinavia and Finland*, Weidenfeld and Nicolson, 1973.

P. Wilkinson, *Terrorism and the Liberal State*, Macmillan, 1977.

7

Assemblies and Governments

Parliamentary Decline

'A THEATRE OF ILLUSIONS' is how one disgruntled member has described the French National Assembly. In saying this, Jean-Jacques Servan-Schreiber no doubt echoes the views of parliamentarians in other countries. The 'illusions', if they are such, are especially relevant to the assemblies of unified systems: the simple corollary of government responsibility to the assembly is that the government should be able to control its decisions—by virtue of its hold over the majority parties. The trappings of legislative power help to sustain the illusions, and it becomes a vexed question to determine just how important such assemblies are in relation to the power of government.

There is another point of weakness evident in unified systems beyond that of straightforward party control: the powers of assemblies over governments are all double-edged. What appears as, and may actually be, a potent parliamentary control can be used by the government to further its influence over the assembly. In fact, we can say that inherent in this version of a balanced system is the underlying theme that no controls are ever completely one-way. In its most elementary *constitutional* form, this is apparent where the assembly has the power to bring down a government, but itself then faces the peril of dissolution. Yet we shall see that the *political* forms of this reciprocal control are of greater importance. Where a system of separation of powers is enforced quite different considerations apply, and the demarcation of functions and personnel makes it more possible for an assembly to stem the influence of government.

However, there is, too, the more general impression that *all* parliaments have declined in stature, that as the scope of government activity has widened, so parliamentary influence has waned. The conclusion: the basis of liberal democracy is threatened. Contrast this with the undoubted prominence of European parliaments in the nineteenth century—the 'golden age' of legislatures.[1] Two factors may explain their special importance then, both at different times helping to secure legislative pre-eminence, but in fact mutually opposed. The earlier of the two was the relative insulation of legislatures from wider social forces; later there occurred the once-for-all, mass entry into politics as the working class won the franchise. In different ways, both phases served to make assemblies

152

the focal point of political life, and the term 'liberal democracy' is a precise indication of the gap between them. The *liberal* state, '. . . was designed to operate by competition between political parties responsible to a non-democratic electorate',[2] and the narrow social base of the electorate meant that political choice could be maintained exclusively within the legislature. The absence of mass parties, party discipline, and even of meaningful party labels, gave the members of the assembly a unique freedom to control government, and since they came from broadly the same social classes, changes of government did not indicate political instability. Thus legislatures were of central importance to the process of government, but the particular circumstances were not to last.[3]

The fundamental shift occurred with the addition of democracy to the liberal state. The demand for a popular voice in government concentrated naturally on securing popular representation in the legislature as the best means of securing government by the people. As the initial battles were fought and won, so parliaments became synonymous with popular sovereignty, and they achieved an enormous symbolic importance. But at the same time the need to organize the popular vote gave rise to national and mass parties. No longer were assembly members able to act as individuals; party government and party discipline meant that the legislature lost its substantial power over government, and gradually, too, its reputation as a 'spearhead' of popular sovereignty. In both of these developments we see that the reasons for legislative pre-eminence were not lasting, and that comparisons with nineteenth-century ideal-pictures can be misleading; the heritage still persists—assemblies remain symbols of power and legitimacy. But the powers and functions of modern assemblies now have to be interpreted in an entirely different context, within the dictates of party democracy and contemporary government.

The usual functions of assemblies continue unaltered in their form—the power to legislate, to vote and control expenditure; yet these traditional weapons are nowhere in Western Europe regarded as of prime importance, and there is a consequent sense of loss; that legislatures really should legislate, otherwise they must be 'weak'. We can call these traditional functions of assemblies the 'direct controls', and they were historically the strong ones. They are 'direct' since it is around them that the work of an assembly is organized. The efforts of, say, the Opposition in Britain are geared to fighting controversial government legislation step-by-step, clause-by-clause, on the floor of the Commons and in committee, even though the final product may not look much different from what the government had originally intended. The apparent 'failure' to secure this control in its direct sense does not preclude the Opposition from securing indirect successes. This can be put another way: without the framework which the exercise of these direct controls gives, the work of Parliament would lack any coherent structure.

The important point is that certain indirect controls are operating alongside the direct ones, and they are only given expression in the course of assembly preoccupation with its allotted functions; they are used latently—but not, of course, unknowingly. First summarizing the direct controls:

> *elective:* the power to decide on the duration of governments, and providing for orderly succession;
> *rules:* the power to make laws and other decisions which are binding on governments, and to see that these decisions are observed;
> *personnel:* the individual and collective responsibility of the members of the government to the assembly gives the latter a power to determine the composition of government; as a corollary, in unified systems the personnel of government are normally recruited from the assembly.

And within these same areas there are a number of indirect controls:

> *elective:* the necessity for the governing party (or parties) to impose discipline to ensure government duration requires also that governments foster continued support—they must heed the wishes of party groups;
> *rules:* the process of rule-making diminishes in importance (in the bounds of what is possible for the legislature), but otherwise peripheral aspects now come to the fore: the assembly is an important channel of *communication,* one allowing for the input of demands and linking all the participants—including the electorate;
> *personnel:* members of the government normally start as members of the assembly—and eventually return there; this common origin, and prolonged experience of assembly life, acts as a strong *socializing* influence, modifying the actions of government.

To complete the picture, we should also draw attention to the *double-edged* nature of all these controls. Most obviously, the government must seek to control the elective function of the assembly in exercising power over the government parties. At the ultimate, this would nullify the elective function, giving the government an almost permanent life, but the constitutional rules impose minimum standards. Secondly, and as a matter of fact, the great bulk of law-making (more accurately, rule-making) belongs exclusively to governments in Western Europe; even the indirect aspects of this, input and communication, governments will naturally seek to control for their own ends. Finally, a government recruits its members principally from the assembly, in doing so it exacts a loyalty from those it promotes, and additionally, encourages support from those who may be recruited in the future—the power of patronage.

These general statements about the functions of West European assemblies make it apparent that there is a complex balance involved. Whilst the 'decline' of assembly power can be measured in terms of an idealized past, simply to write it off as no more than a convenient 'setting' for the display of governmental legitimacy would be wrong. The assembly remains a key factor in securing political balance; we can appreciate this contribution, first by examining how the various European parliaments operate in relation to our broad groups of function and then by viewing the general significance of assemblies in relation to political communication.

Elective Functions

The duration, party composition, and the orderly succession of governments—the elective aspect—is partly determined by constitutional ground-rules. The nearest to complete constitutional determination in a unified system occurs in Switzerland. There, the written constitution fixes the life of the Federal Council, and strong constitutional convention decides the composition of the federal government as well as succession (or rather non-succession) by the institution of permanent collegial government. In other countries, the life of a government is left indeterminate, but with rigorous attention paid to the maximum life of the assembly—sometimes five, normally four years—as the critical constitutional factor. At root, the assembly elective function depends on shifts of support in the electorate from one election to another. The nature of the British party system is such that it reacts passively to these shifts; the elective function is a formal one performed by a mandated college of electors, and an outgoing prime minister usually concedes the election to his opponent before the election returns are complete—true at least until the 1970s.

The British party system is untypical. In all other countries, the election results offer a number of possibilities. In the simplest situation, where there are three parties and none with an absolute majority, there are four quite feasible outcomes, including all-party government, and the permutations rise quickly with the number of parties. A prime minister from a party losing support at an election is by no means inclined to throw in his cards. However, quite apart from the number of parties and coalition possibilities that may be present, we can distinguish between two uses made of the assembly elective function. One approaches the British example by making changes in government dependent on party fortunes at a general election; the other shows little or no relation to election results: governments come and go irrespective of how the individual parties fare.

The leading distinction is that in some countries inter-election changes of government are rare; there is a premium on government and coalition stability until the normal life of the assembly is concluded. In accounting for this stability, it is doubtful if strictly constitutional explanations have much to offer; for example, the idea prevalent at one time that the power to enforce a premature dissolution enhances government stability. Such a 'dissolution-centred' interpretation of parliamentary government is firmly constitutional and implies a separate source of power outside the party system. But this power is inherent either in the position of prime minister as party leader or as a function of all the coalition parties, and as Martin Needler in discussing this issue comments: 'It is party politics which gives the system meaning.'[4] Only where, as in the Fifth French Republic, the power of dissolution was deliberately conceived as operating externally to the party system (in the hands of the president) can it be regarded as a separate factor. In unstable systems, premature dissolution is always a relevant consideration, but one which the parties will seek to control. And we can note that although government stability is as great as in most other countries, there is no provision for early dissolution of the Norwegian Storting. Government stability, and the elective function which contains it, has to be interpreted on a wider canvas.

We can look first at those countries where governments are stable from one election to another. In contrast to British experience, there is a much greater tendency for assemblies to run their full term, and the British resort to early dissolution is in practice a useful tactical weapon to secure an advantage for the majority party in election *timing*, not one reserved for government defeat. The normal pattern is exemplified in the case of West Germany where (except in 1972) every Bundestag since 1949 has lasted its full four-year term. An important inter-election government change did occur in 1966. The Christian Democrats, dominant since 1949, relied normally on the support of the Free Democrats. By 1966 dissatisfaction with CDU Chancellor Erhard became intense, the FDP left the coalition and the new CDU chancellor, Kiesinger, formed a 'grand coalition' with the SPD—far from anyone's intention at the preceding election in 1965. But the move was not simply the arbitrary use of the assembly's elective function: the SPD vote was rising, yet the party had been excluded from office, and support rose still more in 1969, thus showing that the change in government *reflected* a shift in electoral opinion. Since 1969 the SPD and FDP have ruled together, and before the 1972 and 1976 elections they made a *prior* commitment to continue their coalition.

Most countries, and especially Scandinavia—except Finland—show a similar direct dependence on elections; the crumbling of the bourgeois party coalition in Norway in 1971 was an exceptional occurrence. We can complete a picture of the elective function in stable systems by citing the rather different experiences of Austria and the Netherlands. The semi-permanent coalition between the Austrian People's Party and the Socialists from 1945 until 1966 in one sense disregarded electoral will, since the *Koalitionsvertrag* made impossible any other form of government, but the *Proporz* system of dividing up the ministries according to party strength did strike some relation to the election results. And after the eventual breakdown of the coalition, there was a close correspondence between government composition and electoral support. From 1966 to 1970 the ruling People's Party had an overall majority of seats, and in

1970 the roles were reversed with the Socialists emerging as the strongest party, supplying the first Socialist chancellor in fifty years, Dr Bruno Kreisky. Throughout the 1970s the Socialists strengthened their position by gaining a narrow majority in seats and votes.

The highly fragmented nature of the Dutch party system, in contrast with the Austrian, has not prevented the formation of stable three- or four-party coalitions from the dozen or so parties normally represented, and some ministerial figures become almost permanent fixtures—such as Dr Joseph Luns, foreign minister for eighteen years until 1971. Coalition-building in the Netherlands can be a cliff-hanging affair. Before all the various combinations are examined and the potential partners succeed in reconciling their differing priorities and programmes, several weeks, even months, may elapse: in 1977 it took no less than nine months after the election to form a government coalition. On the other hand, that process of detailed negotiation is probably an ingredient for subsequent stability.

What the Netherlands case shows is that the elective function is still firmly retained by the parties and voters have no real idea of the governing majority that will eventually result. Impatience and disquiet were evident in 1977, but earlier, in the 1960s, the party of Democrats '66 arose as a protest against the game of coalition 'musical chairs' played by the larger parties, demanding that the political composition of the cabinet should express the will of the voters—and even proposing that the prime minister should be directly elected. The party also acted as a catalyst on the party system by trying to forge a 'progressive bloc' thus giving voters a clear choice of *government*, not just a party preference.* Yet in the 1970s the problems have become even more intense. The reason may be the changing composition of the party system, in particular the formation of the Christian Democratic Appeal from the three major religious parties: their fusion, although on one level 'simplifying' the plethora of coalition possibilities, also made the new CDA a party which straddled across old divisions. As one consequence the progress towards a two-bloc system, encouraging a clear electoral choice, was checked.

So far we have looked at the elective function in relation to stable government systems; unstable government implies that the elective function is performed by the assembly parties. The cases of Italy, Finland, and Fourth Republic France have much in common: the Italian government formed in August 1979 was the forty-second since 1943, compared with twenty-seven in Finland since 1945 and the twenty-five of the Fourth Republic. A second common feature has been the contrasting stability of the elected assemblies in these periods—an almost *inverse* relationship between assembly life and government life. In Britain, there were ten elections from 1945 to 1974; in the same period, Italy had only

* See above, p. 80.

six, and until 1972 when elections were called a year early all parliaments had run their full term since 1953. The Finnish Eduskunta has a maximum life of only four years, against five in Britain, but there were only eight elections up to 1974 and only two premature dissolutions. And from 1945 to 1958, the French Assembly was dissolved early only once; and two of the five elections which were held were for constituent assemblies—the second necessary because the first draft constitution failed to obtain popular ratification. A third feature they have in common is a straight political one: the continued strength of the Communist parties in all three countries—at least a fifth and sometimes more than a quarter of the vote. These characteristics, length of government, life of assembly, and the Communist vote hold together. Put briefly, one can say that the nature of their electoral politics makes (made in the case of the Fourth Republic) recurrent government 'crisis' preferable to more frequent elections, at which the extremist parties might be the only beneficiaries—and the net effect of elections held in quick succession could itself be a destabilizing influence.

This trait applied to Italian politics. The dominance of the DC, secured through a minority of the vote, entailed coalitions with the diminutive right or the moderate left. Governments were unstable, but resort to elections might weaken the Christian Democrats or potential coalition partners: the unreal crisis of coalition was preferred to an election upset—the Communists never suffered electorally from their political ostracism. As the PCI vote gradually increased, the coalition base of the DC was weakened, eventually forcing the party to serve as a minority government on a long-term basis after the 1976 election. Room for DC manoeuvre disappeared and brought an early election in 1979—instead of 1981.*

The troubles of the Fourth Republic which we examined earlier can be underlined by two relevant assembly features: the size of the anticonstitutionalist opposition and the lack of cohesion in the constitutionalist majority. Governments faced a double opposition, but there was no salvation to be had in referring the issues back to the electorate. The electoral laws, it is true, were rigged to favour the parties of government: although in 1951 the Communist Party secured twice as many votes as the moderate Catholic MRP, it ended up with about the same number of seats, a discrimination which adversely affected the Gaullists as well. An Assembly majority, once elected, had little interest in going back to the electorate again—it could not be sure that the electoral laws would operate so favourably the next time. In this process of distortion, there could be little connection between the type of government people wanted and the leadership that actually emerged. Prior to the 1956 election, a public opinion poll established that 2 per cent of the electorate

---

* For the 1979 election, see below p. 294.

favoured the Socialist Guy Mollet as future prime minister, subsequently he emerged as just that.[5] We can also see how constitutional provisions fail to become applicable. The Fourth Republic constitution required an *absolute* majority to bring down a government, with automatic dissolution if this occurred twice within six months. But this clause remained almost inoperative, since the constitutionalist parties who could rely on two-thirds of the assembly vote found that, although an absolute majority was not against them, it was very difficult to secure *relative* majorities for essential measures—and it was to such hostile votes that they succumbed. The constitutional formula only applied on one occasion, and for most of the time the assembly continued to exercise its independent elective function.[6]

Government instability in Finland is countered by the stability of the presidential office—the present incumbent, Dr Urho Kekkonen, has been elected to five consecutive terms of office, and the president is a separate source of power and legitimacy. The demand in the Netherlands for a directly elected prime minister most nearly approximates to the Finnish position. Since the assembly is only responsible for part of the elective function, Finland can 'afford' frequent changes in government. The stability of the Finnish system may have been aided by the policy of not excluding the Communists from office, and their participation in coalitions has possibly enhanced government stability.

A general conclusion could be that when the assembly parties have much more than a passive elective function, this freedom is readily translated to government instability—yet instability is not a necessary consequence as the Dutch case shows. We can go on to say that the instability is the price the 'governing' parties are willing to pay to keep the system intact. The price they may not be so willing to pay—but just the same exacted—is the lack of consistent policy output—the *immobolisme* to which the Fourth Republic succumbed, but which the others have avoided.

Personnel Functions

The function of recruitment to government is almost exclusively performed by the assemblies in unified systems. The doctrine of 'responsibility' is that much easier to enforce if ministers not only appear in the assembly to answer for government actions, but also really 'belong' there as well. There is little doubt that the influence of recruitment—as well as the process of socialization involved—is one of the most important of assembly controls.

Typically, European assemblies provide a base from which a governing hierarchy emerges, whether or not this is a strict constitutional requirement. In this respect, the British system is the most stringent, but in practice the exceptions turn out to be minor variations. Thus there are 'incompatibility' rules in both France and the Netherlands; a person joining the government simply relinquishes his assembly seat, but apart from losing his vote, his position in the assembly is hardly altered. There are sporadic exceptions to assembly recruitment. Caretaker governments in Finland avoid prejudicing delicate coalition negotiations if they are made up of non-political figures, largely civil servants. In several countries, the occasional non-party person is given a portfolio, and the British system can be 'bent' by awarding a peerage. De Gaulle's first governments contained a number of non-parliamentary 'technocrats', but later de Gaulle himself was to insist that his ministers, even if they were not party politicians, should fight for a constituency seat at elections—promptly resigning the seat, if successful, in order to maintain the incompatibility rule. The fact that the constitutionally unnecessary course of ministers contesting elections was adopted shows the legitimizing power which the assembly carries, and the 'greyness' of non-political figures who are simply co-opted.

The most obvious effect of assembly recruitment to government is the strength of the link forged between the majority parties and government. But there is no formal process by which this is achieved. Instead, the composition of the government, as in Britain, remains the prerogative of the prime minister. However, the realities of coalition-building are such that the influence of the party will vary from one country and one situation to another. Where the coalition parties are of comparable size, coalition negotiations involve a hammering-out not only of policies, but the party share-out of the ministries and the names to fill them as well. If a party stakes a claim to a particular ministry, then the incumbent becomes virtually the nominee of the assembly caucus of that party, and the prime minister will only have a decisive say in the ministers coming from his own party. Thus it was a novelty in Norwegian politics in the 1965–71 coalition, that the member parties nominated people to fill government vacancies, not the prime minister. Inevitably, ministers who arrive in this way will see their main loyalty to parliamentary party rather than to the head of government.

In situations where one party is dominant, the prime minister's power is much greater. Thus the political scene in West Germany between 1953 and 1961 was dominated by the CDU and Chancellor Adenauer—in 1953 the CDU almost, and in 1957 actually, gained a majority of votes on its own account. There was no question that in this period Adenauer firmly controlled his own party, and the fate of the junior coalition partners was in his hands. Federal ministers were 'his' ministers, and the terms of the Basic Law by which, 'The Federal Chancellor determines, and is responsible for, general policy' (Article 65), helped to foster the concept of 'chancellor-democracy'. In fact, this expression is remarkably similar in connotation to the idea of 'prime ministerial government' in Britain—the view that the accretion of powers in the hands of the prime minister and the nature of modern elections (in which all issues polarize around two rival candidates for supreme office), have together made parliamentary, even party government an outmoded expression. Yet both concepts are open to serious criticism. In West Germany it proved to be no more than a label for a particular period, and ended when Adenauer's authority visibly crumbled with the onset of the Berlin crisis in 1961—the occasion of the erection of the Berlin Wall. Shortly afterwards, the CDU lost its Bundestag supremacy, and Adenauer had increasing difficulty with his own party and with the coalition partner, the Free Democrats. No more was heard of chancellor-democracy in the eras of Erhard and Kiesinger, and Brandt, the first post-war Social Democratic chancellor, proved to be in the parliamentary and party mainstream, and the same is true of his successor, Helmut Schmidt.

Nor is it the case that party dominance in the assembly necessarily weakens the major party in relation to the head of government. The leading position of the Italian Christian Democrats has not resulted in a single, powerful figure emerging in recent years. In the course of the prolonged government 'crises', a succession of prominent Christian Democrats in turn will try to form a new government. Cross-currents in the party (numerous entrenched factions, the *correnti*) act against a unified leadership emerging, and the eventual prime minister is not the sole leader of the party—he has to share authority with the secretary-general—a much more permanent figure. Once a government falls, there are several contenders for the premiership, usually former ministers; the decisive merit of any one of them rests on whether he has a broad acceptability within the party *and* whether he can come up with a workable coalition formula.

Where no one party has much of an edge on the others, the paramount influence on ministers will be their own parties, not the government leadership. This factor applies with all the more force in situations of unstable coalition; ministers know that their political future rests with the party, and the fall of the existing government will not preclude them from having another (or even the same) post in the next one. Certain parties, certain people, become indispensable—the Centre Party in Finland, the Catholics in the Netherlands, the Radicals in the Fourth Republic. Contrast this with the period of Adenauer's rule in West Germany: on more than one occasion, the effect of a small party leaving the CDU-led coalition was that the ministers hung on to their posts when their party went into opposition. This is highly exceptional; partly loyalty usually comes first. In several countries, party leadership is strictly divorced from those who accept ministerial office. The reason is apparent: a party serving in coalition has to maintain its identity and morale. One way of doing so is to underline the independence of the parliamentary party—and at the same time reduce the status and authority of those members who become ministers.

In all we have been saying about government leadership and ministerial recruitment, there is a clear point at issue: if there were a general trend towards 'chancellor-democracy', or its national equivalent, then the personnel functions of assemblies would be declining. Yet there is no evidence that this is the case in Western Europe, and recruitment to government remains an important assembly control weapon. All countries have a period when a gifted leader can impose his own pattern for a while—a combination of factors, involving his own relative ability, the structure and traditions of his party, and its strength in relation to others. His lasting influence may be important, but to take the experience of de Gaulle: in order to impose his own pattern he was forced to break up the existing unified system quite deliberately. The quasi-presidential system he bequeathed to his successor—a 'routinization of the charisma' —represents a determined attempt to loosen the hold of assembly parties on government. But other outstanding leaders have been content to work within the parliamentary framework, and consequently when they depart the old practices and controls are reasserted.

A less obvious aspect of the personnel function is the process of socialization. It is no small matter that prior to taking office, ministers may spend several years as full-time professional politicians with seats in the assembly. The values and attitudes they bring with them correspond to their party labels, but they are also subject to an assembly 'embrace'—as their whole parliamentary party has been for decades before them. And the rules of the parliamentary game are too well learned to be forgotten by those who become ministers. There is an element of self regard: ex-ministers will have to return to the assembly one day, or retire from politics. The net result is to moderate the antagonism inherent in the relationship between assemblies and governments. Codes and practices vary, but two essentials are the 'rights' of opposition and the trust necessary between a minister and his parliamentary party. To ride roughshod over both is to court disaster.

One has to introduce a number of reservations to this model picture. It does not apply to all politicians nor to all parties. The longer a party has had parliamentary representation, the more it has shared in office, the less the likelihood it will break the 'rules' when it is in a position of real power. The classic example of non-socialization is the Nazi Party in the Weimar Republic; it fulfilled its promises. We have seen how in a few years the tiny party in the Reichstag suddenly became the largest of all—in uniform and more of a military formation than a political party. It can reasonably be argued that had the NSDAP shown instead a slow growth throughout the 1920s, a greater willingness to play the party game, even to take a minor place in government, might have been evident. It can be objected that such considerations are irrelevant for an extremist and anti-parliamentary movement. This, however, is to ignore the changes that are apparent in European Communist parties. They see a parliamentary solution as the best that can be hoped for, and this road requires them to engage in a long-term parliamentary strategy, electoral pacts with the Socialists, even participation in government as an aim. This attitude is a far cry from the purely tactical share in government that many took at the end of the war, further still from the splendid isolation of the Communist Party in the Weimar Republic: 'After the Nazis, our turn will come!' All the same, to the extent that a Communist party is still rigorously excluded from government, the parliamentary socializing process works in reverse. Permanent opposition becomes an acceptable mode of existence; it is hardly likely to engender any respect for the problems of government. But changes are evident: government participation in Finland and Iceland, active 'support' in Sweden, signatories to multi-party 'pacts' in Italy and Spain—signs of a 'parliamentary communism' still awaiting a rigorous test.

Beyond the obvious socio-economic differences in recruitment from party to party, there are national variations evident in the source of politicians. Most significant of these is the place of the public servant in politics. Once again Britain is quite untypical; it is not a question of the Civil Service being politically neutral in its dealings; British civil servants are politically emasculated as well—besides the position of the judiciary, the one real element of the separation of powers. For historical reasons, and with a different conception of civic rights, the situation in mainland Europe is in sharp contrast. Many nineteenth-century assemblies contributed very few government ministers; these were recruited directly from the government service. Whilst Bismarck was chancellor in Imperial Germany, he was the only minister with a seat in the Reichstag. In Sweden, public officials formed a high proportion of the multi-cameral assembly before 1866, and the Finnish 'caretaker' governments are largely composed of civil servants. The undoubted blurring of function has meant that public officials are often free to pursue an active political career. This is written into the Austrian constitution (article 59/2): 'Public employees, as well as members of the armed forces, do not require release from their posts in order to serve as members of the National Assembly. Should they wish to stand for election to the National Assembly, they are to be granted the necessary free time.' Norway is exceptional in excluding higher civil servants from the Storting, but in many countries it is quite unremarkable to have a proportion of public employees in parliament. In West Germany, this tradition extends to the Land assemblies; an established state official, with a seat in the Landtag, may well find himself speaking in opposition to the Land minister who heads the official's own department.

In former times, the presence of a number of serving officials in a parliament would be an obvious index of weakness in the face of government; now they are certain to be 'party men'. It can mean that the public service is overtly politicized—in Austria, the influence of party reaches fairly deep; this 'political' aspect of the civil service is one we take up in the following chapter. In the parliamentary context, the level of expertise of officials can be a source of talent covering the whole range of government activity, and with a higher degree of competence than possessed by the average parliamentarian.

Nowadays, it seems unlikely that the origin of assembly personnel is a matter which governments can turn to their advantage. The real power of governments is found in the disbursement of ministerial posts. In this, the power of the British government exceeds others. By most standards Britain has a large assembly, yet a high proportion of its members, and up to a third of the majority party, can be recruited for government service. A massive array of senior and junior ministers results. In one way, this dependence makes an assembly stronger, but the reverse is also true—a government can control a key proportion of its voting strength which in Britain even extends to the ranks of Parliamentary Private Secretary, and the promise of eventual preferment goes far wider. This influence of the government is probably more important in Britain since the ministerial team is concentrated in one party; in other countries, fewer posts are available, and the loyalty exacted is to the party in coalition rather than to the government leader.

Rule Functions

Law-making is historically a central function of legislatures; the ability to impose decisions binding on governments was the means by which they rose to a pre-eminent position. But 'rules', in the sense of the totality of binding decisions, do not have to be made through passing laws, and assemblies have little say in all this: 'Not more than perhaps 4 or 5 per cent of rule-making can be ascribed to the British parliament or to most parliaments of Western Europe.'[7] This does not alter the fact that assemblies are firmly attached to the legislative process as if theirs was the primary responsibility. We have said that it is not the case that they are engaged in a futile exercise; even if the outcome has long been decided in the cabinet or inner-party cabals, it is primarily the legislative process which serves as a context within which demands can be voiced and communications passed to the various parts of the political system.

As an extreme example of legislative downgrading to virtual non-competence, we can take the position of the French Assembly of the Fifth Republic in contrast with the Fourth. In the old republic, the Assembly was the fount of all legislative authority, a power which went to it largely by default, since governments foundered one after another in their inability to push through fundamental legislation, and the reaction of the National Assembly was to become excessively concerned with minor measures—understandable in view of the party stalemate and the activity of pressure groups. Philip Williams comments: 'Indeed, it is a sign of the triviality of members' preoccupations in the Fourth Republic that nine-tenths of the bills introduced in its last year, and half of those passed, would have fallen into the domain of regulations.'[8] This 'domain of regulations' is one of the areas of legislation created in the 1958 constitution in an attempt to cut through the tangled web of assembly legislative power.

Essentially, the 'rationalization' of legislative authority in the Fifth Republic shows a parallel with its division in a federal state, though the division is not territorial but between government and assembly. The constitution, mainly in Article 34, gives a comprehensive list of headings under which an assembly can legislate, either to establish 'rules concerning' or 'fundamental principles', but the implementation of these and their detailed expression is achieved by government 'regulation'—in other words, an enormous increase of what in other countries would be delegated legislation. Besides the definition of ordinary law by a number of headings, there is a further category of 'organic law', which although not as fundamental as the constitution, still requires special procedures under Article 46. As in a federal system, the definition of competence and procedures has to be given to an outside body, not the government or assembly. A reading of the constitution would not be of much help in distinguishing a 'principle' from a 'rule' and both from a 'regulation'. This delicate task was laid at the door of the Constitutional Council which can rule on the constitutionality of laws and the appropriateness of procedures, either before a measure comes into force or afterwards.

The government's sweeping powers are made explicit by Article 37: 'Matters other than those regulated by laws fall within the field of rule-making'; thus all residual areas are the responsibility of government, and 'laws' too can be modified by regulation. If this were not enough, the government can also ask the assembly for powers to issue ordinances which encroach on the law-making domain. Shorn of its prime legislative powers in this way, an assembly loses any real pretension to the function of rule-making. It is no longer in a position to haggle over the small print or even to read it; as a consequence, there is a further loss: there is little 'legislative context' for the passing of communications or the voicing of demands.

Fortunately, the complexities of the French provisions are not reproduced elsewhere. But the absence of such severity in other countries does not necessarily make their assemblies that much stronger in relation to rule-making. The sheer amount of legislative activity is a poor guide to its significance, nor can assembly power be inferred from the number of private members' bills introduced. Italy leads the field here, but only around 10 per cent of such bills become law and most are of trivial importance. In Britain, the proportion of total legislation taken by non-government laws is about 5 per cent, higher than in most other countries, and in some others, such as Norway, Austria, and Switzerland, there is no provision at all for private member bills. Even under the stern regime of the Fifth Republic, legislation not sponsored by the government has crept back to over 10 per cent of the whole—as against 30 per cent in the

Fourth Republic. One can even say that a government's readiness to accept assembly initiative is a convenient form of tension-management, giving it an 'illusion' of power. Even if it is conceded that resulting measures are highly worthy, it is hardly a serious index of assembly power.

For that matter, no satisfactory index does exist. A detailed study of European and other assemblies has raised some of the problems.[9] How important are the laws made in a country compared with other forms of rule-making? Given that two assemblies exhibit the same amount of legislative 'activity' (for instance, amount of legislation, the number of amendments passed, length of debate and so on), are the bills of the same importance, and how is this importance to be measured? And in a purely negative sense, what of government bills which are not defeated, but quietly dropped (House of Lords reform and trade union legislation during the British Labour government of 1964–70)? Even if one agrees that, as the study found, in Ireland and Britain the weight of assembly activity is observed 'in fairly long debates and the passage of governmental amendments', it could also be shown that in Sweden, on any other reckoning a country with a strong assembly, neither was the case.

The style of legislative activity in Sweden makes it apparent that we also have to take account of the activities which lead to bills being introduced—the input of demands and ideas which promote legislation; there may be less need for conciliation or the airing of views in the formal passage of a bill if this has taken place earlier. Normally, the basis of legislation is taken to be the prerogative of the ruling parties, but in Sweden the Riksdag itself plays an important part; the emphasis is on the introduction of 'propositions' to be investigated rather than on the government's presentation of ready-made bills. Briefly, any Riksdag member can raise a matter of public importance, requesting government action. A committee reports on this matter, and with Riksdag approval, the proposition is brought to the attention of the government. The normal course is then to set up a Royal Commission whose report is circulated widely for comment by interested parties, the government is then in a position to place detailed legislative proposals before the Riksdag. Even allowing for the fact that a high proportion of the 2,000 propositions which may be made in the course of a year relate to detail, simple electioneering, or to the scaling-up or down of government expenditure, there remains a hard core of proposals which can lead to fundamental legislation. This process makes for a diffusion of the rule-making function in comparison, say, with the British system, not only through the inter-party co-operation involved (perhaps a better word would be 'interaction'), but also in the wide consultation with affected interests. A proposition may fail eventually and yet spark off wide discussion and inquiry—supplementing the even-more numerous official inquiries that the government conducts on its own account.

The Swedish pattern contrasts with the usual form whereby the government majority provides the basis for an announced legislative programme. But there are substantial differences between assemblies here as well. Some of these relate to procedure: the relative importance attached to plenary sessions as opposed to committee; however, it is the variation in the party basis of government which is all-important. Only where single-party government results is it possible to say that the legislative programme is directly related to an electoral mandate. A coalition government can claim no such clear-cut authorization, and actual legislation is the product of difficult negotiation and compromise. The result will vary from a coalition that is little more than a holding-operation, securing only a minimum of essential government business, such as the budget, to one where a detailed programme is decided upon in advance. This latter situation is well-illustrated by Clause 4 of the 1956 Austrian coalition pact: 'Government proposals, about which both coalition parties represented in the government have already agreed in matter and form, are binding for the parliamentary groups of the two coalition parties. Basic agreements to amend them need the agreement of the coalition committee.' Rarely would one expect to see decision-making taken so explicitly outside the realm of parliaments, but it is frequently such a coalition committee (rather than a cabinet) which wields the real power in determining the laws to be passed.

Structural differences are also relevant in assessing the rule function of assemblies. In particular, one gauge of their power, not only in legislation but also as a general control mechanism, lies in the strength of their committee systems. This is one conclusion reached by Blondel: 'The maximum effectiveness of assemblies is obtained if small groups are created.'[10] One might almost say that there is an inverse relationship between the number of assembly committees and the power of government. In general terms, it is not difficult to see why this should be so. A number of small groups is less amenable to government control than a single, large one. A degree of specialization results, and a committee expertise is generated which can soon run counter to party or government policy. We should expect strong committees in the following conditions: where the composition of committees does not reflect the majority in the assembly—alternatively where party discipline is weak; where committees are relatively small and specialized, rather than large and ad hoc, and on which members serve together for long periods with a chairman who is independent of government pressure; finally, where committees have the right of independent access to the bureaucracy and other experts, and themselves have considerable research facilities.

It will be obvious that the foregoing conditions are exactly met by the United States Congress.[11] For these reasons and, of course, because it enjoys a life independent of the president, the American assembly is more powerful than any in Western Europe. Although it has been breached in recent years the 'seniority rule', by which chairmanship of a committee goes by convention to the member of the majority party with the longest continuous service on that committee, concentrates power in a man who is not susceptible to party discipline or presidential blandishments—his long congressional service presupposes that he has the safest of safe seats in Congress. One should also add the power of committees effectively to 'kill' bills, and for the committees themselves to spawn subcommittees. And then there is the existence of the key 'gateway' committees: the Rules and Appropriations committees plus the joint committees of the two houses; through all of these, bills will normally have to make their perilous journey.

On this formidable yardstick, the committees of European assemblies achieve a low rating. Party control at all levels is much more in evidence, and a government committed to a legislative proposal is unlikely to tolerate committee 'obstruction' for long. Yet there are important differences in the systems that have evolved; for illustration, we can take West Germany, Sweden, and France as representative of the possibilities. The West German committee system in the Bundestag is typical of many assemblies in relying on specialized committees. These are fairly numerous, around twenty, and are fairly small with from fifteen to twenty-seven members; almost all have a legislative and inquiry function, and thus have a 'hybrid' character. They cover the whole range of government activity, and the great majority pair neatly with corresponding federal ministries. It is important to realize that the centre of gravity of the Bundestag is to be found in the committee system and not in the plenary sessions—less than a third of the time spent on them compared with the House of Commons. Committee membership depends on qualified expertise; a member may owe his place on the party list, and hence his election to the Bundestag, because his party felt that he could make an expert contribution. And it is in a committee that he will make his parliamentary reputation, not on the floor of the house. Party discipline is strict on most issues and the committees exactly reflect party strength. Nonetheless they are highly effective; sitting in private and with their own secretariat, they hear the evidence of government officials and independent witnesses; ministers attend, though not as chairmen. The net result is to make the committee a focal point for government and opposition, as well as the object of interest representation.

In other systems the division of labour is not so marked. Scandinavian assemblies differ in two respects. Firstly, there are far fewer committees; secondly, there is little attempt to align them with particular government departments. They are still of fundamental importance; thus the basic Finnish Parliament Act of 1928 devotes sixteen detailed articles to their power and composition, although there are only eight specialized standing committees. The present Swedish Riksdag has three of its eleven committees concerned with legislation, and only the finance and foreign affairs committee of the others match the relevant departments of state.

The Swedish system also goes far in dissociating the government from the committees by the rule of 'ministerial disability'—ministers are firmly excluded from taking *any* part in the deliberations of committees. It may be true that this rule is simply a hangover from a strict separation of powers doctrine, but ministerial exclusion and the fact that a chairman need not come from the majority party, may have helped foster the spirit of informed objectivity, *Saklighet*, and in Elder's view: 'The system ... permits the opposition groups a relatively generous right of initiative within well-defined limits; and puts a premium on the arguing through of cases on their merits.'[12]

In case one should doubt the potency of committee power, it is salutary to contrast their position in the Fourth and Fifth Republics. In the Fourth, the heart of any government's troubles was to be found in the activities of committees. Once a bill had been sent to one of the twenty specialized committees, the government virtually lost control over its ultimate fate. In the end, an unrecognizably mangled version could be reported out to the Chamber, and there the government would have to use all its resources to bring back deleted clauses or to remove various provisions added in committee. Even though the party composition of the committee reflected that of the Assembly, few of its members, and quite possibly not its chairman either (who, after all, could reasonably hope to receive the relevant ministry himself once the government fell) would feel themselves bound by the wishes of the government—especially not when opportunities arose to further their particular interests. A further handicap was that ministers did not pilot their own bills through committee and assembly; this latter task would be entrusted by the committee to a rapporteur who could well be hostile to the bill.

The Fifth Republic changed all this. In place of the numerous specialized committees, the constitution set up six very large ones on a broad functional basis, some with as many as 120 members—on the clear supposition that, as a virtual mini-assembly, government control would be that much easier. This move was over-ambitious, and sub-committees have naturally resulted to deal with detailed aspects of bills. Government powers were greatly strengthened: the minister now pilots his own bill through committee and Chamber, and the plenary session considers the government's version of the bill with the committee's view merely as proposed amendments. As an additional precaution, to prevent delaying tactics, the government can call a bill out of committee before it is reported. Finally, the convention whereby the chairmanship of committees bore some relation to party representation was broken after the 1968 election when the Gaullists, enjoying an absolute majority, took them all.

These measures have brought the French system quite close to British practice—the priority given to government measures, the means to secure their passage through committee, and the move away from highly specialized committees. The British approach has been to reproduce the fundamental dualism between Government and Opposition in the committees, and, of course, the dualism is perpetuated best in large, non-specialized bodies in which the government has the whip-hand. This is still true for purely legislative matters; the main question in recents years has been to decide on what terms specialist committees should be allowed to develop in the Commons, in particular, whether they are to relate to specific ministries, or (as in Scandinavia) directly avoiding this. Developments have favoured a series of functional Committees rather than ones specializing on a departmental basis. Thus there is now a large and important Expenditure Committee which has numerous sub-committees. Select Committees also operate for the nationalized industries and race relations, but there has been no move to establish Committees in the realms of defence or foreign affairs or to revive one for agriculture. And whatever specialism results, it is in the field of scrutiny, not legislation.

Whilst the range of European committee systems show different and characteristic emphases, only the American manages to preserve a sharp demarcation between government and assembly. European versions vary from the dualism in Britain to the Swedish emphasis on a genuine assembly input function. Between the two is the West German type, combining expertise with a strict party orientation. The basic choice is whether to insist that control functions are best exercised by securing a 'distance' from government or not. This problem comes to a head in the question of foreign affairs and defence committees. The presence of these is natural if one agrees that control functions are best furthered by an association with government, but the counter-argument—at least for unified systems—is that participation in such committees means that the opposition parties, since they must be taken into the government's confidence, lose their freedom of action; the emergence of bipartisan policies is poor compensation for an unfettered right of criticism.

It is helpful in this discussion to regard second chambers as an extension of the committee idea. In their own right, as a separate mode of class representation or an overt check on the popular assembly, they are largely anachronisms, and the evolution of party government has tended to leave them high and dry. Both Denmark (1953) and Sweden (1970) have rid themselves of their upper houses, and this would have substantially been the effect of de Gaulle's ill-starred referendum in 1969. A second chamber does have a live function where there is a marked territorial power dispersion, providing a political means of resolving differences of view regarding local-central competence.* For the rest, powers of an upper house usually appear greater than they are in reality. The superficially strong bicameralism in Italy, with the government responsible to both

* See 'European Federalism', pp. 211–18, below.

houses, is negated by the fact that the party line-up is roughly the same in both. The same double responsibility exists in theory both in Belgium and the Netherlands; in practice, they are appendages, and both reflect the party situation in the lower house. The British House of Lords, with its built-in Conservative majority is always an implied threat to a Labour government at the tail-end of a parliamentary term. In contrast, Austria, a nominally federal state, has an upper house so weak that, '. . . one can hardly speak of a genuine two-chamber system'.[13]; its veto can be overcome by a simple majority vote of the National Council. Perhaps one of the last attempts to reassert the second chamber as a control on the lower house will prove to have been the French Senate; the constitution made it a mechanism which, on occasion, could be used by the government to circumvent a hostile vote in the Chamber of Deputies.[14]

The idea of a second chamber as a glorified committee of the lower house comes to reality in three Nordic countries: Norway, Iceland, and Finland. In all three, there is no second chamber as such, but the assemblies constitute themselves into two divisions at the beginning of each parliament. In Norway and Iceland, they then function as distinct bodies. The Norwegian Storting elects a quarter of its members to sit separately, but a common membership of committees is retained. The Icelandic Althingi operates as two distinct entities, except for two key committees, and disagreement between the two divisions results in a combined meeting (as in Norway) decided by a two-thirds vote. In both countries, the party proportions are preserved so that the likelihood of confrontation is remote. The Finnish Eduskunta elects somewhat less than a quarter of its members to a Grand Committee, but they still retain their position in the full assembly. The Grand Committee reviews all legislative proposals, but with scrutiny powers only, since the views of the whole Eduskunta finally prevail.

The modest end-point of second chambers in Scandinavia should not obscure one relevant fact: the organization of an assembly into two or more operating parts may be the best way for assemblies to preserve a 'zone of independence', especially in rule-making functions, which is not incompatible with majority party rule. It is, in fact, an extension of the idea of 'internal checks' based on an increased differentiation.

Communications

One way of assessing the political function of assemblies is to regard them as devices for providing and passing on information which will form the basis of decisions reached in other parts of the political system. Indeed, the more one emphasizes the communication function of assemblies, the less one is inclined to see them as decision-making organs at all. This view applies with force to unified systems and to all the functions we have considered so far: an elective function increasingly shifted to the electorate, rule-making as an aspect of majority party power, and the personnel function in unified systems, because of common membership, is uniquely suited to communication rather than to detailed control.

Various writers have expressed the importance of communication in different ways. Dahl, speaking of Britain, finds that Parliament is not a site '... for genuine encounters, so much as it is a forum from which to influence the next election.'[15] Or as Blondel states more generally: 'The primary function of assemblies is one of communication between inputs and outputs, as well as one of feedback from outputs on to inputs.' The most he will allow for traditional rule-making is a 'streamlining' of inputs or a 'clarification of demands, which entails as its by-product a rather greater publicity given to these demands'.[16] European assemblies can be seen as 'nodal points' of communication: the meeting-place of a number of routes issuing from and to the electorate, but others as well which link the parties, organized interests, and the government.

Another associated contribution which assemblies make to the political system is to give the seal of legitimacy to those groupings whose activities relate to the assembly—government and party. And this applies even if its functions are performed quite passively. The legitimizing power of parliaments is well-shown in the lip-service paid to them by dictatorships. In Greece, although national elections were indefinitely postponed, an indirectly-elected and consultative assembly was set up in 1970, and likened to the British Parliament by the deputy prime minster: 'Britain, the cradle of contemporary parliamentarianism, draws her democratic origins from a similar body.'[17] It is apparent, however, that unless an assembly has a number of active controls, or else effectively performs a communication function, it is unlikely to gain wide respect or serve to sanction the actions of political contenders.

It is clear that there is no 'pure' communication function, that it is more a bundle of functions, a resultant of others. Direct comparison of assembly performance in this respect is therefore difficult. Assemblies not only develop individual styles, there is also the probability that no two assemblies, even in unified systems, handle the communication function in the same way. Whatever the particular content, it will be an index of performance for the political system as a whole, and failure in communication can lead to a rapid decline in effectiveness throughout. The British system scores highly in being able at times to achieve a 'sense of occasion' in the momentous 'great debate' which has an immediate impact on the nation. It is argued that multi-party systems in contrast, are necessarily more muffled in their effect, and that they become inward-looking since they must concentrate primarily on the give-and-take of coalition government. But it would be rash to regard the British Parliament as superior for that reason. The natural concomitant of a multi-party system is that the assembly parties have more power to make fundamental decisions. Answers to the questions: 'Which parties will be in the new government?',

'Will this controversial measure be carried?', 'Will the government fall?', all result in immediate and effective communication, and an informed electorate; the occasional 'great debate' may only be a partial compensation.

Even on a more subdued level, the Swedish style of legislation, with the particular attention given to inputs, is likely to draw in a cross-section of opinion only on the fringe of political activity. Again, the Swiss use of the referendum offers a direct means of communication which is often only weakly performed by the parties in exclusively representative systems. An alternative argument is that the sharp dualisms encouraged by the British dichotomy of Government and Opposition (in emphasis, if not in content) are at times counterproductive. The 'informed and rationally-active citizen', can deal with the ploys and counter-ploys involved, but the overall effect on the electorate may simply be confusing, even alienating.

Yet over-emphasis on the British Parliament as a 'forum' may well obscure its effectiveness in more detailed aspects of a communication. The political homogeneity of single-party government gives the members of the majority party the chance of securing the government's undivided attention. For all unified systems, a key aspect of communication is in the contact of party and ministers; it is in the party committees that rank-and-file views can be forcibly expressed to ministers, rather than in the open assembly. For good reasons this type of communication receives minimal publicity, and the same type of process is evident in the coalition committees of multi-party government. This semi-private communication functions as a feedback to government, and is complementary to the public side of assembly transactions. The criticism of public debate is that the proceedings are followed by relatively few, but this objection misses the nature of most political communication: it is rarely direct in the first instance; to begin with, messages are passed horizontally—that is, between élites—and only later do they move vertically, to the general public. In this sense, assemblies are not 'popular', but firmly élitist in their make-up.

All that we have said does not point to a general parliamentary decline. This is not to say that assemblies are powerful in their 'own' right, but indispensable as 'sites' available to all active political participants; that they are élitist is inevitable, since this élitism is a major characteristic of liberal democracy, but the parliamentary system functions to prevent a single unified élite from emerging.

NOTES AND REFERENCES

1. For a representative early view, see Sir Henry Maine, *Popular Government*, 1885.
2. C. B. Macpherson, *The Real World of Democracy*, Clarendon Press, 1966, p. 35. 'There was nothing necessarily democratic about the responsible party system . . . The job of the competitive party system was to uphold the competitive market society, by keeping the government responsive to the shifting majority of those who were running the market society.' p. 9.

3. For the transition in Britain, see A. H. Birch, *Representative and Responsible Government*, Allen and Unwin, 1964, Part II, 'The Traditional Doctrines'.
4. Martin Needler, 'On the Dangers of Copying from the British'. *Political Science Quarterly*, vol. 77, no. 3, September 1962, pp. 379–96.
5. See H.Ehrmann in R. C. Macridis (ed.), *Political Parties: Contemporary Trends and Ideas*, New York: Harper and Row, 1967, p. 154. In the same poll, 33 per cent realistically thought that their vote would have no influence.
6. See S. E. Finer, *Comparative Government*, Allen Lane, The Penguin Press, 1970, pp. 291–5.
7. J. Blondel, *An Introduction to Comparative Government*, Weidenfeld and Nicolson, 1969, p. 356.
8. P. M. Williams, *The French Parliament: 1958–67*, George Allen and Unwin, 1968, p. 57.
9. J. Blondel and others, 'Legislative Behaviour: Some steps towards a cross-national measurement', *Government and Opposition*, Winter 1969–70.
10. J. Blondel, *An Introduction to Comparative Government*, p. 362.
11. See J. D. Lees, *The Committee System of the United States Congress*, Routledge, 1967.
12. N. Elder, *Government in Sweden*, Pergamon Press, 1970, p. 188.
13. E. Machek, *Die Österreichische Bundesverfassung*, Vienna: Cura-Verlag, 1965, p. 40.
14. In the words of Michel Debré, the upper house was to be, '. . . a Senate whose principal role is to support the government in case of need.' Quoted by P. M. Williams, op. cit., p. 29. The proposed Senate of a reconstituted Spanish Cortes (announced by the government in 1976) may also belong in this category.
15. R. A. Dahl (ed.), *Political Oppositions in Western Democracies*, New Haven: Yale University Press, 1966, p. 339.
16. J. Blondel, op. cit., pp. 321 and 325.
17. Quoted in *The Times*, 19th October 1970.

Additional References

J. Blondel, *Comparative Legislatures*, Prentice-Hall, 1973.
K. Bradshaw and D. Pring, *Parliament and Congress*, Quartet Books, 1973.
R. Butt, *The Power of Parliament*, Constable, 1969.
D. Coombes and others, *The Power of the Purse: The Role of European Parliaments in Budgetary Decisions*, Allen and Unwin, 1976.
B. Crick (ed.), *The Reform of Parliament*, Weidenfeld and Nicolson, 1966.
H. Eulau and M. Czudnowski (eds.), *Elite Recruitment in Democratic Polities*. Sage Publications, 1976.
A. Grosser, 'The Evolution of European Parliaments', in M. Dogan and R. Rose (eds.), *European Politics*, Macmillan, 1971.
H. Hirsch and D. Hancock (eds.), *Comparative Legislative Systems*, Glencoe: The Free Press, 1972.
G. Loewenberg, *Modern Parliaments—Change or Decline?*, Princeton University Press, 1966.
G. Loewenberg and C. Limkin, 'Comparing the Representativeness of Parliaments', *Legislative Studies Quarterly*, vol. 3/1, February 1978.
G. Loewenberg and S. C. Patterson, *Comparing Legislatures*, Little, Brown, 1979.
J. P. Morgan, *The House of Lords and the Labour Government, 1964–1970*, Oxford University Press, 1975.

J. Meynaud (ed.), 'The Parliamentary Profession', *International Social Science Journal*, vol. 13, 1961.

G. Sartori, 'The Professionalisation of Italian M.P.'s', in M. Dogan and R. Rose, op. cit.

J. McG. Smyth, *The Theory and Practice of the Irish Senate*, Dublin: Institute of Public Administration, 1972.

J. C. Wahlke and H. Eulau, *Legislative Behavior: A Reader in Theory and Research*, New York: The Free Press, 1959.

S. A. Walkland, 'The Politics of Parliamentary Reform', *Parliamentary Affairs*, Spring 1976.

S. A. Walkland and M. Ryle (eds.), *The Commons in the Seventies*, Martin Robertson, 1977.

K. C. Wheare, *Legislatures*, Oxford University Press, 1968.

8
Executive Power

ALL GOVERNMENTS are concerned to meet two widely different requirements: to provide for efficient administration and the need to secure political direction. Just how these two requirements are fulfilled, and combined, will result in a distinctive government form. The solutions favoured in Western Europe follow a similar pattern: parliamentary systems to give political direction, and a 'constitutional bureaucracy' to provide efficient administration—a term which we examine in the following section. A parliamentary form results in a cabinet system of government which supplies a *general* political leadership; at the same time it sets up a number of *specialized* leadership positions, also of a political nature, through a wide range of ministerial appointments. The doctrines of collective and individual ministerial responsibility incorporate both forms of political leadership; whilst they are analytically and often in practice distinct, they are exercised by the same group of party politicians in power.

The alternative, a non-parliamentary one, is to rely solely on a general political leadership, in which case leaders may or may not come to power by democratic means. We can take three representative examples. Thus the president of the United States exercises all the general leadership functions himself; the heads of the various departments of state, his nominees, are responsible to him alone, and the separation of powers operates to make them non-political in origin in that they are not recruited from Congress; their status in presidential cabinets in the final resort is only advisory. General Franco, the Caudillo of Spain, was the only source of political authority; his governing ministers consisted of non-political technocrats along with army officers, and they were responsible to him alone. In the Soviet Union, the presidium of the Communist Party supplies a permanent collective leadership—though this can be usurped by one man—the Council of Ministers has virtually no collective functions and individual ministers have only a technical competence. In their different ways, all three types of government show a greater concentration of political leadership than for parliamentary systems, and none of them enforces collective or individual responsibility to an assembly.

The evolution of the general and specialized political functions in parliamentary systems has resulted in a broad band of leadership roles which span the administrative system, and this structure has led to the necessity of determining a line of demarcation between political oversight and executive administration. But in practice the division is blurred. The sharp dichotomy between the civil servant and the political minister is not always maintained: as we have seen, Finnish 'caretaker' cabinets regularly contain a high proportion of civil servants; de Gaulle appointed several civil servants as government ministers, and on a smaller scale many European governments include one or two such appointments. Further, top-ranking civil servants, sympathetic to a new government, are frequently found key places in sensitive ministries. This is an admission that the distinction between politics and 'pure' administration cannot be maintained in practice. The difficulty of separation is less evident for the 'big issues', but whenever specialized political leadership becomes involved with the administration the two tend to become inseparable. In the final analysis, some see the function of a civil servant as securing the continuity of the state, and this role implies a basic political competence. The problem of all governments is to retain a firm hold on the political reins, but it applies to parliamentary systems with special force because the nature of the political leadership they supply is subject to administrative influence at many points.

We can usefully mention one approach to this problem of securing political primacy which, in its broad sweep, provides a basis for comparison, namely the theory of 'parallel hierarchies'. It involves creating a *second* bureaucratic hierarchy, exclusively at the service of the political leaders so that they can control the activities of the administration; at the logical extreme, it requires that for every unit and level of administration there should be a parallel control section, with a comparable level of expertise but not duplicating the routine administrative tasks. The reason for its leading importance in Communist administrative thinking has been that the parallel hierarchy would serve to underpin the primacy of the party. Party control is mandatory at all levels and this approach is one way of ensuring that it remains a reality. But such a solution requires a large outlay of resources and manpower, and that is only feasible if the party is assured of permanent power. The possibility of frequent government alternation in western systems makes control impracticable on this scale, although the institution of 'ministerial heads' is similar in principle. Indeed, what is remarkable about these systems is that the party, *as a national organization*, contributes very little to the maintenance of political leadership once its leaders gain power. The party leaders not only experience a loosening of party control over their own actions once they attain office, but the party also relies on this small band of men to secure political leadership without any other precaution or intervention. The party itself does not come to power, only its government representatives.

Yet it is possible to construct a model of liberal democratic politics in which this did happen. It would involve, for instance, the party machine supplanting the policy-making functions of the entire higher civil service and some of the administrative tasks as well; only the lower reaches of the administration would be left intact. A 'superimposed' hierarchy, rather than a parallel one, could result.

It is in the objections to such an arrangement that one appreciates the basis of the system that has evolved. Firstly, it is clear that the frequency of changes in the party complexion of government could lead to a disruption of policy output and a lowering of administrative efficiency. Secondly, it can be argued that the quality of administrative expertise would suffer (although this point assumes that the capability of party machines remained at their present level). Thirdly, there is the possibility that an unmitigated spoils system would result, that connections would prevail over merit; this is not a necessary consequence if the party machine were already organized on a merit-hierarchy basis. Finally, it can be said that the cabinet system of government achieves the same effect as a superimposed hierarchy, but in a much more economical way: it is sufficient if the controlling government positions are taken over by the party, since the administrative machine is geared to political control exercised in such a fashion.

One can also refer to a number of factors which serve to strengthen this type of political leadership. The cabinet itself can be regarded as an insulative device. It is here that the general leadership functions are preserved, and it is in the cabinet that the performance of specialized leadership comes under scrutiny; political ministers in the cabinet are 'amongst themselves', and high-level political decisions are taken with the widest considerations of government and party benefit in mind without the direct influence of the permanent administrators being apparent. Where coalition government is the rule, the cabinet is not a protection against the various party pressures, but in the case of single-party government the cabinet system ensures a partial insulation from both party and administration.

The presence of a party dominant in government for long periods does not necessarily result in strong political leadership vis-à-vis the administration, as the example of the Christian Democrats in Italy shows. Although the bureaucracy is 'colonized' by the permanent governing party, the client relationship favours the party and its affiliates as a whole, not just the national political leadership. A large number of related groups enjoy a special relationship to government power, even showing their influence in the composition of the bureaucracy. This accommodation to a range of party interests means that the national leadership is in competition with its own party. A remedy would be a general party reform, centralized and cadre-oriented rather than dispersed and mass-based. Yet to do this could weaken the party's attractions, and its first priority is to maintain its hold on power at elections.

Two administrative devices can be mentioned which have the effect of concentrating policy functions within the political leadership. One is to make a clear distinction between the policy functions of departments and their 'agency' functions. In principle, this division is a clear-cut distinction, yet only in Sweden is it carried through to the extent that most ministries are concerned solely with policy formulation and oversight, whilst numerous agencies and boards are responsible for detailed administration. But this system does not supply any guarantees: agencies can become very independent and evolve their own policies, and within the ministry the political heads are still subject to the direct influence of the permanent administrator.

It is precisely to avoid this direct influence that the ministerial *'cabinet'* system operates in France. It has the character of a superimposed hierarchy in miniature. Briefly, the minister's cabinet consists of up to a dozen members personally appointed by the incoming minister, each with a specific function. Some simply work as personal aides, and others deal with public relations, the general public, and members of the Assembly. The more relevant figures are those concerned with government administration. One has to remember that French ministries lack the unifying and powerful influence of the permanent secretary in control of British government departments. These ministerial appointees therefore bridge the gap between the numerous departmental heads within a ministration. One has to remember that French ministries lack the unifying and powerful influence of the permanent secretary in control of and who has wide powers to act on his behalf. There are also more specialized personnel: the *conseillers techniques* and the *chargés de mission.* Together, the cabinet has three broad tasks: policy formulation for the minister, supervision of the departments, co-ordination of the work of the ministry internally and with other ministries. Although each member has his own province, they exercise a collective advisory function to the minister.

It might appear that the French ministerial cabinet solves the problem of preserving political leadership. But there are a number of very real objections. In practice, the staff of the cabinet is recruited largely from the civil service. Three-quarters of cabinet directors come from one or other of the *grands corps,* and up to 90 per cent of cabinet members may be civil servants. Whilst this service is obviously invaluable experience to them in the course of their career—about half the departmental heads have served in a cabinet—it hardly answers the problem, and indeed may have, '... excessively strengthened the part played in the state by certain categories of government officials.'[1] It supports the impression that the 'technocrats' of the élitist *grands corps* operate in the critical area between political leadership and routine administration. Only if one is prepared to argue that the *origin* of cabinet personnel is not relevant, that these people are free of 'departmental loyalties', does the cabinet system make a contribution to ministerial supremacy.

The general problem of the parliamentary systems is to ensure that political control is maintained, but there is always the inherent possibility of a 'reverse osmosis'—that the values and aims of the bureaucracy will infect the political leadership. This tendency will be shown in the readiness of ministers to accept the advice of the permanent officials rather than that of the party, to put forward departmental policies rather than party ones, or at least seriously to modify the content of the latter. The question of how a bureaucracy can come to have its own 'values' is one which we consider in a succeeding section on 'administrative élites'; first, the historical context of a civil service should be taken into account.

Constitutional Bureaucracy

It is through its historical evolution that the status and role of a country's administrative personnel can best be appreciated. The key development in western societies has been what Brian Chapman calls 'the depersonalization of the state'.[2] The changing nature of state power, away from the personal authority of a particular ruler towards the exercise of an abstract and 'rational-legal' authority, was seen by Max Weber as one of the typical features of capitalist society, one which replaced the authority of traditional and charismatic rulers. It was in the implementation of this rational-legal power that, according to Weber, a bureaucracy came into its own as the one perfectly rational instrument of government.[3]

For Britain in particular we can say that this evolution led at a fairly early date to the emergence of what Henry Parris terms a 'constitutional bureaucracy'.[4] As the idea of the circulation or alternation of governments became an integral part of the liberal democratic order, so as a corollary there came about a virtual separation of an important part of the government machine: 'From being one strand in the unified executive, the civil service had become a distinct entity, at the service of each successive cabinet.'[5] This implied a permanence for the skilled administrators, but it also meant that they had to be removed from the political arena as a substantive requirement for their continued employment. It is reasonable to say that the idea of a constitutional bureaucracy which this removal caused is a common end-product for the European democracies, whatever particular route was followed. The important differences that still exist derive from the ways in which the civil service became a 'distinct entity' in government. The most notable contrast is, in fact, between Britain and most of the other states in Western Europe.

There are two reasons which we can put forward for the different pattern of British central administration, and each has left its own stamp. One lies in the development of public law, the other in the *phasing* of constitutional development. Britain was outside the European mainstream in not participating in the rediscovery of Roman Law; this divergence was due in part to the fact that the rediscovery from the sixteenth century onwards coincided with the emergence of absolute monarchies in many European states, and Roman Law provided the legal doctrines which could be used to bolster up absolutist claims. And the use of one type of legal system also came to colour administrative styles as Chapman points out: 'There are parallels between Roman and modern European administrative traditions, and Roman Law has exerted a great influence on continental jurists and is the fundamental European tradition.'[6]

The development of modern absolutist states required a high degree of centralization which could only be operated by expert administrators, and with the growth of trade and industry, active government intervention necessitated the specialization of administrative services. By the mid-eighteenth century these administrative techniques had been well-developed in Prussia; her rationalized administrative system, developed by Freiherr vom Stein, was complementary to her military strength and quickly compensated for her late entry as a European power. In France, Napoleon's contribution was of greater import because he created a blueprint which could be, and was, run off for many other states. The Napoleonic system harked back to the Roman system of administration in various ways: the provision of a systematic legal code, the organization of central government along functional lines, the insistence on employing skilled personnel of proven ability. In many ways he reinforced the royal administrative system he inherited: the idea of technical training for specialist administrators, and the prefectoral system had much in common with that of the former royal *intendants*.

Besides developing quite dissimilar legal doctrines, Britain took a different line in her constitutional development. First there was the much earlier establishment of constitutional government than elsewhere. V. Subramaniam has indicated the development of responsible government in Britain as emerging in distinct phases: there was a two-step climb from original absolutist rule to the fully democratic order—the critical intervening phase was the rule by a wealthy oligarchy; in contrast, other European states took a single step only from absolutism to democracy: 'When Britain settled for government by enlightened gentlemen of means, the leading states of Europe evolved into absolute monarchies and developed an efficient modern government machine to make it effective.'[7] This build-up of a powerful state bureaucracy was then carried straight over into the fully democratic era. Even though some states developed wealthy oligarchies at a later date, the administrative framework was by then fully established.

Thus it was in the timing of the intervening period which Subramaniam finds had a decisive influence on the nature of the British civil service, especially as it coincided with a re-awakening of the generalist ideal in education. Both the nature of government and the implanting of a liberal educational tradition were sufficient to impede the growth of a specialist civil service, and this feature has remained as a permanent influence on the nature of the higher civil service in Britain, favouring the 'generalist' rather than the 'specialist'—a contrast we shall examine shortly.

The rather natural growth of the British system, its lack of purposive modelling at least until the latter part of the nineteenth century, made changes consequent upon immediate needs. This gradualism enables Parris to detail the steps by which the civil service came to be depoliticized.[8] It was a halting process, in the nature of successive approximations, and necessarily so, since the parallel establishment of the principle of ministerial responsibility was equally long drawn-out. In the end, the British version of constitutional bureaucracy was clear: there was a sharp distinction between two types of state service. State servants were either political (hence removable) or civil (permanent as long as they remained non-political). In the phase of transition each individual office-holder had to be assessed: would he serve the incoming government as loyally as he had the last?

The nature of the cut-off finally arrived at left no room for a spoils system as it did in the United States where the desire for the spoils of office ensured that a large number of otherwise 'non-political' appointments were available to a victorious party. Jacksonian democracy, with its popularization of the spoils system, can be contrasted with European experience in that the United States reached a fully participatory system much earlier. Parris, in answering the question why no spoils system came about in Britain, advances a number of reasons of which perhaps the most important was the nature of the dominant value system: 'Office was regarded as something closely akin to freehold property. To deprive a man of it seemed only less shocking than to deprive him of goods or land.'[9] Here we see values which were fundamentally opposed to achievement-oriented American society.

Continental practice emerged as not all that different from the British, but for rather different reasons. The permanent nature of absolutist, or at least non-responsible government, made wholesale changes in administrative personnel less likely from the start. A greater reliance on expertise at all levels meant that people would enter the state service as a career for which they had often had specific training in advance. The claim of the civil servant to a permanent post did require of him a special loyalty to the state, but in return he enjoyed a high status in society. There was an additional twist arising from the late development of responsible, parliamentary government: the lack of responsibility meant that there was no good reason for excluding civil servants from top ministerial appointments; indeed, their skill and experience were an added recommendation. We have seen earlier that it was common practice throughout the nineteenth century to appoint civil servants as ministers; theirs was not so much an acknowledged political function as a bureaucratization of politics—a tradition that lies not far from the surface and which naturally comes into its own again whenever parliamentary government shows signs of faltering. Such discontinuities of the parliamentary system have not affected Britain in modern times, and the easy conclusion to draw is that a completely non-political service shows the virtues of British government stability to be rewarded.

This idea can be challenged. Anyway, it is agreed that in those West European countries where leading civil servants do have some political function, the situation could never lead to a spoils system—all European bureaucracies are too well-protected for that to happen. The British view is that absolute loyalty can be maintained on the basis of absolute neutrality—as a statement of faith on the part of the civil servant. The extent to which a British civil servant 'becomes' non-political is well-illustrated by the appointment of a Labour peer, Lord Rothschild, as head of a Central Policy Review body to serve the Conservative cabinet: 'He did not see any conflict in a Labour Peer working for a Conservative Government. . . . "I shall be a Civil Servant and the politics of a civil servant are irrelevant." '[10] That view rather slurs over the distinction between a passive loyalty and an active commitment. If British parties had less common ground, in particular if the Labour Party had sought to make 'revolutionary' changes, then doubtless ideas of civil service neutrality would have been modified. Other countries acknowledge that their senior servants do have political views, and their services are made use of accordingly, even if this entails a switching-around of top level administrators after a change in government.

Ferrel Heady contrasts the British and American administrative systems with the majority of those in Europe; the former he sees as being firmly in the 'civic culture' tradition,* the main traits of which he regards as the effects of 'the gradualist pattern of political development on public administration', and as a result: '. . . the administrative system was also able to shape feature by feature in a way that reflected political changes and was consonant with them. Political and administrative adaptations were concurrent and fairly well-balanced, but the political theme was dominant.'[11] This view, that the predominance of the political element early on made civil services more dependent on social development is echoed by Hans Daalder with particular reference to the possibilities of party control over bureaucracy: 'The British civil service was from the outset below party; the French and German bureaucracies were to a very real extent above it.'[12] The power of such bureaucracies meant that when party government did come the political function of the bureaucracy continued.

It is this question of political predominance which Heady sees as a cardinal difference between the civic culture tradition and continental bureaucracies cast in the Weberian form. But as David Coombes has pointed out, in terms of objectivity, impartiality, and discretion, 'The standards of the British civil service have been far closer to the classical type of

* See above, pp. 6–7.

career service than those of its Continental counterparts.'[13] One unfortunate consequence of taking a 'classic' view of *any* bureaucracy is the tendency to play down the links which civil servants have with the rest of society. The view that they can be insulated from social life or become what Michel Crozier terms 'closed systems of social action' is only true for limited periods. Such a role as that of an independent agent of social and political renewal is also likely to be transient. The more permanent position is that of an élite which reflects the distribution of power in wider society.

Administrative Élites

Constitutional bureaucracies in the European tradition conform to a similar pattern in the way a civil service is run. A first requirement is that the conditions of service should be standard throughout. Within these conditions, uniformity is best ensured where recruitment is centrally organized, and quite separate from the individual ministries. Hiring and firing at will is unthinkable, and promotion according to personal whim scarcely less so. Successful candidates are chosen on merit alone, and once appointed at a relatively early age, there is little likelihood that they will ever be dismissed. Promotion strikes a balance between merit and seniority. In return for this favourable treatment civil servants are expected to abide by the formal rules and procedures, and never to challenge (or undermine) the political authority. These conditions of service dovetail with Weber's itemized definition of bureaucracy,[14] and the process of bureaucratization since the nineteenth century represents the successful imposition of those terms of service. The bureaucracy becomes a 'closed', career service from which 'outsiders' are excluded, and an administrative élite runs the state machine.

Before we look at the social and political implications of this élite, we should appreciate the importance of individual variations which make for differences in the type of bureaucracy which emerges. These variations occur in several ways: the degree of centralization, the extent of competitive recruitment, the nature of training, and the forms of post-entry specialization all have an effect.

Britain has a highly-unified service, and is in almost every respect fully centralized. This applies to the method of recruitment, to Treasury control, and to the relative lack of 'field' or regional deconcentration. A leading contrast is with the civil service in a federal state where the federal service will be quite small in comparison with the state services, each of which will be responsible for its own recruitment. Thus each West German Land is directly responsible for its own civil servants, a term which also includes teachers and judges, and well over 80 per cent of public administration personnel (that is, excluding those engaged in public enterprise) are employed by the Land and local authorities. However, overall conditions are fixed by federal law, and strong trade unions ensure that none of the Länder gets out of line in respect of remuneration and grading. The dispersion necessary in a federal state is an important component of European 'administrative' federalism which we look at later;* in the unitary states, the civil service is never broken up in this way, but only geographically dispersed for administrative convenience. Only a small proportion of the French civil service is located in Paris, the majority dispersed to the departments: 'Both before and since the Revolution, external services have enabled French governments to pursue a policy of direct administration in the provinces.'[15] This geographical dispersion possibly makes for a greater independence of the individual ministries rather than for the local units.

The Swedish alternative, as already indicated, does give subordinate units greater independence. Administration is in the hands of numerous agencies, and their independence from the parent ministry is further underlined by the fact that recruitment is not centrally organized, though other conditions of service are laid down nationally. Decentralized recruitment can work two ways: it can lead to an undesirable local nepotism at its worst, but at best it can lead to a more open type of recruitment, possibly with less social bias. Sweden perhaps accords to this latter type, and Italy to the former.

The way in which people enter the civil service varies considerably from one country to another: according to whether it is by means of competitive selection or by the possession of prior qualifications, and allied to this, whether provisions are made for training, preceding formal entry, post-entry, or not at all. Sweden relies on qualification only, with little specific training except in the trading agencies. In Italy, entry is competitive with no prior or post-entry training. British entry is highly competitive, but with only rudimentary in-service training as yet. The German system has a developed scheme of advanced pre-entry training, but non-competitive entry. And France operates in reverse—intensive post-entry training with highly competitive entry. From this variety, it is doubtful if any sure conclusion could be drawn, but the really fundamental similarity is the tie-in of civil service recruitment with the system of higher education for all countries, and an examination of the relationship to education helps to explain some of the variations.

In neither Sweden nor Germany is competitive entry a feature, but in both countries there is a tradition of strong government influence on the content of university training. For the majority of German students the final educational qualification is the 'state examination' in the relevant faculty. In effect, this is a passport enabling them to enter state service in a capacity determined by their specialism. It is not vocational training, but vocationally-relevant, with the needs of government influencing the content of the course. The same is true for Sweden, especially in relation to uni-

* See below, p. 212.

versity law courses, and we shall see that this is still the prime source of recruitment for the majority of services. The German emphasis on pre-entry training is, however, probably unique. Typically, and especially for those seeking a legal qualification for state service, a first state examination is followed by an extended period of pre-entry, practical training lasting for three or more years. In this time the *Referendar* (probationer) spends some time in each of a number of administrative departments and in the courts. Finally, he takes his second state examination, and, if successful, becomes an established civil servant. The ambit of such training is wide for it takes in future high officials in federal and state service, the judiciary, local government and the legal profession itself. Chapman draws attention to the effects: 'This common background produces a closely knit and cohesive governing cadre with ramifications in all fields of public life. . . . In most other countries it would be unbelievable to find people capable of going through this training process working in local government.'[16]

The contrast with the French system is striking, all the more so when one considers that at least for the senior civil servants just as cohesive a governing cadre emerges. The relationship of the state to the universities is markedly different. We can say in fact that the state does not place a reliance on them; instead it has built up its own parallel educational system which in some fields is more highly regarded than what can be offered outside. One should distinguish here between those candidates who will finally be placed in one of the most important of the technical corps and those who will join the general administrative corps. The former will normally qualify first by winning a place in fierce competition to an institution such as the *Ecole Polytechnique*—this as an alternative to university entrance which is *not* competitive. From there, if the successful student wishes to have a career in the state service, he will go to one of the specialized colleges associated with particular technical corps as a form of postgraduate training before receiving his first posting. Thus the decision to enter state service usually has to be taken in the final years at school, but such is the reputation of, say, the *Ecole Polytechnique* that a 'polytechnician' can always switch on completion of his training to private industry—and be welcomed as a valued acquisition. The French term, *pantouflage,* neatly expresses the facility with which a civil servant can safely 'parachute' to a leading post in the private sector.

Parallel with the great technical schools is the *Ecole Nationale d'Administration* (ENA), providing an in-service training for those who have already graduated at a university in Law, Economics, or Politics. Highly-competitive entry requires additional, specialized preparation at one of the Institutes of Political Science attached to the universities. The ENA course itself is once again competitive, and those who pass out near the top have the pick of which of the *grands corps* they will enter. Thus the administrative élite, whether from the ENA or the technical schools, is based on intellectual excellence over a broad range of disciplines.

In Britain, the complete divorce that existed between the needs of state administration and what the universities provided, led to the university traditions themselves coming to dominate the civil service, with particular emphasis on an education in the humanities. The generalist ideal assumes that academic background prior to entry is irrelevant to administrative arts, but that general excellence is ensured by competitive entry. Even though the post-Fulton reforms should weaken the generalist-specialist dichotomy that runs through the service, the fact that this problem has not emerged in other European countries is worth noting.

The continental equivalent to the British generalist is the civil servant who has had a legal training, for he will normally be found near the top of the administrative hierarchy. But this will not be because of the 'general' qualities which a degree in law will foster in him, rather it is that as an administrator he is expected to be well-versed in law as one of the tools of his trade. Thus the basic difference between a judge and a legal-administrator is that one applies the law in the course of litigation and the other applies it in the course of his administrative duties—hence the common training which they undergo in several countries. It is the state service which dominates the legal profession rather than the other way round: in Sweden, just under two-thirds of the legal profession are employed by the state, either as judges or administrators, and within the service the jurists heavily outnumber all other groups. But the importance of a legal training in Scandinavian and other countries does not mean that those who are technically qualified are thereby downgraded as 'mere' specialists. We have seen the high status of the technical corps in France, and Ridley points out that the only losers are likely to be members of the newer professions, such as town-planners, who face the entrenched status of the élite corps.[17]

How significant are these differences? They may result in differences of technical competence, but against this one has to bear in mind the different administrative traditions of various countries: administrative legalism would be foreign to the British approach as would the British generalist be at sea in German administration. The real issue is the *social* function and origin of the administrative élite. Dahrendorf makes this comparison: 'In principle, the law faculties of German universities accomplish for German society what the exclusive Public Schools do for the English, and the *grandes écoles* for the French. In them an élite receives its training.'[18] There is then a 'functional equivalence' between them, but the similarity does not stop there. Common to all the West European states has been the close connection between wealth, education, and administrative power; the line which can be drawn in Britain from the public schools, through the older universities, to the generalist administrators—at least until the very recent past—simply finds a different formula in other countries. Entry based on 'merit' only highlights differences in educational opportunity, and a civil service geared to a university training has always discriminated in favour of the middle class.*

The discrimination was not entirely accidental, and this fact becomes apparent when one looks back to the nineteenth century: the large-scale reforms—including the merit system of open competition—did not really alter the balance which favoured the privileged, and were not intended to do so. At the time of the Northcote-Trevelyan reforms in England, Gladstone defended the introduction of open competition on the grounds that the new method, '. . . would not entail a lowering of social standards in the service—a substitution of *parvenus* for "gentlemen"—but would rather "strengthen and multiply the ties between the higher classes and the possession of administrative power".' Asa Briggs comments, 'The civil service was to be thrown open not to the "raw" middle classes but to the new educational élite of the public schools and universities . . .social stratification was to remain.'[19] This view of the social function of the civil service found a contemporary echo in France: 'The higher classes, as they call themselves, are obliged to acknowledge the right of the majority, and they can only maintain their political dominance by invoking the right of the most capable. . . . The tide of democracy must encounter a second line of defence . . . of superior qualities whose prestige cannot be gainsaid.'[20]

The bias has not been eliminated with the passing of the years, only the middle class is no longer 'raw'. Sweden may be regarded as one of the more socially-progressive of the European states, yet the composition of the civil service, which Neil Elder concedes as a 'mildly élitist state of affairs',[21] means that the highest social group with only 5 per cent of the population supplies some 50 per cent of the senior officials, and the working-class percentage actually fell between 1949 and 1961.

Obviously changes are taking place. To a limited extent a greater fluidity will result in Britain with the abolition (in 1971) of the three traditional classes—administrative, executive and clerical—each linked to a certain educational standard; in the past, inter-class mobility was limited since each class had its own career structure. The new system, at least in theory, does not make lower, formal educational attainments an absolute bar. But the willingness to make reforms does not ensure their success. The French ENA was set up in 1945 partly to end the nepotism of individual corps recruitment and also to make the intake more socially representative. Yet students of a direct working-class origin are still a rarity: 'The student intake of the ENA, which is one of the most prestigious shortcuts to high office in existence, tends to be exclusively middle class.'[22] Only seldom do applicants with a working-class or rural background enter the ENA; a certain social narrowness accompanies the Schools' reputation for fostering 'meritocratic' ability. To a lesser extent the same is true for the technical

---

* For a comparison of educational opportunity at university level, see the table on p. 263.

schools; the French civil service is firmly rooted in the Parisian middle class.

The social elitism is enhanced by the amount of inbreeding which takes place. Often the family traditions show a constancy for a considerable period, thus maintaining the social composition of the service intact. Dahrendorf records the 'overwhelming' fact that, 'In Imperial Germany, the Weimar Republic, and the Federal Republic about one half of all civil servants were recruited from the families of civil servants. This is the real inner continuity of German officialdom.'[23] Similarly, up to a third of the successful candidates to the ENA are the sons of higher officials, and a greater proportion if one includes all grades of public official.

Whilst the social composition of many services is not at all representative of their communities, the bias is passive and the general quality of the services is not open to dispute. This contrasts with the situation in Italy, still in the stage of positive discrimination: 'It is assumed that connections and recommendations are necessary to get anywhere in public or private life. This distrust of the impartiality of the examination process is bolstered by the fact that some offices in various ministries appear to be populated largely by individuals coming from a particular province or a particular private group. There is a sort of colonization of jobs.'[24] The malaise which Kogan sees in the Italian civil service goes deeper. Lack of respect for Italian officials is often apparently confirmed by the number of scandals involving civil servants. The aspiring candidate sees the security offered by state service as the summit of his ambition; lacking is a further sense of public service: his authority is for use against a disrespectful public. Almond and Verba have shown the wide range of attitudes towards bureaucracy; whilst the overwhelming majority of British respondents believed they would receive fair treatment from civil servants, and almost two-thirds of the West German sample thought so too, barely half of the Italians thought that impartiality was likely.[25]

Quite opposed views are held about the *political* power of civil servants. The terms on which a constitutional bureaucracy was established in the first place seem to exclude the overt use of political power. In Britain, the civil servant is regarded as a political cypher, and where civil servants are admitted to be at all influential, this ability is applied to their individual characteristics rather than to the nature of bureaucracy. At the other extreme, Max Weber advanced the view that, 'Under normal conditions the power position of a fully developed bureaucracy is always overtowering'.[26] Part of the confusion arises from the *way* an administrator treats a political problem; he does not offer a political solution but an administrative one, as Mannheim puts it: 'The attempt to hide all problems under the cover of administration may be explained by the fact that the sphere of the official exists within the limits of laws already formulated. Hence the genesis or the development of law falls outside the scope of his activity,'[27] This does not at all prevent him in engaging in legislative activity or any other political decision-making, but it will not be expressed by him in these terms, and since the problems are defined administratively, an issue will inevitably be played down by him, though his power is not less for not receiving open recognition. One can go too far in this direction and build up a composite picture of the all-powerful civil servant, a 'fallacy of aggregation' in which as Parry observes, '. . . evidence of the planning powers of French officials, the policy-forming opportunities of British civil servants and the independence of the old German officialdom are compounded to produce a picture of the political power of the bureaucracy as such.'[28]

We can, however, postulate four major conditions under which a bureaucracy is likely to be strong, although no one by itself will lead to an independent power position:

if the political authorities are weak and governments are unstable;
if the service is unified, grounded in a common pattern of recruitment and training;
if it is socially homogeneous—though one should note here that when it is fully representative of a dominant social class, the harmony which results will not give the bureaucracy power in its own right;
if, conscious of its corporate identity, the service can develop an 'autonomous sense of purpose'.[29]

It is clear that most European bureaucracies have some of these conditions in their favour, and if we add as an alternative to the first of these that the government may actually favour active intervention by civil servants, then one can appreciate that the exercise of bureaucratic power is a real eventuality. Blondel, in fact, concludes that France, '. . . seems a country where the possibility of "technocracy" is not remote.'[30] He uses the term 'technocracy' in regarding bureaucracies as 'managerial enterprises with an autonomous sense of purpose that sets them aside from the rule-makers', and the administrators are regarded as the 'technicians'. The French situation is one in which all our conditions for bureaucratic power may be met. Blondel argues that the French and British bureaucratic models are at the two extremes of a spectrum, and that, '. . . the question of managerial influence has been minimised in the UK and other Anglo-Saxon countries and maximised in France and some other Continental countries because of the relatively lower status of technicians in the managerial hierarchy of the former countries.'[31] The acceptance of a lower status depends on various factors. The 'sectional demands' of the technicians will be weakened by strong parliamentary pressures, but also where, as in Britain, the humanistic university training weakens the technical ethos. The weak substitute for this ethos, membership of a professional association, does not offer a sufficient stimulus within the public service; the influence of the technician is simply dispersed to a number of administrative agencies.

The contrast with France is marked. Unity of the technicians is bolstered by the pre-eminence of certain forms of technical training, by the solidarity of the technical corps, and by the fact that the products of this technical élitism spill over into wider society, making social control that much more difficult. And in the French circumstances these effects were multiplied by the government instability of the Fourth Republic, and by the search for administrative solutions in the Fifth. All the same, if Britain and France represent polar points with respect to the exercise of 'technocratic' power, the dissimilarities are not so pronounced when one considers only the social-class 'representative' nature of the two,[32] and many would hold that it is the social composition of a civil service which in the end is decisive for the role which it plays in society.

Politics and the Military

The armed forces in Western Europe are almost everywhere in a quiescent condition, accepting the decisions of the political leaders with docility. It is hardly the case in other parts of the world, and two questions we have to answer here are, why this happy situation should exist, and whether it is a permanent state of affairs. We need only to bear in mind the recent history of France, the dictatorship in Greece and the military backing to the regimes in Spain and Portugal, and latterly the rule of the Portuguese Armed Forces Movement—to be aware that the feasibility of military intervention in politics, even of military rule, is nowhere quite impossible. Even if, unlike the army in developing countries, the military in Europe cannot easily don the guise of 'modernizing agents', in principle there are various pretexts they can use to justify political action.

The readiness of the armed forces to take a back seat politically is not something new; in fact, active intervention, though always striking when it occurs, is very much the exception in European history. To explain this, Andreski draws attention to the early view advanced by Gaetano Mosca, who '. . . considered the subordination of the military to the civilian authority to have been one of the most distinctive and crucial features of the European civilisation. . . . It was proof of Mosca's genius that, diverging from all current opinions, he put forth the view that the relative docility of the European armies depended on the rigidity of class divisions in their midst.'[33] Thus on the one hand the military leaders were an integral part of the ruling social order, yet on the other they were always 'divided from their men by an impassable economic and cultural abyss.' These different facets of cohesion and division served to neutralize the army as a political force.

Other factors can be added to this basic orientation. For instance, Janowitz explains the subordination from an early time as arising from, '. . . the low specialization of the military profession [which] made it possible for the political élite to supply the bulk of the necessary leadership for the armed forces'.[34] Further, the ability of the political system to avoid 'sharp discontinuities' meant that there was no prolonged period when this leadership was not in evidence. However, a precondition of stability in *all* cases is the social homogeneity of the political rulers and the military élite; without this, the tensions between the political and the military orders are likely to become acute—such was the case in Spain, Portugal, and Greece.

The particular problem in Western Europe was to secure the continued subordination of the military into the democratic era; the close link which the armies had with conservative traditions, as part of a pre-democratic and feudal order, provided no promise at all that the military would meekly accept a new political establishment. Whilst Mosca's formulation helps to show the difficulties of an officer class in effecting a successful coup, this applies much more to the period before the onset of political democracy when the political leaders and the military ones had an identical social background. It was still true in the democratic era that the continuing rigidity of class divisions within armies meant that they were never a cohesive force; this division made intervention more risky, yet not necessarily less desirable, from a right-wing and military viewpoint.

In assessing the political role of the military and its degree of subordination to the democratic political order, there are three areas of explanation which we can usefully consider:

the social background of the officer class;
the leading values of the military, and their concept of what is a 'legitimate' political order;
the degree of 'isolation' of the armed forces from wider society, both in a social and technical sense.

We should expect that the military could take on an independent political colouring in conditions where its recruitment is from the privileged classes, where it regards the democratic order with suspicion, and where, in its isolation, it becomes 'a state within a state' developing military values as the yardstick of its judgement. Each of these conditions has to be related to the actual course of development in the various countries.

As far as the social background of top military personnel is concerned, what is immediately apparent for Europe is that there was no sudden democratization of recruitment. What happened in most European states was a relatively gradual shift from the predominance of the nobility towards one of the middle class, a shift that lasted for the best part of a century. The important point is that the change in composition was gradual, yet at the same time it was for the most part an unhindered process. C. B. Otley has shown the wide variations from one country to another.[35] Thus in the Netherlands, middle-class officers were already in a large majority in the last quarter of the nineteenth century, but this was exceptional. For Britain in the same period, the nobility and the middle class shared high-ranking military positions in about equal proportions. At the other extreme, the German army élite was almost exclusively of the nobility—well over 90 per cent in 1872. Otley's figures show that there was a gradual, but never dramatic shift in the twentieth century, and in Britain it was actually at a slower rate than for other European countries. Exceptionally again, even by 1939 the German nobility still supplied a third of the high-ranking officers. In all European countries, it has been only in the most recent past that the top positions have covered all sections of the middle class; the slow transfer was from the nobility to the upper middle class in the first place; of course, lower class recruitment to top positions is still an extreme rarity.

The significance of the changing pattern is twofold. In most states, the widening social background of the officer class meant that an increasing proportion came from the same background as the new political leaders; secondly, the gradual nature of the change did not present a challenge to leading military values—to some extent the middle-class officers were happy to accept them—and no sudden crisis in the status of the military resulted. The continuity of military traditions was also protected by the considerable inbreeding amongst the officer class; family background is very important in the decision to take up a military career, and anything from a third to a half of military leaders have some prior connection with the armed forces. A conclusion to the question of social background and the political involvement of the military is that whilst it is important that a socially representative officer hierarchy should emerge, the terms on which it does so are of equal importance.

The second determining feature is the 'legitimacy' of the civilian rulers. This authority is not something which the military has a free hand in interpreting, and which it can call into question at will. Of importance here is the historical subordination of the military élite to the political leaders, for this was largely taken over into the democratic era, and where the democratic institutions were peacefully grafted on to the older system, the transfer of legitimacy occurred without question; at no stage did the military face a sharp clash of loyalties. Just as important as the military view of the civilian order is the civilian view of its own institutions, in other words the relative maturity of the political culture. As Finer has put it, 'The greater the degree of consensus in society and the width and organization of this opinion, the less the likelihood of a military intervention and the less likely, in the event, its success.'[36] The extent to which organized opinion can be gauged is another matter; it depends on the cohesion of the party system, the ability to marshal public opinion, and on the presence of strong secondary groupings such as trade unions. All three of these will help deter the military from intervening, and should it nevertheless do so, the extent of civilian resistance may weaken the army's resolve—especially that of the lower ranks who will be much less disposed to question the civilian norms.

The third area of explanation depends partly on the other two. We have called this the degree of 'isolation' of the military, and it is related to the social basis of recruitment and to the prevailing civilian consensus. But the isolation can lead to the armed forces defining their own role in society, not just allying themselves with an old and threatened social order. Blondel terms this independence a form of 'professionalism': 'The isolation of the military from the rest of the nation tends to increase the professional nature of the army. . . . It will tend to develop its own values and attitudes to greater extremes than it would otherwise do.'[37] A 'professional' army of this kind has its own code—foremost, it will see itself as the sole guarantee of national honour. However, the forces acting against it being able to do so are considerable. Firstly, there are the basic socializing influences to which the military leaders are subjected, and these are specifically reinforced by the strict idea of obedience which characterize any army. In Britain, this subordinating function was for long performed by the public schools, of which Otley says, '. . . although they did not lack militaristic features were basically *class* training centres. . . . (They) provided a general training for the performance of "diffuse" leadership roles.'[38] Where this subordination was not achieved, the military role was not clearly defined, and the obedience which military leaders could command was at their disposal in defining their own role.

The other force acting against the development of an isolated and professional army may be called 'technical'. Superficially, it might appear that any technically-advanced army would become more professionalized. But the nature of modern warfare has made the armed forces less rather than more self-sufficient. In order to develop its techniques the military is forced to maintain a range of contacts with non-military groups. There is no longer any *special* military mystique, only multidisciplinary, military technicians. Increasingly, modern armies are unable to operate effectively unless they can secure co-operation from their civilian counterparts, and this involves the army at all points; it cannot retreat into a shell of its own myth-making.

It is instructive to examine those cases where the subordination of the military has *not* been so much in evidence, and we can take the French and German armies to illustrate the application of the three general conditions we have already outlined. At the present time, it appears that the armed forces in both countries now fully accept the primacy of the political and democratic order, but in both cases the transfer was far from smooth. We have already drawn attention to the social composition of the German military élite in the early part of the century; the preponderance of the nobility meant that the armed forces at the disposal of the politicians of the Weimar Republic were simply unreliable; the military still believed in the values of Imperial Germany, and if a restoration of the monarchy was impossible, this only served to increase the isolative tendencies in the German Army. Before the German defeat in the First World War, this isolation was not in evidence; instead there was a 'dual legitimacy'—'a civilian government linked to the assembly and military men directly responsible to the Emperor'.[39]

Yet the military representatives of the old ruling class did not resort to an open attack on the Weimar Republic. The Kapp Putsch of 1920 was not engineered by the German High Command, and its failure can be directly ascribed to the strength of the 'civilian consensus'. But even at that time one can see the army's own definition of its role, especially in the attitude of the German High Command towards the attempted coup. The answer to the government's request to deal with it was simply: 'The Reichswehr does not shoot at Reichswehr'. If the army leaders did not go so far as to topple the civilian government themselves, it was certain that they would do little to save it either.

The German Army came to regard itself not just as a servant of the state, but identical with it; in the eyes of the military, the political game was played out on a lower level entirely. This is not to say that the military leaders remained aloof from politics; in particular, there were the manoeuvrings of the military camarilla round the ageing President Hindenburg as well as the machinations of General Schleicher, both in his role as minister for the Reichswehr and later as short-lived chancellor. But the various manoeuvres were in the nature of a high level deal: how to keep Hitler out or, alternatively, on what terms he should be allowed in; the military did not itself seek direct political power.

Although by 1933 many of the junior officers were affected by the Nazi enthusiasm, the High Command was not. Nevertheless, a general transfer of loyalties was enforced, from the values of Imperial Germany to the personal oath of loyalty to Hitler—in the end an élite subservience. Earlier we referred to the 'liquidation' of the German military élite as one of the consequences of fascism,* and the effects of this can be seen in post-war Germany. The pattern of recruitment has moved decisively in favour of the lower middle class, and the 'double rupture' suffered by the German military in 1918 and 1945, '... left its traces in the career patterns and social outlook of its élite'[40]—the 'retired' officers got themselves permanent civilian jobs, unlike their predecessors in 1918 who flocked to the 'Free Corps'. The new army personnel is largely conscript, and the Bundeswehr does not enjoy the high status of the Reichswehr in West German society: 'There can be no doubt that the Federal Republic is one major country where the military is least influential,' and there has been a dramatic drop in the status of officers, in the public view, in relation to comparable professions.[41] In all three respects: social composition, ideas of legitimacy, and in its lack of social isolation, the German Army has lost the basis for an independent political role.

There are important points of difference between the French and Ger-

* See above, p. 130.

man experience of the military. The estrangement of the French Army was not primarily caused by its social composition; a statute of the Third Republic required the officer intake to be made up by the promotion from the ranks of a third of the total, and generally, up to the Second World War French recruitment was more middle class than that for the German Army. For all that, the conflict with the ruling political authorities was more long-lasting. The French Army's loyalty to the Third Republic was suspect in its early years, and its attitude was shared by all the conservative forces in France. The line-up of pro- and anti-republican forces was shown with sharp relief by the onset of the Dreyfus Affair at the end of the century; here were the 'dual legitimacies' in their French context. But the showdown was averted, and it was only in the collapse of the Third Republic in 1940 that the bulk of the French Army threw in its lot with the conservative-authoritarian Vichy regime. Thus on the counts of social composition and legitimacy, the army for the most part learned to live with political democracy.

A new phase was evident after 1945. The normal post-war retrenchment made the officer class socially more homogeneous, for there was a sharp increase in those having a military background, and the temporary influx of non-professionals during the war was reversed. It is in this situation that the isolative tendencies of the military can become apparent, and the trigger to this process was the long and painful phase of decolonization in which the army bore the full brunt in the decade of the 1950s. Mauled in Indo-China, and robbed of success in the Suez escapade, the French Army had no intention of facing a further drubbing in Algeria. And it was there that the army was able to develop its own conception of its role. Answerable to no one, and certainly not to the politicians of the Fourth Republic, it proceeded to rule Algeria and fight the Algerian war in its own way; in a limited sense, the French armed forces in Algeria constituted a 'state within a state'.

Like the German Army at the end of the Weimar Republic, the French military was in a unique position to influence events —but likewise unable to control them—as the attempted putsch in Germany of 1944 and the abortive Algerian rising of 1961 were to show. Having once handed power over to de Gaulle, the rebels were powerless to prevent the complete reversal of the army's Algerian policy. Their 'moment' had been in 1958, at a time when the army's isolative role had reached its full expression and when the legitimacy of the Fourth Republic had reached its lowest ebb. Once de Gaulle had assumed legitimate power, he was quite able to deal with the army, just as Hitler had squashed the German High Command as an independent force. The circumstances were entirely different, the effect was the same.[42] In neither case was the army able to rule alone, and in both the long term effect of military intervention has been to bring them into line with the other European states. In this, they appear not simply to be politically neutral, but politically neutralized.

The Portuguese case shows the difficulty of neutralizing the military after it has enjoyed a long period of political influence. Once the army itself had overthrown the watered-down dictatorship of Salazar's successor, Caetano, in April 1974, a unique form of rule emerged: the rudiments of party life were allowed to coexist with the revolutionary Armed Forces Movement, the MFA. Both the junior officers in the MFA and the Communist Party shared an impatience with, even an abhorrence for, parliamentary democracy. For the army, the strains of fighting hopeless colonial wars in Africa led to a rapid politicization—and in fact the army was widely influenced by the left-wing ideas of the liberation movements which it had failed to put down. Consequently, the Communist Party seemed a natural ally to those officers who wished to bring about a social revolution in Portugal. But the MFA leadership was not representative of the military hierarchy as a whole, and although the verbiage of the 1974 revolution was enshrined in the constitutional 'pact' reached with the parties in 1976, in fact the MFA ceased to have a political significance. Instead, the military was content to retain a watching-brief in the person of the president of the republic, General Eanes, elected by popular vote.

A gulf separates Portugal from the prevailing order in Western Europe. National armies are less the guarantors of national honour and strength, more the pledges for international commitment[43]—an unmilitary view of the military and at the polar extreme from militarism. If this were permanently to be true, then the politicians could 'forget about' the military to an extent that is not possible in the rest of the world. This may be wishful thinking; whilst it may be the case that the army, like the bureaucracy, has no wish to supplant the political rulers, its influence may well extend along bureaucratic lines. Indeed, its very dependence on outside social and economic interests may lead the military élite to play an active, if discreet, part in political affairs—no longer an overt threat to political democracy, but one of the more effective of organized interests. And even then, there is no guarantee that some of the conditions which are favourable to the army taking an active political role will not also obtain at some future date.

Controlling Executive Power

There are two quite different aspects of the control of the executive; one is the *political* limit set on governments, the other is a *policing function* which acts on the detailed exercise of executive powers. Of the two, it is the political controls which are the more fundamental, since without them the possibility of calling a government to account is non-existent, and if that is the case then any other controls are only allowed by the grace of the government—by the nature of things it will always seek to protect itself and its servants. In the preceding chapter we have seen how, in parliamentary systems, the political controls are given expression in the relations between assemblies and governments; the life-blood of this relationship is the operation of the party system, and as a *control* function, the party system revolves around the twin pivots of 'government' and 'opposition'. In its constitutional form, the basis for the control is embedded in the principle of collective responsibility of government to assembly—a starting-point from which any parliamentary system must proceed to define the precise nature of its own political controls.

We can term the political controls the 'macro' aspect of the system, since implicitly it is the fate of whole governments and whole policies which are at stake. The policing function is naturally a 'micro' one: it questions particular actions of the executive, the implications of certain policies, and seeks redress for those who have been harmed. But it stops short of passing judgement on the government of the day. In principle, the distinction is clear-cut; in practice, there is a considerable blurring between the two: the questioning of a government's fitness to govern is partly a matter of regarding the activities of the executive as a whole, and the particular policies favoured by a government are bound to effect the *behaviour* of government; the only way to make the government behave may be to turn it out. The overlap is also evident in the actual working out of the two principles of collective and individual ministerial responsibility. Although a minister is in general charged with the sole responsibility for the work of his department, once he is on the parliamentary rack for the shortcomings of his civil servants, the issue can easily be translated— by government or opposition—to a question of confidence in the government.

Since we have dealt with the issue of political control in several contexts already, we can concentrate here entirely on the policing function, and how it is implemented. Really it is a problem of securing administrative rather than political responsibility, although it may entail the use of political institutions. In fact, we can make the fundamental distinction between devices for administrative control which are geared to political, usually parliamentary, techniques and others which operate explicitly to avoid such a connection. What is more, the European states differ considerably in the emphasis they place on one or the other.

The tradition of parliamentary control over administration is a strong one, and it is used in a variety of ways, ranging from the full plenary session to individual contact between assembly members and government officials. In the first category are the instruments of full debate and various methods of interpellation. Unless the issue is primarily of political importance, plenary sessions are expensive and blunt weapons for detailed control. But it is apparent from the British use of Question-Time that the 'details' are always potentially of wider importance. Formally, it is a request for information, possibly a demand for action, but questions have an implicit political function as well. Ministers are judged by the kind of performance they put up, and the use of questions is one aspect of the forum-like qualities of the Commons, articulated to highly-public exchanges. It is because Question-Time is not just about straight answers to specific questions that it does not transplant readily to other assemblies.

Generally, the more effective control of the administration is secured by the use of specialized committees with the power to interrogate officials, to send for 'persons, papers, and records'. The problem here is to differentiate between the work of the officials and the political responsibility of the government. As a control device it may simply be too effective; the searchlight of the politicians may be too blinding and result in officials lacking in nerve or, alternatively, in officials who themselves become too well-versed in playing politics. The protective shield of *ministerial* responsibility is of use in averting both tendencies. The other way in which detailed control of the administration is possible within the parliamentary framework is through the work of individual members of the assembly, or through the work of their common agent, the Ombudsman—a figure who has come to symbolize the control of the executive by parliamentary means.

The Swedish version of this office is based on somewhat different considerations from the later imitations. Most obviously lacking in Sweden has been the full doctrine of ministerial responsibility, arising from the neat separation of the policy-making ministries and the executive agencies which are free from ministerial control, so that the latter cannot be controlled by the Riksdag via the relevant minister. The long history of the office covers periods when the Ombudsman was little more than a royal nominee; only since 1809 has he been securely a servant of the Riksdag, but in this time he has emerged not just as one more parliamentary official, but a person enjoying a popular standing in his own right, '. . . almost as a Tribune of the People, a protector against the abuses of those in authority.'[44]

What really marks out the Swedish Ombudsman is the considerable power of initiative he possesses. He has the power of independent investigation, that is to say, he can make unsponsored tours. His counterpart for the armed forces, the Military Ombudsman, is in this sense even more of a trouble-shooter, for the great majority of his cases arise in the course of his tours of investigation, but even for the civilian Ombudsman the proportion of 'discovered' cases, as opposed to those 'referred' to him, is as high as a third. The British version is very much watered-down. The main differences can be itemized: the Parliamentary Commissioner has no right of initiative—he must wait until cases are referred to him by Members of Parliament; large areas of the administration are excluded from his jurisdiction, the most important are the armed forces, the police, and the local authorities; he is answerable to a Parliamentary Select Committee, and this it has been said, '. . . could conceivably blur the clarity and finality of his judgements.'[45] His terms of reference are more circumscribed and also less well-defined; his brief of 'maladministration' precludes judgements on the merits of a case. The manner in which the British system still has to grope its way forward is indicated by Marshall in the assumption that, although '. . . the merits of a decision may not be questioned if it is reached without maladministration, it is, it seems, now permissible to infer that if a decision has no merits at all, there *must* have been maladministration in the way it was reached.'[46] The fact is that the institution cannot yet be finally judged in the countries which have copied Sweden—Denmark (1953) and Norway (1962), and France now has the equivalent office of the *mediateur*.

Even so, it is a mistake to regard the Ombudsman as simply a legislative offshoot, one way of plugging gaps in a deficient parliamentary system of control. Properly conceived, it is a political institution on a par with others, with the assembly only providing a protective base, but the office itself a legally competent entity. The institution can combine popular, legal, and bureaucratic elements, and it works well within the bureaucratic ethos. The Swedish Ombudsman has power to start court actions against officials and he relies heavily on the weapon of publicity. Both of these features are notably absent in the British case, and it is not unfair to conclude that there the office is a prop to Parliament, rather than an attempt to secure a genuine innovation.

The Ombudsman in Sweden is a genuine hybrid of parliamentary and legal-administrative types of control. Typically, those countries which favour parliamentary control also favour strictly legal controls on the executive, that is to say controls by the ordinary courts to check the misuse of executive power. Like Britain, the states of Ireland, Denmark, the Netherlands, and Norway have no developed system of administrative law. It may be that for most of the monarchies, there has been a greater tendency to insist on parliamentary and external court jurisdiction, avoiding royal influence and the apparatus of a 'star chamber' where possible. However the differences arose, there is now a considerable contrast between those countries which operate a parliamentary plus legal check and those which seek administrative solutions to the problem of controlling the executive.

The idea of 'administrative law' needs some explanation and illustration. We can take the French *Conseil d'Etat* as the model of administrative law in action,[47] and as an example of a type of body which in one form or another is common to most West European states. As is the case with the other Councils of State, the French Conseil combines in one organ advisory, legislative, and judicial functions. We are not concerned here with its substantial powers of vetting draft laws and controlling delegated legislation, but all the functions are linked. Blondel points out that, 'France was exceptional in having developed, almost by accident, a general administrative court in the nineteenth century',[48] and its general nature meant that detailed application was left to a large number of minor, specialized courts. The result was that the Council of State emerged at the apex of an appeals system, the infrastructure of which remains the specialist and provincial courts. The consequence is a dual judicial system, both with their well-defined competence: the ordinary and criminal courts co-existing with a system of administrative courts.

At a maximum, and as it exists in France, a developed system of administrative law, with its related court system, involves the following features. There must be a *complete* jurisdiction over the public service, and correspondingly a rigorous exclusion of the ordinary courts. There has to be the power to judge whether a public authority has acted within the law or regulation, to see that discretionary powers are not misused, and that there is no wilful misuse of power. Complementary to these powers, the administrative courts should have the ability to award damages and ensure that adequate redress is made to those who have suffered through the fault of officials.

This is a 'model' view, and various deviations are evident in practice. The mere existence of a Council of State is no guarantee of standards. This is true of the Italian Council—a conservative body with recruits from prefects and other state officials near the end of their career whilst the French Council is a highly professional body. But one feature they must share if a bona fide system of administrative law is to exist: the decisions must be binding on governments, however unpalatable they may be. Thus the Netherlands, with no administrative law system, has only a weak Council of State with advisory powers. Its findings are made public, but this only forces governments to justify their decisions, not change them.

West Germany may be used as an illustration of the structure of administrative courts, though it operates without a Council of State. The Constitutional Court has a share in supervision over the administration, since the entrenched constitutional rights (especially those applying to individual liberties) may be infringed by the federal executive or those of the Länder. At the same time, there are a number of administrative courts running parallel to the main areas of public administration. The structure of the general administrative courts is three-tier, necessitated by the federal system: local courts, Land courts, and finally the Federal Administrative Court in Berlin. Besides the general courts, there are a number of specialized ones: Labour Courts, which include the private sector, Social Courts, concerned with social security questions, and the Finance Courts, with a jurisdiction in all taxation matters. The normal three-tier system gives a channel of appeal; a fourth-tier, the Supreme Federal Court, to iron out differences between the regular and administrative courts, has still not been set up.

Similar administrative court structures are to be found in other countries, such as in both Sweden and Finland. Denmark differs, and her system is noteworthy in two respects. Firstly, there is an elaborate system of intra-departmental appeals, with a de facto independence from ministerial influence and a flexibility not enjoyed by formal administrative courts.

Secondly, the Danes do not make the sharp distinction between ordinary and administrative law: 'The attitude of the Danish Courts towards a number of fundamental principles of administrative law have, over the last forty years, indirectly been influenced by the ideas underlying the jurisprudence of the *Conseil d'Etat*.'[49]

In the Danish case, one sees that the possibility of moving to a system of control based on administrative law is not inherently difficult, and Belgium Council of State was set up only in 1945. But the real issue is whether such controls are compatible with parliamentary and legal controls. The short answer from Sweden, which uses the full armoury, is that they are. In the final analysis, it is the independence of an administrative court which is in question; but there is little logic in recognizing the independence of the normal court system and yet not appreciating that the 'administration' is hardly a monolithic block. Critics of the adequacy of parliamentary methods as controls argue also that the major effect is a downgrading of public law, and Mitchell puts the case strongly: 'The question, quite bluntly, is whether we want to restore the place of law in government. That restoration demands a susceptible law and a susceptible body which administers that law, a body which at the same time is aware of the real needs of government and of the value of the individual. That is what, behind its technicality, *Droit Administratif* is about; it is what the Conseil d'Etat tries to be.'[50]

Behind the debate on the relative virtues of parliamentary and administrative forms of control is the fundamental issue of whether it is necessary to secure a 'political distance' between the agent and its control. One of the tenets of liberal democracy has always been of institutional separation and balance; yet we saw in our discussion of European consitutionalism that it is the internal checks which have been instrumental in fostering constitutional development. In a similar way, it can be argued that it is *within* the bureaucracy itself that some of the most powerful controls are to be found.

NOTES AND REFERENCES

1. A. D. de Lamothe, 'Ministerial Cabinets in France', *Public Administration*, Winter 1965, vol. 43 pp. 365–81.
2. B. Chapman, *The Profession of Government*, George Allen and Unwin, 1959, p. 26. This depersonalization of the state, 'encouraged a rapid growth in the field of public law.' Previously no clear distinction existed between public and private law.
3. H. Gerth and C. Wright Mills, *From Max Weber: Essays in Sociology*, Routledge and Kegan Paul, 1948, pp. 214–16.
4. H. Parris, 'The Origins of the Permanent Civil Service, 1780–1830', *Public Administration*, Summer 1968, vol. 46, pp. 143–66. (Also as the first chapter of *Constitutional Bureaucracy*, George Allen and Unwin, 1969.)
5. Parris, op. cit., p. 164.
6. Chapman, op. cit., p. 9.

7. V. Subramaniam, 'The Relative Status of Specialists and Generalists', *Public Administration*, Autumn 1968, vol. 46, pp. 331–40.

8. Parris, op. cit., particularly 'The case of the Treasury', pp. 161–3.

9. ibid., p. 151.

10. Quoted in the *Daily Telegraph*, 30th October 1970.

11. F. Heady, *Public Administration: A Comparative Perspective*, Englewood Cliffs, N. J.: Prentice-Hall, 1966, p. 46.

12. H. Daalder, 'Parties, Elites, and Political Developments in Western Europe', in J. LaPalombara and M. Weiner (eds.), *Political Parties and Political Development*, Princeton University Press, 1966, p. 60.

13. D. Coombes, *Towards a European Civil Service*, Chatham House; PEP, 1968, p. 59. This does *not* imply that civil servants are to be 'impartial' as between government and opposition.

14. On the characteristics of bureaucracy and their relation to the conditions of service, see R. Bendix, *Nation-Building and Citizenship*, New York: Wiley, 1964, pp. 107–15. We can summarize the essential aspects of Weber's view of 'bureaucracy': organization determined by rules, competence, and hierarchy; and the bureaucratic office is a 'vocation' based on special knowledge and training, with the office distinguished sharply from the incumbent.

15. F. Ridley and J. Blondel, *Public Administration in France*, Routledge and Kegan Paul, 1964, p. 59.

16. Chapman, op. cit., p. 107.

17. See F. F. Ridley (ed.). *Specialists and Generalists*, George Allen and Unwin, 1968, pp. 128–30.

18. R. Dahrendorf, *Society and Democracy in Germany*, Weidenfeld and Nicolson, 1968, p. 236.

19. Asa Briggs, *The Age of Improvement, 1783–1867*, Longmans, 1962, p. 443.

20. Quoted by T. B. Bottomore, *Elites and Society*, Penguin Books, 1966, p. 88.

21. N. Elder, *Government in Sweden: The Executive at Work*, Pergamon Press, 1970, p. 118. See also, J. Board, *The Government and Politics of Sweden*, Boston: Houghton Mifflin, 1970, pp. 164–7.

22. P. Avril, *Politics in France*, Penguin Books, 1969, pp. 206–7.

23. Dahrendorf, op. cit., p. 252

24. N. Kogan, *The Government of Italy*, New York: Thomas Crowell, 1962, p. 110.

25. See G. A. Almond and S. Verba, *The Civic Culture: Political Attitudes and Democracy in Five Countries*, Princeton University Press, 1963, pp. 106–14.

26. Gerth and Mills, op. cit., p. 232.

27. K. Mannheim, *Ideology and Utopia*, Routledge and Kegan Paul, 1960, p. 105.

28. G. Parry, *Political Elites*, George Allen and Unwin, 1969, p. 83.

29. J. Blondel, *An Introduction to Comparative Government*, Weidenfeld and Nicolson, 1969, p. 399.

30. Blondel, op. cit., p. 405.

31. ibid., p. 402.

32. See V. Subramaniam, 'Representative Bureaucracy: A Reassessment', *American Political Science Review*, December 1967, pp. 1010–19.

33. S. Andreski, *Elements of Comparative Sociology*, Weidenfeld and Nicolson, 1964, pp. 131–5.

34. Morris Janowitz in Jacques van Doorn (ed.), *Armed Forces and Society*, The Hague: Mouton, 1968, p. 25. The élite to which Janowitz refers was an aristocratic one.

35. C. B. Otley, 'Militarism and the Social Affiliations of the British Army Elite' in *Armed Forces and Society*, pp. 84–108. Otley gives a summary of class backgrounds of British, Dutch, German, Italian, and Swedish army élites.

36. S. Finer, *Comparative Government*, Allen Lane, 1970, p. 536. Finer distinguishes

four levels of political culture, of which two, the 'mature' and the 'developed' are relevant to European conditions. In 'Armed Forces and the Political Process', *Penguin
Survey of the Social Sciences,* Penguin Books, 1968, pp. 16–33, he relates the four
types to variations in per capita GNP; this shows an inverse relationship of the level
of GNP and the likelihood of a military coup.

37. J. Blondel, *An Introduction to Comparative Government,* op. cit., p. 417.
38. C. B. Otley, *Armed Forces and Society,* p. 107.
39. J. Blondel, op. cit., p. 421.
40. Dahrendorf, op. cit., p. 254.
41. Ludwig von Friedeburg, 'Rearmament and Social Change: Observations on Civil-
    Military Relations in Western Germany', in *Armed Forces and Society,* pp. 174–9.
42. The preceding argument is based on Kurt Lang, 'The Military Putsch in a
    Developed Political Culture: Confrontations of Military and Civil Power in Ger-
    many and France', in *Armed Forces and Society,* pp. 202–28.
43. See M. Janowitz, *The Professional Soldier: A Social and Political Portrait,* Collier-
    Macmillan, 1964, p. 418, for a discussion of the 'constabulary concept'.
44. B. Chapman, op. cit., p. 247.
45. G. Marshall, 'Parliament and the Ombudsman', in A. H. Hanson and B. Crick
    (eds.), *The Commons in Transition,* Fontana/Collins, 1970, p. 114. Marshall con-
    cludes, however, that the 'collective interventionism' of the Commissioner and the
    Select Committee is efficacious.
46. Marshall, op. cit., p. 123.
47. See Ridley and Blondel, op. cit., pp. 146–59, for an account of the judicial functions
    of the Conseil d'Etat.
48. J. Blondel, op. cit., p. 456.
49. I. M. Pedersen in D. C. Rowat (ed.), *The Ombudsman: Citizen's Defender,* George
    Allen and Unwin, 1968, p. 231.
50. J. D. B. Mitchell, 'The Real Argument about Administrative Law', *Public Ad-
    ministration,* Summer 1968, vol. 46, pp. 167–8.

Additional References

D. Allen, 'Ministers and Their Mandarins', *Government and Opposition,* Summer
1977.
W. G. Andrews (ed.), *European Political Institutions: A Comparative Government
Reader,* Princeton: Van Nostrand, 1966.
J. A. Armstrong, *The European Administrative Elite,* Princeton University Press,
1973.
J. Blondel, 'Types of Governmental Leadership in Atlantic Countries', *European Jour-
nal of Political Research,* 5/1, March 1977.
Sir R. Clarke, *New Trends in Government,* HMSO, 1971.
M. Crozier, *The Bureaucratic Phenomenon,* Tavistock Publications, 1964.
S. A. de Smith, *Judicial Review of Administrative Action,* Stevens (3rd ed.), 1973.
M. Dogan (ed.), *The New Mandarins of Western Europe: The Political Roles of Top
Civil Servants,* Sage Publications, 1976.
K. Dyson, *Party, State and Bureaucracy in Germany,* Sage, 1977.
H. Eulau and M. M. Czudnowski, *Elite Recruitment in Democratic Polities,* Sage
Publications, 1976.
R. Gregory and P. Hutchesson, *The Parliamentary Ombudsman,* George Allen and
Unwin, 1975.
B. Headey, *British Cabinet Ministers: The Roles of Politicians in Executive Office,*
Allen and Unwin, 1974.

M.-C. Kessler, 'Recruitment and Training of Higher Civil Servants in France: The *Ecole Nationale d'Administration*', *European Journal of Political Research*, 6/1, March 1978.

J. D. Kingsley, *Representative Bureaucracy*, Yellow Springs, Ohio: Antioch Press, 1944.

J. LaPalombara (ed.), *Bureaucracy and Political Development*, Princeton University Press, 1963.

B. Peters, *The Politics of Bureaucracy*, Longman, 1978.

R. Putnam, *The Comparative Study of Political Elites*, Prentice-Hall, 1976.

M. Rendel, *The Administrative Functions of the French Conseil d'Etat*, Weidenfeld and Nicolson, 1970.

F. F. Ridley (ed.), *Government and Administration in Europe*, Martin Robertson, 1979.

R. Rose, 'Models of Governing', *Comparative Politics*, 5/4, 1973.

D. C. Rowat (ed.), *The Ombudsman: Citizen's Defender*, George Allen and Unwin, 1968.

B. Schwartz, *French Administrative Law and the Common Law World*, New York University Press, 1954.

E. Searls, 'The Fragmented French Executive: Ministerial *Cabinets* in the Fifth French Republic', *West European Politics*, May 1978.

P. Self, *Administrative Theories and Politics*, George Allen and Unwin, 1973.

G. Smith, 'A Model of the Bureaucratic Culture', *Political Studies*, vol. XXII/I, March 1974.

J. Stanyer and B. Smith, *Administering Britain*, Martin Robertson, 1976.

E. N. Suleiman, *Politics, Power and the Bureaucracy in France*, Princeton University Press, 1973.

M. Walles and A. M. Hanson, *Governing Britain*, Fontana, 1978.

European Journal of Political Research, 'Political Elites in Europe', March 1978 (whole issue).

THE EUROPEAN MILITARY

J. S. Ambler, *The French Army in Politics*, Ohio State University Press, 1966.

F. L. Carsten, *The Reichswehr in Politics, 1918–1933*, Oxford University Press, 1966.

R. Fields, *The Portuguese Revolution and the Armed Forces Movement*, New York: Praeger, 1977.

W. Goerlitz, *History of the German General Staff 1657–1945*, Pall Mall Press, 1969.

G. Harries-Jenkins, 'Armed Forces in European Society' in S. Giner and M. Archer (eds.), *Contemporary Europe: Social Structures and Cultural Patterns*, Routledge, 1978.

G. Harries-Jenkins and J. van Doorn (eds.), *The Military and the Problem of Legitimacy*, Sage Publications, 1976.

S. P. Huntington (ed.), *Changing Patterns of Military Politics*, New York: The Free Press, 1962.

K. Medhurst, 'The Military and the Prospects for Spanish Democracy', *West European Politics*, 1/1, February 1978.

O. D. Menard, *The Army and the Fifth Republic*, University of Nebraska Press, 1967.

S. G. Payne, *Politics and the Military in Modern Spain*, Stanford University Press, 1967.

R. Porch, *The Portuguese Armed Forces and the Revolution*, Croom Helm, 1977.

D. B. Ralston (ed.), *Soldiers and States: Civil-Military Relations in Modern Europe*, Boston: D. C. Heath, 1966.

J. Wheeler-Bennett, *The Nemesis of Power: The German Army in Politics, 1918–1945*, Macmillan, 2nd ed., 1964.

9

The Local-Central Axis

The Territorial Dispersion of Power

OUR DISCUSSION in preceding chapters centred on the question of the dispersion of power, or alternatively its concentration, at the *national* level; these aspects are seen particularly in the nature of assembly-government relations and in the organization and control of central executive power, but the idea of 'balance' in the liberal democratic state permeates all political institutions. We should now see how this dispersion operates along the territorial axis and before looking in detail at the European arrangements governing central-local relations, appreciate some of the theoretical perspectives and contemporary pressures involved. To start with, it would be incorrect to regard the territorial dispersion of power as necessarily of a lower order than what can be achieved at a national level—nevertheless the former is usually regarded as a quite subordinate issue, often merely as an appendage of 'local government'.

The essential parity of the two forms has been demonstrated clearly by Arthur Maass.[1] He shows how all the major terms of a 'national', or as he terms it, a 'capital division of powers'—by process, function, and constituency—can be reproduced on a territorial level to give an 'areal division of powers'. The fact that it is at least feasible to construct a model of this kind in which power can be distributed territorially, makes it necessary to differentiate both between the various *levels* at which an areal dispersion is employed and between the *types* of dispersion used; taken together, these two give the characteristic features of any system of local-central relations. At the extremes, there will either be complete local autonomy or the wholly-centralized state, and Fesler points out the implications of both: 'Total decentralization would require the withering away of the state, whereas total centralization would imperil the state's capacity to perform its functions.'[2] It is not difficult to see why both should be true: 'complete' local autonomy would make it almost impossible to hold the state together when differences of interest arose; total centralization is likely to be an inefficient and expensive solution if all decisions have to be referred to the centre, and normally an unpalatable one for those who are so governed.

The question of levels we can best leave until we have examined the various types of dispersion possible. A first distinction is between powers granted on an 'original' or on a 'devolved' basis. By powers granted to an area on original terms, it is implied that its structure and functioning exist independently of the central government—most obviously they will be spelled out in the constitution, and in most cases will be beyond the immediate reach of the government of the day. These guarantees of local autonomy may possibly have originated with the state itself or simply be added later by constitutional amendment. Clearly, original powers are most closely associated with some form of federalism, but in principle it could apply to any level of areal distribution. Later, when we examine European federal systems, we shall see that the term 'federalism' covers at least two quite different concepts and that although both can be labelled 'original', in fact, one shades off towards a devolution.

Devolution of power may be no less far-reaching in its effect than an original allocation, but the cardinal difference is that it is a grant of power by the national political authorities and as such its continuance finally depends on its acceptability to these authorities, central government and national assembly; the area unit has no entrenched rights. The devolution of power also involves two distinct types of power distribution: 'deconcentration' and 'decentralization'. The *deconcentration* of power is a simple delegation of authority from one level of the administrative hierarchy to a lower one which is spatially remote from the centre. The delegation of such authority, which can take place at various levels, need not involve the use of marked discretionary power: the field services of the central government may be closely controlled in order to ensure a national uniformity. But where the central government maintains a single local personage as its representative, his powers of decision-making will often be very wide.

In contrast with the deconcentration of power, *decentralization* implies some measure of self-government, or at least of self-administration, for the local area; it represents a sub-division of the national state, a segmentary structure with the control of the segments resting on local constituencies. Obviously, there can be varying degrees of decentralization; at the minimum, local assemblies will be restricted to decisions on petty local matters, have few financial powers, and be quite unimportant in comparison with the central government's field agencies. And at a higher level, regional councils may have little more than advisory planning powers. However, at the maximum a whole range of government activity will be decentralized and large areas may enjoy what is virtually 'home-rule'. We can set out the requirements of a strong form of decentralization as follows:

1. *direct* election of representatives to a regional or provincial assembly;
2. control over the subordinate local government organs in the area;
3. a provincial executive authority responsible to the assembly;
4. an area administration under the control of the executive;
5. powers to finance activities in the region.

If none of these is granted by the national authority, then what emerges can be little more than an advisory council. However, even if only one of these requirements is met, the basis for an effective decentralization exists. The direct election of representatives is perhaps the critical ingredient, for as long as this element is absent, the legitimacy of a regional or equivalent body will remain incomplete; appointed or seconded members will owe their first loyalty elsewhere. This outline of decentralization will prove useful later when we come to examine regional structures in Europe—the status of Northern Ireland, regional experiments in Belgium, France, and Italy.

In practice, both government deconcentration and decentralization exist alongside one another. They may even pass each other by: if the functions allocated to the two types of dispersion are quite distinct, then local field administration of the central government service need bear no relation either to the structure or the areas of the decentralized organs; this parallelism can be described as a system of 'dual hierarchies'.* Alternatively, there can be a correspondence between the two so that not only are there similar areas for the field services and the decentralized government but the patterns of authority for the two hierarchies can be 'fused' at one or more points. The fusion may take place around a single figure or office, and this authority represents both the forces of deconcentration and decentralization. The two types, fused and dual, make for two quite distinctive patterns of local and regional government systems.[3] Contrast the institution of a state-appointed provincial governor or the prefect of a French department with the complete dualism which characterizes the British system.

From a consideration of the two main types of the areal distribution of power, original and devolved and their chief sub-types, we can turn to the number of levels to which power can be dispersed. Just as the arrangements at a national level are amenable to complex sub-division, so there is hardly any limit to the sub-divisions on a territorial basis. In practice, however, actual division keeps to a few, distinctive levels, not all of them represented in any one country; the full range of power distribution can be represented as:

1. Supranational authorities
2. National government
3. Federal state units
4. Regional government or administration
5. Upper-tier local government (province or district)
6. Intermediate government *administration*
7. Lower-tier local government (commune or municipality)
8. Sub-communal units (parish councils).

---

* See below, p. 225, for diagrams illustrating various types of hierarchy.

At one extreme, Switzerland has a very simple structure (virtually only 2, 3, and 7), whilst West Germany (with 1, 2, 3, 5, 6, and 7) has one of the widest spreads. Even within a country there is scope for variety with the main urban areas having the fewest levels—the city of Hamburg is a unit of local government and at the same time one of the component states of the Federal German Republic. And as already indicated, the same unit in a fused system combines decentralization and deconcentration. Four main levels can be taken for later comparison. At the highest level, that of supranational authority, some special considerations apply, but the territorial component is still present and supranationalism can provide the basis for some form of federal association; we shall look at the particular problems of political integration in the following chapter. The other three important levels: federalism, regionalism, and local government (5 and 7 above), all involve special considerations and are best treated separately in subsequent sections.

No one country's arrangements can really be put forward as exemplary and the range of possibilities open defeats a simple categorization. But beyond the practical difficulties there is an added complication, since the apparent dichotomy of 'central' and 'local' authority conceals the fact that the arguments for centralization are frequently of a *different order* from those favouring local power. Narrowly conceived, the argument could be one about 'local democracy' versus 'central efficiency'. Yet democracy, both in the sense of popular control and the dispersion of power, is compatible with a 'capital division of power' as well as its areal division. In turn, maximum administrative efficiency can only be attained by avoiding an undue concentration at the centre. Thus any move towards a central-local 'balance' is not necessarily the outcome of direct conflict between the two, and for this reason it is impossible to set up a particular areal division of power as a model. At the very least, account also has to be taken of the terms on which the capital division of powers operates.

A further twist is evident. The demand for local power, in the guise of 'freedom', may result in powerful local interests holding sway—and these will be directly opposed to the popular voice at the national level. The term 'efficiency' is also capable of holding different meanings. It can be interpreted in a purely static sense—current economy in the use of resources to achieve the goals of the community. However, one such widely-held goal is to secure the economic and social development of the nation, and this, according to Leemans, '... needs more than just efficiency; it also requires the promotion of active popular participation as well as the integration of governmental activities for the various geographical areas and governmental tasks ... In European countries, greater weight is generally given to democracy and efficiency; economic and social development is gaining ground.'[4] Whilst economy in supplying static services may require a high concentration of administrative resources and a minimum of duplication, the broad aim of 'development' may necessitate a measure of dispersal. Thus it can result that the dictates of democracy may be increasingly satisfied at the national level at the same time as the goals of the community indicate increased local power. From this it can be concluded that the apparently competing demands for 'efficiency', 'economic and social development', local 'freedom' and 'democracy' only partly impinge on one another; the realization of one aim does not necessarily imply the others—nor preclude them either. A broad band of central-local relations, representing various actual systems, will show how the various optima are combined; the location of any one system depends partly on the nature of the national balance attained as well as on the priorities of the particular society.

The European countries generally favour a unitary system of government in which power is devolved to area units; the powers, structures, functions, even the existence of these units are matters which ultimately are decided nationally. Nor is the drift of socio-economic forces particularly favourable to localist sentiment: nationwide markets, central planning, improved communications are accompanied by an increase in mobility from one part of a country to another and they lead to a growing social homogeneity. These are all factors which give a national focus to political life; the consciousness of being a Bavarian takes second place to the political line-up at Bonn. All the indications are that the urban-rural dichotomy is rapidly disappearing, and with it one of the main props of local loyalty. This process can be illustrated in the case of Finland, on many counts one of the lesser industrialized of West European countries; according to Allardt and Pesonen, 'Finnish society has become more and more homogeneous. A majority of the population still lives in what are administratively defined as rural communes, but the differences between "rural" and "urban" concepts are shrinking. . . . Geographical mobility, especially to urban areas is considerable: only one fourth of the present inhabitants of Helsinki or Tampere were born in their city, the majority being born in rural communes.'[5] Such changes in society are reinforced by the needs of government: the scope and depth of government intervention requires ambitious national planning and the deployment of a large number of centrally-organized services. Together, both social and governmental outlooks appear to be antithetical to the creation of strong, self-contained territorial units.

But the pointers are not all one way. The pace of economic and social change is the cause of sharp national imbalance with hardship resulting for certain areas. The threat of social dislocation, the knowledge of being in an economic backwater, leads to demands for a local say in decisions. Furthermore, the planning undertaken by the central authorities has to be related to the requirements of the sub-national areas; the idea of 'regionalism' is one response—a recognition that national planning is likely to be neither adequate nor acceptable if it is dictated entirely from the centre. Even at the periphery—at the level of local government—there are strong European traditions of local self-administration. Some of the extravagant claims for local democracy must be discounted, but the fact remains that local government in Western Europe has accumulated considerable expertise and prestige. The main 'crisis' of local government is seen as one of outmoded functions and areas; fundamental reform in these respects, possibly linked to new, higher-level structures, could have important long-term effects on the central-local balance. Before examining these possibilities, we should assess the importance of the federal idea as it is implemented in Austria, Germany, and Switzerland.

European Federalism

The distinguishing feature of a federal system is that the barriers which are erected against the intrusions of central government or national assembly are independent of their continued goodwill; neither the whims of the government of the day nor particular party constellations, nor even the continuing hold of local traditions are crucial factors for the survival of a federal state. Whilst it is true that their mainstay, the constitution, can be amended, the majorities needed may be very difficult to secure, and, as in the Federal German Republic, the constitution may stipulate that the federal system itself is beyond the reach of amendment. Yet there can be no absolute guarantees of original federal powers, since in the final analysis the territorial distribution of power runs up against the will and power of the national political authority, and the powers of constituent states are continually subject to erosion either by consent or by the tacit acceptance that the central government must assume certain responsibilities.

The conventional model of a 'pure' federal system requires three features to be present:

1. a clear specification of the powers of the states and of the federation, and also that the powers of the states should be significant ones;
2. supportive institutions (such as a constitutional court) in order to preserve the demarcation between the federation and the states;
3. a distribution and division of powers within the federal state so that, according to Wheare, '. . . the general and regional governments are each, within a sphere, co-ordinate and independent.'[6]

On such criteria, a 'strong' federal system will be seen as one in which the states exercise a wide range of powers quite independently of the federation with a whole gamut of institutional checks serving to keep the balance between the two—preventing the system flying apart or keeping the central government in its place. 'Weak' systems will be seen as those where the powers of either the federation or the states are excessively modest, where the supportive institutions lack an effective jurisdiction, and where the failure to secure powers for each level within a 'closed sphere' results in a lack of clear definition of responsibilities.

Insistence on the presence of all three features leads to the conclusion that if they are not, then the system is not only 'weak' but also that it is not 'genuine'. We shall be able to judge the suitability of one appellation or another to European systems in the course of relating the details of their arrangements, but we should appreciate first the defect of setting up one 'pure' federal model as the single standard of judgement. It may be that a variety of 'federal-type' solutions are of relevance to present-day problems of power distribution, rather than an archetype of mainly historical significance. It can be conceded directly that the European systems fail on the third requirement, since there is a considerable intermeshing of state and federal activity. In this respect they contrast considerably with the federal concept of the United States whose constitution was conceived in quite different circumstances.

G. F. Sawer, in dealing with the distinctive 'stages' through which federalism can pass, uses the terms 'co-ordinate', 'co-operative', and 'organic'.[7] The first of these conforms to the conditions we have already set out; the second, co-operative federalism, requires the states to have some 'bargaining capacity' in order that the joint authority exercised by the centre and the states should not hide a simple domination by the federation; in the third case, the organic type, the capacity to bargain is substantially lost, and, in effect, the states will become the administrative agents of the central government. At that point, one has to consider whether the guarantees of the federal structure and the extent of original powers are sufficient to warrant the federal label. An alternative description of the third stage is that of 'administrative federalism', since it draws attention to the essential nature of centre-state relationship, with total initiative really left to the federation, but the federal structure still preserved.

The three European federal systems are probably to be allocated to the third stage. Their main strength is in the character of the supportive institutions, and the states are losing, or have lost, their bargaining capacity. This is undoubtedly true for Austria, possibly for Switzerland, less certainly for West Germany. In all three, the powers of the national governments are very wide, leaving the component states only small areas of autonomy. But both the enforced co-operation and centralization are modified by the presence of supportive institutions, guarantees which make it difficult for the national governments to do as they please with the states.

Historically, the association of the Swiss cantons since 1291 is of importance, but for most of the time the links were external and confederal only. In its modern form the confederation draws directly on the experience of the United States, and the powers of the national government were fully determined as recently as 1874. The parallels with the

United States are in the legislative institutions: there is the same form of territorial representation—the upper house, the Council of States, represents the interests of the cantons and has coequal powers with the National Council which is elected on the basis of population. Express powers are granted to the federation (Switzerland remains a confederation in name only) and residual powers to the cantons. The Swiss federal government has a very long list of enumerated powers, and these have been supplemented by convention and constitutional amendment to give a strong centralist drift.

A major difference lies in the area of constitutional jurisdiction. We have seen earlier that the Federal Tribunal has no power to invalidate legislation, and that instead the referendum is used for this purpose.* It is a moot point whether this is an effective check. Obviously, where there are fundamental issues at stake, the referendum will provide a potent counterbalance, but on lesser issues the challenge may not be made, and the sum total of these over the years gives a centralist impulse. The impetus can be maintained by the ploys open to the federal government to avoid challenge by referendum—notably in the use of decrees (*arrêtés*) in place of 'laws' as the former escape by being declared 'urgent' or 'not universally binding'. This subterfuge has often been necessary in the field of finance, since although actual functions are weighted heavily in favour of the federation, the constitution divided the powers of taxation between the federation and cantons, and the financial powers of the federation have not been commensurate with its responsibilities. As a consequence, the federal government for long had to rely on makeshifts of 'once-for-all' and 'crisis' taxes, avoiding challenge on the grounds of urgency; only in recent years has the position been regularized by formal amendment to the constitution. As the national government has taken on greater responsibilities in economic policy and social welfare, so have the cantons looked to the centre for positive initiatives, while their own powers showed a relative decline.

The federal structure has worked well as a containing force because the federation has always avoided becoming a power set up against the interests of the cantons. If, as is alleged, a Swiss national is proud *not* to know the name of the president of the Confederation in the current year (the office is a rotating one from members of the Federal Council), this at least underlines the passive nature of federal government in popular thinking, even if this does not accord with reality. The terms on which the federal power can act 'nationally yet neutrally' have to be appreciated in historical, political, and constitutional senses. We have already referred to the consensual framework within which the social cleavages are contained—the religious and linguistic differences, and in the past the potential, and sometimes actual, conflicts among the cantons and between the classes. It is now true to say that these conflict sources have reached a

* See above, p. 120.

minimal point. It has helped that the lines of cleavage have overlapped, rarely giving a clear-cut division and a simple polarization. To this one has to add the determined lack of external involvement, a united front of non-entanglement. Swiss parochialism has helped to maintain her stability.

The political basis for the neutralization of the federal government stems from the permanent government coalition; this never-ending collegial caucus is made possible by the lack of full government responsibility to the Federal Assembly—an arrangement which serves to take much of the heat out of national politics; local issues tend to loom large and the voters (and parties) find much political stimulation within the cantons. The powers of the upper house, directly representing the cantons, and the use of the referendum also act to neutralize the centripetal tendencies of federation, and even if national government emerges as the prime force, all the factors we have mentioned help to ensure that it is never a sudden shift.

The actual powers of the cantons are relatively modest; any well-developed local government administration would be capable of handling the reserved powers, chiefly education, cultural affairs, and police. But that would considerably underestimate the true position. To the considerable financial powers of the individual cantons, one also has to add their wide *administrative* powers and responsibilities. The bureaucracy which serves the federal government is relatively small; by the nature of a federal system, it is not possible to proceed by a simple deconcentration of central government services. Instead, the services must be decentralized, and the bureaucracy thus becomes an integral part of each canton, with central control through powers of inspection. The cantons have a wide administrative competence, and it is this responsibility which continues to give the cantons a real base, with localist sentiments and constitutional guarantees acting as supports.

The idea of 'administrative' federalism is one that can usefully be applied to the Swiss system to distinguish it from strong 'co-ordinate' types. This is also true for West Germany, but there are several differences in other respects from Switzerland. The most important contrast is the lack of strong localist loyalties in present-day Germany. The federal system which was resurrected in 1949 owed as much to the influence of the United States, in her role as an occupying power, as to the precedents of the weak federalism of the Weimar Republic or that of Imperial Germany. The argument favoured by the United States was that since Nazi Germany had imposed a strictly unitary system, a federal form of democracy would be the best protection against an undesirable centralism. The Weimar system had been deliberately devised as a weak federal form—in order to escape the predominance that Prussia had enjoyed in the Bismarck period and later, a hegemony rather than federalism. One of the few, easy agreements reached by the wartime allies was that the Prussian state should not be recreated after

1945. The component parts of the Federal German Republic were put together from the three zones of occupation of the western allies, with the later addition of the Saar. Some of the states, such as Bavaria and the Hanseatic cities of Hamburg and Bremen, had historical sanction, others were virtually new creations. It was rather a hotch-potch with great variation in size from the small city-states to the mammoth North-Rhine Westphalia having some 30 per cent of the total population. Nor did the states have any option but to join—Bavarian separatist inclinations were ignored.

The sharing of powers between federation and states is complex. The Basic Law gives specified powers to the federation and the residue to the states (Länder). The residual powers are mainly concerned with cultural affairs—religion, education, and the mass media. But there is a further category of concurrent powers (including: nationalization, transport, nuclear energy, civil and criminal law) on which both the federation and the states are free to legislate, with the important qualification of Article 31 that, 'Federal law overrides Land law'. The Basic Law also gives another category of federal legislation, so-called 'framework laws', by which the general principles are laid down by the federal government and each Land is then free to fill in according to its own wishes by state legislation.

The idea of the framework law gives the keynote to German federalism, and there are other provisions which empower the federal government to delegate functions to the Länder, even where the powers belong exclusively to the federation. And the constitution explicitly makes the states the responsible agents for the execution of federal law. As in Switzerland, this gives them a strong administrative base and a wide executive competence. Similarly, the Länder have their own constitutionally-guaranteed sources of revenue (a range of indirect taxes plus inheritance taxes and an entrenched proportion of the income tax yield); however the federal government is better provided for than in Switzerland, and the federation has the power to equalize financial burdens between the richer and poorer Länder. A picture emerges of each Land with its own large civil service administering the bulk of the nation's internal affairs; each one with its own responsible government headed by a minister-president, its own court system and police force, considerable revenue, along with the full guarantees of a federal state.

These guarantees are provided by the presence of a constitutional court and the second chamber of the federal parliament, the Bundesrat. We have already seen that the Federal Constitutional Court, although a new creation, has wide powers of judicial review which also preserve the central-local balance. The Bundesrat provides a political balance, and it does this in a novel way by giving a direct representation to the *governments* of the states with some weighting according to their size. The Bundesrat has been described by Heidenheimer as, 'The only chamber in the world which is in effect a continuous congress of state (Land) ministers who vote in accordance with the instructions of their governments.'[8] This gives the state governments a powerful federal platform, a direct link to the federal authorities, and an opportunity to form a common front against incursions from the centre. And the governmental flavour of the Bundesrat is further underlined by the stipulation that all the members of a state delegation must vote the same way—of particular importance as Land governments are usually based on coalitions.

The powers of the West German Bundesrat are fewer than those of the Swiss Council of States. But it does have equal powers in some matters, over constitutional amendments and over proposals affecting the apportionment of tax revenues. In all other questions it has a qualified veto, which, depending on the size of the negative vote in the upper house, will require the Bundestag to override it with a simple or a two-thirds majority. A crisis over this blocking-power of the Bundesrat almost came to a head in the course of the legislation on the ratification of the treaties consequent upon Brandt's Ostpolitik in 1972.* The potential power of the Bundestrat to obstruct the policies of the federal government is undoubtedly great. In recent years the CDU-CSU opposition has had a majority in the Bundesrat, and this situation has often led to confrontation. The party line-up has been the operative factor rather than any real threat to the interests of the Länder governments. However, the usual emphasis is more on co-operation with the federal government; a large part of the work of the Bundesrat takes place in committee and in liaison with central government officials; moreover, civil servants from the Länder can deputize for their ministers in Bundesrat committees. Administrative solutions will be sought, not political confrontation, and the Bundesrat acts as a useful clearing-house.

Austrian federalism has superficial similarities with the West German, but in almost every respect it is weaker—in relation to the powers of the states and the supporting institutions. The present system is a revival of the one in operation during the inter-war years, and as in Germany there is little historical sanction for the constituent Länder. The nine states are on average far smaller than the corresponding ones in West Germany, and to a large extent they depend on financial aid from the federal government to perform their functions. Their original powers are few; only minor cultural and planning matters are reserved to the states, whilst the federation has all major police powers and control of the educational system, and the judicial system is completely federal.

Central controls are more powerful too: the federal government has a direct veto over many Land activities, including a financial veto, and the Länder are subject to central inspection and control in most of their activities as well as to the audit of the Central Accounting Office (*Oberster*

---

* See below, p. 281.

Rechnungshof), though this body is itself independent of the federal government. As in West Germany, the position of the states is guarded by a constitutional court, but there is less to protect, and historically the court has favoured the claims of the centre. The other supportive institution is the Bundesrat, but this body is very weak in comparison with its West German counterpart, a suspensory veto which can be overcome by a simple majority in the lower house, and its members are elected from the provincial assemblies on a party-proportional basis, so it is a party line-up in the Bundesrat, not the voice of the state governments.

At this modest level, one is entitled to ask whether a federal system is really in operation at all, to say that the trappings are there without the content. One might go even further and be tempted to relegate all three European federal states as 'weak' forms, perhaps with the additional comment that *all* forms of territorial pluralism represent a phase in a country's development, that in the long run the centripetal, national forces are too strong to be denied. Indeed, even where the powers of the states are firmly entrenched, the effect may be just to create an obstacle to a more rational re-allocation of powers and functions which is always possible in a unitary state. And with a continually changing socio-economic balance, it is desirable that a constant re-definition should take place. Even where federalism has some historical justification, the criterion of the success of the federal form often appears to be the extent to which it acts as a solvent on local loyalties, and the continued erosion of these is in the end resisted only by backward-looking localist parties, out of touch with the problems of a modern state.

Forceful as these arguments are, they probably rely too much on the 'co-ordinate' view, that it is pseudo-federalism unless the states have strong original powers, distinctive functions, and powerful supports. But the alternative model of 'administrative' federalism may be more relevant to developed societies, where the need to secure a decentralization of central government power is admitted on grounds of 'efficiency' as well as to secure economic and social development. The merit of administrative federalism is that it ensures a complete decentralization of the bureaucracy, not just its deconcentration, and usually in units large enough to be viable. Whilst it is possible to stop short of providing guarantees of this decentralization, their merit is that (whether by second house, constitutional court, or referendum) the local units are encouraged to preserve their identity. The effects of a wide measure of administrative decentralization are also apparent in the calibre of those who actively participate at the state level; recruitment from the ranks of those who have served in state assemblies and governments offer a broader base than is available in a unitary system, whilst service in local government only exceptionally provides this opportunity—Belgium is a good example. In spite of the national supremacy of two major parties in West Germany, experience in Land assemblies provides an alternative channel of recruitment for national political figures—three of the five post-war chancellors first rose to power at the Land level.

We shall be considering the problems of regionalism later, but the meeting-point between the 'weak' forms of federalism and this new level of decentralization is apparent. The contribution of the regional factor is simply that it makes the area of decentralization dependent on relevant socio-economic factors, not an accident of demarcation. The major contribution of the European type of federalism is the solution it provides to the problem of avoiding administrative concentration.

Government at the Grass Roots

At the level of local government, the picture of European systems can be presented as a choice between one of deconcentration allied to local government, typical of the 'fused' model, and the alternative of local self-administration in certain respects, quite divorced from the central government's field services, and giving a system of detached or 'dual' hierarchies. Despite the enormous number of individual variations, particularly with regard to the allocation of powers, both types of system work generally within a two-tier structure. Switzerland is the main exception, where the municipality is the only level below the canton; within individual countries, some urban areas are single tier, with the city acting as an all-purpose authority. Often the second, or upper, tier is the chief unit of government deconcentration, so that it is the commune or municipality—the lower, or first, tier—which is the real focus of local government.

The traditions of the commune are almost everywhere very strong, and as a consequence extremely resistant to change. For many states, the problem of adaptation to changing circumstances appears intractable, but others, notably England, Sweden and Denmark, have carried through fundamental reforms. The communes in most countries are often very small, but vary wildly in size, and whilst they are frequently regarded as quite inadequate units of government, they insist on their continuing indispensability. In Switzerland, there are some 3,000 municipalities, ranging from only fifty people to over half a million inhabitants, and their existence is guaranteed in the constitutions of several parent cantons. Local attachment is an integral part of the Swiss political structure: it was after all the small, valley municipalities of central Switzerland which formed the nucleus of the original confederation. Likewise in Belgium, the myths of the commune are exalted: 'A student of Belgian history finds that the equivalent of the Magna Carta or the Declaration of Independence was a document of the Middle Ages assuring that the rights of the communes would be respected.'[9]

France, with around 37,000 communes, probably has the greatest ratio of local government units to population; West Germany has some 24,000

Gemeinde, and the smaller countries have been 1,000 and 3,000 local units. This proliferation is not usually reproduced at the second tier level.
Here West Germany leads the field with over 400 *Kreise*, or districts, with
140 large towns and cities in addition functioning independently of the
second tier and designated as *kreisfrei* urban areas. This is quite exceptional, for France has only 95 departments and Italy 91 provinces; most
of the smaller states have around ten upper-tier authorities, though some
such as Sweden, have twenty or more. In general, the same argument is
held to apply, that the provinces are too small for modern government, but
there has been little attempt at regrouping at the second level, and where
this has occurred, in France, it has resulted in an additional 'regional' tier
without much affecting the old departmental format.

Root-and-branch reform of local government is a rarity, even where the
existing structure is patently inadequate; stop-gap devices are used: ad
hoc authorities are created, intercommunal co-operation encouraged, and
voluntary amalgamation made easier. The apparent inadequacy of the
small units arises from the greater number of services which local government is expected to provide, and the small units simply do not have the
financial or administrative resources. It also arises from the changing
patterns of settlement, particularly in the rapid growth of urban areas
which can make nonsense of time-honoured communal traditions.

We can trace three stages in the thinking about local government in its
rural and urban context. The first stage, at the origins of local government,
was the conception of parity, and this naturally resulted in the nation-wide
distribution of uniform communal government. With the growth of large
towns, the need for differential treatment became apparent—to encourage
the urban and preserve the rural—and resulted in the urban-rural
dichotomy; this is seen typically in the English county borough, divorced
from its partially-rural county hinterland, with a similar pattern in Germany (the *Kreisfrei* cities). The third, and current, stage is to reverse this
town-country split and to make the city the focal point for a large local
government area.

But a recognition of the implications of an urban society does not point
to any model applicable to all countries—as the concept of the 'city-
region' might imply. On the one hand there are the totally-urbanized and
very large conurbations in Western Europe (including always the capital
cities); these require a different treatment from the relatively isolated, but
large, towns with a considerable rural catchment area. In England, the
reforms enacted in 1972 have had the result that the large conurbations
(with some two-fifths of the total population) are served by two-tier
authorities. Outside the conurbations, the numerous county boroughs
were simply absorbed into the surrounding counties, although a two-tier
structure was preserved. In the latter case, city-regions did not result,
rather a lack of firm differentiation between town and country; only at the
communal level does the urban-rural distinction continue to exist.

The French solution to the problem of purely urban government has been to create a special category for the larger conurbations, the *communautés urbaines*, a new tier above the level of the existing commune. Much the same effect is obtained in West Germany by the setting-up of such bodies as the Greater Hanover Federation. Broadly then, as far as the cities are concerned, there are two types of solution; one involves the creation of specifically urban government, usually two-tier as with the Greater London Council, and with much extended boundaries; the alternative is to incorporate the cities as part of a larger urban-rural framework, with the city-region as one possibility. This has been the result of current reforms in England and it has a parallel in the process of *Wiedereinkreisung* in West Germany, a reincorporation of many towns into the *Kreis* structure. Such solutions are in most countries reached in a piecemeal manner, but the rapidity of urban growth puts on a pressure for general reform.

Sweden provides an example of drastic overhaul. Before 1962, the Swedish system was based on 2,500 lower-tier municipalities, varying greatly in population, and organized into twenty-four provinces (twenty-five with Stockholm which has the status of a province). The provinces were left intact, but the number of municipalities was drastically cut to 1,000. A further reform launched in 1964 planned to reduce this number to 262—a total reduction of almost 90 per cent on the original figure. The basis of the restructuring was the creation of viable *kommunblocks*, formed by the amalgamation of existing municipalities. As far as possible, the new communal blocks were devised so that each would have a minimum population (and we comment on the size of this minimum later) with sufficient tax resources, and various minimum figures were calculated for the economic provision of services. Finally, every communal block was to consist of a distinctive economic or geographic region, with a city or town to provide a natural centre. Although the criteria were laid down nationally, the implementation was left at the provincial level, co-ordinating the views of all the local units—for this reason the second reform was not planned as an overnight operation.

Similar far-reaching reforms were made in Denmark and came into effect in 1970. Previously she had one of the most outdated systems of local government in Europe. Although it had been a nominally two-tier structure, the communal authorities varied greatly in status and power, and for such a small and compact country a prolific number of them—about 1,000 rural and urban communes. The aim of the 1970 reforms was to secure a completely rationalized structure; the number of second-tier authorities was cut from twenty-five to fourteen and the communes to about a quarter of the original figure. The new authorities, all of comparable status and function, are based broadly on the city-region idea, with the obvious exception of Copenhagen.

These two examples tell us something of the likely emerging pattern for local government, especially at the communal level: increased size to ensure functional competence and an end to the rural-urban dichotomy. To some extent, these reforms can be regarded as no more than a *technical* matter: the retention of a two-tier structure points to the particular problems of spatial organization, with an upper level needed for wide planning and for the provision of services needing a large catchment area. The need for this upper tier in many countries is made greater by the requirements of central government, both as a unit for the deconcentration of government services and as a vantage point for the supervision and control of local government. The 'technical' argument for the lower tier is that as the size of the unit increases, so there are decreasing returns to scale beyond a certain point. The problem here is that 'decreasing returns' are particularly difficult to quantify; vague feelings of 'remoteness' may result in the serious under-use or even misuse of services. Thus, although in general terms it is clear that a two-tier structure can maximize economies of scale of two quite different orders, it is not so clear what the size of each should be, nor how the functions should be shared between them.

From the criteria of efficiency, we can turn to the other argument for the lower tier, that of territorial affiliation, the sense of belonging which a local community imparts. The problematic issue here is whether any local unit, but especially an urban one, even if vested with strong powers, will be able to encourage a sense of community. One measure of 'community feeling' may be the turnout at local elections. There are some interesting contrasts. Despite the large measure of local competence, highly-urbanized England shows low polling at local elections—about 40 per cent of the electorate voting—and compares unfavourably with most other countries. With compulsory attendance at the polling booth (though with no obligation to vote), the Netherlands has reached 90 per cent. Even without this degree of compulsion, high figures are the rule for other countries: Ireland 60, Germany 70, France 75, and Sweden 80 per cent. The British position is even less impressive when one considers the large number of seats that go uncontested, as a result of local one-party dominance.

It would be difficult to find any one convincing explanation for this disparity. It may be traced in part to the effects in Britain of the simple-majority system of voting, which on a *local* level favours one-party dominance and thus creates voting apathy. Another explanation could be that the very detachment of English local government from the central administration makes for a greater reliance on local élites, the presence of national parties notwithstanding; and this local élitism leads to an indifference on the part of the majority towards local politics. One also has to admit that there is a substantial difference in the idea of what a 'commune' stands for in fused systems. There is inevitably a closer connection with the central government; communal officials are public as well as local officials, since the commune is an expression of government deconcentration as well as of decentralization. Often the commune is treated (in theory) as having a *general* competence in law simply because it is a unit of public administration.

How sharply this view contrasts with the English position can be seen in a key sentence in the Redcliffe-Maud proposals for the reform of English local government: 'The only *duty* of the local councils would be to represent local opinion.'[10] Such 'no-power' councils were, in the event, rejected by the government in favour of a two-tier system with shared powers. The novelty of the Maud proposal that local councils, at the communal level, should act primarily as 'demand articulators' (though not precluded from exercising other functions delegated by the upper tier) draws attention to a polarity of views about the nature of local government. At the other extreme, the function of local government is seen as to encourage a maximum of local commitment and active responsibility for self-administration—seen in its ultimate form in the *Amtszwang* (duty to take office) which still obtains in some very small Swiss municipalities.

Anyway, if the 'voicing' of local opinion were to be the only major function of the commune, it is arguable that it could only succeed if a quite different range of machinery was available to voice demands effectively and to provide for adequate feedback. Neither the representative principle by itself nor the mounting of disguised public-relations exercises from a higher level is likely to achieve a strong community-effect. It is possible that other channels of communication can give a more realistic expression of communal views: the initiative, the referendum, the office of a local ombudsman.[11] This still leaves unresolved the question of how far the commune is a suitable unit for self-administration.

The 'suitability' of the commune as an administrative unit is related directly to the critical problem of size. And here we should look more closely at the argument that the efficiency of local government increases with the size of the unit, a view that larger units is the general panacea for the 'crisis' in local government. What stands out in contrast to prevalent British thinking, is the generally lower population-size acceptable as the basis for communal administration. The Redcliffe-Maud proposals for England envisaged a minimum population of 250,000 for the provision of all major services—far higher than that in most other countries outside their metropolitan areas. One only has to look at recent reforms in Scandinavia to appreciate the disparity in optimum size.[12] Thus the Swedish reforms, although drastically cutting the number of authorities, ended up with *kommunblock* groupings of around 8,000 population, and the Swedish changes were based on numerous investigations to determine an acceptable size for the provision of services. A comparable minimum was arrived at in Norway with the rationalization which took place in 1968, reducing the number of communes by a third. The large size of these countries and the scattered nature of the populations may invalidate anything but the crudest comparison; however, more-compact Denmark based the

1970 reform on a minimum population of 5,000. Nor should one forget the wide and general competence of most communal authorities. This is true for West Germany which 'manages' with a large number of both first and second-tier authorities—although a paring-down of these is now under way.

Few people would make a simplistic equation between size and 'efficiency', since efficiency has so many alternative criteria. The research studies carried out by the Redcliffe-Maud Commission failed to show a 'statistically demonstrable correlation' between population size and efficiency in terms of cost-effectiveness. And in his dissenting opinion Derek Senior concluded: 'The fact must be faced that no objective basis exists on which to attribute any material significance to population size as a factor in any way influencing the performance of existing major authorities'.[13] There are numerous ways in which the communal efficiency of relatively small communal populations can be enhanced: the potential of inter-communal co-operation, the widening of the financial tax base, a more generous interpretation of 'social' development, and, in fused systems, the possibility of government deconcentration to small local units, with a second tier providing a unit of co-ordination. Of course, it is precisely the flexibility of the 'tier' system which should be available to take account of low and high population for the requirements of different services. The over-ready acceptance of quantifiable scale-economies (with little attention paid to less quantifiable diseconomies) leads to mammoth second-tier authorities complemented by weakly 'community councils' at the communal level.

At various points we have touched on the relationship of local government to the central administration, particularly in the idea of fused and dual systems of administration,* and we can take this as one of several ways in which English local government differs from most others in Western Europe; to some extent the causes of these differences are related. The most obvious contrast is found in the English reliance on the tradition of 'government by committee'—indeed, 'government by, of and through committees'.[14] The committee system involves the local representatives as a body (not just a few of them and not just the party in a majority) with the work and decisions of the permanent executive personnel. This association is not an accidental feature, for it is a natural expression of the detached as opposed to the fused hierarchy—a total responsibility for the functions of local government borne by the council as a whole. A consequence of the committee system is that there can be no unified executive, either political or administrative, only the weak substitutes of a majority-party caucus and the town-clerk.

In other countries, the unified executive is the rule with the unification seen in one person who can come to office in various ways: direct popular

* See also the illustrations on p. 225.

election, election by the council, appointment by the council of a 'professional' administrator (e.g. the Irish 'manager'), appointment by the central government. The Länder in West Germany use all of these methods for their municipalities except the last; however, direct government appointment, especially at the upper-tier, is quite usual in many countries. Thus there is a contrast in the responsibility which the English system places in the council as a whole as against the vesting of this responsibility in a single individual where some degree of fusion exists—the prefect of a French department, the mayor of the commune.

A further major difference is in the absence of a *general* central government supervisory power in England. Central government ministers act individually in supervising the services provided by the local authorities which concern their departments, and the Department of the Environment has a co-ordinative and advisory rather than a directive function. The more usual practice is for a particular ministry to have strong regulative powers over local authorities, and this authority is usually underpinned by the presence of a government-appointed 'governor' or similar person at the provincial level. Even if the fusion is incomplete, some kind of government hierarchy is implied which at one point has to come to terms with the local representative system. An important result we have already noted: since the local-central antithesis is blurred, local authorities have wide powers, albeit under the umbrella of central government control. This wide local competence is evident for West Germany and to some extent for France, with an apparent difference in focus from that of British local government: 'The French approach to local government emphasizes the community to be administered, not the services to be run.'[15] The same wide powers are available in Sweden—the obverse of which is that the decisions of the local authority can be voided by the appeal of individual citizens to a higher organ, with the Supreme Administrative Court acting as the final arbiter.

The most complete expression of fused authority structures is found in the French prefectoral system. The departmental prefect, a career civil servant, stands at the meeting-point of central and local pressures. As an agent and representative of the central government, he has both general and particular responsibilities for government services in his department. He also becomes responsible for the quality of local government in his area, and almost as much the department's representative towards the central authorities as the other way round. But at no time is he responsible to the elected department council for his work; he wields his power on behalf of the central government, and his administrative and co-ordinative functions are considerable—a typical prefect will be expected to chair up to a hundred committees, a task which will be shared with the sub-prefects. The prefectoral apparatus becomes a ubiquitous feature of departmental life: 'The prefecture is a focus of power: it is a combination of local Whitehall and County Hall. The citizen of the French provinces

Dual Systems

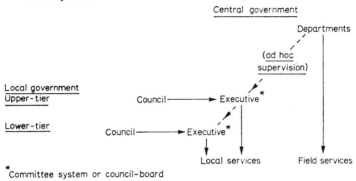

*Committee system or council-board

Fused Systems

Split Hierarchy Systems

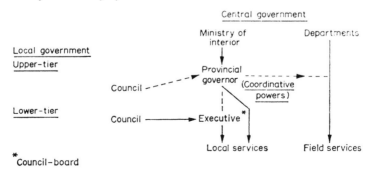

*Council-board

can look to the prefecture as a seat of government when in Britain he must look to London.'[16]

Yet the prefect is not a miniature Napoleon. Counterbalancing his power in relation to the departmental council—which can at best use budgetary sanctions—is the fact that the council contains political personalities, frequently members of the National Assembly. The council is a powerful expression of local interests, and the prefect will want to come to terms with them, for both he and they wish to further the interests of the department. Nor is the prefect in an all-powerful position with regard to the rest of the central administration located in his department since this largely exists as a result of the deconcentration to the level of field service on the part of various ministries. Thus in 1964 it had to be reasserted that, 'The Prefect, representing all the ministries is granted real and direct authority over all the heads of services operating in the department.'[17] At times, it becomes impossible to integrate satisfactorily government administration both horizontally and vertically at the departmental level. And the prefect has to contend with several aspects of central government: the various operating ministries, the Ministry of the Interior, and the Council of State. At the level of the commune, the fusion is only partly complete, but the prefect has wide powers over communal activity, and the mayor of the commune also personifies national authority; although he is elected by the local council, he cannot simply be dismissed by it. Historically, too, the post was originally an appointment made by the government.

The basis of this fused, prefectoral pattern is seen in a number of countries that have been influenced by France. In one of these, Italy, the system does not result in a high quality of administration or uniformly-adequate local government. The system is a replica of the French one with the main difference that at the upper level, the province, there is a form of dualism, that is, both a prefecture and a separate executive council, with a president, chosen by the provincial council. This arrangement proves to be an uneasy division of authority, with the prefect the more powerful of the two, and as Adams and Barile point out, able to intervene almost at will in the affairs of local government: 'The prefect's inclusive powers over the deliberations of the provincial and communal governments rests on the legal fiction that the local governments are purely administrative bodies and that as such all their acts, even the deliberations of the councils, are reversible by a higher administrative body, always on the grounds of illegality, and sometimes on their lack of merit.'[18] Italian local government appears to be under a system of tutelage with the prefect usually having to give positive approval to proposed local government measures.

Unlike the French arrangements, the Italian prefect appears to be more of a device set up against local government, though the degree of this opposition largely depends on the party-political composition of the local council; there is little antagonism between the two in Christian-Democratic strongholds, but it comes to a head where local government is in Communist hands. Paradoxically, the balance of forces which then obtains may result in better administration overall, since the chances of collusion are minimized which is certainly not so in areas where the prefect develops a *clientela* relationship* with the dominant Christian Democrats.

In countries such as Spain and Portugal, the absence hitherto of independent parties meant that the system went beyond a fusion towards a virtual deconcentration. At the communal level, the mayor was a government appointee and he had wide powers over the local council, and at the provincial level central government dominance was complete. As one moves northwards from France, so the position of the chief executive changes. In the Netherlands, the local burgomaster is still a career-official appointed by the central government, and a government commissioner heads each of the eleven provinces. But at both levels the official works alongside a board with executive powers, elected by the municipal or the provincial council. Formally, the same system applies in Belgium as well, but the established practice is for the council at the communal level to nominate its own executive head who is confirmed in office by the government.

The council-board system is prevalent in the Scandinavian countries, and at the lower tier a chairman is appointed by the council to head the board. At the provincial level, the picture is a mixed one, usually the governor is appointed by the government, but Sweden has recently opted to change this to having an elected representative. These modes of selection of the executive are a fair indication of the degree of fusion which is in operation. As a general rule, there is less fusion of the local and administrative hierarchies where appointment at both levels is in the hands of the local councils. But this rule should not be taken too far; the principle of fusion is quite compatible with a degree of local freedom in the appointment of a council executive. This is true for West Germany where administration at the local level makes little distinction between decentralization and deconcentration, and where the executive head (only rarely an appointment made by a Land government) enjoys a powerful position in relation to the elected board members, irrespective of how he comes to office.

These different traditions of local government have resulted in structures which are only partially comparable with one another; it would be very difficult to graft a single feature of any one on to the system used in another country without upsetting the whole balance. Nevertheless, what all West European countries face in common is the impact of urban development on local government. Whatever the balance of argument in respect of the size and functions of the first-tier units, and even the second, there is a common predicament of having to plan and develop over areas much larger than either. This need results in a higher level of administration

* See above, p. 59.

and possibly of self-government which can no longer be described as 'local', an awkward half-way house below national government, which in the idea of 'regionalism' has yet to find any definitive solutions.

Regionalism

As we use the term here, 'regionalism' is not put forward as a doctrine along with other 'isms', but an expression of two quite different sets of forces which meet at a regional level; one is an argument for greater decentralization of government involving an extension of local autonomy upwards; the other is an attempt to deconcentrate the machinery of central government, not so much for the day-to-day running of field services—although there are proven advantages in having large, standard areas to ensure interdepartmental co-ordination—but mainly in order to formulate and implement national economic planning. These two separate forces, democracy and administration, are not entirely divorced from one another: the need for a regional component in national planning is made pressing because serious regional imbalances are present, and it will be most probably the people in those areas which appear to be losing out in comparison with the economic growth enjoyed by others who will be in the vanguard with demands for a greater say in their own affairs.

The problem of uneven regional development affects almost every country to a greater or lesser degree, and it is not only a matter of a few peripheral areas being permanently in the doldrums, but also the rapidity with which the general process of urbanization is proceeding, and the regional differences this involves. Figures for the original six EEC countries are fairly representative of mainland Europe: 'The Community's farming population, which in 1958 accounted for 20 per cent and in 1967 for 15 per cent of the total population, will be down to 7 per cent by 1980.'[19] Behind the massive occupational shift, the net result of which will be a commensurate increase in the service sector with the industrial labour force on balance relatively unchanged, there will be an inevitable and rapid urban growth—left to itself, leaving some centres untouched with others acting as considerable magnets. As the European Economic Commission sees it, 'One of the aims of regional policy is to enable such urbanization to take place within the region, so as to avoid excessive migration and greater congestion in large cities.'[20]

These are essentially the problems of prosperity, and generally quite recent ones. The most deep-seated structural problems resulting in territorial extremes of wealth and poverty are to be found in France and Italy—the two states where regional ideas have been developed most. Both countries have been clearly split between the poor and the more prosperous parts. In France, the line of demarcation is from Le Havre, through Grenoble, and thence to Marseilles, with the whole area south and west of this line showing a higher proportion engaged in agriculture, with lower incomes, and a static or declining population. The disparities are now diminishing partly as a result of regional policies begun in the early 1950s. A similar problem affects the Italian *Mezzogiorno*, all of Italy south of Rome together with the islands of Sicily and Sardinia. There has for long been the contrast of endemic poverty in the Italian south with the prosperity and industrial growth in the north; the imbalance has been relieved by the high rate of southern emigration to the northern cities and abroad. Soon after the war, the South was singled out for special government assistance, but as in France, the areas involved are too vast to be called 'regional': the relatively impoverished areas both have the same proportion of population—about one third of the whole—and the malaise has affected a number of regions, all suffering from an identical blight.

We shall shortly consider the specific remedies adopted in these two countries; first we should look at the more general picture of regional solutions, whether of decentralization or of deconcentration. Regional decentralization requires that a number of important decisions should be taken by a representative body with a constituency based on the whole region. We have already outlined the requirements for strong decentralization,* and it will be apparent that these are rarely fulfilled in European forms of decentralization. The former structure of government for Northern Ireland is the best example—with some of the most deplorable results. In miniature, the government of Northern Ireland reproduced most of the functions of central government, except those which by definition fall outside the province of home-rule: defence and foreign affairs. The powers of the Stormont government were further limited in respect of control over foreign trade and exchange. Unlike the position in a federal state, all the enabling powers of the government of Northern Ireland stem from a statute of the British Parliament: the Government of Ireland Act of 1920 and subsequent British legislation. These powers can be amended or rescinded without the express consent of the Northern Ireland Stormont or Government: 'direct rule' from Westminster could be imposed at any time, as in fact occurred in March 1972. In all matters, save the essential constitutional position of Northern Ireland, there is only the right to be consulted. Under Section 1 of the Ireland Act of 1949, however, the British government is committed to obtain the consent of the Northern Ireland Parliament in any matter affecting Northern Ireland's status as an integral part of 'His Majesty's dominions and of the United Kingdom', thus precluding the unification of Ireland except on terms acceptable to the Protestant majority in Northern Ireland. Her economic weakness, plus the fact that the power of the British government is needed to guarantee a continued existence, always forces the authorities in Northern Ireland to lean heavily on the British government for support.

* See above, pp. 207–8.

In many ways the Northern Ireland government until 1972 acted as an administrative agent for the national government, routinely providing services similar to those for the rest of the United Kingdom, even if the authority for these requires separate legislative treatment. The resulting freedom of action may appear somewhat limited, but it is as well to bear in mind that the European federal systems do not amount to much more in practice—a great deal of the activity of the German Länder is concerned with administering federal laws, and the exercise of concurrent powers under the constitution, as well as the device of the 'framework' law, acts as a disguised form of devolution. Indeed, the government in Northern Ireland was in some ways stronger: its ability to use the Special Powers Act to restrict civil liberties went beyond what the government of a German Land could accomplish, and unlike the position in West Germany there is no protection of a constitutional court. In this respect, such an advanced form of government decentralization may result in greater 'freedom' (for the Protestant majority) but not a democratic consensus for all sections of the population—short of the imposition of 'direct rule', the minority in Northern Ireland might feel that it is the direct representation in the British Parliament which serves their interests better.

There is an understandable hesitancy on the part of central governments to engage in regional experiments of decentralization; only in circumstances of peculiar difficulty are they likely to concede very much in this direction. The Belgian example is a case in point; only when the rise of the linguistic parties had begun to threaten the cohesion of the party and political systems, did the major parties, themselves subject to internal pressures, make radical constitutional reforms to meet the demands of the two language communities, providing for regional cultural autonomy and economic decision-making.* The difficulty of making the constitutional changes, requiring a two-thirds majority in the Belgian Parliament, is counter-balanced by the fact that, now once secured, they are even more difficult to upset. The clear language frontier in Belgium makes the regions linguistically homogeneous and thus does not present an acute problem of having to redress the balance for minorities at the national level.

The strong forms of regional decentralization are exceptional, and we can postpone further discussion until we look at the Italian example. The weak forms are those which fail to meet any of the five conditions we have set out for effective decentralization. In this latter category fall the proposals for English local government envisaged by the Redcliffe-Maud Commission; these would involve setting up eight English provinces above the highest level of local government. However, they would be indirectly-elected from lower-level units, provide no services themselves, and would chiefly act as planning and consultative bodies. Even these modest moves to decentralization were shelved indefinitely.[21]

* See below, pp. 269–70.

The case against an extended regional decentralization of British government has been put by Sir Richard Clarke. Firstly, he argued that there is little popular demand for this; secondly, at least for England, it would be impossible to have units small enough for local identification, and yet sufficiently large for law-making and administration. His third argument concerns the provision of social services; these are geared naturally to the central government: 'Indeed, a change of system towards regional government would almost certainly be resisted by the poorer regions which would then have less scope for bringing pressure on central government to provide ad hoc support. There is no middle course in this area: either there is responsible regional government in the social services or there is not.'[22] Naturally, one would expect a leading figure in the British Civil Service to view the fragmentation of a unified and efficient service with some dismay, and the argument against the 'middle course' is parallel to the co-ordinate view of federalism, a particular view of power distribution, for which the 'administrative' type is an alternative.

A natural response of the central government to regional problems is to seek a measure of deconcentration of government services. Thus Scotland, in spite of its distinctive character and problems, has never been given a decentralized government form; instead, there has been a sporadic process of purely administrative devolution dating from the middle of the nineteenth century, and this dispersal has built up to the extent that, besides the Secretary of State for Scotland, there are a number of junior ministers concerned solely with Scottish affairs. They and the civil servants concerned administer certain services direct or with the appropriate local authorities. Since much of this activity takes place in Scotland, the extent of deconcentration is high. Yet the ministers are firmly part of the central government and the civil servants, although preponderantly Scottish, are members of a unified service. Similarly, British governments long held out against popular pressure for directly-elected assemblies for Scotland and Wales, but as one result of the report of the Royal Commission on the Constitution made in 1973, assemblies for both are to be established as part of a programme of devolution.[23] A more pressing reason for action was the large increase in support for the Scottish and Welsh national parties.

We can relate the discussion of government deconcentration to the earlier distinction made between 'fused' and 'dual' hierarchies of administration. The fused system combines elements of deconcentration and decentralization in the same office or area; the formula for building up a system of regions by grouping together a number of second-tier units, as has been the case in France, works well since the machinery of government administration is already articulated along these lines. Dual systems do not easily adapt to this type of regional deconcentration, and local government bodies will prefer to deal with the ministry direct rather than with an intervening layer of regional administrators—this the Scottish system of devolution avoids. Where matters of economic planning are involved, as distinct from the administration of services, the differences between fused and dual systems are not so marked. The regional components of a national plan require wide consultation. To this extent, the British 'Economic Planning Regions' enable a harmonious deliberation of government with an assortment of organized interests and local government organs.

It is quite different with the implementation of policies; for the fused systems, with or without regional level of administration, the co-ordination is partly ensured by the existence of a government representative standing in a direct and general relationship to local government. In dual systems, policy implementation requires either the creation of ad hoc agencies, or else each ministry separately carrying out its share of the agreed plan and dealing individually with the local authorities. The danger of a powerful regional administration is that it may lack flexibility—we have already seen the problems of co-ordination within the French department—and much will depend on the discretionary power the central government ministries are prepared to give the regional offices. Where they are considerable, a regional hierarchy makes sense, but if it just becomes a cumbersome intermediate apparatus, then the fragmentation associated with dual systems is likely to work better.

Our discussion of regionalism so far has made very little mention at all of the situation in France and Italy. Taken together, their experience provides a useful commentary on a number of the general points already considered, and in both a key concern is with balanced national development. The essence of French regionalism is that it is an integral part of national planning and administration, a deconcentration rather than decentralization.[24] Although French national planning got under way soon after the war, the early versions, such as the Monnet plan (1946–1953), were concerned with the modernization of industry rather than with social and regional development. Regional planning was only integrated with national planning as a consequence of the Third Plan (1958–1961) and the Fourth (1962–1965). Basic to the regional contribution was the creation of planning units larger than the existing departments. What finally resulted was a structure of twenty-one regions, grouping together from two to eight of the ninety-five administrative departments. Each region has its own prefect (usually the senior prefect of one of the constituent departments), and his task is to co-ordinate rather than to administer; to coordinate the regional aspects of the Plan he acts in liaison with two major bodies: a Regional Administrative Conference, consisting of the departmental prefects and the highest level government (field) representatives in the region, and a Regional Development Committee (CODER). The latter is a body specifically concerned with the articulation of local interests and is made up of local office-holders, representatives from industry, commerce, and the trade unions, plus a number of individually-nominated persons. It is not a decision-making body, but one which the regional prefect has to consult. At a less official level, there are also Regional Expansion Committees composed of local authorities and private interests.

How much of this intensive regional planning activity survives or is 'lost in the post' by the time the overall national Plan is promulgated is difficult to say because there are so many facets besides the regional problems: the constraints and uncertainties affecting the whole economy, the claims of particular industries, and so on; regional interests have to take their place in the queue, with the harmonization of claims occurring at the national level. The central planning machinery is also complex. Although the centrepiece is the Planning Commissariat, there are a large number of subordinate committees dealing with various sectors of the economy ('vertical'), and with broad economic considerations ('horizontal'); these have to coexist with the Economic and Social Council, a Planning Council (composed of leading establishment figures of the public and private sectors), and last, and probably least, with the National Assembly.

In this welter of consultation, bearing in mind that the implementation of the Plan is centrally-directed, regional aspirations become muted. The upshot of the Plan may be a series of cautious generalities. Thus the Sixth Plan (1971–1975) was described by President Pompidou as not amounting to a fixed intent, rather, 'It is an appreciation of our ambitions, our possibilities ... The Plan constitutes a solemn undertaking of the nation.'[25] Forecasting increases in the gross national product can be a political hazard, but despite the inevitable dilution of regional claims by the various constraints, their place in the total matrix is assured.

What is questionable is whether the planning apparatus alone can ever lead to a decentralization of government. The careful hierarchy of the planning process makes for equitable treatment; it may do little to increase local competence or awareness. The Sixth Plan aroused little national enthusiasm, even less on a local level. There is little in the regions to arouse solidarity, for, with the notable exceptions of Brittany and Alsace, they are mainly areas of administrative convenience. The total effect of regional planning may be to make the regions even more aware of their financial dependence on the central government, and the reality of 'regional politics' simply a technique for increasing the size of central government subsidy.

The proposed reforms of 1969, eventually defeated by referendum, took a tiny step towards decentralization. The projected regional councils would have had important powers in social and economic affairs, but no provision was made to give any regional autonomy in finance, and the councils were to be indirectly elected (parliamentary deputies of the region along with representatives of the departmental councils). The new regional councils would have resembled the departmental ones written a little larger, and still be faced by a regional prefect who held most of the strings. A general point to be made here is that traditions of a fused hierarchy are always a barrier to regional bodies achieving substantial power.

At first sight, the Italian creation of regional governments may be regarded as a much bolder move altogether, since they had their origin in the 1948 constitution, were set up by direct election, and they were never so enmeshed in the planning requirements of national government. Although the constitution provided all the necessary sanctions, only five regions came into being without delay and the full complement of twenty was not reached until 1970. Part of the reason for the long postponement was the unwillingness of the Christian Democratic government to have a number of left-wing regional governments sniping at its authority. The regions first set up all showed some cultural distinctiveness, besides being on the periphery: Val d'Aosta, Terentino-Alto Adige, Friuli-Venezia Giulia in the north, and the islands of Sardinia and Sicily. All had particular localist features, some were very small—one with a population of around 100,000, and were hardly representative of how regional government might develop over the whole country.

A reading of the constitutional provisions (Articles 114–133) does give some indication of their character, and they are modelled on the existing provices. The regional assembly elects an executive junta, headed by a president; there is also a regional commissioner representing the central government, a figure armed with powers similar to those of the prefect in respect of local government, especially over legislative activity. Although the constitution gives the regions power to levy taxes, regional administration is expected to remain skeletal, using local government for detailed administration. The regions do not have a permanent territorial status; new ones can be created by mergers proposed by local initiative and confirmed by referendum. The most important protection the regions have is the constitutional court; this helps to guaranteee their existence (to this extent the Italian regions come close to enjoying the guarantees of federalism); and the court also acts as arbiter when the central government has disallowed regional legislation or administrative actions.

Powers given to the regions by the constitution are not very great: control over agriculture and extractive industry, transport, tourism, police, housing, and education. More important have proved to be the planning powers as they have developed in Sardinia and Sicily, and their originating statutes gave them wider powers in this respect than were listed in the constitution. But the impetus has come just as much from the central government's own commitment to regional development and from its own resources and machinery set up to cope with the economic problems of the *Mezzogiorno*. Regional governments were in no position to become the spearheads of regional planning.

The principal agent of government policy is the *Cassa per il Mezzogiorno*[26]; this is a semi-autonomous public body charged with developing the public utilities and agriculture. Picturesquely described as a 'giant watering-can', the *Cassa*, by means of government funds and the raising of large loans, first injected money to build up the primary economy and later moved on to projects of direct industrialization. This latter development, a distinct shift from the original aim of securing the economic infrastructure, has meant that the *Cassa* became closely involved with local consortia—local authorities acting in conjunction with private interests—to finance key industrialization schemes. Regional governments have been able to play some part in this in Sardinia and Sicily as they do have their own financial powers, and by using discriminatory devices they can bring influence to bear on the private sector.

A curious relationship has developed between the regional (as well as the local) governments and the regional arm of the central government development agencies, for it is one which tends to bypass the normal administrative hierarchy, and it has led to a partnership in which the relatively weak local and regional government can benefit from the competent supervision of the *Cassa*, as well as from the free flow of funds. Such a body may be government deconcentration in disguise, but its operational freedom may show a greater compatibility with regional self-government.

These remarks apply with particular force to the *Mezzogiorno* as an area which is quite unable to lift itself by its own bootstraps. To the general poverty and the often-admitted weakness of local government, one has to add the lack of faith in private development alone being able to redress the balance with the north. It can be argued that the sheer magnitude of the problems in Sardinia and Sicily are likely to make the long-term importance of regional government much greater than in other areas with less cultural unity and with fewer pressing economic problems.

The rather different versions of 'regionalism' which have come about in France and Italy make it evident that the term is likely to continue to span a variety of structures. Some, notably the smaller countries and those with a federal system, are unlikely to develop strong regional forms; neither Denmark nor Sweden took the opportunity of introducing regional levels when they extensively remoulded their local government systems. In federal states, the existence of regional government would be anomalous, and the most to be expected is a rationalization of local government as is now proceeding in most West German Länder.[27] It is in the large, unitary states that the strongest case can be made for regional government, but, as the experience of Britain shows, the traditions of centralized administration run counter to a significant devolution of power.

The advantage of the unitary system is that areas of devolution are in principle quite flexible, whilst federal states face the problem that state boundaries are virtually immutable and can become an increasing hindrance to rational planning and cooperation. The most glaring example of this inadequacy is metropolitan New York. The fact that this conglomeration bestrides three separate states points to the need for a drastic solution, and a solution, extremely difficult to implement, would be to create a fifty-first state of the union.[28] In Europe, such problems may in the future cut across existing national boundaries; a current example is the Aachen-Liège-Maastricht triangle which involves three countries, but, with growing economic interdependence, the European states will find that the spatial problems of government are closely linked to others. Here we are approaching the supranational aspects of the subject of government power; it is in the concept of supranationality that ideas of 'deconcentration' and 'decentralization' have, so to speak, to be tilted on their heads, to give levels of concentration and centralization above the level of national government; to this question of political integration we can now turn.

NOTES AND REFERENCES

1. A Maass (ed.), *Area and Power: A Theory of Local Government*, Collier-Macmillan, 1959.
2. J. Fesler, 'Centralization and Decentralization', in *The International Encyclopedia of the Social Sciences*, Collier-Macmillan, 1968, vol. 2, p. 371.
3. The terminology of 'fused' and 'dual' hierarchies is used by A. F. Leemans, *Changing Patterns of Local Government*, The Hague: The International Union of Local Authorities, 1969, pp. 52–8. He also refers to 'split hierarchies'—those having some levels only concerned with government deconcentration, at others only local government.
4. ibid., pp. 24–5.
5. E. Allardt and P. Pesonen, 'Cleavages in Finnish Politics', in S. M. Lipset and S. Rokkan (eds.), *Party Systems and Voter Alignments: Cross-National Perspectives*, Collier-Macmillan, 1967, p. 333.
6. K. C. Wheare, *Federal Government*, Oxford University Press, 1953, p. 11.
7. G. F. Sawer, *Modern Federalism*, C. A. Watts, 1969, pp. 117–30.
8. A. J. Heidenheimer, *The Governments of Germany*, New York: Thomas Crowell, 1961, p. 119. The Bundesrat, as Heidenheimer points out, is a 'throwback' to an earlier form of princely representation.
9. G. L. Weil, *The Benelux Nations: The Politics of Small-Country Democracies*, New York: Holt, Rinehart and Winston, 1970, p. 77.
10. A recommendation of the *Royal Commission on Local Government*, (Redcliffe-Maud), HMSO, Command 4040, June 1969, vol. 1, para 5. For a rebuttal of the argument for single 'all-purpose' authorities, see Derek Senior's 'Memorandum of Dissent', published as volume 2.
11. In England, a 'local ombudsman' was established in 1974—The Commission for Local Government Administration. See, *Your Local Ombudsman*, Commission for Local Administration, 1975.
12. See I. B. Rees, *Government by Community*, Charles Knight, 1971, pp. 138–9.
13. *Royal Commission on Local Government, op. cit.*, vol. 2, para 268.
14. S. Humes and E. Martin, *The Structure of Local Government: A Comparative Survey of 81 Countries*, The Hague: The International Union of Local Authorities, 1969, p. 48.
15. F. Ridley and J. Blondel, *Public Administration in France*, Routledge and Kegan Paul, 1964, p. 100.
16. ibid., p. 93.
17. This was a government decree of 14th March 1964, quoted by M. Anderson, *Government in France: An Introduction to Executive Power*, Pergamon Press, 1970, p. 131.

18. J. C. Adams and P. Barile, *The Government of Republican Italy*, Boston: Houghton Mifflin, 1966, p. 117.

19. Hans von der Groeben, *Regional Policy in an Integrated Europe*, European Community Information, November 1969, p. 4.

20. idem.

21. One pertinent reason for not considering the establishment of English Provinces was that the government should await the report of the *Royal Commission on the Constitution* (Kilbrandon) which eventually appeared in 1973.

22. Sir R. Clarke, *New Trends in Government*, HMSO, 1971.

23. The Kilbrandon Report of 1973 (the Royal Commission on the Constitution) formed the basis for the specific government proposals made in November 1975: *Our Changing Democracy: Devolution to Scotland and Wales* (Command 6348). The proposals envisaged a large degree of devolution for domestic affairs, an elected assembly for Scotland and for Wales. But the failure of the 1979 referendum on the devolution plans effectively buried them—see page 314 below.

24. For a comparative treatment of national planning, see J. Hayward and M. Watson (eds.), *Planning, Politics and Public Policy: The British, French and Italian Experience*, Cambridge University Press, 1975.

25. Quoted in *The Times*, 29th April 1971.

26. For a detailed account of the operation of the *Cassa*, and an assessment of regional planning, see M. M. Watson, *Regional Development Policy and Administration in Italy*, Longmans, 1970.

27. West Germany local government reform centres on the amalgamation numbers of second-level *Kreis* units of which there are at present a very large number. This can be done by making use of the existing *Regierungsbezirke*. These are purely administrative districts, but can be adapted to an enlarged *Kreis* structure with a minimum of dislocation. However, a commission of inquiury has also examined the feasibility of restructuring the present Länder; eventually, this could lead either to amalgamation or at least the redrawing of certain Länder boundaries.

28. See P. Hall, *The World Cities*, Weidenfeld and Nicolson, 1966.

Additional References

K. J. Allen and M. C. Maclennan, *Regional Problems and Policies in France and Italy*, Allen and Unwin, 1971.

P. A. Allum and G. Amyot, 'Regionalism in Italy: Old Wine in New Bottles', *Parliamentary Affairs*, vol. XXIV, Winter 1970–1.

T. J. Anton, *Governing Greater Stockholm*, California University Press, 1974.

W. G. Andrews, 'The Politics of Regionalization in France', in M. O. Heisler (ed.), *Politics in Europe*, New York: David McKay, 1974.

D. Ashford, 'French Idealism and British Pragmatism: Financial Aspects of Local Government Reorganization', *Comparative Political Studies*, vol. 11/2, July 1978.

J. C. Banks, *Federal Britain? The Case for Regionalism*, Harrap, 1971.

V. Bognador, *Devolution*, Oxford University Press, 1979.

C. E. B. Brett, 'The Lessons of Devolution in Northern Ireland', *Political Quarterly*, vol. 41, no. 3, July–September 1970.

T. H. Caulcott and P. Mountfield, 'Decentralized Administration in Sweden', *Public Administration*, vol. 52, Spring 1974.

B. Chapman, *French Local Government*, George Allen and Unwin, 1953.

J. Cornford (ed.), *The Failure of the State: On the Distribution of Political and Economic Power in Europe*, Croom Helm, 1975.

T. Dalyell, *Devolution: The End of Britain?*, Jonathan Cape, 1977.

C. J. Davies, 'Comparative Local Government as a Field of Study', in *Studies in Com-

parative Local Government, (IULA) vol. 4, no. 2, Winter 1970 (bibliographical essay).

H. M. Drucker, 'Devolution and Corporatism', *Government and Opposition*, Summer 1977.

I. D. Duchacek, *Comparative Federalism*, New York: Holt, Rinehart and Winston, 1970.

G. Flämig, *Report on Regional Planning: A European Problem*, Strasbourg: The Council of Europe, 1968.

R. C. Fried, *The Italian Prefects: A Study in Administrative Politics*, New Haven: Yale University Press, 1963.

D. Green, 'The Seventh Plan—The Demise of French Planning?', *West European Politics*, February 1978.

N. Hansen, *French Regional Planning*, Edinburgh University Press, 1968.

A. J. Heidenheimer, H. Heclo, C. Adams, *Comparative Public Policy: The Politics of Social Choice in Europe and America*, Macmillan, 1976.

D. Hill, *Democratic Theory and Local Government*, George Allen and Unwin, 1974.

G. Ionescu, *Centripetal Politics*, Hart-Davis, MacGibbon, 1975.

M. Kolinsky (ed.), *Divided Loyalties: British Regional Assertion and European Integration*, Manchester University Press, 1978.

J. Lagroye and V. White (eds.), *Local Government in Britain and France*, Hutchinson, 1979.

J. LaPalombara, *Italy: the Politics of Planning*, New York: Syracuse University Press, 1966.

W. S. Livingston, *Federalism and Constitutional Change*, Oxford University Press, 1956.

H. Machin, *The Prefect in French Administration*, Croom Helm, 1977.

A. H. Marshall, *Local Government Administration Abroad, Report of the Maud Committee on the Management of Local Government*, vol. 4, HMSO, 1967.

Lord Redcliffe-Maud and B. Wood, *English Local Government Reformed*, Oxford University Press, 1974.

P. Richards, *The Reformed Local Government System*, Allen and Unwin, 1975.

F. F. Ridley, 'Integrated Decentralization: Models of the Prefectoral System', *Political Studies* vol. XXI/I, March 1973.

W. H. Riker, *Federalism: Origin, Operation, Significance*, Boston: Little, Brown, 1964.

R. Rose and D. W. Urwin, *Regional Differentiation and Political Unity in Western Nations*, Sage Publications, 1974.

L. Saville, *Regional Economic Development in Italy*, Edinburgh University Press, 1968.

G. F. Sawer, *Modern Federalism*, C. A. Watts, 1969.

L. J. Sharpe (ed.), *Decentralist Trends in Western Democracies*, Sage, 1979.

J. Stanger, *Understanding Local Government*, Martin Robertson, 1976.

S. Tarrow, *Between Center and Periphery: Grassroots Politicians in Italy and France*, Yale University Press, 1977.

10
Political Integration

Models of Integration

THE SPATIAL aspects of politics we considered in the preceding chapter in relation to national politics apply equally to political integration which cuts across existing national boundaries. From this point of view, the political development of Europe is of particular relevance. The broad sweep of European history from the Romans, through the eras of Charlemagne and Napoleon, to the twentieth century shows the continual potency of a European-wide concept. Yet at the same time Europe also has to be regarded as the home of the nation-state, each country jealous of its sovereignty, and unlikely to accept for long a unity imposed by force. The effect of these two opposed ideas has been to set up lasting tensions which the two 'world' wars of this century, equally to be thought of as European civil wars, only partially dispelled. Neither armed force nor national expansionism has brought about a unified Europe. The use of force to forge one Europe came to its ultimate expression in Hitler's attempt to impose his 'new order' on the European states. Since that time there has only been one anachronistic echo on the occasion of the French Army's Algerian rising: 'The paratroops will create the real Europe!'

This does not mean that the attempt to secure a unified Europe by coercion will never be made again, but that the present era is well-suited to negotiation and the use of reason. At least for Western Europe there have been various pressures at work in recent years acting towards a growing unity. Of these, the economic considerations have probably been uppermost: the need for the wider markets, the harnessing of investment potential, the desirable mobility of labour and capital—all of these make the boundaries and restrictions of the nation-state an increasing hindrance to the fulfilment of economic possibilities. Alternatively, the economic pressures can be viewed as a continuing crisis to which the process of 'capitalist internationalization' is a response, as Miliband sees it: 'The European Economic Community is one institutional expression of this phenomenon and represents an attempt to overcome within the context of capitalism one of its major "contradictions", namely the constantly more marked obsolescence of the nation-state as the basic unit of international life.'[1]

Seen only in this light, the success of economic partnerships, technical

239

co-operation, and political ventures is altogether unremarkable. And it can be further argued that remoteness of the new organizations established makes them far less amenable to popular pressures than are the individual governments of the countries concerned. Nevertheless, this may be offset by the heightened expectations which economic advance brings in its train. Popular demand to share in the benefits of growing material abundance could make the 'distributive state', and its supranational counterpart, a live object of political pressure. To achieve this, new political structures will have to come into being at the same time as old concepts of national sovereignty are abandoned and the apparatus of the nation-state is dismantled.

Considered from two aspects, the 'undoing' of the nation-state is particularly relevant to Western Europe. Here are concentrated a great proportion of the world's most advanced nations, but at the same time it is largely an assemblage of small and medium-sized states; the chequerboard of their boundaries is an impediment to economic rationalization. If for no other reason, the economic influences are likely to modify the national political structures, although, as we shall see in the following section, there have been other influences at work in Western Europe as well.

We should start by examining the meanings that can be attached to the term 'integration' and the alternative processes by which it can be achieved. Ultimately, full political integration involves the adoption of a common political authority, with similar structures and processes for all the previously independent states. Once achieved, there is a considerable political simplification, but whilst the development is still under way, the coexistence of authorities, and of more or less competitive structures, will lead to a more complex situation. This is especially true for Western Europe, since the form of integration which has emerged so far is still open-ended. At the other extreme, in the crude sense of 'primitive' integration—by conquest or imposed hegemony—the simplification can take place without any intermediate stages; integration is direct, structures and processes are laid down centrally, and the only delay is in securing a common loyalty to the new state form.

Any other mode of integration has to allow for an intermediate coexistence of authority. This duality raises a number of questions: How is the coexistence to be effected? Is the coexistence of authority to be based on a static or a changing balance? How far are the political authorities in a position to regulate the balance? What final political forms are likely to emerge?

To attempt an answer to these questions, we can first refer to the classic solution of securing integration by political means—the federal blueprint. Federalism is one example, and in some ways the most practicable, of securing full political union outright. It involves the immediate creation of a central political authority, a territorial dispersion of power, and a binding commitment to irrevocable union. The initial conception is necessarily static: on the one hand the right to secede must be denied, and on the other, the founding members cannot countenance an erosion of their stated powers from the word 'go'. Just the same, this territorial pluralism, even if conceived as a genuine balance, appears as a period of extended transition, within which national loyalties become paramount and the powers of the central authorities become decisive. At some point, the instruments used to secure a territorial power dispersion, although *formally* operating as was originally conceived, at length assume a secondary importance. Distinctions between such 'advanced' federal states and unitary ones can still be made, but the territorial aspects of the federal state lose out in the end to the national division of powers.

The leading feature of federalism, besides its detailed power arrangements, is the emphasis on a final idea of the political system. The strong alternative to this finality is not really a 'confederation' of states, because this requires the member states to be distinct entities, without any loss of sovereignty; it amounts to a series of treaty relationships amongst fully responsible states, and a purely instrumental, or even non-existent, authority at the centre. As with federalism, a confederation lays down a final political form.

The real alternative is a form of integration which does not detail the extent of integration nor carry a conception of the end-product—what is usually labelled a 'functional' solution. As this description implies, integration proceeds by the harmonizing of *particular* governmental structures and policies. In principle, it is never final, never total, but a steady aggregation; nor is the process of necessity overtly political. The harmonization can take place in a variety of social and economic sectors, and to a large extent leave the political structure of the nation-states apparently unaffected. At the minimal level, the functional form of integration can be defined as, 'a union with joint, but limited liability for a particular activity'.[2] But it is clear that this version given by Mitrany represents only a point of departure. One cannot remain long with the fiction that membership from one activity to another will vary at random: the nature of one partnership will affect later ones both with regard to membership and content. It is also more than probable that there will be preconditions at the outset, making some type of partnership desirable and some potential members unacceptable. And although the unions are 'limited', they do represent common goals—ones which at least must be consonant with the goals in the non-integrated sectors.

A new element is brought into play when political integration is defined by Calleo as, '. . . the process by which member states give up making key public policies independently and instead make them jointly within a supranational cadre or pass them on to a new supranational administration.'[3] Here one has the germ of a *general* political authority, extremely limited if the 'public policies' in question relate only to one sector, but with great potential if the supranational authority becomes multifunctional. Even here, however, the emphasis is on the coexistence of this new authority with the pre-existing ones of the nation-states. What is quite different from the federal version of coexistence is that the functional form avoids any head-on confrontation with the national political authorities; instead there will be a whole series of minor conflicts and compromises. And the 'confrontation' need never occur if the *final* political form is never given a specific rendering. Because the functional system of integration at no stage seeks a solution embracing, '... the totality of political responsibilities in the field of foreign policy or defence, nor looking to a federal super-state as its ultimate objective', the form of the system may remain open indefinitely.[4] An approximation to federalism might only emerge when political integration had become an established fact in many other ways; full political union could then resemble more a topping-out ceremony.

A third rendering of political integration gives an indication of what these 'other ways' might be. Ernst Haas defines it as, '... the process whereby political actors in several distinct national settings are persuaded to shift their loyalties, expectations and political activities towards a new centre, whose institutions possess or demand jurisdiction over pre-existing national states.'[5] This version of integration extends the meaning considerably, away from an exclusive focus on institutions to the people involved, and it underlines what is particularly true for functional integration that the required change in behaviour and attitudes will be gradual, an assimilation to the new centre. In sum, there is a dual development which is interconnected: the modification of behaviour goes together with the building-up of new, supranational institutions.

The questions we posed originally about the coexistence of authority in the intermediate stages of integration appear to be partly answered. Functional integration allows for coexistence, since it does not set up new, general political authorities, but allows for a gradual redistribution of authority, in effect, a sector-by-sector approach. There is a continually changing balance, and the 'final' political form, although still nominally open, is related to how this balance evolves.

The question that remains to be answered is: How far are the political authorities in the member states in a position to regulate the balance? This can be put in other ways: Does functional integration have a dynamic of its own, or can a limit to further integration be imposed? Is the undermining of their sovereignty inevitable? Functional integration is certainly not irreversible, even if it does generate its own dynamic. To use the analogy made by Walter Hallstein, at one time the leading exponent of the Community viewpoint within the Commission, integration is like riding a bicycle: the choice is simply between going forward or falling off.[6] One can accept that at any point an individual government can cry 'halt', and only if coercive pressure exists at the centre can a member state be forced to remain within the fold; yet the nature of functional integration precludes the setting-up of a general coercive power so that basic freedom of action is preserved right up to the point of declared political union.

Less radically, a goverment may attempt to put a stop to further integration—by veto, non-co-operation, the 'empty chair'. Such possibilities are not eliminated by the majority voting, since the attempt to apply a majority verdict to disputed policies can prove too costly; the consensual element is vital as long as governments cannot be coerced. Thus a cut-off point can be dictated by individual governments, and this resistance can hold up the *formal* process of integration indefinitely. But at a more fundamental level the development may continue unchecked; in particular, as we have just seen, it depends on the attitudes and behaviour of *all* political participants, not only those operating at the top level of decision-making, and at the informal, social levels they may not be readily amenable to government influence.

There are two other factors which serve to make functional integration progressive. The first of these has been termed the 'spillover' effect; that is, integration in one sector encourages a like process in similar or related sectors. For example, the implementation of common economic and trade policies may lead to a demand for definite social safeguards; social provisions will be made, and it will be desirable to have a common policy in all member states. The second factor is the 'enmeshing' of the activities of *parallel* institutions in the participating states. Such institutions may be private agencies or ones of government; there will be increasingly close relations between opposite numbers in particular integrated fields, and as new developments take place these relations will be strengthened. Patterns of initiation and response are formed which go beyond a simple co-operation towards a permanent relationship.

These two effects are supplemented by a third—the creation of supranational cadres; no significant degree of integration could take place without the provision for personnel to administer the integrated sectors. And once these officials are appointed they will tend to develop a loyalty to the organization rather than to the states of their origin, at least with regard to their own area of work. This development is a first sign of a political will emerging within the supranational organization.

We can conclude that there is an independent dynamic of integration; with the cumulative effect of this movement, it is realistic to admit that at some stage a point of no-return will be reached. When and how this would be determined is problematic. One view is that it would be unlikely to occur through the mere accumulation of institutions, but the resolution of the issue would depend on a combination of institutional development, plus the onset of a particular economic or political crisis which would either cement or fragment the system. In this crisis there would be a test of the most fundamental index of integration, of loyalties.

This view, that 'crisis-cum-institution' will in the end mark the transference from sovereign nation-state to a new super-state, is only one possibility. Thus it can be argued that the widespread 'need' to have a recognizable national sovereignty—typical of the era of the nation-state—may lead to fallacious ideas of sovereignty when it is placed in the context of functional integration: the vision of Western Europe one day emerging as a kind of super-state can be regarded as a simple extension of the nation-state syndrome. Both nationalism and the nation-state were functional to the growth of industrial society, but is it necessary to look for an equivalent in 'post-industrial' society? It could equally be the case that the transition to advanced capitalism requires the muting of strong national attachments; if this were so, then the final unit of integration could emerge quite unlike existing state forms, neither explicitly claiming sovereignty, nor requiring strong political attachments.

Even if it is maintained that the final unit would have to acquire state-like qualities if it were to survive in a world of other states, there is still an alternative argument that the co-existence of two types of authority, national and supranational, need not reach a crisis-point. It is simply that member governments find it increasingly difficult to act independently—even in those areas which are wholly within their own province. The power of these implied limitations, a form of 'seepage' which runs from the integrated to the non-integrated areas, is that governments see that it is in their own interests to act in common. Earlier commitments are likely to induce common attitudes and interests *in advance* of the question of the non-integrated areas being raised, the more so if this process operates over an extended period of time. Thus the assertion of sovereignty, though always feasible, need never become a live issue.

This general discussion of political integration can now be related to the actual developments that have taken place within Western Europe. Before we look at the practical implications of the functional model, as seen in the European Community, it is helpful to look at the background to European integration—in the eyes of the idealists and the realists.

European Perspectives

That Western Europe does form a recognizable entity has been an assumption underlying all the comparisons we have so far made in this book, and it is further shown by the increasing cohesion shown by many of the states since 1945; the central question concerning us here is the political form which is likely to result. A number of alternative models is available, all with a relevance for the not-too-distant future. Is a new Europe to be basically a 'Europe of States', conveniently sheltering behind an umbrella of association? Or is it to emerge as a tightly-knit federal union? Again, is the political basis likely to be a direct expression of democratic will, or rather the apparatus of a remote and manipulative bureaucracy? And whatever form it takes, is a new Europe to be identified as a world force or one preoccupied with its own backyard? Answers to

these questions lead to radically different views as to what integration
could mean in practice. But important as the questions are, they do not admit of simple and direct answers. An assessment has to take into account
a range of factors: the general drift of West European development in recent years, the weight of formal integration so far achieved, the basic compatibility of the nation-states, and the degree to which a common political
culture is a necessary ingredient.

The outcome of the Second World War was important in two respects.
It was a turning-point for Western Europe, now relegated to a secondary
place in world affairs; the new global balance between the Soviet Union
and the United States made the one concerned with Western Europe as
extended frontier to be sealed off, and the other interested to secure
Western Europe as a political and military ally. A second, and related
effect was to bring about an equality of power *within* the area; there was
no West European 'victor' able to impose its hegemony or willing to give
decisive leadership to the other states. Both developments made European
statesmen aware of their subordinate position in world politics; some saw
that their main hope of self-assertion, even survival, lay in making collective approaches.

This is one strand in the reorientation; there are two others which serve
to give a more rounded picture. At one extreme there was the vision of a
united Europe on the part of idealists. From their point of view the new
equality after 1945 presented an unrivalled opportunity to achieve full
political union, a federal system of government. This union would at last
give expression to the 'European Idea', the institutional realization of a
common European culture. For the idealists political integration was the
culminating step in an age-old mission, but for realists at the other extreme
it was the third strand in the reorientation which was conclusive: that the
needs of advanced capitalism made the old political boundaries outmoded; the real advances towards integration would only be secured by
economic imperatives. We do not necessarily have to choose between
these competing versions. None of the three favours the nation-state as a
suitable vehicle for future development, and the strength of the movement
towards European integration lies in the fact that at different times each of
these diverse motives has preserved the initial momentum.

This momentum can be traced ultimately to the critical rapprochement
between France and Germany; without this scarcely any permanent advance could have been made, and from it has resulted the most tangible set
of integrated institutions. It is worth reviewing the terms on which reconciliation came about. The lever was undoubtedly the shift in allied, chiefly
American, policy towards the western zones of occupied Germany from
1946 onwards—a shift occasioned by the complete rupture of the western
allies from the Soviet Union. Later than her allies, who early on began to
appreciate the cost to themselves of a permanently weakened Germany,
the French government slowly began a reversal of the historic policy of

reparation and annexation: the economic fusion of the Saar with France soon after the war was still in the classic mould of Franco-German relations. Given the history of these relations between the two countries, this policy was understandable. Its reversal was dramatic, but it did not mean an abandonment of French aims. The point of the new strategy of reconciliation which French governments began to pursue was made crystal-clear by the Socialist, André Philip: 'The only way to ensure that a new Germany shall not dominate Europe is to see that Europe dominates the Ruhr'[7]—a Europeanization of the 'German Problem'.

The efforts made by the United States to secure a rehabilitation of Germany were at first economic, but the political and military implications soon became apparent; full statehood for West Germany meant that her willing participation could only be achieved if she were an equal partner. But this change would only be accomplished if it were on terms with both French and German thinking. To successive French governments the postwar instability of France and weakness of her economy appeared to be more immediate dangers than those from a weakened and truncated Germany. A planned reconciliation could give economic and political benefits outweighing transient gains of a continued and solitary reprisal.

At first sight, West Germany might appear as simply the passive object of policies laid down by the western allies—forced willy-nilly to accept their definition of European realities. But from 1949 onwards an increasingly independent German voice had to be taken into account; the German electorate had a choice between two leaders whose policies were opposed, Kurt Schumacher and Konrad Adenauer. For Schumacher, the Social Democrat leader—never able to achieve power—a West German government should *prove* itself to be independent of the occupiers, and follow a policy directly aimed at German reunification. For Adenauer, in power for the whole of the critical period, the considerations were different. As he was a Rhinelander and a Catholic, one can possibly doubt the strength of his commitment to a reunified Germany. It can be said that, in effect, he practised a separatism for the whole of West Germany in a fashion parallel to the separatism he had briefly supported for the Rhineland after the First World War. His decision to side unequivocally with the western powers brought the taunt from Schumacher that he was 'the chancellor of the allies'; on this view he forfeited the remote possibility of reunification which a neutralist policy would have offered.

One of the first fruits of the Franco-German accord was the Schuman Plan put forward by the French government in May 1950 to pool European coal and steel production under the control of a supranational authority. In the words of its sponsor, it was designed 'to end Franco-German hostility once and for all'. The 1951 treaty setting up the European Coal and Steel Community (ECSC) was specifically designed, according to Schuman, '. . . to enable Germany to accept restrictions on her own sovereignty which is gradually being restored to her.'[8] Thus the High

Authority of the ECSC served to replace the more direct supervision exercised by the Allied High Commission in Germany. It would be a mistake to see the ECSC in these instrumental terms alone, as only concerned with the regulation of basic production and representing a disguised 'occupation' of Germany. With its nucleus of six states, it was to be a model for later integration, and was then the first step of an open-ended 'jump into Europe'.

The ECSC was a strange amalgam of idealism, hard-headed calculation of economic benefit, and an attempt to gain strategic security— precisely the three strands of reorientation we noted earlier. But it was hardly a manifestation of a popular mandate, rather an attempt to forge European unity 'by stealth'—especially on the part of the idealists who saw that their first attempts to secure outright political unity were unlikely to get off the ground. Later developments were to show that supranational devices could be advocated too far in advance of national acceptability. The Pleven Plan, put forward in October 1950, aimed to create a European Army, with an eventual extension to a 'Political Community' as well, and it foundered on just these national susceptibilities. The main proposal in the Pleven Plan for a European Defence Community—a military equivalent of the ECSC—would have solved the dilemma of securing German military participation without the embarrassment of a German national army, but it was eventually rejected by the French National Assembly in 1954.

This failure apart, the ECSC proved to be the successful prototype for the technical co-operation of 'Euratom' (1956), and in the multi-functional European Economic Community (1957). There was a threefold link between the Communities: a common membership, the structural solutions arrived at, and the underlying purpose of securing ever-wider integration. But the smooth evolution in organization and areas of competence was matched by the continuing problem of creating a purposive *political* instrument from this supranationalism; the 'community approach' which was successful in functional terms was not the means to secure a rapid political unity. It was a disillusion for the idealists, but not for the governments or the economic interests concerned.

If the original six EEC countries represented an 'inner ring' of successful functional integration, the larger number outside this ring was made up of states for which these tight commitments were for long unacceptable, and these countries preferred looser alliances such as the European Free Trade Association and the Nordic Council, with strictly limited aims and no supranational authority. Even in a modified way such organizations, together with military treaties and the setting-up of various intergovernmental bodies, also have some passive integrative effect; attitudes and behaviour are affected by this limited co-operation, and the co-operation can be seen as a prelude to a later, and more explicit, integration of the 'outer ring'. The reasons for many countries being unwilling or unable to take on additional commitments were various: traditional policies of 'neutrality' in the case of Sweden and Switzerland, the delicate international position of Austria and Finland, the political unacceptability of Greece, Portugal, and Spain. For the United Kingdom it was the strength of her other commitments which made for hesitation. Denmark and Ireland were contingently affected by British reluctance because of their dependence on trade with Britain.

With such a mixed-bag of political viewpoints, it was little wonder that the original landmark—some would say the graveyard—of political unity, the Council of Europe, proved a failure. At the time it was founded, in 1949, the Council promised to be a strong unifying influence. Its wide membership of ultimately eighteen countries gave it a truly European representation and as many points of view. Its constitution meant that it could never become a decision-making body. The Consultative Assembly, composed of members from the national parliaments, has no mandatory powers; and the Committee of Ministers, representing the member governments, can only proceed on a unanimous basis; the veto of a single member can always block a substantive proposal.

Faced with this impasse, it is tempting to write off the Council of Europe as little more than a supranational debating society. This would be to neglect two contributions. The first is the large number of conventions which the Council has sponsored, later to be ratified by the member countries; most spectacularly these have included the Convention on Human Rights and the European Social Charter; later the emphasis changed to the study of a number of detailed projects under the general heading of inter-governmental 'Work Programmes'. With some sixty specialized committees, some idea of the range of interest of the Council can be gauged. The second contribution links directly to this: the Council acts as a sounding-board for informed opinion; whilst its popular appeal is almost nil, the Council of Europe operates at the level of parliamentarians, civil servants, and governments. It is this function of communication which it has to pursue, not that of formal integration: 'How ridiculous to ask the Committee of Ministers . . . to set up international political authorities, when almost half of those ministers have stated quite formally that they are not in favour of this.'[9] Thus complained Paul Henri Spaak, 'Mr Europe', after one frustrating year as President of the Consultative Assembly. It soon became clear that one had to look to the European Economic Community for the development of formal integration.

Political Features of the European Community

On one level, the institutional structure of the Community is relatively straightforward, on another, in terms of its future evolution, it represents a complex of possibilities. We can first set out the basic institutional arrangements and then take account of some of the imponderables. The keynote principle is that of supranationalism, by which a permanent executive body exists, independent of the member states, and able to take a range of decisions on its own account. This feature is integral to the 'Community Method' which David Coombes defines as: 'A process of unification by which "supranational" institutions, acting initially within limited sectors, are expected to have wide-ranging effects on political behaviour and by this means to provide an impetus for growing political union.'[10] It entails, 'progress towards political unity by integrating one sector at a time'; the Community Method is an extremely subtle instrument because it combines a pragmatism in determining the nature and the timing of the sectors to be integrated with an overall strategy contained in the cumulative effect of sector integration.

In one area after another substantial developments have taken place. Fundamentally, the creation of a single free market affects policy in a number of related spheres: in transport, capital and labour movement, regional development, and ultimately in general economic management and monetary policy. At the same time, there has to be a harmonization of law and of social policy. In some of these respects common policies are still only tentative, but once the hurdle of securing a managed market in agriculture had been passed, all the essentials of an Economic Community were established. And to this has to be added the effect of the pre-existing 'Communities' in Euratom and the ECSC, now effectively merged with the EEC. The Community in the 1970s therefore stood at a new stage of development in which higher questions of economic policy became matters of supranational concern. The 1970 report of the Werner Committee, in tackling the issue of economic and monetary union in the EEC, envisaged, rather prematurely, that an increasing number of cardinal economic decisions would be taken at Community level: budget formulation, taxation, and monetary policies. The conclusion reached by the committee was that this centripetal tendency had, '. . . a fundamental political significance, and implies the progressive development of political union. The economic and monetary union, therefore, has to be seen as a generator for the development of a political union . . . Political and monetary union are an irreversible process.'[11] Such implications extend outside the economic sphere to a possible third stage—the harmonization of defence policies and of foreign affairs. Thus the Davignon Report proposed twice-yearly consultations between the foreign ministers of the member states, with more frequent meetings of senior officials, and a logical step was to set up permanent Community machinery in these areas.[12]

The political framework consists of four main institutions: a European Parliament, a permanent executive Commission, the Council of Ministers, and a Court of Justice. Our analysis will be concerned with the first three as they share an active political function. Of the three, the European Parliament has hitherto been the weakest, in effect a consultative body. Its one sanction, by a two-thirds majority, is to enforce the resignation of the thirteen members of the Commission en bloc, a nuclear weapon too vast to be of practical importance, and an unreal one as Parliament has no complementary power of appointment to the Commission. Actual powers are limited to debating the annual report of the Commission, suggesting amendments to the Community budget (though these are not mandatory), making detailed studies of particular topics in specialist committees, and questioning individual members of the Commission in the area of their responsibility. Until the direct elections of 1979 the members of the European Parliament were seconded from their national assemblies—underlining parliamentary impotence: 'Nobody is going to get worked up over debates which have no outcome conducted by non-elected nominees.'[13] Inevitably, 'political union' involved grasping the nettles of direct election *and* the powers of the European Parliament. As a consultative body it did not carry more effective weight than the numerous specialized committees, nominated by the member governments, which advise the Commission on various aspects of policy. Amongst these are the Economic and Social Committee, flanked by ones concerned with monetary policy, short and medium-term economic policy, budgetary questions, transport, scientific and technical matters, and agriculture. Their expert nature gives them a considerable weight with the Commission, and at the highest level they correspond to a form of functional representation with which even the reformed parliamentary body will have to compete.

The permanent Commission is a hybrid of administrative and political competences. Coombes summarized its main functions as threefold:[14]

1. Initiation of Community legislation. The Commission makes policy proposals to the Council of Ministers. The Council can only make amendments by unanimous vote; otherwise the Commission proposal has to be accepted or rejected. This procedure ensures that thorough negotiation takes place before proposals are laid on the table.
2. A 'mediating' function. This aspect follows directly from the first: the need to negotiate at a sub-ministerial level to iron out the differences of interest amongst the member states.
3. Implementation of Community legislation. Once policy has been agreed, the Commission can take consequent 'Decisions' and make 'Regulations'—both important forms of delegated legislation. In cases of breach of Community law, the Commission can intervene and if necessary refer the case to the Court of Justice.

To these can be added the technical and advisory functions of the Commission, generally that it acts to co-ordinate the actions of member states in particular fields, and the Commission's status as the diplomatic representative of the Community.

Behind all these functions lies the theme that the Commission represents the 'conscience' of the Community, serving its interests rather than those of any member states. This infusion, quite apart from the political powers, distinguishes the Commission from a normal bureaucracy. Members of the Commission are appointed for a four year, renewable term by agreement amongst the member governments, and with a regard for national balance. But they are in no way subordinate to the governments—Commission members are explicitly barred from taking outside instructions. Nor do they seek anonymity; on the contrary, they are expected to emerge as figures in their own right, and in this respect the calibre of Commission personnel has been noteworthy, not only because it has included a proportion of committed 'Europeans', but individual members are frequently important political or administrative figures in their home country. Beneath this collegiate body is the administrative and research staff of the various Community projects, some ten thousand in all, seven thousand of these forming the central bureaucracy.

The Council of Ministers (usually composed of the foreign ministers of the member states) remains the basic decision-making body of the Community. It provides the locus of sovereignty, since the Council is not responsible to any Community institution; its members are only answerable to their own governments. Whilst majority voting is the rule, weighted according to the size of state, in practice unanimity has to be secured on any matter which a single country defines as fundamental to its interests. The working relationship between the Commission and the Council of Ministers is maintained by the Council's subordinate offshoot, 'Coreper', the Committee of Permanent Representatives. Formally, this is not a decision-making organ, but because the Council only meets infrequently, and anyway changes composition according to the subject under consideration, the Committee will make a number of recommendations many of which the Council will later approve 'on the nod'. The importance of these government nominees (civil servants, diplomats, and 'experts') on Coreper is seen in that, 'They are not only their countries' representatives in Brussels but also in a sense the Community's representatives in their own capitals. As almost all committee business passes through their hands, they are in a position to bring influence not only on each other but also on their governments and on the European Commission.'[15] The Committee of Permanent Representatives thus makes for a continuity, and possibly for a homogeneity as well, which the Council of Ministers by itself could not impart. Coreper represents a real centre of power, and with some justice it can be said that this is the true location of the 'technocrats' and not the Commission.

This general outline of Community institutions is sufficient as a basis for comparison with national institutions, and it is apparent that none of the three main organs has an exact equivalent at national level. Popular representation was for long absent, the Commission is more than a civil service but less than a government, the Council of Ministers is neither a government nor really a legislature. Above all, there is the almost complete lack of *reciprocal controls*, and this deficiency is aggravated by the blurred division of legislative responsibility between Council and Commission. Finally, Coreper occupies a shadowy, if strategic, halfway house between the two, exercising functions which nominally belong to the others.

Some institutional parallels can be drawn, most obviously with the two federal states, West Germany and Switzerland. Thus the German Bundesrat can be linkened to the Council of Ministers: both consist of essentially governmental delegations, acting in a legislative capacity and with a power of veto (individual ministers in the case of the Council, but the body as a whole in the case of the Bundesrat). But there the similarity ends, for the Bundesrat faces a federal goverment with considerable powers of its own, which the Bundesrat can only marginally affect, and the federal government is also politically responsible to an elected body, the Bundestag. The European Commission, if for the moment it is likened to the federal government, lacks this connection with the European Parliament, and the latter, in turn has lacked it with the electorate.

Another parallel can be drawn with the Swiss Federal Council; in some ways it shows a resemblance to the Commission: this is seen in the collegial nature of both and the guaranteed terms of office, as well as in the fact that the Federal Council, like the Commission, lacks the normal attributes of a parliamentary executive—this is shown by the 'qualified' responsibility which governs its existence. In its permanence, the Swiss system of federal government comes nearest to what one might term an administrative form of democracy, and thus has some likeness to the Commission. The missing requirement here is that the personnel of the Commission do not emanate from the European Parliament, either as a source of recruitment or in the actual mode of appointment.

Problems of Development

The conclusion must be that the institutions of the Community, compared with what has evolved on a national level, are still inadequate to bear the weight of extended *political* integration. That judgement does not imply any breakdown: a tailing-off in the rate of sector integration and a fall in demand for new political institutions could well leave the system functioning for an indefinite period. The increase in the number of Community members from the original six to nine in 1973 with the accession of Britain, Denmark and Ireland (ten with Greece in 1981) and with the probability of Spain and Portugal joining later, creates continuous and long-term problems of adjustment so that radical changes of institutional structure may be shelved—especially since the unanimous agreement of member governments is required. However, we can examine some of the issues raised by 'development'.

The specific demand for the direct election of the European Parliament, as provided for in the original Treaty of Rome, has now been met. Obviously the new Parliament will not be content with a consultative role. But what direction should it take? The assembly may strengthen its control powers at the same time as 'legitimating' the Community as a whole. In Hallstein's view the Parliament should 'dramatize and popularize the great decisions'[16]—with the implication that this function was the prime one. But such a dramatization would work only if the assembly were really *linked* to the decision-making process. Any parallel with the *actual* weakness of national parliaments is misleading, for they have an historical legitimacy, a live relationship to their executives, informal controls, party discipline, a common legislative-executive recruitment. In future the European Parliament will necessarily seek real powers in two areas: political responsibility and financial controls.

The vexed question of political responsibility can be shunted around in various ways. The obvious solution of having the European Commission solely responsible to Parliament would have an immediate impact on the power of the Council of Ministers. This implication is quite unacceptable to some governments, and Georges Pompidou argued for a totally opposed solution, claiming that executive power should rest with state-appointed European ministers rather than with an 'independent' Commission. Only in the 'final' phase might such ministers, '. . . have nothing but strictly European duties and no longer be a part of a national government', and only *then* would it be necessary to have a strong European Parliament.[17] Explicit here is the mistrust of both a strong Commission and a popular assembly—not surprisingly the Commission and the European Parliament are often regarded as in alliance for a more 'European' solution than governments will countenance.

However the question of political responsibility is solved or just left unanswered, the role of the Commission remains ambiguous. Coombes regarded its particular functions as coming under two general and opposed heads: *promotive* functions, requiring normative judgements and powers of initiative, and an *implementative* function involving pure administration and neutral mediation.[18] These roles tend to be mutually exclusive; emphasis on more active promotion weakens its bureaucratic tendencies, and when the latter predominate, the Commission will be unable to maintain a political stance. There are phases when one or other has been to the fore, but one can argue that there is also a long-term shift from the promotive to the implementative, a loss of political momentum which could only be restored to the Commission by a substantial redefinition of Community institutions in which direct elections were only a first token.

At present the 'dialogue' between the Commission and Council may still appear to be formally on the basis of equality, but the reality is seen differently: 'For several years the Council has been eroding the Commission's powers, reducing its proposals to preliminary drafts which the Permanent Representatives re-examine and re-shape before passing them to the Council for final approval.' The strategic power of Coreper is well in evidence. That Altiero Spinelli who made this diagnosis and who wrote as a member of the Commission was unhappy with this shift is apparent: 'The time has come to end this political downgrading. It is the Commission's duty to consult the Permanent Representatives among other bodies before submitting its proposals, and its right to withdraw them for modification if the Council is not prepared to accept them. But the proposal must remain permanently in the Commission's hands, and it is on its proposal that the Council must vote in the last instance.'[19]

The troubles of the Commission can be traced to the fact that it exists in a political vacuum, a result of the 'failure' to settle the question of securing political responsibility. The other matter, that of securing financial controls is just as intractable, but concerns the Assembly not the Commission. Historically, the power of financial control has been central to the evolution of parliamentary institutions, but the scope for this in the Community arrangements is limited.

It is difficult to see how the European Parliament could extend its financial authority without upsetting the whole Community system. The vast sums collected by the member states and paid into Community funds are largely earmarked in advance for established support schemes—chiefly farming subsidies which account for some three-quarters of the Community's budget—and those schemes can only be altered by inter-government agreement. With important national interests at stake—as with the Common Agricultural Policy—it is hard to visualize member governments conceding authority to the European Parliament. Even though the aim of the present arrangement was partly to make the Community financially independent—giving permanent sources of revenue rather than contributions from the member states—the result has been to impart an inertia to the system. The Community budget has to be agreed by the Council of Ministers and the scope for intervention by the European Parliament is limited. It does have the power, by a two-thirds vote, to reject the entire draft of an annual budget and request a re-submission, but that right is mainly of symbolic value. Parliament also has direct control of a small part of the Community's budget (relating mainly to administration and information services) and use of the European Court of Auditors to scrutinize Community revenues and expenditure. But since the question of political responsibility remains unresolved, the gobbets of financial power given to the European Parliament are lacking in real substance: a ritual dance of 'blustering confrontation' results which does not affect the substance of inter-governmental agreement.

Much depends on the nature of the evolving *European* party system—on whether the idea of 'transnational' parties has substantial meaning.[20] Any assessment will have to depend on the experience of two or more directly-elected European Parliaments,* but it is clear that any transnational party is affected by its double basis of loyalty: national interest and party interest. Those two interests do not necessarily coincide, and resort to majoritarian decision-making and discipline within a party group would be an invitation to fragmentation. Yet unless the transnational parties can develop supranational qualities, the ability of the European Parliament to assert its authority over the other Community institutions will always founder on the assertion of national interest. Paradoxically, however, if any one 'European' party—conservative or socialist, say—did emerge as dominant in the Parliament, then *national* governments of a different political persuasion would be all the more concerned to resist parliamentary encroachments on their authority. The potential of the various cross-currents make it evident that precise parallels with existing party systems, and the terms of their evolution, are not to be drawn.

There are other problems of Community development. One source of unease is associated with the bureaucratic and possibly 'illiberal' tendencies of the Community which may in part result from the political weakness of the Commission and Parliament. An expression of the 'bureaucratization' process is seen in panacea of creating a 'harmony' of regulation throughout the Community—a 'harmonization madness' as Ralf Dahrendorf has called it. Dahrendorf saw the underlying fault in the original conception of the 'First Europe', with its predeliction for supranational solutions. Thus whilst still a member of the Commission he wrote: 'No one talks any more about the beginnings of a European Government ... As long as not much was being decided on a European level the member states tolerated the fiction ... But to the extent to which European matters have become more important to the member states, the states have withdrawn decisions from the Commission or have arranged for them to be taken elsewhere ... The illogical route (to securing political unity) which many wanted to follow has led us into a dead end ... Only the peasants are left as proof that Europe exists'.[21]

The germs of a more realistic 'Second Europe' were seen by Dahrendorf to reside in the growing emphasis on 'international' rather than supranational integration. This shift was made evident in the Davignon 'formula' which proposed more effective cooperation between the *member governments* especially in the important non-integrated sectors of foreign relations and defence. Dahrendorf favoured an explicit emphasis on 'European' ministers representing the individual states as the best way to proceed in creating the Second Europe, a conception not far removed

* For the results of the European elections held in June 1979, see p. 261.

from Pompidou's view of a desirable evolution. Moreover, the enlarge-
ment of the Community has made it even more important to coordinate
the policies of governments and to carry all members along in the establishment of clear priorities for the Community.

One indication of the preference for inter-governmental initiative is the
procedure that has been adopted for regular 'summit' meetings of the
heads of government which take place twice a year in the various capital
cities. These 'European Council' meetings (in addition to the frequent
meetings of foreign ministers and others of a more specialized competence)
are significant in giving the Community a political profile besides acting as a
springboard for new approaches to integration.

There is a fundamental conflict between the supranational approach
and the inter-governmental alternative, for inevitably the Council of
Ministers is strengthened and the Commission is relegated to an instrumental role. Nevertheless, the success of a more 'logical' process of integration brings with it the need for permanent implementation, and some
of the objectives, for instance the commitment to 'political and monetary
union' as first set out by the Werner Committee, could only in the initial
stages be entrusted to inter-governmental agreement. Yet the actual
machinery set up to implement new policies may or may not enhance the
Commission's role; it is conceivable that various ad hoc arrangements
will be devised, such as the European Monetary System of 1979, to
avoid a concentration of authority within the permanent Commission
which otherwise might become a monstrously blown-up 'substitute'
government.

One indication of an alternative route was given in a special report
presented by the Commission in June 1975; in essence the Commission
proposed the creation of an 'independent' European government—that is,
independent of the governments of the member states. In effect such a
body would amount to a fusion of the Commission and the Council of
Ministers since it would combine the policy and executive functions of
both. A parallel report adopted by the European Parliament called for 'a
single decision-making centre which has the character of a real European
government'. Both sets of proposals assumed a directly-elected
assembly—to which any such 'decision-making centre' would ultimately
have to be responsible. Although neither report can be treated as more
than an adumbration of possibilities, both show an inclination to set up
entirely new institutions. Any substantial development, however, would
have to take the commitment to political and monetary union 'by 1980'
as the *beginning* of an extended stage of transition during which any new
body would have to co-exist with the existing Council of Ministers, a
directly-elected assembly, and the Commission as well.[22]

A European Political Culture?

At the present time the whole political structure of the Community still resembles a delicate piece of tracery rather than the product of powerful social forces: 'One day much bigger political and social forces will inevitably appear on the stage of European unification than are to be found there today. . . but so far they are still absent.'[23] It is the hiatus between the facts of integration and the orientation of social forces which provides the main imponderable for the future. Once these are marshalled, a new dynamic will be at work; they remain the missing parts of the jigsaw.

Yet one could hardly expect to see the pressing of popular demands and expressions of solidarity to come about before there were adequate means for them to be articulated and aggregated; and they require a definite focus for activity. So far, the Community has attracted interest group attention on a consultative basis—over three hundred such groups operate in Brussels. The first 'popular' manifestation may have been in March 1971 when some 80,000 farmers converged on Brussels in a violent demonstration over the Community's agricultural pricing policies. Conceivably, this was an advance indication that Community politics were entering the mass era.

Apart from such outbursts, a necessary step towards a new era of 'European' politics would be the reorientation of national institutions. A natural shift in interest representation is to be expected; without further ado these will gravitate to new decision-making centres, although their best approach is still to lobby the member governments. Other institutions are less mobile: the parties are geared to certain channels of action, the formal decision-making process, and bound by their own national traditions and concerns. Only direct elections from a *single* European-wide constituency would really throw the parties in the European Parliament into a melting-pot. They have developed a number of transnational federations: the Confederation of Socialist Parties, the Federation of Liberal and Democratic Parties (ELD), the Christian Democratic European People's Party (EPP)—together with the wider European Democratic Union (EDU) which in addition to the Christian Democrats brings in the British Conservatives. The Communists on the other hand have rejected any such formal ties on the grounds that they are artificial and have purely an electioneering value. It remains to be seen how far the commitments to common policies and European election programmes develop beyond a loose cooperative intent. It is interesting that those parties espousing 'working-class solidarity' have been the least inclined to subordinate themselves to a federal party.

Even if this transfer to a European scene of operations were to be a prolonged process, the underlying compatibility of the institutions is not really in question. It applies to the political parties, and their history is one of commitment to the institutions of liberal democracy and to the parliamentary system. Alongside these major uniformities, individual variations appear insignificant. Differences are real in such aspects as the form of legal system, the role of a civil servant, the detailed means of controlling executive power, but these are particular flavours, political styles, not evidence of different political values.

Institutional modification is only one aspect of the refashioning of political cultures which 'integration' implies. In the definition we took earlier from Haas, its full expression requires that 'expectations and political activities' would shift to a new centre, and the same applies to the other ingredient he includes, namely the 'loyalties'. As the centres of power change, we can expect that the direction of political activities and expectations will shift along with the modification of institutions, but the question of 'loyalties' is more difficult to evaluate. There are two related problems: Are the new loyalties a necessary constituent of the type of integration which is now taking place in Europe? Is there a likelihood of a loyalty emerging with a distinctive European colouring?

We have already seen that the nation-state can be viewed as a product of of various forces, and this applies to the concomitant of 'nationalism', the apex of domestic allegiance; the European context of the form of the nation-state is a product of changes in economy and society over several hundred years. Yet the development of advanced capitalism points to a weakening of the loyalty demanded by the nation-state; the growing inability of the West European countries to wage war on their own account at least points to the redundancy of chauvinism. But it does not follow that a reduction in these national loyalties must have an equal compensation—a simultaneous heightening of 'European' awareness. The requirements of a diffuse and functional system of integration do not pose sharp questions of commitment.

Strong pressures to full political union to be successful would need to build on this wider identity. Anyway, the relatively modest integration that has already taken place did need a certain commitment on the part of some politically-relevant people. The point is: who are these people likely to be? At successive stages in the course of integration different sets will be involved. A possible scheme applying to European integration involves three distinct stages. The initial steps were the concern of several élite groups. Some of these had a purely propaganda value out of all proportion to their numbers, and advocated outright federal union. Other groups, more concerned with concrete benefits, operated within the national governments as politicians or top administrators. Together these groups secured the initial, formal advances. Once these had been made, wider circles were involved in the maintenance and extension of the institutions.

This first stage of development involved the minimum number of people to set the process of functional integration under way. The two other stages involve a much wider public. The second requires the acceptance, even a desire for integration by 'informed' public opinion; and the third stage needs the extension of these attitudes to the broad mass of the people—in the end that integration becomes a part of ordinary thinking. To make something more than an analogy: the three stages correspond to the 'two-step' model of political communication which draws attention to the indirect path by which political messages are transmitted and attitudes changed. The initial phase of élite commitment and mass passivity is quite in line with the functioning of liberal democratic politics. Yet the original impetus given by the élites may falter. This, in fact, was one conclusion reached by Karl Deutsch and his colleagues in a study of élite attitudes in European countries, chiefly France and Germany.[24]

This concentration on specific élite groups may, however, neglect a fundamental reorientation elsewhere. From the three-stage model we should expect the impetus to further change to come from within 'informed' public opinion. Survey findings have shown consistently that the young, the more-informed and the better educated sections of a community have tended to favour European integration.[25] This category is necessarily diffuse in character and cuts across established party lines, but its lack of specific relationship is probably advantageous in bringing about fundamental changes of attitude in the population as a whole.

This leaves the third stage, mass acceptance, as a remaining doubtful quantity. We originally introduced this discussion in terms of 'loyalty', but it is apparent that this term can have different connotations. At the minimum there can be the readiness to co-operate with the political authorities, providing support in the willingness to pay taxes. At the other extreme, political support implies 'loyalty' in a strong sense of active commitment. What has yet to be decided is whether European integration is ever likely to need this powerful sense of identity, the characteristics of the nation-state, and further whether new political authorities could ever successfully promote it. It is not too much to say that the definition of Europe's world role in the future depends on the precise nature of her new political culture.

NOTES AND REFERENCES

1. R. Miliband, *The State in Capitalist Society*, Weidenfeld and Nicolson, 1969, p. 14.
2. D. Mitrany, quoted in A. Buchan (ed.), *Europe's Future, Europe's Choices*, Chatto and Windus/The Institute for Strategic Studies, 1969, p. 164.
3. D. P. Calleo, *Europe's Future: The Grand Alternatives*, Hodder and Stoughton, 1967, p. 56.
4. A. Buchan, op. cit., p. 162.
5. E. B. Haas, *The Uniting of Europe*, Oxford University Press, 1958, p. 16.
6. W. Hallstein, quoted by A. Sampson, *The New Europeans*, Hodder and Stoughton, 1968, p. 55.
7. Quoted by F. R. Willis, *France, Germany and the New Europe, 1945–1967*, Oxford University Press, 1968, p. 58.
8. ibid., p. 104.
9. J. H. Huizinga, *Mr Europe: A Political Biography of Paul-Henri Spaak*, Weidenfeld and Nicolson, 1961, p. 235. For an account of the Council of Europe, see O. Crawford, *Done This Day*, Hart-Davis, 1970.
10. D. Coombes, *Politics and Bureaucracy in the European Community*, George Allen and Unwin/PEP, 1970, p. 26.

11. The Commission's *Werner Committee Report* (October 1970) proposed a three-stage plan for economic and monetary union to be completed by 1980, with a central authority for economic policy and a Community system of central banks.
12. The *Davignon Report* of the European Commission was adopted by the EEC in October 1970. One should note that its effect is essentially to increase co-operation between *member governments* rather than act as a form of supranational integration.
13. N. St John-Stevas, 'Parliaments without Power', in *The Times*, 12th February 1971.
14. D. Coombes, op. cit., pp. 78–82.
15. Peter Strafford in *The Times*, 13th March 1970.
16. W. Hallstein, quoted by D. P. Calleo, op. cit., p. 70.
17. Quoted in *The Economist*, 30th January 1971.
18. C. Coombes, op. cit., p. 240.
19. *The Guardian*, 18th November 1970.
20. See G. Pridham and P. Pridham, 'Transnational Parties in the European Community: The Development of European Party Federations', in S. Henig (ed.), *Political Parties in the European Community*, Allen and Unwin, 1979.
21. Ralf Dahrendorf in *Die Zeit*, 9th and 16th July 1971. His reference to the 'peasants' is an implied stricture of the Common Agricultural Policy.
22. The Tindemans Report (January 1976) on 'European Union' shows one approach to the 'stage of transition', proposing that the 'European Council' (the heads of government at their regular summit meetings) should be integrated with Community institutions, so that the distinction between 'political' matters and formal treaty obligations would disappear. Once the European Council had reached *broad* agreement, the Council of Ministers (foreign ministers) would proceed, as necessary, to majority voting on *specific* matters, and hence would become the single decision-making centre.
23. Altiero Spinelli in *The Guardian*, 18th November 1970.
24. K. Deutsch and others, *Political Community and the North Atlantic Area: A Study of Elite Attitudes on European Integration*, New York: Scribner, 1967.
25. See R. Inglehart, 'Long-Term Trends in Mass Support for European Integration', *Government and Opposition*, Summer 1977, also 'Political Generations in Europe', *European Journal of Political Research*, June 1977 (whole issue). More generally, see R. Inglehart, *The Silent Revolution: Changing Values and Political Styles Among Western Publics*, Princeton University Press, 1977.

Additional References

B. Burrows (and others), *Federal Solutions to European Issues*, Macmillan, 1978.
D. Coombes, *The Political Significance of the EEC*, Macmillan, 1979.
P. Dagtoglu (ed.), *Basic Problems of the European Community*, Blackwell, 1975.
J. Fitzmaurice, *The European Parliament*, Saxon House, 1978.
J. Fitzmaurice, 'Direct Elections and the Future of the European Parliament', *West European Politics*, May 1978.
Lord Gladwyn, *The European Idea*, Weidenfeld and Nicolson, 1966.
W. Hallstein, *Europe in the Making*, Allen and Unwin, 1972.
Hansard Society, *The British People: Their Voice in Europe*, Lexington Books, 1977.
S. Henig, 'The Institutional Structures of the European Communities', *Journal of Common Market Studies*, 12/4, 1974.

V. Herman and J. Lodge, *The European Parliament and the European Community*, Macmillan, 1978.

V. Herman and R. von Schendelen, *The European Parliament and the National Parliaments*, Saxon House, 1979.

G. Ionescu (ed.), *The European Alternatives*, Alphen aan de Rijn: Sijthoff, 1979.

E. Kirchner, *Trade Unions as a Pressure Group in the European Community*, Saxon House, 1977.

R. Morgan, *West European Politics since 1945: The Shaping of the European Community*, Batsford, 1973.

C. Sasse (and others), *Decision Making in the European Community*, New York: Praeger, 1977.

M. Shanks, *European Social Policy*, Pergamon, 1977.

H. Wallace, M. Wallace and C. Webb (eds.), *Policy-Making in the European Communities*, John Wiley, 1977.

Elections to the European Parliament, June 1979

Distribution of Seats and Votes

	Bel- gium	Den- mark	France	Ger- many	Ire- land	Italy	Lux- em- bourg	Neth- er- lands	U.K.	Party seats	Party vote (%)
Socialists	7	3	21	35	4	13	1	9	18	111	26.6
Christian Democrats	10	—	7	42	4	30	3	10	—	106	29.5
Conservatives	—	3	—	—	—	—	—	—	60	63	6.2
Communists	—	1	19	—	—	24	—	—	—	44	13.5
Liberals	4	3	19	4	—	5	2	4	—	41	10.6
Progressive Democrats	—	1	15	—	5	—	—	—	—	21	3.5
Non- attached	3	5	—	—	2	9	—	2	3	24	10.1
Seats allocated	24	16	81	81	15	81	6	25	81	410	100.0
Electorate (millions)	6.6	3.7	35.2	42.1	2.1	40.9	0.2	9.5	40.1	=	152.3
Votes (millions)	5.4	1.7	20.3	27.9	1.3	35.0	0.2	5.7	13.4	=	110.9
Turnout(%)	91.4	47.8	60.7	65.7	63.6	85.5	88.9	57.8	32.6	=	72.8

Notes. The vote shown for the non-attached (10.1%) includes the share (4.6%) of those parties failing to win seats. Since the election the Christian Democrats in the European Parliament have become the group of the 'European People's Party', and the Conservatives have become the 'European Democrats'. The European Progressive Democrats consist mainly of the French Gaullists and the Irish Fianna Fail. Apart from the UK (except Northern Ireland) all countries used a national system of proportional representation. In Belgium voting is compulsory. For an analysis of the results, see *Government and Opposition*, 'After the European Elections', Autumn 1979 (whole issue).

The Nations of Western Europe

THE MATERIAL in this section gives a range of background information about the individual West European countries: major socio-economic and constitutional comparisons as well as specific political information. The table of socio-economic comparisons generally provides data for a particular recent year, and where possible this should be supplemented to show comparative rates of change. Besides the sources mentioned, an amount of statistical and comparative information is contained in:

C. Cook and J. Paxton (eds), *European Political Facts, 1918–1973*, Macmillan, 1975.
Europa Yearbook (vol. 1), Europa Publications.
T. Mackie and R. Rose, *The International Almanac of Electoral History*, Macmillan, 1974.
OECD, *Main Economic Indicators*.
C. L. Taylor and M. C. Hudson, *World Handbook of Political and Social Indicators*, Yale University Press, 1972.

The table of constitutional comparisons is necessarily couched in general terms as all countries show particular variations under a given head. Portugal and Spain are included, although obviously the constitutional situation in both countries may not yet be as permanent. The 'national profiles' are designed to give a brief historical and political outline of each of the states, and the main developments have been taken into account until October 1979. The summaries of election results are based on information supplied by *Keesing's Contemporary Archives*. The short reading list for each country can be supplemented by the various chapter references.

1. European Socio-Economic Comparisons

	1 Population (millions)	2 Population Density (per sq. km.)	3 Percentage of Population in Cities over 100,000	4 Population Increase (% Annual Average 1963–73)	5 Employment in Agriculture etc. % of Labour Force	6 Trade Union Strength % of Civilian Labour Force	7 Industrial Disputes (days lost per 1,000 employees)	8 Telephones per 1,000 population	9 Television sets per 1,000 population	10 Newspaper circulation per 1,000 population	11 Secondary Education Enrolment as % of 15–19 age group	12 Percentage of Students of Working-class origin in H.E.	13 Infant Mortality per 1,000 live births	14 Doctors per 10,000 population	15 Suicide rates per 100,000 males	16 Predominant Religion
Austria	7.5	90	31	0.5	11.8	50	—	304	247	328	32.0	5.5	16.8	18.5	33.3	1
Belgium	9.8	322	30	0.5	3.3	46	466	300	255	260	61.3	22.8	15.3	15.4	21.5	1
Denmark	5.1	118	38	0.7	9.1	39	868	494	308	361	57.4	10.1	8.7	14.4	30.2	2
Finland	4.7	2	22	0.3	12.9	34	1362	409	306	419	60.8	21.3	12.0	10.2	39.0	2
France	52.9	96	33	0.9	9.6	15	288	293	268	237	54.6	9.0	11.4	13.4	23.3	1
Germany	61.5	248	34	0.8	6.8	30	80	344	306	319	41.5	5.3	15.5	17.2	26.3	3
Greece	9.1	69	29	0.6	28.4	—	—	238	126	77	45.4	12.0	20.3	16.2	3.9	4
Iceland	0.2	2	48	1.4	14.2	45	—	411	234	449	—	—	9.6	14.5	11.3	2
Ireland	3.2	45	26	0.7	23.1	36	870	150	192	233	50.0	8.3	15.7	10.2	4.3	1
Italy	56.2	186	27	0.7	15.9	18	2182	271	213	133	40.8	15.4	17.7	18.1	8.2	1
Luxembourg	0.4	137	30	0.8	5.9	34	—	442	257	463	33.5	3.2	10.6	10.6	20.4	1
Netherlands	13.8	338	31	1.2	6.3	27	120	391	259	311	62.7	9.4	9.5	12.5	10.0	3
Norway	4.0	12	19	0.8	9.0	39	18	366	255	390	63.6	23.9	10.5	13.8	13.0	2
Portugal	9.7	105	12	−0.5	32.5	—	—	119	65	71	33.4	7.4	38.9	9.1	13.4	1
Spain	36.2	72	31	1.1	20.7	—	—	239	184	98	35.5	7.5	15.6	13.4	6.7	1
Sweden	8.2	18	28	0.7	6.1	60	62	689	352	534	56.3	14.3	8.0	13.6	29.4	2
Switzerland	6.3	154	18	1.1	8.5	41	2	634	273	384	68.2	13.8	9.8	14.2	28.2	3
United Kingdom	56.0	229	58	0.4	2.7	42	1036	394	320	528	44.6	27.2	14.1	12.3	9.2	2
Japan	113.8	303	48	1.1	11.9	27	238	426	235	519	70.9	8.7	8.9	11.3	19.4	5
United States	215.1	23	57	1.1	3.6	22	1372	721	571	297	72.0	26.6	15.2	15.6	16.7	2

Notes and Sources for table on p. 263

1. OECD *Observer*, no. 91, March 1978; 1976 figures.
2. OECD *Observer*, 1978; 1976 figures.
3. Based on information in the UN *Demographic Yearbook*. Both Reykjavik (Iceland) and Luxembourg Ville have rather less than 100,000 inhabitants.
4. OECD *Observer*, 1975.
5. OECD *Observer*, no. 97, March 1979. (Includes fishing and forestry.) 1977 figures*.
6. Estimates of trade union membership have been made from various sources.
7. Department of Employment Gazette, December 1974. Average for each country, 1969–1973.
8. OECD *Observer*, 1979; 1977 figures.
9. OECD *Observer*, 1979; 1977 figures.
10. UN Statistical Yearbook 1973 and UN Statistical Papers, 'Comparison of Social Statistics' 1967.
11. OECD *Observer*, 1979; figures for 1975–6.
12. These estimates have to be treated with some reserve. See OECD, *Group Disparities in Educational Participation*, STP (70)9. They refer to the early 1970s.
13. OECD *Observer*, 1979; figures mainly for 1976 and 1977.
14. WHO, *World Health Statistics Annual*, vol. III, 1974. Figures for 1970. UK figures for England and Wales only.
15. WHO, *World Health Statistics Annual*, 1975. Figures for 1972. Male rates have been shown since females rates are lower and show less disparity. Northern Ireland female rates (2.0 per 100,000) are the lowest in Western Europe.
16. 1 = predominantly Roman Catholic.
    2 = predominantly Protestant.
    3 = approximate Roman Catholic and Protestant parity.
    4 = Greek Orthodox.
    5 = Buddhist (Japan).

* The extent of the changes in agricultural (and fishing) employment affecting some countries can be judged by comparing the corresponding percentages of 1970: Austria 18.3; Belgium 4.8; Denmark 11.4; Finland 22.7; France 14.0; Germany 9.0; Greece 48.2; Iceland 19.0; Ireland 27.5; Italy 19.6; Luxembourg 11.1; Netherlands 7.2; Norway 13.9; Portugal 33.0; Spain 29.6; Sweden 8.1; Switzerland 7.0; United Kingdom 2.9.

2. European Constitutional Comparisons

	State Form	State Structure	Head of State	Effective Executive Head	Leg.-Executive Relationship	Second Chamber Composition	Second Chamber Powers	Constitutional Jurisdiction	Constitutional Change	Direct Methods	Voting System
Austria	1	7	9	13	16	21	30	31	39	50	57
Belgium	2	6	8	13	16	22	28	33	40	49	59
Denmark	2	5	8	13	16	26	26	34	43	47	59
Finland	1	5	9	14	16	25	30	34	40	52	60
France	1	5	9	14	17	21	27	32	39	51	54
Germany	1	7	10	13	16	23	29	31	42	52	56
Greece	1	5	10	14	17	26	26	35	40	51	61
Iceland	1	5	9	13	16	25	30	34	41	49	59
Ireland	1	5	9	13	16	21	30	35	38	48	55
Italy	1	6	10	13	16	22	28	31	42	46	59
Luxembourg	2	5	8	13	16	26	26	33	40	52	60
Netherlands	2	5	8	13	16	21	28	34	40	52	58
Norway	2	5	8	13	18	25	30	34	40	49	60
Portugal	1	5	9	3	17	26	26	12	42	52	57
Spain	2	6	8	13	16	20	30	32	42	51	60
Sweden	2	5	8	13	16	26	26	34	41	49	59
Switzerland	1	7	11	15	18	20	27	31	38	45	60
United Kingdom	2	5	8	13	16	24	30	35	37	52	53

Key

1. Republic. 2. Monarchy. 3. Council of the Revolution with prime minister. 4. Prime minister (with substantial powers of monarch). 5. Unitary state. 6. Unitary state, with constitutionally entrenched regions. 7. Federal system. 8. Hereditary monarchy (Luxembourg, a grand duchy). 9. President, by popular vote. 10. President, by legislature (and other representatives). 11. Rotating presidency, from Federal Council. 12. Council of the Revolution. 13. Prime minister or equivalent. 14. Hybrid or mixed: president and prime minister. 15. Collegial executive. 16. Unified system (in Finland, president forms partial exception). 17. Partial unification, no assembly powers over executive actions of president. 18. Partial unification; in Switzerland fixed life for Federal Council, in Norway fixed life for Storting. 19. Government domination. 20. Directly-elected second chamber. 21. Indirectly-elected, usually from local government (Ireland, functional). 22. Mixed: direct, indirect, appointed. 23. Appointed by state governments as their representatives. 24. Hereditary and/or government appointed. 25. By and from assembly (quasi 'second chamber'). 26. No second chamber. 27. Co-equal with lower house (in France, this depends on governments). 28. Nominally co-equal, in practice subordinate. 29. Co-equal for certain matters, otherwise qualified veto. 30. Suspensory powers only. 31. Full constitutional court (in Switzerland, no power over federal legislation). 32. Constitutional Council (legislation) and Council of State (administration). 33. Council of State (administration), courts (basic rights); Luxembourg Council of State has suspensory powers over legislation. 34. Advisory bodies on legislation and courts. 35. Courts only; no power

to query legislation. 36. Essentially arbitrary jurisdiction. 37. No special procedure, as for ordinary legislation. 38. Legislative process plus referendum (in Switzerland, a majority of voters in a majority of cantons). 39. Special majority in legislature, or an ordinary one with referendum. 40. Intervening election and special legislative majorities. 41. Intervening election, no special majorities. 42. Special majority in legislature. 43. Intervening election and referendum. 44. By referendum used at government discretion. 45. Full rights of challenge, but only constitutional initative at federal level. 46. Rights of challenge to legislation and initiative. 47. Challenge to legislation, on initiative of minority in assembly. 48. Referendum on constitutional changes and on other basic issues. 49. On initiative of assembly, consultative (on basic constitutional issues). 50. Popular initiative. 51. On government initiative. 52. No use made of direct methods (or no recent use). 53. Relative majority in single-member constituencies. 54. Second ballot in single-member constituencies. 55. Proportional Representation by system of Single Transferable Vote in multi-member constituencies. 56. Effectively proportional, combining relative majority in single-member constituencies with straight party list; the latter is used to secure overall proportionality. 57. Proportional Representation with straight party list. 58. PR, with one national constituency, 59. PR, with sub-national constituencies; overall proportionality by allocation of remainders. 60. PR, sub-national constituencies, no overall proportionality ensured. 58–60 all provide freedom (to varying degrees) for voters to express individual preferences or vote the straight party list. 61. PR, but with second distribution of seats to leading parties; effectively non-proportional.

Note: In Portugal the President is the leading figure in the Council of the Revolution. The 1976 Constitution established a Constitutional Commission which acts in an advisory capacity to the Council.

3. Political Profiles

AUSTRIA

The first Austrian Republic came into being in November 1918 on the collapse of the Austro-Hungarian Empire; the parliamentary system of government which resulted from the constitution of 1920 proved to be unstable and constitutional amendments in 1925 and 1929 sought to rectify this—the 1929 amendment by providing for a directly-elected president with reserve powers. However, the causes of instability were more deep-rooted. The truncated state had Vienna as its capital city, with about one third of the country's total population; it was the contrast between this large metropolitan centre—'Red Vienna'—and the largely rural and clerically-dominated remainder of Austria which set the pattern to politics in the inter-war years. On an extra-parliamentary level the conflict was seen in the clashes between the two paramilitary formations, the anti-Socialist *Heimwehr* and the Socialist *Schutzbund*. The uneasy balance between the two major parties, the Christian Socials and the Socialists, was broken in 1933 when Chancellor Dollfuss (Christian-Social) suppressed the constitution, replacing it in 1934 with an authoritatian system. But at the last election to be held, in 1930, neither the Austrian Nazis nor the *Heimwehr* made any impact, and the ruling Christian Socials were clerical-conservative rather than fascist. On the left, the Socialists united the working class, with the tiny Communist Party of no importance.

In March 1938 Austria was incorporated into the Third Reich, and with its collapse the country was immediately occupied by the wartime allies. The Second Austrian Republic was set up in 1945 and the former constitution reactivated. Nevertheless the occupation continued until 1955, and only with the signing of the Austrian State Treaty in that year was full sovereignty restored; the peace treaty enforced on Austria a 'permanent neutrality' making her ineligible to join any military or political alliance. Whilst the protracted treaty negotiations dragged on, Austrian self-government was early restored and elections were first held in November 1945. It should be noted that, although Austria is formally a federal state with nine constituent Länder, political life is highly centralized and dominated by the national parties. The two contestants of the inter-war years remained: the Socialists and the People's Party (formerly Christian-Socials), but the old bitterness disappeared, and in the special conditions of the post-war period they ruled jointly in 'permanent' coalition from 1945 until 1966, after which the People's Party ruled alone with an absolute majority in the Nationalrat until 1970.

The 1970 election led to the first purely Socialist administration, a minority government dependent on the small, right-wing Freedom Party. Subsequent elections in 1971 and 1975 gave the SPÖ an absolute majority in the Nationalrat. In the 1974 presidential election the socialist-sponsored candidate was elected with 51.7 per cent of the popular vote (in a 94 per cent poll); the SPÖ has supplied all the presidents of the second republic. The chancellor throughout the period of Socialist domination has been Dr Bruno Kreisky—with his strong personal leadership he has presided over the fast-growing Austrian economy rather than the implementation of radical policies. He suffered a dent in his prestige in November 1978 when the government's nuclear energy policy was rejected in a referendum (50.5 per cent against), and an early election was called. Surprisingly, the Socialist Party actually strengthened its position in the May 1979 election and established a record of winning an absolute majority at three consecutive elections. Its success was due in part to the inability of the People's Party to find a convincing leader to challenge Kreisky.

Elections to the Nationalrat, May 1979

	1979 Seats	1979 %	1975 %	1971 %	1970 %	1966 %
Socialist Party	95	51.0	50.4	50.0	48.4	42.6
People's Party	77	41.9	43.0	43.1	44.7	48.4
Freedom Party	11	6.1	5.4	5.5	5.5	5.4
Communist Party	—	1.0	1.1	1.2	1.0	0.4
Others	—	—	0.1	0.2	0.5	3.9

Reading

E. Barker, *Austria, 1918–1972*, Macmillan, 1973.

W. T. Bluhm, *Building an Austrian Nation*, Yale University Press, 1973.

G. Brook-Shepherd, *Dollfuss*, Macmillan, 1961.

F. L. Carsten, *Fascist Movements in Austria: From Schönerer to Hitler*, Sage Publications, 1977.

F. C. Englemann, 'Austria: The Pooling of Opposition', in R. A. Dahl (ed.) *Political Oppositions in Western Democracies*, New Haven: Yale University Press, 1966.

P. J. Katzenstein, 'The Last Old Nation: Austrian National Consciousness since 1945', *Comparative Politics*, vol. 9/2, January 1977.

G. B. Powell, *Social Fragmentation and Political Hostility: An Austrian Case Study*, Stanford University Press, 1971.

P. Pulzer, 'Austria', in S. Henig and J. Pinder (eds.), *European Political Parties*, PEP/George Allen and Unwin, 1969.

K. Shell, *The Transformation of Austrian Socialism*, Univ. of New York, 1962.

K. R. Stadler, 'Austria', in S. J. Woolf (ed.), *European Fascism*, Weidenfeld and Nicolson, 1968.

K. R. Stadler, *Austria*, Ernest Benn, 1971.

K. Steiner, *Politics in Austria*, Boston: Little, Brown, 1972.

R. P. Stiefbold, 'Segmented Pluralism and Consociational Democracy in Austria', in M. O. Heisler (ed.), *Politics in Europe*, New York: David McKay, 1974.

M. A. Sully, 'The Austrian Parliamentary Election of 1975', *Parliamentary Affairs*, Summer 1976.
M. A. Sully, 'The Socialist Party of Austria' in W. E. Paterson and A. Thomas (eds.), *Social Democratic Parties in Western Europe*, Croom Helm, 1977.

BELGIUM

Belgian independence resulted from the successful revolution in 1830 against William I of the Netherlands. Since 1831 Belgium has been a constitutional monarchy and the relatively liberal form of that constitution has been maintained ever since. The monarchy was only once seriously in question in the dispute subsequent to Leopold III's wartime behaviour, and this crisis was only finally resolved by his abdication in 1951. The predominantly Roman Catholic allegiance of the population has given the progressive Social Christian Party a leading place in Belgian politics for much of the past century, and it has been almost always the dominant governing party, in coalition with the Liberals (Party for Liberty and Progress) or the Socialists. The strict unitary form of the Belgian state and the power of these three parties has only masked the underlying social tensions resulting from the language question. The linguistic frontier is clearly marked: Flemish is the language of the majority of the population (about 55 per cent) in the north of the country, and French in most of the remainder; Brussels is a predominantly French-speaking enclave within Flanders. Over the years numerous reforms have been made to meet the demands of the two language communities, particularly those of the underprivileged Flemish. A measure of the growth of discontent is provided by the rise of the linguistic parties, the Flemish *Volksunie* and the *Rassemblement Wallon* of the French-speakers. They received only 2.2 per cent of the vote in 1954 but reached a high-point of 22.4 per cent in 1971.

Their subsequent decline has been entirely offset by the divisions affecting the major parties (Social-Christians, Socialists, and Liberals)—all three have developed autonomous linguistic wings. The linguistic issue is therefore the main cause of contention both within and between parties and a factor which has been a cause of governmental instability. Composition of governments has had to reflect a linguistic balance: strict parity in cabinets, separate ministers for education and culture, as well as for the relations between the two communities.

Major constitutional reforms were agreed in 1971 which, although falling short of a federal solution, gave a large degree of devolved power to the linguistic areas—guaranteed regional autonomy for cultural, educational, and regional economic affairs, and the establishment of elected councils for the regions; responsibility to main parliament would be restricted to budgetary matters. Guarantees also had to be worked out for the French-speaking minority, for their deputies would inevitably be in a minority in parliament. The regulation of Brussels was central to the new constitutional formula: the city was designated as a third region and given an official bilingual status, but the city's limits were permanently fixed to prevent further Francophone encroachment into surrounding Flemish areas.

The constitutional compromise settled the principles of reform, but agreement on the detailed legislation required proved just as difficult to reach. In particular, the position accorded to Brussels satisfied neither side: the French-speaking population regarded the permanent restriction on Brussels as artificial, whilst Flemish-speakers continued to regard Brussels as an integral part of Flanders and saw the creation of Brussels as a third region to be a denial of the Flemish majority position in the country as a whole. Since 1971 successive governments have stumbled on the problem of passing detailed implementing laws relating to the constitutional changes.

Subsequent to the 1977 election, a very broad coalition was formed controlling some four-fifths of the parliamentary vote: Social Christians, Socialists, *Volksunie*, and the Brussels *FDF*. The inclusion of the linguistic parties augured well for the coalition and its chances of reaching a definitive agreement. One result was the conclusion of a *Pacte Communautaire* which promised to resolve outstanding differences: provisions for the Belgian Senate to represent the language communities with voting requirements guaranteeing the position of the French-speaking minority; the election of regional assemblies; a strengthening of the regional Cultural Councils; the creation of an Arbitration Court to adjudicate between the various representative organs; proposals to overcome the difficulties concerning Brussels. However, some of the provisions were ruled unconstitutional by the Council of State, and the Pact as a whole could not be implemented.

In consequence, a further election was held in December 1978, but no party benefited substantially. If anything it appeared that the electorate was tiring of 'regional niggling' and that the national economy was just as important a preoccupation: in that case, the pressure will be on the parties to settle their differences to avoid electoral disaffection.

Elections to the Chamber of Representatives, December 1978

| | 1978 | | 1977 | 1974 | 1971 |
	Seats	%	%	%	%
Social Christians (CVP/PSC)	82	36.3	35.9	32.3	30.0
Socialists (BSP/PSB)	58	25.3	26.4	26.7	27.3
Liberals (PVV/PLP)	37	16.3	15.6	15.2	15.1
FDF/*Rassemblement*	15	7.0	7.1	11.0	13.0
Volksunie	14	7.0	10.1	10.2	11.1
Communist Party	4	3.3	2.7	3.2	3.1
Others	2	4.8	2.2	1.5	0.4

Notes: Voting at elections is compulsory. The *Rassemblement* (RW) is the Francophone party in Wallonia, and for Brussels the equivalent is the FDF (*Front des Francophones*); the votes and seats for the two parties are shown together. In 1978 'Others' includes the ultra-Flemish *Vlaamsche Blok* and an 'anti-tax' protest party—both parties won one seat. The 1978 election was inconclusive since party strengths remained the same; nevertheless it took over three months to form a new coalition—the three largest parties together with the FDF/*Rassemblement*.

Reading

R. Anstey, *King Leopold's Legacy*, Oxford University Press, 1966.

M. O. Heisler, 'Institutionalizing Societal Cleavages in a Cooptive polity', in Heisler (ed.), *Politics in Europe, op. cit.*

K. Hill, 'Belgium', in *European Political Parties*, op. cit.

K. Hill, 'Belgium: Political Change in a Segmented Society', in R. Rose (ed.), *Electoral Behavior: A Comparative Handbook*, Collier–Macmillan, 1974.

S. Holt, *Six European States*, Hamish Hamilton, 1970.

R. Irving, 'The Contemporary Belgian Political Scene' in R. King (ed.), *Benelux*, Hull University Press, 1977.

R. Irving, 'The Belgian General Election of 1978', *West European Politics*, 2/2, May 1979.

V. R. Lorwin, 'Belgium: Religion, Class and Language in National Politics', in *Political Oppositions to Western Democracies, op. cit.*

X. Mabille and V. R. Lorwin, 'The Belgian Socialist Party' in Paterson and Thomas (eds.), *Social Democratic Parties in Western Europe*, op. cit.

X. Mabille and V. R. Lorwin, 'Belgium' in S. Henig (ed.), *Political Parties in the European Community*, Allen and Unwin, 1979.

V. Mallinson, *Belgium*, Ernest Benn, 1970.

A. Mughan, 'Modernization and Ethnic Conflict in Belgium', *Political Studies*, March 1979.

D. W. Urwin, 'Social Cleavages and Political Parties in Belgium: Problems of Institutionalisation', *Political Studies*, vol. xviii, no. 3, September 1970.

G. L. Weil, *The Benelux Nations: The Politics of Small-Country Democracies*, New York: Holt, Rinehart and Winston, 1970.

DENMARK

Denmark is one of the oldest European states in having a continuous national sovereignty for several hundred years; from the fourteenth century until early in the nineteenth she was a major European power with considerable possessions in Scandinavia and northern Germany. Already in the twelfth century a unified royal power had emerged, one which for a time coexisted with the provincial assemblies, or Landstings. Early evolution was marked by full government participation for the nobility and the decline of the popular assemblies. Government by king and council of the nobility resulted; moreover, the monarchy was an elective position. In 1660 there was a shift to royal absolutism and the Act of Royalty which resulted transformed the Danish monarchy from a constitutional force to a completely autocratic one, a situation which continued until well into the nineteenth century; it was an enlightened despotism—compulsory elementary education was introduced in 1814. Just as suddenly, in 1849, there was a reversion to full constitutional rule, with elections to parliament on a democratic franchise. However, the principle of government responsibility to the lower house, the Folketing, was not established until 1901. The main political cleavage was initially between the conservative Right and the Left (the Venstre) supporting progressive and agrarian intersts. The Venstre split in 1905 to give a Radical Left which voiced the interests of small farmers and urban liberals. The fourth historical party, the Social Democrats, quickly rose to prominence and formed its first government in 1924. With its rise, both the Venstre and the Radical Left became gradually more bourgeois in orientation, but for long the Social Democrats were able to rule with the support of the Radical Left.

In the earlier years of the post-war period the Social Democrats were in a dominant position, but gradually the system developed the form of a balanced cluster: the Conservative, Venstre, and Radical Left parties represented the bourgeois interests, whilst on the left the Social Democrats were flanked by the Socialist People's Party, the Left Socialists, and the Communists. In 1968, the bourgeois parties formed a coalition government which in 1971 was replaced by a minority Social Democratic one, with the support of the Socialist People's Party. The new constitution of 1953 reduced parliament to one house only, the Folketing, and at the same time provided for the use of the referendum as a popular check on the legislature; constitutional changes were also made subject to approval by referendum. Danish accession to the European Community was decided by a constitutional referendum held in October 1972 and resulted in a large vote in favour, 63.7 per cent. However, this decisive result was actually accompanied by a growing diffusion of the party system, as was clearly demonstrated in the subsequent elections.

Elections to the Folketing, October 1979

	1979		1977	1975	1973
	Seats	%	%	%	%
Social Democrats	69	38.3	37.0	29.9	25.6
Progress Party	20	11.0	14.6	13.6	15.9
Liberal Democrats (Venstre)	22	12.5	12.0	23.3	12.3
Conservative People's Party	22	12.5	8.5	5.5	9.2
Centre-Democrats	6	3.2	6.4	2.2	7.8
Socialist People's Party	10	5.9	3.9	5.0	6.0
Communists	0	1.9	3.7	4.2	3.6
Radical Liberals	10	5.4	3.6	7.0	11.2
Christian People's Party	5	2.6	3.4	5.3	4.0
Single-Tax Party	5	2.6	3.3	1.8	2.9
Left Socialists	6	3.6	2.7	2.1	1.5

Notes: In addition to the 175 Danish deputies, the Faroe Islands and Greenland each send two representatives. In 1979 there was a poll of 85.1 per cent. The qualifying level for seats is 2 per cent of votes cast. The voting age was lowered in 1978 to eighteen by referendum.

Only five parties were represented in the 1971 Folketing, ten in 1973 and 1975, and eleven in 1977. The situation of 'electoral chaos' showed an extent of disaffection from the traditional parties without giving any pronounced polarization. The sudden rise of the maverick Progress Party (anti-tax, anti-government) to be the second largest in the Folketing was indicative of the fragmentation. After 1971 the governments have been mainly minority Social Democratic administrations, but they lacked sufficient authority to deal with Denmark's pressing economic problems (large unemployment and high rate of inflation). The Social Democratic vote recovered in 1977, and the party continued a minority government until August 1978 when an 'unlikely' coalition was formed with the Liberal Democrats, which stayed in office for a year. The coalition was unpopular with the trade unions, and after the 1979 election the strengthened Social Democrats instead looked for support from the moderate left. Both extremes (Progress Party and Communists) lost in 1979, and the peak of fragmentation in the party system seemed to have passed.

Reading

N. Andrén, *Government and Politics in the Nordic Countries*, Stockholm: Almqvist and Wiksell, 1964.

K. H. Cerny (ed.), *Scandinavia at the Polls Recent Political Trends in Denmark, Norway and Sweden*, Washington: American Enterprise Institute, 1977.

J. Fitzmaurice, 'Denmark', in S. Henig. *Political Parties in the European Community*, op. cit.

S. Hurwitz, *The Ombudsman*, Copenhagen: Det Danske Selskab, 1968.

C. Jarlor and O. P. Kristensen, 'Electoral Mobility and Social Change in Denmark', *Scandinavian Political Studies*, new series, vol. 1/1, 1978.

W. G. Jones, *Denmark,* Ernest Benn, 1970.

K. E. Miller, *Government and Politics in Denmark*, Boston: Houghton Mifflin, 1968.

N. Petersen, 'Attitudes Towards European Integration and the Danish Common Market Referendum', *Scandinavian Political Studies*, n.s., vol. 1/1, 1978.

G. G. Rusk and O. Borre, 'The Changing Party Space in Danish Voter Perceptions, 1971–73', *European Journal of Political Research*, No. 2/1974.

A. H. Thomas, 'Social Democracy in Denmark' in Paterson and Thomas (eds.), *Social Democratic Parties in Western Europe*, op. cit.

See also, *Scandinavian Political Studies*, vols. 1–9, Helsinki: Academic Bookstore/Gumpert, 1966–1974, and Columbia University Press.

FINLAND

Until 1809 Finland was a province of the Swedish monarchy, and from then until an independent republic was declared in December 1917, she was an autonomous Grand Duchy of Imperial Russia. For the several hundred years which Finland was a part of Sweden, a strong representative system was maintained, although a more authoritarian form of government resulted from the constitution acts of 1772/89. These acts remained the basis of later tzarist rule which was exercised by a governor-general with an estate system of representation and this form persisted until 1906. The 1906 Parliament Act effected a sudden transformation—proportional voting and a single-chamber assembly—a modern political form which gave full expression to national aspirations. At the same time there was a rapid political mobilization and the Social Democrats quickly became the largest political party. Following independence, and under the influence of the Russian Revolution, a bitter civil war ensued between the right-wing monarchist and nationalist forces, the 'Whites', and the 'Reds' who wished to follow the Soviet example. A new Constitution Act of 1919 gave the basic form of mixed parliamentary and presidential government which has remained unaltered. Party politics in the inter-war period were dominated by the cleavages of the civil war, and although the republic did not quite succumb to these pressures, there was a marked shift to the right, especially seen in the Lapua Movement, the para-military Civil Guards, and support for these from the regular army. There was considerable harassment of the left, with the Communist Party banned from 1930 onwards. Since 1945, some of the deep divisions in Finnish society have been healed, but in spite of the multi-party system a moderate social polarization remains apparent. Unstable left-of-centre coalitions have been the rule; however, the 1919 innovation of a strong president (popularly-elected, actually via an electoral college) existing alongside parliamentary government has mitigated the effects of government instability. The president is an integral part of the Finnish system, particularly as he can represent the national viewpoint in relations with the Soviet Union. The latter is an active factor in Finnish politics and is naturally hostile to Finland becoming involved in western treaty organizations.

The looming presence of the Soviet Union enforces cohesion on the fragmented party system. Coalitions are always very broadly based, usually made up of four or five parties. The Centre Party represents the pivot of most coalition possibilities, the exact colouration depending on shifts in electoral preference. However, governments are short lived, reflecting the difficulty of harmonizing the differing viewpoints especially in economic matters. The People's Democratic League (SKDL) has frequently participated in governing coalitions—the desirability of placating the Soviet Union has to be remembered—but the SKDL, although Communist in orientation, is a wide alliance with three semi-autonomous factions.

The unity and continuity provided by President Urho Kekkonen is impressive. He was first elected to office in 1956 and commands wide popular support. Exceptionally, in 1973, the Eduskunta agreed to extend his term of office by a constitutional amendment which required a five-sixths majority in the assembly, an indication of his acceptability to most parties; Kekkonen was elected for a further four-year term in

1978. The president is influential in determining the composition of coalitions, and the frequent punctuation of non-party 'caretaker' governments enables him to take a controlling interest on occasion. For some years the left-wing parties have been in the ascendant, thus making centre-left governments the rule. In the March 1979 election, however, there was a pronounced shift to the right favouring the Conservatives, Christian Union, and the Rural Party.

Elections to the Eduskunta, March 1979

	1979 Seats	1979 %	1975 %	1972 %	1970 %
Social Democrats	52	23.9	24.9	25.8	23.4
SKDL (Democratic League)	35	17.8	18.9	17.0	16.6
Centre Party	36	17.4	17.5	16.4	17.1
Conservatives	47	21.6	18.4	17.6	18.0
Swedish People's Party	10	4.6	5.0	5.3	5.6
Liberal People's Party	4	3.7	4.4	5.2	6.0
Christian Union	9	4.8	3.3	2.5	0.9
Rural Party	7	4.6	3.2	9.2	10.5
Party of National Unity	—	0.3	1.6	—	—
Constitutional People's Party	—	1.2	1.7	—	—

Notes: There was a turnout of 82 per cent. Election alliances within electoral districts significantly distort the proportionality of the electoral system. The Conservatives are otherwise known as the National Coalition. The Swedish People's Party represents the Swedish linguistic minority, and the Constitutional People's Party was a breakaway from it—in protest at the party's support for the continued re-election of President Kekkonen. The Party of National Unity is a split from the Rural Party.

Reading

E. Allardt and P. Pesonen, 'Cleavages in Finnish Politics', in S. M. Lipset and S. Rokkan (eds.), *Party Systems and Voter Alignments*, Collier-Macmillan, 1967.
N. Andrén, *Government and Politics in the Nordic Countries*, op. cit.
D. Arter, 'All-Party Government for Finland?', *Parliamentary Affairs*, 31/1, Winter 1978.
D. Arter, 'The Finnish Centre Party: Portrait of a "Hinge Group",' *West European Politics*, 2/1, January 1979.
W. E. Griffith (ed.), *Communism in Europe*, Pergamon Press, 1967.
R. Helenius, 'The Finnish Social Democratic Party', in Paterson and Thomas (eds.), *Social Democratic Parties in Western Europe*, op. cit.
J. H. Hodgson, 'The Finnish Communist Party and Neutrality', *Government and Opposition*, vol. 2, no. 2, January–April 1967.
P. Kastari, *Constitution Act and Parliament Act of Finland*, Helsinki: Ministry for Foreign Affairs, 1967.
P. Kastari, 'Finland's Guardians of the Law', in D. C. Rowat, op. cit.
D. G. Kirby, *Finland in the Twentieth Century*, C. Hurst, 1979.
W. R. Mead, *Finland*, Ernest Benn, 1968.
J. Nousiainen, *The Finnish Political System*, Harvard University Press, 1971.

P. Pesonen, 'Party Support in a Fragmented System', in R. Rose (ed.), *Electoral Behavior*, op. cit.

L. A. Puntilla, *The Political History of Finland, 1809–1966*, Heinemann, 1975.

K. Törnudd, *The Electoral System of Finland*, Hugh Evelyn, 1968.

A. F. Upton (ed.), *The Communist Parties of Scandinavia and Finland*, Weidenfeld and Nicolson, 1973.

See also, *Scandinavian Political Studies*, vols. 1–9.

FRANCE

When it was first approved by popular vote in September 1958, the constitution of the Fifth French Republic was regarded by most observers as a stop-gap contrivance, a form of legitimation for the exercise of personal power by de Gaulle, the 'lesser evil' in view of the threat from the Army in revolt in Algeria. The apparently cyclical pattern of French politics since the Revolution of 1789 by which: 'Constitutional Monarchy gives way to Republic and the Republic in turn is replaced by some form of dictatorial government',* appeared to show the decline of parliamentarianism of the Fourth Republic (1946–1958) and its replacement by a non-democratic form. The new constitution made certain institutional innovations, the total effect of which was to create a new balance of power and a form of presidentialism in which all other institutions were aligned against the party system in the Chamber of Deputies; it was these parties which were held responsible for the troubles of the Third Republic (1871–1940) and the Fourth. Whilst all previous attempts to create a strong executive power had resulted in dictatorship, the Fifth Republic showed the possibility of integrating the party system with a strong, directly-elected president. Once de Gaulle was firmly in power, he deliberately avoided making the army the basis of his support, and this showed in his determination to liquidate the Algerian problem; he instead relied on popular approval for his actions, by the use of the referendum, and extended its use to a form of general policy approval.

1958 (September)	The new constitution	79.25% in favour
1961 (January)	Algerian policy	75.00% in favour
1962 (April)	Algerian settlement	90.70% in favour
1962 (October)	Method of presidential election	62.00% in favour
1969 (April)	Reorganization of Senate etc.	53.15% against

To these results should be added that of the presidential election of December 1965 when de Gaulle won 55.2 per cent of the vote at the second ballot. The turning-point in securing the fortunes of the Fifth Republic came with the 'events' of May 1968, starting with student unrest, pitched battles with the riot-police, and escalating into a general

* D. Pickles, *The Fifth French Republic*, Methuen, 1962, p. 10.

strike. Although the government made some concessions, the sweeping nature of the Gaullist election victory in June 1968 showed the underlying strength of the regime. Paradoxically, the electoral success was accompanied by a weakening hold of de Gaulle over the electorate—as was shown by the defeat of his reform proposals in the 1969 referendum, a reverse which led directly to de Gaulle's resignation. His successor, Georges Pompidou, previously prime minister, was elected with an impressive majority in June 1969 (58.2 per cent at the second ballot, but on a low poll). The result indicated that the presidential system was taking root, since Pompidou managed to hold the Gaullist electorate together even though he lacked de Gaulle's personal appeal.

Gradually the parties were re-asserting their position and the run-up to the March 1973 Assembly election promised a formidable swing to the Left against the ruling UDR. The Socialists and Communists put forward a joint election programme and undertook to form a coalition government if they secured a majority. In the event, the Gaullists did lose their overall majority but were able to rely on the support of the independent Republicans and the Democratic Centre to maintain their hold on government. Even so, the left-wing parties managed almost to double their representation.

Elections to the Chamber of Deputies, March 1973

| | 1973 | | 1968 |
	Seats	%	%
UDR (and majority affiliates)	183	27.4	43.6
Independent Republicans	55	6.9	4.1
Centre Démocratie et Progrès	30	3.7	—
Réformateurs (previously Centre-PDM)	34	12.4	10.3
Left-Wing Radicals		2.7	0.7
Socialists	102	19.0	16.5
Other Left		3.3	3.9
Communists	73	21.4	20.0
Others (*non-inscrits*)	13	2.8	0.6

Notes: Percentages in both years are for first ballot and do not relate to number of seats a party obtained. The *Mouvement réformateurs* was composed of the *Centre démocrate* (Lecanuet) and the *Radicals* (Servan-Schreiber), forming parliamentary group of *Réformateurs démocrates sociaux*. Socialists and Left-Wing Radicals formed a common parliamentary group.

The death of President Pompidou in April 1974 immediately reopened the struggle for power, yet there was a new twist to the competition: Was a Gaullist candidate the best contender on behalf of the 'parties of the majority' to ward off the challenge from the 'United Left'? The Gaullist image had become somewhat tarnished, and the leader of the Independent Republicans, Valéry Giscard d'Estaing, proved better able to appeal to uncommitted voters. Giscard secured a very narrow win over

François Mitterrand, leader of the Socialist Party who was supported by the Communists.

Presidential Election, May 1974

Candidates	Main Support	Ballots	
		I %	II %
V. Giscard d'Estaing	Independent Republican UDR, CDP	32.60	50.81
F. Mitterrand	Socialist, Communist	43.24	49.19
J. Chaban-Delmas	UDR	15.10	—
Others	various	9.06	—

Notes: 'Others' consisted of nine candidates representing extremes of right and left as well as some non-party candidates. The poll at the second ballot was 87.33%, a record for any French election.

As set by the terms of the 1974 presidential election, the French party system came to resemble a 'two-bloc' formation. But the constituent parties bore an uneasy relationship to their supposed allies. The Gaullists smarted at the indignity of having to serve in 'second place' to a non-Gaullist president in a government which eventually had a non-Gaullist prime minister as well. There was a similarly uneasy relationship existing between the Socialists and Communists, for the latter perceived the danger to themselves of allowing Mitterrand to make the running for the Left, and they became increasingly alarmed that their predominant position in the alliance would be eroded. Left-wing cohesion was maintained until the strain of the 1978 election campaign began to tell, and from a predicted 'near certain' victory the Communists and Socialists drifted into a posture of mutual recrimination: partly in consequence, the 'parties of the majority' were again successful.

Elections to the Chamber of Deputies, March 1978

	First Ballot %	Second Ballot %	Assembly Seats*	
Gaullist RPR	22.6	26.1	143 + 11	
Giscardien UDF	21.5	23.2	108 + 16	
Other pro-Presidential	2.4	1.4		
Communist Party	20.6	18.6	86	
Socialist Party	22.6	28.3	102 + 11	
Left-Wing Radicals	2.1	2.3	(*in addition 14 not attached	
Extreme Left	3.3	—	to a party group)	
Environmentalists	2.1	—		
Others	2.8	—		

Notes: Changes in the party formations make comparisons with earlier years misleading. The UDR changed its name to RPR (*Rassemblement pour la République*).

The 'presidential' *Giscardien* UDF (*Union pour la Démocratie Française*) is a 'federation' including the Independent Republicans, the Radical Party, and the 'Centrists' (CDS). Candidates not securing 12.5 per cent at the first ballot were eliminated; those securing 50.0 per cent were elected at the first ballot. Broadly, inter-party agreements between first and second ballots meant that the leading candidate for the parties in alliance went forward to the second ballot, whilst any others stood down: RPR for the UDF, or vice-versa, Socialist for Communist or vice-versa. In consequence, second ballot votes often vary considerably from the first ballot recorded for any one party. In the Assembly there are four party groups with a number of *apparentés*, not strictly belonging to the party, attached to them.

Reading

M. Anderson, *Conservative Politics in France*, Allen and Unwin, 1975.

J. Ardagh, *The New France: De Gaulle and After*, Penguin Books, 1973.

B. E. Brown, *Protest in Paris: Anatomy of a Revolt*, New Jersey: General Learning Press, 1974.

J. Charlot, *The Gaullist Phenomenon*, George Allen and Unwin, 1971.

P. Coffey, *The Social Economy of France*, Macmillan, 1973.

S. E. Finer, *Comparative Government*, Allen Lane, 1970.

J. E. Flower (ed.), *France Today: Introductory Studies*, Methuen, (3rd ed.) 1977.

J. Frears, 'The French National Elections of March 1978', *Government and Opposition*, Summer 1978.

J. Frears, *Political Parties and Elections in the Fifth French Republic*, St. Martin's Press, 1977.

C. Hauss, *The New Left in France: The Unified Socialist Party*, Westport, Conn. The Greenwood Press, 1978.

J. Hayward, *The One and Indivisible French Republic*, Weidenfeld and Nicolson, 1973.

J. Hayward and V. Wright, 'Les Deux France and the French Presidential Election of May 1974', *Parliamentary Affairs*, Summer 1974.

R. Irving, 'The Centre Parties in the Fifth Republic', *Parliamentary Affairs*, Summer 1976.

H. Machin, *The Prefect in French Administration*, Croom Helm, 1977.

P. Naville, 'France', in *Contemporary Europe: Class, Status and Power*, op. cit.

D. Pickles, *The Government and Politics of France*, Methuen, 1972–3.

F. Ridley and J. Blondel, *Public Administration in France*, Routledge, 1964.

D. Thomson, *Democracy in France since 1870*, Oxford University Press, 1969.

M. Vaughan and M. Kolinsky, *Social Change in France*, Martin Robertson, 1980.

P. M. Williams, *Crisis and Compromise: Politics in the Fourth Republic*, Longman, 1964.

P. M. Williams and others, *French Politicians and Elections, 1961–1969*, Cambridge University Press, 1970.

V. Wright and J. Hayward, 'Governing from the Centre', *Government and Opposition*, Autumn 1977.

V. Wright, *The Government and Politics of France*, Hutchinson, 1978.

V. Wright (ed.), *Conflict and Consensus in France*, Frank Cass, 1979.

T. Zeldin (ed.), *Conflicts in French Society*, George Allen and Unwin, 1971.

THE FEDERAL GERMAN REPUBLIC

The Federal German Republic came into existence in 1949 with the promulgation of an Occupation Statute by the three western occupying powers, the United States, Britain, and France. Its area was therefore defined by their zones of occupation, with the later addition of the Saarland. Complete sovereignty did not come to the new state until 1955 when the Occupation Statute was withdrawn and West Germany became a full member of NATO. The period 1945 to 1949 was marked by the slow reactivation of political life, 'democracy under licence', beginning with the licensing of acceptable political parties (including the Communist Party) and proceeding to the establishment of Länder governments. As western relations with the Soviet Union worsened, so there was increasing pressure to set up a West German state. A decisive step was the creation of a German 'Bizonal Economic Council' in 1947 as a rudimentary government form for the British and American zones. West German delegates drafted a Basic Law, approved by the western powers, which was intended as a temporary constitution pending a peace settlement and the reunification of East and West Germany; this came into force in 1949. In many ways the new constitution was in marked contrast with that of the Weimar Republic (November 1918–March 1933). For a strong president with wide reserve powers, it substituted a weak figurehead; this change was deliberate, since the aim was to create a strong government leader, a chancellor, who although responsible to the lower house, the Bundestag, would have a decisive say in government policy. Unlike most other states, there is no provision for popular initiative or referendum, since they were felt to undermine the representative institutions. Like the Weimar Republic, West Germany is a federal state, but the system is securely based on a constitutional court and a powerful upper house, the Bundesrat. An apparent consequence of these innovations has been stable government; although governments are responsible to the Bundestag, none have been defeated by assembly vote and all parliaments have run their full term (except in 1972). However, social and economic factors are equally relevant in accounting for stable political life.

German economic recovery in the 1950s and 1960s was reflected politically in the assimilative power of the two major parties, the Christian Democrats and the Social Democrats, and a rapid run-down in the number of parties. Extremist parties of left and right were uniformly unsuccessful, and just as significant was the failure of the so-called 'Refugee Party' appealing to those uprooted either from East Germany or from the lost territories. This assimilation was at its height in the Adenauer era (1949–1963); thereafter the hold of Christian Democracy weakened under Chancellors Erhard and Kiesinger, and subsequent to the 1965 elections (in 1966) the Social Democrats entered into a 'Grand Coalition' with the CDU.

In 1969, the Christian Democrats were finally ousted from office, and the Free Democrats joined the SPD in coalition with Willy Brandt as chancellor. The 'social-liberal' coalition had only a slim majority over the CDU–CSU which was further narrowed by defection to the opposition, mainly caused by the government's attempt to fashion a positive Ostpolitik. The reconciliation with Germany's eastern neighbours resulted in treaties with the Soviet Union and Poland (ratified in June 1973) which confirmed the territorial status quo east of the Oder-Neisse line. A four-power pact guaranteeing the special position of Berlin was concluded in June 1971, and this eased the way for an important agreement with the German Democratic Republic, the 'Basic Treaty', which effectively gave official recognition to the existence of two German states. Brandt's Ostpolitik led to a succession of parliamentary confrontations (including an attempt to remove Brandt by a vote of constructive no-confidence) and the erosion of the coalition's majority forced an early election in November 1972; at this time the terms of the Basic Treaty were made public and became a central issue in the campaign.

The result of the election was a convincing victory for the SPD–FDP coalition. The Basic Treaty was ratified by the Bundestag in May 1973, and declared valid by the Constitutional Court in July 1973 (on the grounds that it did not conflict with the Basic Law, because the commitment to eventual reunification was maintained by the Federal Republic and since the Democratic Republic was nowhere in the treaty recognized as a foreign state).

Brandt resigned as chancellor in May 1974 after the discovery of an East German spy on his personal staff, although he remained leader of the SPD. His successor, Helmut Schmidt, was successful in maintaining the SPD–FDP coalition intact, but with a sharply reduced majority at the 1976 election.

Elections to the Bundestag, October 1976

	1976		1972	1969	1965
	Seats	%	%	%	%
Social Democrats	214	42.6	45.8	42.7	39.3
CDU–CSU	243	48.6	44.9	46.1	47.6
Free Democrats	39	7.9	8.4	5.8	9.5
NPD	—	0.3	0.6	4.3	2.0
Others	—	0.6	0.4	1.1	1.6

Notes: In 1976 there was a poll of 90.7 per cent. The CSU (Christian-Social Union) is the Bavarian partner of the CDU and holds 53 seats. Parties with less than five per cent of the total vote do not gain representation; that was the fate of the extremist National Democratic Party (NPD), most notably in 1969. 'Others' in 1976 includes the Communist Party (DKP) and other left splinter groups. West Berlin does not participate in federal elections, but sends representatives who take part in committees, although they have no vote in plenary sessions of the Bundestag.

Schmidt's term as chancellor was marked by the economic difficulties following the oil crisis, the rising incidence of terrorist activity in West Germany, and by the continuing controversy on the issue of employment of radicals in the public service (the so-called 'Berufsverbot'). The difficulties of the coalition were made more acute by the powerful position of the CDU–CSU in the Länder—and consequently in the Bundesrat. However, Schmidt's strong leadership won popular approval, and an endemic leadership problem beset the CDU–CSU opposition. In 1979 Franz Josef Strauss, leader of the right-wing CSU, became the CDU–CSU chancellor candidate for the 1980 federal election.

Reading

K. von Beyme and M. Kaase (eds.), *Elections and Parties*, Sage Publications, 1979.

K. von Beyme, 'The Politics of Limited Pluralism? The Case of West Germany', *Government and Opposition*, vol. 13/3, Summer 1978.

K. E. Birnbaum, *East and West Germany: A Modus Vivendi*, Saxon House, 1973.

W. Brandt, *People and Politics*, Collins, 1978.

A. Burkett, *Parties and Elections in West Germany*, C. Hurst, 1975.

C. Carl-Sime, 'Bavaria, the CSU and the West German Party System', *West European Politics*, vol. 2/1, January 1979.

K. H. Cerny (ed.), *Germany at the Polls: The Bundestag Election of 1976*, Washington: American Enterprise Institute, 1978.

D. P. Conradt, *The German Polity*, New York: David McKay, 1977.

K. Dyson, *Party, State and Bureaucracy in Western Germany*, Sage, 1977.

E. J. Feuchtwanger (ed.), *Upheaval and Continuity: A Century of German History*, Oswald Wolff, 1978.

W. Graf, *The German Left since 1945*, Oleander Press, 1976.

A. Grosser, *Germany in Our Time: A Political History of the Post-War Years*, Penguin Books, 1974.

R. Irving and W. Paterson, 'The West German Parliamentary Election of October 1976', *Parliamentary Affairs*, Spring 1977.

G. Kloss, *West Germany: An Introduction*, Macmillan, 1976.

N. Johnson, *Government in the Federal Republic of Germany: The Executive at Work*, Pergamon, 1973.

G. Loewenberg, *Parliament in the German Political System*, Cornell University Press, 1967.

P. H. Merkl, *German Foreign Policies, West and East*, Oxford, ABC-CLIO, 1974.

W. E. Paterson, *The SPD and European Integration*, Saxon House, 1974.

G. Pridham, *Christian Democracy in Western Germany*, Croom Helm, 1977.

G. Pridham, 'Ecologists in Politics: The West German Case', *Parliamentary Affairs*, Autumn 1978.

P. Pulzer, 'Responsible Party Government and Stable Coalition: The Case of the Federal Republic', *Political Studies*, vol. 16/2, June 1978.

H. K. Schellenger, *The SPD in the Bonn Republic*, The Hague: Martinus Nijhoff, 1968.

G. Schweigler, *National Consciousness in Divided Germany*, Saxon House, 1975.

G. Smith, *Democracy in Western Germany: Parties and Politics in the Federal Republic*, Heinemann, 1979.

G. Smith, 'West Germany and the Politics of Centrality', *Government and Opposition*, 11/4, 1976.

K. Sontheimer, *The Government and Politics of West Germany*, Hutchinson, 1972.
J. Sowden, *The German Question: 1945–1973*, Bradford University Press, 1975.
R. Tilford (ed.), *The Ostpolitik and Political Change in Germany*, Saxon House, 1975.

GREECE

Greece achieved her independence from the Ottoman Empire in 1827, and after a short period as a republic, became a monarchy in 1831. Since 1862, with sharp discontinuities, the line has been that of the House of Gluckbörg, and styled the 'King of the Hellenes'. This idea of a greater Greece did not accord with the boundaries of the original small state, and much of Greek political development until the 1920s was related to the problems of realizing the 'Great Idea' and resulted in foreign entanglement and dissension at home when the ambitions were unsatisfied. This nationalism has particularly affected the armed forces which became involved in politics at an early date. Disaffection in the army and navy over the failure to secure Crete led to a revolt against the parliamentary system and the monarchy (1909–1911); the effect of this however was to lead to a more democratic constitution in 1911, replacing that of 1864. As a result of the war with Turkey, beginning in 1912, Greece expanded her national territory considerably with the addition of Crete and Macedonia. With the accession of King Constantine I (1913–1922) there began a pattern of constitutional government, coup, and military dictatorship, which has repeated itself ever since. The whole period from 1917 until 1935 was marked by active military intervention, especially after the defeat of the Greek army in Asia Minor in 1922. A new (Second) republic was declared in 1924; this persisted until 1935, punctuated by attempted military coups. The elections of 1935 gave the pro-monarchist parties a majority and led to the return of King George II who had ruled previously from 1922–1924. The constitutional system was then undermined from within: rising to power by constitutional means as prime minister, General Metaxas became the strong man of Greek politics from 1936 until 1941. He assumed dictatorial powers, using the pretext of the growing internal threat of the Communist Party. In the war years, the common struggle against the Italian and German occupiers did not obscure the cleavage between left and right; from 1943 onwards the resistance groups were often locked in their own battles. The return of the government in exile and its attempts to disarm the resistance groups and reimpose national order were hardly effective. Elections held in 1946 gave the monarchist groups a majority, but large numbers of the electorate did not vote; following a referendum King George II once more returned to the throne. It was a signal for open warfare between the Communist 'Free Democratic Government' against the British-backed Greek National Army, and from 1947 the Americans began their permanent involvement in Greek politics.

By 1949, the Communist challenge had been defeated, and from 1950 until 1967 a stable parliamentary system was maintained under a new, and liberal constitution, though the Communist Party continued to be out-lawed. Fairly moderate conservative governments were the rule, first un-der the banner of the National Rally and then with the National Radicals led by Constantine Karamanlis who was prime minister from 1955 until 1963. This stability was superficial; the monarchy had lost none of its ability for becoming involved in politics, and this led to the resignation of Karamanlis. Social discontents were also growing; in 1964 the new, radical Centre Union under Giorgios Papendreou obtained an absolute majority. On dubious constitutional grounds King Constantine forced Papendreou out of office, but was then faced with the problem of finding a more amenable prime minister who could command an assembly majori-ty. For fear that the Centre Union and the left (EDA) would be returned with greater strength in the elections announced for April 1967, the military took power. The king's attempt at a counter-coup a few months later, although it failed, showed the gap between the military and the monarchy. The military junta appeared to gain some popular support when a new constitution it devised was overwhelmingly accepted (92 per cent) in 1968. In practice, the constitution remained a dead letter, with the leader of the junta, George Papadopoulos, exercising increasing personal power. A republic was declared in June 1973, later confirmed by referen-dum, and Papadopoulos became president. However, he was in turn deposed by an army coup in November 1973 following a savage repres-sion of student disorders. The new leaders of the regime, proved to have few ideas and little popular backing, and the dictatorship collapsed in the course of the confrontation in 1974 between Turkey and Greece over Cyprus; Greece was simply not in a position to defend her interests on the island, and the military government lost all credibility. Power was handed back to the civilians in July 1974, Constantine Karamanlis returning from exile to become prime minister. The relief at the end of the military dic-tatorship brought a refreshing moderation to Greek politics, but several ringleaders of the 1967 coup were subsequently tried for treason and imprisoned.

Political life was soon fully restored: the Communist Party was able to operate freely for the first time since 1947. Elections to a constituent assembly were held in November 1974 and the moderate parties were overwhelmingly successful. A referendum on the form of state followed in December and by a large majority (69.2 per cent) the electorate opted for a republic rather than a restoration of the monarchy.

In the 1974 election the victorious party was the New Democracy movement which had rapidly built up around the person of Karamanlis. New Democracy was also helped by the provisions of the electoral system—a 'reinforced proportional' type by which the largest parties (those receiving more than 17 per cent of the vote) qualified for an additional share of seats. Of the remaining parties the one formed by Andreas Papendreou was the most significant: his Pan-Hellenic Socialist Movement (Pasok) promised an alternative of democratic socialism to the broadly conservative outlook of New Democracy and the revamped Centre Union.

A new constitution was approved by the Constituent Assembly in July 1975, but there was bitter opposition in the assembly to the introduction of specifically presidential elements—a suspicion that it was tailor-made for Karamanlis, although in fact he subsequently remained prime minister. The president is elected by the assembly (for a five-year term and by a two-thirds majority) but he can only be removed by impeachment. The president can dissolve the assembly, without requiring the assent of the prime minister, and he is able to initiate a referendum on any fundamental national issue. The president may also proclaim martial law—and he has final control over the armed forces. This presidential injection has potential similarities with the Fifth French Republic.

A further election was held in November 1977. Even though New Democracy retained its overall majority in the assembly, Pasok made a spectacular advance, and the left-wing vote as a whole rose to 37.4 per cent. The way was thus open for a simple bi-polarity in Greek politics, a conclusion which is supported by the decline of the Centre Union and the subsequent fragmentation of its parliamentary group. A particular issue dividing the two groupings was the attitude taken towards Greek entry to the European Community. Although negotiations were completed late in 1979 (Greece will become a full member in 1981), the opposition demanded that the issue be put to a referendum. Pasok was deeply opposed to Greek entry and over a whole range of issues Papendreou insists on taking a strong national line, especially on Cyprus and relations with Turkey.

Elections to the Parliament of the Republic, November 1977

	1977 Seats	1977 %	1974 %
New Democracy	173	41.9	54.4
Pasok	92	25.3	13.6
Democratic Centre	15	12.0	20.5
National Rally	5	6.8	(1.0)
Communist Party	11	9.4	} 9.5
Left-Wing Alliance	2	2.7	
New Liberals	2	1.1	—
Others	—	0.8	1.0

Notes: There was a turnout of 88.3 per cent. Pasok is the Pan-Hellenic Socialist Movement. The Union of the Democratic Centre was formed from the 1974 Centre-

Union/New Forces. The National Rally is monarchist and right-wing—its nearest predecessor in 1974 was the National Democratic Union. In 1974 the Communist left was in alliance as the United Left, but the two major components fought separately in 1977. The more successful of the two was the Communist Party of Greece (Exterior) which is Moscow-oriented; the Communist Party of the Interior, broadly Eurocommunist, went under the banner of the 'Alliance of Progressive and Left-Wing Forces'. The New Liberal deputies joined up with New Democracy some time after the election, and the same applied to a section of the Democratic Centre.

Reading

J. P. C. Carey and A. G. Carey, *The Web of Modern Greek Politics*, New York: Columbia University Press, 1968.

R. Clogg, 'European Elections—Greece', *West European Politics*, 1/1, February 1978.

R. Clogg and G. Yannopoulos (eds.), *Greece under Military Rule*, Secker and Warburg, 1972.

N. Mouzelis, *Modern Greece: Facets of Underdevelopment*, Macmillan, 1977.

N. Mouzelis, 'Rise and Fall of the Greek Junta', *New Left Review*, no. 96, April 1976.

N. Mouzelis and M. Attalides, 'Greece', in *Contemporary Europe: Class, Status and Power*, op. cit.

E. O'Ballance, *The Greek Civil War, 1944–1949*, Faber and Faber, 1964.

A. Papendreou, *Democracy at Gunpoint: The Greek Front*, André Deutsch, 1971.

L. Tsoukalis (ed.), *Greece and the European Community*, Saxon House, 1978.

ICELAND

After many centuries of Danish rule (since 1381), Iceland became substantially independent in 1918, still sharing the Danish king as a common sovereign. In 1944, the country became an independent republic, and although the present constitution dates from that year, the roots of her parliamentary institutions go back to the tenth century, especially the popular assembly, the Althingi. The government is responsible to the assembly, but a popularly-elected president has reserve powers.

The major and traditional parties of government since 1918 have been the Independence Party and the Progressives, broadly corresponding to conservative and centre-agrarian outlooks respectively. However, the Icelandic party system is particularly hard to categorize, and domestic political issues are dictated by special concerns. With only one per cent of the total land area under cultivation, and the great bulk of the population concentrated in Reykjavik, fishing is the basis of the Icelandic economy—a factor which explains the intensity of the 'cod wars' with Britain in the 1960s and 1970s. The presence of a large American NATO base on the island also acts as a continual political irritant for the left-wing parties. Although Iceland has full employment, she is dogged by the most severe rate of inflation in Western Europe, so that the economic performance of successive governments is a major factor in explaining party fortunes.

Elections to the Althingi, June 1978

	1978		1974	1971	1967
	Seats	%	%	%	%
Independence Party	20	32.7	42.8	36.2	37.5
Progressive Party	12	16.9	24.9	25.2	28.1
People's Alliance	14	22.9	18.3	17.1	13.9
Social Democrats	14	22.0	9.1	10.4	15.7
Liberal-Left Union	—	3.3	4.6	8.9	—
Others	—	2.2	0.3	2.0	4.8

Notes: The People's Alliance is a Marxist party, whilst the left-wing Liberal-Left Union is not.

Although the Independence Party and the Progressives shared in coalition from 1974 until 1978, their aggregate share has fallen over the years thus necessitating wider coalitions, including the People's Alliance and the Liberal-Left Union. Thus the governing coalition formed in August 1978 and composed of Progressives, Social Democrats, and the People's Alliance, broke up in October 1979.

Reading

N. Andrén, *Government and Politics in the Nordic Countries*, Stockholm: Almsqvist and Wiksell, 1964.

G. Gislason, *Iceland, 1918–1968*, London: University College, 1968.

J. C. Griffiths, *Modern Iceland*, Pall Mall Press, 1969.

C. C. Hood, 'British Fishing and the Iceland Saga', *The Political Quarterly*, vol. 44/3, July–September, 1973.

J. Madeley, 'European Elections—Iceland', *West European Politics*, vol. 2/1, January 1979.

S. A. Magnusson, *Northern Sphinx. Iceland and the Icelanders*, C. Hurst, 1977.

J. Nordan and V. Kristinsson (eds.), *To Mark the Eleventh Centenary of the Settlement of Iceland*, Reykjavik: Central Bank of Iceland, 1975.

The Constitution of the Republic of Iceland, Reykjavik: Information Office of the Ministry for Foreign Affairs, 1948.

THE REPUBLIC OF IRELAND

After many centuries of English domination, a measure of Home Rule was eventually granted to Ireland in 1914, suspended until after the war, with civil war in Ireland intervening in the meanwhile. The civil war underlined the differences between the loyalist Irish, mainly Protestant and concentrated in Ulster, and the nationalist-dominated south who were

Roman Catholic. The Government of Ireland Act of 1920 took account of this division and set up a parliament for Northern Ireland in Belfast as well as one in Dublin. The fighting which followed led to the repeal of the 1920 Act and the granting of virtual autonomy to Southern Ireland by the passing of the Irish Free State Act of 1922. At the same time, Northern Ireland was granted Home Rule, still sending representatives to the British Parliament. Effective independence had thus been gained for 26 of the 32 Irish counties. In the remaining six counties, the majority favoured continued allegiance to Britain, but this part of Ulster also contained a large minority of Roman Catholics, who if not necessarily republican or nationalist in sympathy, represented a sharp and permanent basis of cleavage in Northern Irish society. A new constitution for Southern Ireland was approved by referendum in 1937, becoming Eire, that is, the Irish Republic, and the constitution affirmed that the national territory included Northern Ireland as well (Article 2). Until 1949 the Irish Republic was still regarded as a part of the Commonwealth. The Ireland Act, passed in Britain in 1949, confirmed the status of the Republic of Ireland, although she was not to be treated as a foreign country, nor her citizens as aliens. Additionally, the Ireland Act reiterated the position of Northern Ireland as an integral complement of the United Kingdom, and her constitutional position could not be altered without the consent of the Northern Irish parliament.

The political scene in the Irish Republic has for long been dominated by the two republican parties, Fine Gael (United Ireland) and Fianna Fail (Soldiers of Ireland); their different viewpoints are largely historical in origin: Fine Gael supported the Treaty with Britain to set up the Irish Free State, whilst Fianna Fail rejected its terms for the partition of Ireland. Both parties have lost any radical image they once had, although Fianna Fail is perhaps more progressive in the social basis of its support. The continued domination by these two parties gives a party system unlike any other in Western Europe, since the class basis of politics is scarcely apparent. There are also strong localist and personal elements which are strengthened by the voting system, a single transferable vote in multi-member constituencies; this system enables party supporters to put the candidates of their party in order of preference.

Although both Fianna Fail and Fine Gael are constitutionally and historically committed to a united Ireland, neither does much actively to promote the cause. There is an important political fringe, the Sinn Fein, which has this aim exclusively. The Irish Republican Army is itself illegal, but enjoys an amount of clandestine support and it serves an ideal which the major parties could never disown.

For much of the post-war period Fianna Fail, and indeed since the early 1930s, has been in a dominant position. But the impact of the crisis in Northern Ireland weakened the party's unity and authority, and in 1973 Fine Gael and the Labour Party were successful in forming a socially progressive coalition. However, Fianna Fail was swept triumphantly back to power in 1977, partly because of electoral dissatisfaction with the economic situation, but also through the personal appeal of the party's leader, Jack Lynch. Fianna Fail may also benefit from its more aggressively republican image.

Elections to the Dail, May 1977

	1977 Seats	1977 %	1973 %	1969 %	1965 %
Fianna Fail	84	50.6	46.4	45.7	47.8
Fine Gael	43	30.5	35.1	34.1	33.9
Labour Party	17	11.6	13.7	16.9	15.4
Independents	4	7.3	4.8	3.3	2.9

Notes: There was a poll of 76 per cent. Sinn Fein and various left-wing parties contested the election without winning any seats. For the 1977 election the voting age was lowered from 21 to 18. The percentages shown refer only to 'first preferences' which under the Single Transferable Vote system need not tally at all with the number of seats obtained.

Two important referenda have been held in recent years. One, in June 1972, resulted in an overwhelming vote in favour (80 per cent) of Irish membership of the European Community. The second, in December 1972, approved the amendment of Article 44 of the constitution which had accorded a 'special position' to the Roman Catholic Church (84.4 per cent in favour). The deletion was interpreted as a gesture of reconciliation towards the Protestant community on Northern Ireland. But it should be stressed that successive Irish governments have not felt able to take much positive action to secure unity. The imposition of direct rule over Northern Ireland was generally welcomed in 1972, and in 1973 the British proposals for its constitutional future did envisage a 'Council of Ireland' which would have involved all-Irish participation. However, Irish governments wish neither to risk an open breach with Britain over the issue of unity, nor to countenance the risk of violence spreading across the border to the republic. Fianna Fail takes the strongest line in calling for an eventual British withdrawal from Northern Ireland.

Reading

M. Ayearst, *The Republic of Ireland: Its Government and Politics*, University of London Press, 1971.

B. Chubb, *The Government and Politics of Ireland*, Oxford University Press, 1973.

B. Chubb, 'Ireland' in S. Henig (ed.), *Political Parties in the European Community*, op. cit.

A. Cohan, *The Irish Political Elite*, Dublin: Gill and Macmillan, 1972.

T. P. Coogan, *The I.R.A.*, Pall Mall Press, 1970.

B. Farrell, *The Irish Parliamentary Tradition*, Dublin: Gill and Macmillan, 1973.

B. Farrell, 'The Irish General Election of 1977', *Parliamentary Affairs*, 31/1, Winter 1978.

M. Gallagher, *Electoral Support for Irish Political Parties*, Sage Publications, 1977.

C. D. Greaves, *The Irish Question*, Lawrence and Wishart, 1973.

J. Jackson, 'Ireland', in *Contemporary Europe: Class, Status and Power*, op. cit.

M. Manning, *Irish Political Parties*, Dublin: Gill and Macmillan, 1972.

A. H. Marshall, *Local Government Administration Abroad*, op. cit.

J. A. Murphy, *Ireland in the Twentieth Century*, Dublin: Gill and Macmillan, 1975.

E. Norman, *A History of Modern Ireland*, Penguin Books, 1973.

J. D. O'Donnell, *How Ireland is Governed*, Dublin: Institute of Public Administration, 1974.

A. Orridge, 'The Irish Labour Party', in Paterson and Thomas (eds.), *Social Democratic Parties in Western Europe*, op. cit.

P. Pyne, 'The Bureaucracy in the Irish Republic', *Political Studies*, March 1974.

D. E. Schmitt, *The Irony of Irish Democracy*, Saxon House, 1974.

J. Whyte, 'Ireland: Politics Without Social Bases', in R. Rose, *Electoral Behavior*, op. cit. cit.

See also, Northern Ireland (United Kingdom).

ITALY

The unification of Italy was finally achieved in 1870 as a monarchy under the House of Savoy until 1946 when she became a republic. The period until the First World War was one of domination by the anti-clerical Liberals, the popular force of national unification; modern mass parties scarcely existed, parliamentary majorities were 'managed', the electorate was restricted, and there was a Papal prohibition on Catholics participating at all in political life. By 1919 this had all changed and the sharp political cleavages were given full expression; the transition to a stable parliamentary system based on mass parties faced severe problems. The contending forces of the Nationalists, Fascists, Catholic Populists, Socialists (and, from 1921, the Communists) shared nothing of the governmental experience of the rapidly declining Liberals. The political and industrial turmoil of the post-war years soon led to a radicalization of Italian politics. The inability of the moderate left and moderate right to work together, Socialists and Catholics, even though these were the two largest parties, gave the lever to the small Fascist movement, which through its militia succeeded in imposing its own version of order on large parts of the country, often with the connivance of local prefects. In October 1922 the King offered the premiership to Mussolini, and the March on Rome which followed was a display of fascist power. The government remained nominally parliamentary until 1924. Elections was held in April, but these took place in an atmosphere of Fascist terror, and under a law made for the benefit of the Fascists which stipulated that the party winning 25 per cent of the votes would be allotted two-thirds of the seats in the

Chamber of Deputies. From January 1925, the system of Fascism and personal dictatorship under Mussolini was instituted, whilst still preserving the symbols of the monarchy and the Pope. The Vatican, indeed, welcomed Mussolini, for the Lateran Treaties of 1929 restored all the privileges of the Church that had been swept away in 1870—the Vatican had been the enemy of a united Italy.

In the period of reconstruction after 1945, a popular plebiscite voted for a republic in 1946, and a new constitution came into effect in 1948. This provided for full parliamentary government, extensive democratic rights, a constitutional court, and far-reaching provisions for regional government. From the beginning, political life has been focused on the powerful Christian Democratic Party which has been in power since the first elections in 1946, though almost always in coalition; for a brief spell (1948 until 1953) it actually had a majority of seats. This stability has to be matched against the deep political cleavage between Christian Democracy and the powerful Communist Party, the strongest in Western Europe. However, the polarization has never come to full effect, since the Christian Democrats have avoided becoming a clerical-conservative party. This was shown clearly from 1962 onwards when it initiated a policy of seeking an opening to the left, that is, left-of-centre coalitions which stopped short of the extreme left. It is the question of co-operation with the Christian Democrats which in turn has divided the left, essentially into three groupings: the excluded Communists, Socialists willing to join a Christian Democratic coalition, and Socialists who regarded such coalitions as divisive of working-class unity.

At the other end of the political scale, the left-inclination of the Christian Democrats has given some encouragement to the extreme right, especially the MSI (*Movimento Sociale Italiano*) which arose as a splinter party but which harbours a considerable neo-fascist potential. Various combinations of the centre-left formula have been applied in recent years—the Christian Democrats with one or more other parties: the Social Democrats, the Socialists, the Republicans, though not all the minor parties have been represented in every coalition.

The extreme difficulty of fashioning a majority can be illustrated by the presidential election which took place in December 1971. The Italian president is elected for a seven-year term by an electoral college consisting of the two houses of the Italian Parliament with representatives from the regions, 1,008 in electors in all. The 1971 election resulted in twenty-two inconclusive ballots before a Christian Democrat was elected at the twenty-third attempt. (For details, see *The Times*, 21/22 December 1971.) However, the powers of the Italian president are not very great; his importance lies in his ability to help build coalitions, and the stability of his office offsets the instability of government which has become an endemic feature of Italian politics.

Prime Minister	Party composition	date taking office	number of government
Colombo	DC, PSI, PSDI, PRI	Aug. 1970	32
Andreotti	DC*	Feb. 1972	33
(Election, May 1972)			
Andreotti	DC, PSDI, PLI	June 1972	34
Rumor	DC, PSI, PSDI, PRI	July 1973	35
Rumor	DC, PSI, PSDI	March 1974	36
(Divorce Law Referendum, May 1974)			
Moro	DC, PRI*	Nov. 1974	37
Moro	DC*	Feb. 1976	38
(Election, June 1976)			
Andreotti	DC*	June 1976	39
Andreotti	DC*	July 1977	40
Andreotti	DC, PSDI, PRI*	March 1979	41
(Election, June 1979)			
Cossiga	DC, PSDI, PLI*	Aug. 1979	42

Notes: All prime ministers have come from the Christian Democratic party. The 'numbering' of governments dates from the first post-fascist government in 1943. The asterisk denotes a minority government formation.

A feature of the early 1970s was the gradual undermining of the DC's dominant position, resulting in wide and generally short-lived coalitions and made more precarious by the gradual rise in the Communist vote. However, the most significant development was shown in the result of the referendum on the Divorce Law held in May 1974. The Christian Democrats and the Roman Catholic hierarchy both supported the repeal of the more liberal divorce law which had been enacted. But the referendum resulted in 59.1 per cent voting in favour of retention (19 million to 13 million with a high poll of 88.1 per cent). Defeat for the abolitionists was also a defeat for Christian Democracy, and it was apparent that many of the party's supporters had defected on this occasion.

The reverse in the Divorce Law referendum was followed in June 1975 by serious setbacks in the regional and municipal elections. The Communists recorded massive gains—becoming the largest party in seven of the fifteen regions contested. In consequence the PCI, often in alliance with the Socialist Party, was able to win control of several regional governments as well as a number of important cities.

The PCI had already embarked on a new strategy before the electoral tide began to move so markedly in its favour. The leader of the PCI, Enrico Berlinguer enunciated the terms of an 'historic compromise' in 1973. The 'compromise' was based on the idea of winning alliances with *all* progressive elements in Italian society, a pluralistic view rather than one based on the necessity of encouraging working class—and therefore PCI—hegemony. Thus the strategy implied a collaboration with the DC under certain conditions rather than an insistence that Christian Democracy should be supplanted. Moreover, the 'historic' nature of the proffered compromise implied much more than a tactical concession: the new line was based on a long-term view of Italian economic and social development—and the economic and social crises which appeared to be endemic.

The PCI received a further endorsement in the national election of June 1976. Although the DC vote remained at roughly its previous level, that of the PCI jumped from 27.3 per cent in 1972 to 34.4 per cent in 1976: a position of near parity to the DC. The dilemma facing Christian Democracy was apparent: it was impossible for the party to rule with the Communists, but it was equally impossible to rule without them either. Any move to bring the PCI directly into government might well have fragmented the DC, but by itself the DC scarcely had the authority to govern. Whilst in the wake of the 1976 election it would have been just about feasible to form a DC coalition without the PCI, that governing majority would have had no mandate to tackle Italy's pressing and deep-rooted economic problems. The interim solution adopted was to establish a conventional DC minority government, but in fact it was generally realized that such a government would have a useful existence only if it could be assured of support from the other parties, especially the Communists.

Tangible evidence of this support came in July 1977 when a six-party 'pact' came into being (DC, PCI, PSI, PSDI, Republicans and Liberals). The pact was mainly concerned with agreement on economic and industrial measures deemed necessary to bring about Italian recovery. In effect, the pact represented a disguised all-party coalition and was the one acceptable way of bringing the PCI into open association with the DC in government.

The working out of the 'historic compromise' however soon set up a political reaction, both from the extreme left and the far right. Of the two, the left-wing reaction was immediately the more portentous. The point of crisis came with the abduction and subsequent murder of Aldo Moro in February 1978. Moro, a previous prime minister and at the time of his assassination president of the DC National Council, was the major figure responsible for reaching an accord with the PCI. That action of the 'Red Brigades' struck at the heart of the 'compromise', although the immediate consequence was, if anything, to increase the general mood of solidarity.

In January 1979 the PCI withdrew its support from the DC government, fearing the electoral effects of continued association. The anxiety proved justified since the PCI vote fell abruptly in June 1979 after decades of almost uninterrupted growth. Other parties such as the MSI also lost ground, whilst the Radical Party, a somewhat unorthodox political formation, introduced a new element. Government formation proved as difficult as ever and several months elapsed before even a temporary 'truce' DC administration was agreed. (See table page 292.)

Elections to the Chamber of Deputies, June 1979

	1979		1976	1972	1968
	Seats	%	%	%	%
Christian Democrats (DC)	262	38.3	38.7	38.3	39.1
Communists (PCI)	201	30.4	34.4	27.3	26.9
Socialists (PSI)	62	9.8	9.6	9.5	14.5
Social Democrats (PSDI)	20	3.8	3.4	5.2	
MSI	30	5.8	6.1	8.7	4.5
Republicans (PRI)	16	3.0	3.1	2.9	2.0
Liberals (PLI)	9	1.9	1.3	3.9	5.8
Radicals	18	3.4	1.1	—	—
Democratic Proletarians	6	1.4	1.5	1.9	4.5
South Tyrol People's Party	4	0.6	0.5	0.5	0.4
Others	2	1.6	0.3	1.1	2.3

Notes: The 'Democratic Proletarians' are the successor to the PSIUP (Socialist Party of Proletarian Unity) which contested the 1972 and 1968 elections. The PSIUP was originally a breakaway from the Socialist Party. The Socialists and the Social Democrats briefly formed a unified party in 1968; the PSDI is now a party well to the right on the political spectrum. The South Tyrol People's Party represents the German-speaking minority and is usually allied with the DC.

Reading

J. C. Adams and P. Barile, *The Government of Republican Italy*, Boston: Houghton Mifflin, 1972.

P. A. Allum, *Italy—Republic without Government?*, Weidenfeld and Nicolson, 1973.

P. A. Allum, *Politics and Society in Post-War Naples*, Cambridge University Press, 1973.

P. A. Allum, 'Italy', in S. Henig (ed.), *Political Parties in the European Community*, op. cit.

S. H. Barnes, 'Italy: Religion and Class in Electoral Behavior', in R. Rose (ed.), *Electoral Behavior*, op. cit.

G. Di Palma, *Surviving without Governing: The Italian Parties in Parliament*, University of California Press, 1977.

P. Flores and F. Moretti, 'Paradoxes of the Italian Crisis', *New Left Review*, April 1976.

D. Hine, 'Social Democracy in Italy', in Paterson and Thomas (eds.), *Social Democratic Parties in Western Europe*, op. cit.

D. Hine, 'Socialists and Communists in Italy—Reversing Roles?', *West European Politics*, 1/2, May 1978.

P. Lange and S. Tarrow (eds.), 'Italy in Transition: Conflict and Consensus', *West European Politics*, October 1979 (whole issue).

A. Marradi, 'Italy's Referendum on Divorce', *European Journal of Political Research*, vol. 4, March 1976.

P. Nichols, *The Politics of the Vatican*, Pall Mall Press, 1968.

G. Pasquino, 'Capital and Labour in Italy', *Government and Opposition*, vol. 11/3, 1976.

G. Pridham, 'The Italian Christian Democrats after Moro', *West European Politics*, 2/1, January 1979.

A. Ranney and G. Sartori (eds.), *Eurocommunism: The Italian Case*, Washington: American Enterprise Institute, 1978.

M. Santuccio and S. Acquaviva, *Social Structure in Italy*, Martin Robertson, 1975.

G. R. Urban (ed.), *Eurocommunism: Its Roots and Future in Italy*, Maurice Temple Smith, 1978.

F. R. Willis, *Italy Chooses Europe*, New York: Oxford University Press, 1971.

E. Wiskemann, *Italy since 1945*, Macmillan, 1971.

S. J. Woolf (ed.), *The Rebirth of Italy, 1943–1950*, Longman, 1972.

R. Zariski, *Italy: The Politics of Uneven Development*, Hinsdale, Illinois: Dryden Press, 1972.

LUXEMBOURG

From the fifteenth century onwards Luxembourg was controlled by a succession of foreign powers. In 1815 it was created a Grand Duchy with the Dutch king as the first Grand Duke. Following the Belgian secession from the Netherlands, Luxembourg became independent as well. The country's independent existence dates from 1839, but as a much smaller entity than was the case in previous centuries. The main spoken language is German and the Letzeburgesch dialect, but there are strong cultural ties with France and strong economic ones with Belgium—a customs union has been in force since 1921. Luxembourg shed the neutral status it had tried to maintain since 1867 after the Second World War and joined the Benelux union in 1947. The country was also a founder member of the European Coal and Steel Community and of the EEC. As she has entered these external commitments, so has her international position increased in importance. The Grand Duke is a purely representative monarch and the government is responsible to the Chamber of Deputies. The assembly is unicameral and there is an unusual legislative checking device whereby the legislation has to be passed by the assembly a second time, with a three-month interval. If this procedure is not adopted, then the administrative body, the Council of State, has a suspensory veto. The party system follows a typical European pattern: Christian Socials, Socialists, Liberals, and Communists. The Christian Socials are the largest party and until 1974 had participated in every government since 1919, and since 1945 had supplied every prime minister. The normal pattern was a coalition with either the Liberals or the Socialists, a formula which broke down in 1974 with a sharp fall in the Christian-Social vote.

Elections to the Chamber of Deputies, June 1979

	1979 Seats	1979 %	1974 %	1968 %	1964 %
Christian Socials	24	34.9	28.0	35.3	33.5
Socialists	14	24.6	29.0	32.3	38.0
Liberals (Democrats)	15	21.6	22.1	16.6	9.9
Social Democrats	2	6.1	9.1	—	—
Communists	2	5.9	10.4	15.5	12.6
Others	2	6.9	1.4	0.4	6.0

Notes: Voting is compulsory. The voting age was reduced to 18 in 1974. The Social Democrats, formed in 1971, was a breakaway from the Socialists on the question of cooperating with the Communists at a local level.

A liberal-socialist coalition was formed after the 1974 election, exceptionally forcing the Christian Socials into opposition. However, the 'normal pattern' was restored in 1979 and the Liberals joined in coalition with the major party.

Reading

M. Hirsch, 'Luxembourg' in S. Henig (ed.), *Political Parties in the European Community*, op. cit.

S. Holt, *Six European States*, Hamish Hamilton, 1970.

A. Herchen, *History of the Grand-Duchy of Luxembourg*, Luxembourg: Linden, 1950.

P. King (ed.), *Benelux*, Hull University Press, 1977.

G. L. Weil, *The Benelux Nations: The Politics of Small Country Democracies*, New York: Holt, Rinehart and Winston, 1970.

MALTA

Malta became a British colony in 1814 after the island had been taken from the French. In 1947 she was granted self-government with a British-appointed governor who had powers in foreign affairs, defence, and currency. In 1955 the Maltese Labour Party came to office and made a radical proposal for the full integration of Malta with the United Kingdom and this proposal received the support of three-quarters of the voters at a referendum in 1956. The constitution was suspended in 1958 following the breakdown of negotiations towards integration, and by the 1960s there was a general desire for independence. The opposing Nationalist Party came to power in 1962 and full independence was gained in 1964 with a new constitution making the government responsible to the single-chamber House of Representatives. The Nationalist government negotiated a Defence Agreement with Britain, the main importance of which for the Maltese was a financial contribution to the underdeveloped economy of Malta. She suffers from a relative overpopulation—a third of a million people and little more than 100 square miles. The Nationalist Party was returned to power in 1966, but the position was reversed in 1971 and the Labour Party, despite its narrow majority, has since become the dominant force in Maltese politics.

Elections to the House of Representatives, September 1976

| | 1976 | | 1971 |
	Seats	%	%
Labour Party	34	51.2	50.8
Nationalist Party	31	48.8	48.1
Others		—	1.1

Notes: 95 per cent of the electorate voted. The electoral system is that of the Single Transferable Vote in multi-member constituencies. The age of voting was lowered to 20 in 1976.

In December 1974 Malta became a republic, thus severing her connection with Britain. The president of the republic is elected for a five-year term by the House of Representatives. His powers are substantially those of the former governor-general. In fact, all real power emanates from Dom Mintoff, the leader of the Labour Party. He has followed a strongly neutralist line for Malta in some respects—favouring close links with China and Libya. He asserted Maltese independence by demanding a revision of the defence agreement with Britain, with the threat of closing the NATO defence establishment on the island. Eventually, in March 1972, a new agreement was reached with Britain (and interested NATO partners) to last for seven years; Britain finally withdrew her forces in 1979.

Political life in Malta is sharply polarized, although disagreement on foreign policy is rather a question of emphasis. The opposition claims that the Labour Party is determined to stay in power at all costs. After the 1976 election the Nationalist Party sought to bring a complaint concerning alleged election irregularities to the Constitutional Court. Thereupon the Labour Government promptly dismissed two of the Court's three judges—replacing them with its own nominees.

Reading

D. Austin, *Malta and the End of Empire*, Frank Cass, 1971.
E. Dobie, *Malta's Road to Independence*, University of Oklahoma, 1967.

THE NETHERLANDS

Although the modern state of the Netherlands dates from 1815, when the existing Stadtholder, William of Orange-Nassau, was created monarch of the north and south Netherlands, her period of greatness was in the seventeeth century as a leader in trade and science. From the late sixteenth century onwards the Dutch Republic, composed of the seven United Provinces, was more of a confederacy than a unified state. A parliamentary system was only established in 1814, and this was not substantially democratized until 1848. The fragile union of the north and south Netherlands was broken when the south revolted in 1830, and became the independent state of Belgium in 1831. The bicameral system of the States-General was reformed in 1848; the estate system of representation was abolished in favour of direct suffrage, whilst the upper house was elected by members of the provincial councils as it continues to be at present. At the same time, the principle of ministerial responsibility to the States-

General was established. As the franchise was extended between 1887 and 1919, so the modern parties took shape, but the party system which resulted was based on the peculiarities of the cleavages in Dutch society, especially those of religion. In this, a fundamental feature was that the political élites, Calvinist or Catholic, have not been identified with a single state church. This religious pluralism has made for a political pluralism; both Protestants and Catholics had to face powerful secular influences, and these three together compose the three 'pillars' of Dutch society—any one of them is a minority so there is a natural tendency to compomise.

Thus despite the apparently introverted nature of the various religious parties, this isolation is modified by the necessity to work in harmony with others or to risk political exclusion. Initially, and until the First World War, the alliance was between Catholics and Calvinists against the Liberals, fought over the question of education, with both groups alternating in office. Fear of the Socialists drove the religious parties together with the Liberals, and for most of the inter-war period it was the Socialists who were excluded, and the wide class appeal of the religious parties prevented the Dutch Labour Party from obtaining more than a quarter of the vote.

In the post-war period coalitions have become more broadly based, frequently with the participation of the Labour Party. The gradual decline of the three major religious parties has led to a general diffusion of the party system: in the 1950s they accounted for about half the vote compared with about a third in recent years. The three religious parties (one Catholic and two Protestant) joined together in 1976 to form the Christian Democratic Appeal, but this consolidation did not improve their position materially in 1977. In contrast, the Labour Party has emerged as the strongest political force.

The diffusion of the party system has caused intense difficulty in the formation of coalitions: after the 1972 election it took some five months to reach agreement, in 1977 no less than nine months. Dutch practice requires detailed negotiation over the government's programme: thus in 1977 the coalition which eventually resulted between the CDA and the Liberals needed prior settlement of 150 relevant questions.

Although the party system does have diffused characteristics, its core is made up of Labour, Christian Democrats and Liberals, and there are indications of a 'two-bloc' balance: CDA and Liberals on one side and the Labour Party with its allies (Democrats '66 and the Radical Political Party) on the other. However, the new CDA has not yet settled its political direction and severe internal stresses were set up in the party by the decision to enter the coalition with the conservative Liberals.

Elections to the Lower Chamber of the States-General, May 1977

	1977 Seats	1977 %	1972 %	1971 %	1967 %
Labour Party	53	33.8	27.4	24.6	23.6
Christian Democrats (CDA)	49	31.9	31.3	36.7	44.6
Liberals (Freedom and Democracy)	28	17.9	14.4	10.4	10.7
Democrats '66	8	5.4	4.2	6.8	4.5
State Reform Party (Calvinist)	3	2.1	2.2	2.4	2.0
Radical Political Party (Catholic)	3	1.7	4.8	1.8	—
Communist Party	2	1.7	4.5	3.9	3.6
Reformed Political Assn. (Calvinist)	1	0.9	1.8	1.6	0.9
Pacifist Socialist Party	1	0.9	1.5	1.4	2.7
Farmers' Party	1	0.8	1.9	1.1	4.8
Democratic Socialists '70	1	0.7	4.1	5.3	—
Roman Catholic Party	—	0.4	0.9	—	—
Party of the Middle Classes	—	—	0.4	1.5	—

Notes: The Christian Democratic Appeal first came into being for the 1977 election; it was formed by an amalgamation of three parties: the Catholic People's Party, the Protestant Anti-Revolutionary Party (ARP), and the Protestant Christian Historical Union (CHU). The separate results for the three in the earlier elections have been combined in the table; in detail they are: 1972—Catholics 17.7%, ARP 8.8%, CHU 4.8%; 1971—Catholics 21.8%, ARP 8.6%, CHU 6.3%; 1967—Catholics 26.5%, ARP 9.9%, CHU 8.2%.

The representation of a number of very small parties is made possible by treating the whole country as a single constituency and by an effective quota of considerably less than one per cent of total votes cast.

Reading

P. Baehr, 'The Netherlands', *in European Political Parties*, op. cit.

H. Daalder, 'The Netherlands', in S. Henig, *Political Parties in the European Community*, op. cit.

H. Daalder, 'The Netherlands: Opposition in a Fragmented Society', in *Political Oppositions in Western Democracies*, op. cit.

Digest of the Kingdom of the Netherlands: Constitutional Structure, The Hague: Netherlands Government Information Service, 1966.

L. E. Dutter, 'The Netherlands as a Plural Society', *Comparative Political Studies*, 10/4, January 1978.

K. Gladdish, 'Two-Party versus Multi-Party: The Netherlands and Britain', *Parliamentary Affairs*, January 1974.

J. Goudsblom, *Dutch Society*, New York: Random House, 1967.

S. Holt, *Six European States*, Hamish Hamilton, 1970.

F. E. Huggett, *The Modern Netherlands*, Pall Mall Press, 1971.

P. King (ed.), *Benelux*, Hull University Press, 1977.

A. Lijphart, *The Politics of Accommodation: Pluralism and Democracy in the Netherlands*, Berkeley and Los Angeles: University of California Press, 1968.

A. Lijphart, 'The Netherlands: Continuity and Change in Voting Behavior', in R. Rose (ed.), *Electoral Behavior*, op. cit.

A. H. Marshall, *Local Government Administration Abroad*, op. cit.

G. L. Weil, *The Benelux Nations: The Politics of Small-Country Democracies*, New York: Holt, Rinehart and Winston, 1970.

S. B. Wolinetz, 'The Dutch Labour Party: A Social Democratic Party in Transition' in Paterson and Thomas (eds.), *Social Democratic Parties in Western Europe*, op. cit.

NORWAY

Although Norway has one of the oldest and least-amended constitutions of Western Europe, dating from 1814, in fact her history until recent times has been one of foreign domination. Prior to 1814, Norway had been under Danish rule for several centuries, and from then until 1905 in union with Sweden. The periods of Danish and Swedish influence left their mark on Norwegian culture and politics. the strong oppositional elements showed in the reaction to the Danish-dominated city-life, bureaucracy, and language in counter-movements of cultural defence and language outside the main cities. There were also the struggles between the assembly, the Storting, and the Swedish monarchy, with the assembly a focus for national demands. This role it could take because the 1814 constitution gave a system of representation which was the most democratic in Europe, almost all men over the age of twenty-five had the vote. Both the cultural and national issues came to the fore in the nineteenth century. By 1884, the principle of government responsibility to the Storting was recognized, and in 1905, using a consultative referendum, the country opted to become an independent monarchy (of Danish origin). The Norwegian party system has been heavily influenced by historical factors, and cultural and constitutional issues were supplemented by class ones.

The first party divisions were represented by the Right (Höyre) against the Left (Venstre), the one conservative and pro-union with Sweden, the other liberal and agrarian. These were joined by the Norwegian Labour Party which first won representation to the Storting in 1903; it soon showed its strength in making an appeal to fishermen, small farmers, as well as the urban worker. In 1927 it became the largest party, and dominated Norwegian politics from 1933 to 1965; apart from the war period it was in office for all but four weeks. Until 1961, the Labour Party had an absolute majority in the Storting, but in 1965 it was replaced by a coalition of the bourgeois parties: Right-Conservative, Venstre-Liberal, Centre-Agrarian, and the Christian People's Party. That these non-socialist parties had never been able to form a united and single opposition party to Labour underlines the various bases of cleavage in Norwegian politics, not least territorially and culturally.

The new coalition represented the actualization of the 'two bloc' system in Norwegian politics. However, the alliance broke up early in 1971, caught up in the turmoil over the question of membership of the European Community. Deep divisions were evident within the parties, and the result of the referendum held in September 1972 (53.5 per cent against joining) indicated a sharp territorial cleavage: northern and rural areas were most deeply opposed. Although a clear majority in the Storting favoured membership, the referendum result was treated as binding.

There then followed the 'electoral earthquake' of the 1973 election in which the Labour Party received its lowest vote in forty years and the Liberal Party was almost annihilated. The Labour Party formed a minority administration following the election, and since there is no provision for an early dissolution of the Storting, its position was relatively secure. In the 1977 election the European Community issue was no longer live, and the Labour Party was able to regain much of its former strength.

Elections to the Storting, September 1977

	1977 Seats	1977 %	1973 %	1969 %	1965 %
Labour Party	76	42.4	35.3	46.5	43.1
Conservative (Höyre)	41	24.7	17.5	19.6	21.1
Centre (Agrarian)	12	8.6	11.0	10.5	9.9
Christian People's Party	22	12.1	12.2	9.4	8.1
Socialist People's Party	2	4.1	⎰ 11.2	3.5	6.0
Communist Party	—	0.4	⎱	1.0	1.4
Progress Party	—	1.9	5.0	—	—
Liberal (Venstre)	2	3.2	3.5	⎰ 9.4	⎰ 10.3
New People's Party	—	1.7	3.4	⎱	⎱
Others	—	0.9	0.8	0.1	0.1

Notes: The Communist Party participated in a Socialist Election Alliance in 1973 but fought alone in 1977. The New People's Party was formed from a Liberal split in 1973. The Progress Party was formerly 'Anders Lange's Party for the Reduction of Taxes, Duties, and Government Intervention'. The system of proportional representation in Norway slightly favours the larger parties and penalizes the smaller ones.

The result of the 1977 election saw the reassertion of the two-bloc formation, and the gains of the Labour Party were matched by those of the Conservatives. The Labour Party continued in office as a minority government and was well-placed to survive on the basis of seeking specific 'majorities for the occasion', but the problems surrounding the Norwegian economy—the embarrassment of riches consequent upon the exploitation of oil reserves—are likely to be intense: the concern for the environment versus the highest projected growth rate for Western Europe.

Reading

T. Andenaes (ed.), *The Constitution of Norway*, Oslo: Norwegian Universities Press, 1962.

N. Andrén, *Government and Politics in the Nordic Countries*, Stockholm: Almqvist and Wiksell, 1964.

K. H. Cerny (ed.), *Scandinavia at the Polls: Recent Political Trends in Denmark, Norway and Sweden*, Washington: American Enterprise Institute, 1977.

T. K. Derry, *A History of Modern Norway*, Oxford University Press, 1973.

T. K. Derry, 'Norway', in *European Fascism*, op. cit.

H. Eckstein, *Division and Cohesion in Democracy: A Study of Norway*, New Jersey: Princeton University Press, 1966.

K. Heidar, 'The Norwegian Labour Party: Social Democracy in a Periphery of Europe', in Paterson and Thomas (eds.), *Social Democratic Parties in Western Europe*, op. cit.

R. B. Kvavik, 'Interest Groups in a "Cooptive" Political System: The Case of Norway' in M. O. Heisler, *Politics in Europe*, op. cit.

J. Madeley, 'European Elections—Norway', *West European Politics*, vol. 1/1, February 1978.

N. Ørvik (ed.), *Norway's No to Europe*, International Studies Association, University of Pittsburgh, 1975.

A. Os and A. Rudd, 'Norway's Ombudsman', in D. C. Rowat, op. cit.

N. R. Ramsøy, *Norwegian Society*, C. Hurst, 1974.

H. Valen and S. Rokkan, 'Norway: Conflict Structure and Mass Politics in a European Periphery', in R. Rose (ed.), *Electoral Behavior*, op. cit.

S. Rokkan, 'Geography, Religion and Social Class: Crosscutting Cleavages in Norwegian Politics', in *Party Systems and Voter Alignments*, op. cit.

S. Rokkan, 'Norway: Numerical Democracy and Corporate Pluralism', in *Political Oppositions in Western Democracies*, op. cit.

H. Valen and D. Katz, *Political Parties in Norway*, Tavistock Publications, 1964.

See also, *Scandinavian Political Studies*.

PORTUGAL

Portugal has had a cohesive national existence since the eleventh century and was a monarchy until 1910. The overthrow of the monarchy led to one of the most unstable parliamentary systems in European experience. From 1910 to 1926, 'There were six presidents, forty prime ministers and two hundred cabinet ministers. In all political changes the action of the military was critical.'* In this period there were also twenty-four revolutions and coups d'état. The army finally put paid to the republic in 1926, and this soon resulted in the rise to power of Dr Antonio de Oliveira Salazar, first as finance minister and finally as dictator from 1932 onwards. The form of the new state (*Estado Novo*) was given expression in the constitution of 1933. The legislature consisted of a corporate (functional) upper house and a lower one elected on a limited franchise. Power rested with the prime minister and the sole legal political organization, the *Uniao Nacional*. All the elections (and all the seats) were always won by the ruling party by use of the 'block vote' (a relative majority in multi-member constituencies), and opposition groups were only allowed to form for the

---

* G. L. Field, *Comparative Political Development: The Precedent of the West*, Routledge and Kegan Paul, 1968, p. 141.

period of the election campaign. The post of president was reserved for a leading member of the armed forces. Salazar stayed in power as prime minister until 1968 when he was succeeded by Dr. Marcello Caetano. In 1971 Caetano attempted various measures of cautious liberalization, including a greater freedom to the press and religious tolerance. The most intractable problem was that of the Portuguese African empire which was officially regarded as an integral part of Portugal. Although the overseas possessions were of great economic value, their continued subjugation was extremely costly and required a large army to keep the various nationalist movements in check. The post-Salazar era of moderate dictatorship succeeded mainly in fomenting the frustrations felt throughout Portuguese society, and Caetano was overthrown by a military coup in April 1974. The coup was engineered by some 400 officers, largely junior in rank, and they led the revolutionary Armed Forces Movement (MFA).

The MFA was determined to take an active part in shaping the new republic, but the armed forces themselves contained disparate political tendencies. A right-wing military coup was thwarted in September 1974, and for the following year the left-wing of the MFA held sway. Elections to a national assembly were held in April 1975, but the MFA—and in particular its Supreme Revolutionary Council—had no intention of handing over power to the parties: 'We are going to have socialism in the next three to five years ... the country can choose something else afterwards.' The 1975 election was treated by the MFA as 'a pedagogic exercise', although the leading parties continued to play a part in the provisional government.

As the revolutionary mood of the Portuguese people subsided, more moderate elements in the MFA rose to power, and in its turn a left-wing military coup was scotched in November 1975. There was a general reaction against the wholesale nationalization and the sweeping land expropriations which had taken place. Moreover, the hard-line Communist Party appeared intent on instituting a state where liberal freedoms were absent: the Communist Party leader, Alvaro Cunhal, declared that there was no place in Portugal for western-style democracy. At that stage, with the country plunged into a dire economic crisis, the moderate military leaders resolved to hand over substantial power to the parties whilst at the same time preserving a political role for the armed forces.

There were two immediate consequences. One was the calling of a fresh election, held in April 1976, to determine the composition of a party government. The other was a 'constitutional agreement', drawn up between the parties and the armed forces. This provisional constitution was to be in force until 1980 when a newly-elected constituent assembly might make revisions. The leading features of the constitution included: the direct election of a president (expected to be a member of the armed forces); the setting-up of a civilian government responsible to the elected assembly *and* to the president; the formation of a 'Council of the Revolution' composed of the president, representatives of the chiefs of staff of the three services plus a number of delegates from the MFA. The function of the Council was shadowy—to 'guarantee' the democratic institutions and to preserve 'the spirit of the Revolution' of April 1974.

The two elections, for the assembly and the presidency, took place in April and June 1976 respectively. Both showed the superiority of the moderate forces: the Socialists became by far the largest party, and the new president, General Ramalho Eanes, was supported by the three leading parties and won 60.8 per cent of the popular vote. Shortly after his election, Eanes appointed the Socialist leader, Mario Soares, to be prime minister. Soares rejected all possibilities of coalition with other parties, fearing that his version of democratic socialism would be compromised. Eventually, in December 1977, his government was defeated in the assembly and thereafter he was forced into coalition with the centrist Christian Democrats. At length, in October 1978, President Eanes intervened since the coalition appeared to be inadequate to solving the continuing economic crisis. A period of non-party, 'technocratic' government followed the party stalement. (The Socialists were wary of an alignment with either the Communists or the centre-right). Resort to non-party government could presage a form of presidential rule if party coalitions cannot be sustained.

Elections to the Assembly of the Republic, April 1976

	1976		1975
	Seats	%	%
Socialists	106	35.1	37.9
Social Democrats (PSD)	71	23.9	26.4
Christian Democratic Centre	41	15.9	7.6
Communists	40	14.6	16.6
Popular Democratic Union	1	1.7	0.8
Others	0	4.0	3.7
Invalid votes	–	4.8	7.0

Notes: There was a poll of 83.3% (91.7% in 1975). In 1975 the MFA encouraged voters to return blank ballots if they did not favour party competition. 'Others' in 1976 includes six parties of the extreme left. The election in 1975 was for a constituent assembly. The Communist vote in 1975 includes 4.1% which went to its offshoot, the Democratic Movement.

Reading

A. de Figueiredo, *Portugal: Fifty Years of Dictatorship*, Penguin Books, 1975.
T. Gallagher, 'Portugal's Bid for Democracy. The Role of the Socialist Party', *West European Politics*, vol. 2/2, May 1979.
L. S. Graham, *Portugal: The Decline and Collapse of an Authoritarian Order*, Sage Publications, 1975.

R. Harvey, *Portugal: Birth of a Democracy*, Macmillan, 1978.

M. Kay, *Salazar and Modern Portugal*, Eyre and Spottiswoode, 1970.

H. Martins, 'Portugal', in *European Fascism*, op. cit.

R. Robinson, *Contemporary Portugal: A History*, Allen and Unwin, 1979.

P. C. Schmitter, *Corporatism and Public Policy in Authoritarian Portugal*, Sage Publications, 1974.

M. Soares, *Portugal's Struggle for Liberty*, Allen and Unwin, 1975.

The Sunday Times, *Portugal*, Penguin Books, 1975.

SPAIN

Spain ceased to be the leading European power in the seventeenth century and gradually lost her European possessions. In the nineteenth century there was considerable internal strife, revolution and civil war with the main protagonists the monarchists and the liberals. These conflicts were not resolved and after 1900 there was the additional cleavage of socialism, represented by a parliamentary wing and by a powerful anarchist movement. After the First World War, a succession of corrupt and incompetent governments led to a coup by General Primo de Rivera in 1923 which was accepted by the monarch, King Alfonso XIII. A period of fairly mild dictatorship then followed until 1930 when de Rivera was forced from office, and a year later the Second Republic was declared (the First Republic was a short-lived one from 1873–4). Although the change was mainly a result of growing left-wing support and militancy, the republican government that followed was primarily liberal-republican and anti-clerical, rather than socialist, and in its attempt to deal with numerous strikes and uprisings it became reactionary. Its success in dealing with disorder was nullified by the growing social discontent. Elections were held in 1936, but the results did nothing to resolve the basic social tensions. The party system was extremely fragmented, with no less than twenty identifiable party groupings represented as a result of the election. However, there were two major alignments: the Catholic and conservative National Front against the left-wing Popular Front. The government which resulted represented a victory for the republican forces, with increasing left-wing influence; both Communists and Anarchists appeared to wield greater influence in the post-election period, and there was a marked increase in civil strife, centering on the question of agrarian reform. This, together with the lack of cohesion of the party system, indicates that even without Franco's intervention, the prospects for parliamentary government were dim. The undoubted shift to the left in Spanish politics between 1931 and 1936 was regarded with foreboding by the Church hierarchy, the army, and by landed interests—about 1 per cent of the population owned half the land in Spain. The army revolt against the Republic began in July 1936 in Spanish Morocco and was led by General Franco; civil war began in earnest and continued until March 1939. Franco's dictatorship was initially influenced by the examples of German and Italian fascism and by the help he had received from these countries in winning the war.

Francoism implanted an essentially conservative, military dictatorship which left Spanish society substantially unchanged. Towards the end of his long rule Franco attempted cautious reforms: a minority of seats in the Cortes were made subject to direct election, and in 1966 an 'organic law', approved by referendum, provided for the eventual restoration of the monarchy. In 1973 a prime minister was appointed, although Franco remained head of state. When Franco died in November 1975 he was succeeded by King Juan Carlos. A period of controlled but intensive liberalization then ensued which the Falange traditionalists and military diehards were powerless to resist. Political parties were allowed free expression and the government embarked on a series of reforms culminating in the election of a constituent assembly in June 1977. The parties were in broad agreement over the nature of the parliamentary system and in particular on the desirability of retaining the constitutional monarchy. The constitutional reform proposals were submitted to a referendum in December 1978 and were approved by 87 per cent of those voting in a (low) poll of 68 per cent. That consensus cleared the way for a further election held in March 1979.

Elections to the Cortes, March 1979

	1979		1977
	Seats	%	%
Democratic Centre Union (UCD)	167	35.2	34.7
Socialists (PSOE)	120	29.4	29.2
Communists (PCE)	23	10.7	9.2
Democratic Coalition (CD)	9	5.5	8.3
Catalan Conservatives (CU)	9	2.5	3.7
Basque Nationalists (PNV)	8	1.5	1.6
Basque Extremists (HB)	3	0.9	—
National Union (UN)	1	2.0	0.3
Others	10	12.3	13.7

Notes: 'Others' includes various regional and left-wing parties. In 1979 there was a poll of 66.4 per cent (78.4 per cent in 1977). As a result of the 1979 election the UCD still failed to obtain an overall majority, but continued in office with the support of the Catalan CU.

The transition to parliamentary democracy depended critically on the cooperation of the parties—the survival of the UCD minority government from 1977 until 1979, the inter-party 'Moncloa Pact' of October 1977 as the basis for industrial peace, the widespread agreement on the form of the new constitution, and above all the positive attitude of the Communist Party towards the parliamentary system. Their willingness to work together was partly to be explained from the fear of sparking off a right-wing reaction, since neither the army nor the bureaucracy had been reformed after Franco's death, and any faltering of the democratic order might invite intervention. The problems were intensified by the regional aspirations of Catalonia and the Basque country. The measures for regional autonomy granted in the constitution were approved by large majorities in referenda held in both provinces in October 1979.

Reading

J. Amodia, *Franco's Political Legacy from Fascism to Democracy*, Allen Lane, 1977.
R. Carr (ed.), *The Republic and the Civil War in Spain*, Macmillan, 1971.
M. Gallo, *Spain under Franco*, George Allen and Unwin, 1973.
S. Giner, 'Spain', in *Contemporary Europe: Class, Status and Power*, op. cit.
R. Herr, *An Historical Essay on Modern Spain*, California University Press, 1974.
A. Hottinger, *Spain in Transition: Prospects and Policies*, Saxon House, 1975.
J. Maravall, '*Spain: Eurocommunism and Socialism*', *Political Studies*, June 1979.
J. Maravall, 'Political Cleavages in Spain and the 1979 General Election', *Government and Opposition*, Summer 1979.
K. Medhurst, 'The Military and the Prospects for Spanish Democracy', *West European Politics*, 1/1, February 1978.
K. Medhurst, *Government in Spain: The Executive at Work*, Pergamon, 1973.
S. G. Payne (ed.), *Politics and Society in Twentieth Century Spain*, Croom Helm, 1977.
B. Pollack, 'Spain: From Corporate State to Parliamentary Democracy', *Parliamentary Affairs*, Winter 1978.
P. Preston (ed.), *Spain in Crisis: The Evolution and Decline of the Franco Regime*, Harvester Press, 1976.
H. Thomas, *The Spanish Civil War*, Penguin Books, 1965.
H. Thomas, 'Spain', in *European Fascism*, op. cit.

SWEDEN

Sweden provides an example of relatively smooth political development over a long period of time. A national monarchy was established in 1523 in winning independence from the Danes, and since that time Sweden has been free from foreign domination. Apart from her one excursion as a great power in the seventeenth century, Sweden has avoided external entanglement, pursuing a policy of neutrality since 1814. The main representative institution, the Riksdag, dates from the fifteenth century, and for a period in the eighteenth century there was a strong, though not democratic, system of parliamentary government. Modern political development dates from the constitution of 1809, itself a reaction against a spell of royal absolutism. Whilst the king was given full executive power, the constitution provided a system of checks and balances; especially important were the financial powers of the Riksdag, the institution of the Ombudsman, and the open publication of public documents. However, the Riksdag itself was based on an estate system of representation with four chambers: nobility, clergy, burghers, and farmers; the first two of these were based on privilege and the whole system was quite unsuited to the development of parliamentary government. The reform of 1866 created a bicameral system, but until 1921 the upper house was based on a limited franchise of wealth and it shared full powers with the lower one. Thus in spite of the power balance given by the constitution, Swedish government was oligarchical throughout the nineteenth century. Moreover, the principle of government responsibility to a parliamentary majority was not finally established until 1917. Modern parties date from the reforms of 1866. At first the conflict was between the conservative groups of privilege and the liberals who sought a democratization of the Riksdag and parliamentary government. The Swedish Social Democrats (founded in 1889) made common cause with the Liberals, but once the franchise had been widened the Social Democrats quickly became the largest party in the lower house of the Riksdag (from 1914) and the Liberal Party declined in importance. The fourth strand in the party system was added in 1913 with the formation of the Agrarian Party (later Centre) which saw itself as a parallel to Social Democracy in protecting the interests of the farming community and for this reason has often joined forces with the Social Democrats.

After first sharing in government in 1917, the Social Democratic Party has been almost continuously in power since 1932. Early on, the party became reformist, and the class-compromise has been a feature of Swedish politics in this century. From being economically one of the most backward European states in the last century, on most counts Sweden is now the most advanced. The long period of office enjoyed by the Social Democrats has led to the development of a high 'distributive capability', in social welfare and insurance, not seriously questioned by the other parties. Fundamental constitutional reforms have taken place in recent years: a unicameral Riksdag with three instead of four-year terms, and provision to remove governments by simple majority no-confidence votes which was previously impossible. Other constitutional changes came into force in 1975 which had the effect of making the Swedish monarchy purely representative in character, and in case of government crisis the power of initiative is given to the Speaker of the Riksdag.

The 1976 election brought about a dramatic change in the political balance. After ruling for 44 years, the Social Democrats were forced out of office by an alliance of 'bourgeois' parties (Centre, Liberals, and Conservatives). Even though the coalition broke up (in 1978 on disagreement over nuclear energy policy) at the 1979 election the bourgeois bloc still held its own, outnumbering the Social Democrat-Communist alliance by a narrow (one seat) margin in the Riksdag. The important change from former years is the growing strength of the Conservatives.

Elections to the Riksdag, September 1976

| | 1979 | | 1976 | 1973 | 1970 |
	Seats	%	%	%	%
Social Democrats	154	43.5	42.7	43.6	45.3
Centre Party	64	18.2	24.1	25.1	19.9
Conservatives	73	20.4	15.6	14.3	11.5
Liberals	38	10.7	11.1	9.4	16.2
Communist Left	20	5.6	4.8	5.3	4.8
Christian Democrats	—	1.3	1.4	1.8	1.8
Others	—	0.3	0.3	0.5	0.4

Notes: Under the electoral system parties are excluded if they secure less than 4 per cent of the total vote or 12 per cent in at least one constituency. The Riksdag is elected for a three-year term. The size of the Riksdag elected in 1976 was reduced by one seat to avoid the deadlocked voting which occurred in the previous assembly—when the ties had to be decided by lot.

Reading

N. Andrén, *Modern Swedish Government*, Stockholm: Almqvist and Wiksell, 1968.

J. B. Board, *The Government and Politics of Sweden*, Boston: Houghton Mifflin, 1970.

F. G. Castles, 'The Political Functions of Organised Groups: The Swedish Case', *Political Studies*, vol. xxi/i, March 1973.

K. H. Cerny (ed.), *Scandinavia at the Polls: Recent Political Trends in Denmark, Norway and Sweden*, Washington: American Enterprise Institute, 1977.

N. Elder, 'The Swedish General Election of 1976', *Parliamentary Affairs*, Spring 1977.

N. Elder, *Government in Sweden: The Executive at Work*, Pergamon Press, 1970.

H. Hancock, *Sweden: The Politics of Post Industrial Change*, Holt, Rinehart and Winston, 1973.

R. Huntford, *Brave New Sweden*, Penguin Books, 1974.

W. Korpi, *The Working Class in Welfare Capitalism*, Routledge, 1978.

L. Lewin and others, *The Swedish Electorate 1887–1968*, Stockholm: Almqvist and Wicksell, 1973.

G. Petri and P. Vinde, *Swedish Government Administration*, Stockholm: SI-Prisma, 1978.

D. C. Rowat, op. cit., various contributors, 'Sweden's Guardians of the Law'.

B. Särlvik, 'Sweden: The Social Bases of the Parties in a Developmental Perspective', in R. Rose (ed.), *Electoral Behavior*, op. cit.

R. Scase, 'Social Democracy in Sweden', in Paterson and Thomas (eds.), *Social Democratic Parties in Western Europe*, op. cit.

N. Stjernquist, 'Sweden: Stability or Deadlock?', in *Political Oppositions in Western Democracies*, op. cit.

See also, *Scandinavian Political Studies*.

SWITZERLAND

The Swiss confederation originated in the thirteenth century as a treaty of alliance between three independent cantons. By the sixteenth century there were sixteen members, and twenty-two in 1815. For a short time after 1798, Napoleon imposed a centralized government, but the peace settlement of 1815 reintroduced the confederal form. The modern state form dates from 1848; this constitution created a federation, and a revision in 1874 further increased the powers of the federation at the expense of the cantons. In principle, the cantons are self-governing, but their area of autonomy is very limited. However, the constitutional structure is such that minority influences are given full weight. The Federal Assembly is composed of two houses with coequal powers, the National Council and the Council of States. In the latter, the twenty full cantons have two seats each and the six so-called 'half-cantons' one seat apiece;* this gives the smaller cantons, and in effect the language and religious minorities, a majority in the upper house. A second feature is that the federal government, the Federal Council, has emerged as a form of permanent collegial government, the membership so devised that its members come from different cantons, besides preserving a linguistic and religious balance. Its seven members represent a coalition of the four major parties in approximate relation to their strength in the National Council. The built-in stability is further enhanced by the fact that, although the Federal Council is 'responsible' to the Federal Assembly, it is not dismissable within its four-year term. The national referendum was introduced in 1874, and although this gives the possibility of popular challenge to federal legislation and of proposing constitutional changes, measures will only be carried if they receive a majority of votes in a majority of the cantons.

These various constitutional provisions and conventions, when added to the extreme localism of Swiss political life, help explain the coexistence of potentially divisive factors. Of approximately 5.5 million inhabitants, over 3 million are German-speaking, over 1 million French-speaking, with small minorities of Italian and Romansch. The other line of division is religious, with approximately 55 per cent Protestants and most of the remainder Roman Catholics. The intense conservatism of Swiss political life is shown by the fact that female suffrage was only finally approved by popular referendum in February 1971 by a two-to-one majority (in 1959 it had been rejected by a similar proportion); on a cantonal level the preponderantly Italian and French-speaking cantons had already given women the vote. A current stress in Swiss political and social life is the heavy reliance on a foreign labour force (mainly Italian) which accounts for a third of the whole. A referendum aimed at sharply restricting immigrant labour failed in June 1970, but the result was close: 655,000 against and 558,000 in favour, with a high referendum poll of 74 per cent. But a further referendum held on this issue in 1974 was decisively rejected by a 66 per cent vote against. Nevertheless, the federal government felt obliged to bring in several measures of its own aimed at 'stabilizing' the immigrant population.

---

* The total of twenty-six includes the new full Canton of the Jura created in 1978, meeting demands for autonomy of the Francophone minority in the Canton of Bern.

Elections in recent years have confirmed the position of the four leading parties, and parties active in the campaign to curb immigration have been notably unsuccessful. The extension of the vote to women on a federal level first in 1971—has made little difference to party fortunes.

Elections to the National Council, October 1979

	1979 Seats	1979 %	1975 %	1971 %	1967 %
Social Democrats	51	24.9	25.4	22.9	24.7
Radical Democrats	51	24.0	22.2	21.7	23.2
Christian Democrat People's Party	44	21.1	20.6	20.6	21.5
Swiss People's Party (Peasants')	23	11.5	10.1	11.1	12.2
Independents' Party (Landesring)	8	4.2	6.2	7.6	9.2
Liberal Democrats (Old Liberals)	8	2.8	2.3	2.2	2.4
Republican Movement	1	0.6	3.0	4.0	–
Party of Labour (Communists)	3	2.1	2.2	2.6	3.0
Evangelical People's Party	3	2.3	2.0	2.1	2.0
National Campaign	2	1.4	2.5	3.2	0.6
Progressive Alliance (Extreme Left)	3	2.1	1.3	–	–
Others	3	3.0	2.2	2.0	1.1

Notes: In 1979 there was a low poll, under 50% (compared with over 70% in earlier years). The first four parties listed form a permanent coalition with seats on the Federal Council in the ratio of 2:2:2:1, a proportion which has remained constant since 1959. The Christian Democrats were formerly the Catholic People's Party. The Republican Movement has ideas similar to the National Campaign against Foreign Domination of People and Homeland. 'Others' in 1979 includes one seat for the Environment Group.

Reading

B. Barber, *Freedom in the Alps*, Princeton University Press, 1974.

G. A. Codding, *The Federal Government of Switzerland*, George Allen and Unwin, 1961.

H. E. Glass, 'Consensus and Opposition in Switzerland', *Comparative Politics,* 10/3, April 1978.

H. P. Hertig, 'Party Cohesion in the Swiss Parliament', *Legislative Studies Quarterly*, 3/1, February 1978.

C. Hughes, *The Federal Constitution of Switzerland*, Oxford University Press, 1954.

C. Hughes, *The Parliament of Switzerland*, Cassell/The Hansard Society, 1962.

C. Hughes, *Switzerland*, Benn, 1975.

H. Kerr, *Switzerland: Social Cleavages and Partisan Conflict*, Sage Publications, 1974.

H. Kerr, 'The Structure of Opposition in the Swiss Parliament', *Legislative Studies Quarterly*, 3/1, February 1978.

M. Mowlam, 'Popular Access to the Decision-making Process in Switzerland', *Government and Opposition*, Spring 1979.

I. B. Rees, *Government by Community*, Charles Knight, 1971.

D. Sidjanski, 'The Swiss and Their Politics', *Government and Opposition*, Summer 1976. 1976.

J. Steinberg, *Why Switzerland?*, Cambridge University Press, 1976.

J. Steiner, *Amicable Agreement versus Majority Rule*, Oxford University Press, 1973.

THE UNITED KINGDOM

Unlike the great majority of European states, British constitutional and political development has shown a relatively peaceful evolution over several centuries, and in this respect most nearly resembles the Scandinavian countries, notably Denmark and Sweden—in all three political advance was unhindered by foreign intrusion. Unlike the other two countries, however, the British constitutional system does not stem from a particular date, has not been codified, and has the peculiarity of being quite flexible. For this reason it is necessary to refer to a number of constitutional landmarks such as: the Magna Carta of 1215, the Petition of Right (1628), the Bill of Rights (1689), the Act of Settlement (1701), and the Parliament Acts of 1911 and 1949. The net effect of these was first to create a constitutional monarchy, and later a parliamentary system of government (which by the terms of the 1911 and 1949 Acts gave legislative supremacy to the House of Commons). But much of the constitutional system has developed by means of convention rather than by statute, in particular the idea of a cabinet system of government responsible to the party with a majority in the House of Commons. Although the roots of the party system are to be found in the eighteenth century, the full acceptance of responsible and majority party government dates from the 1830s and was a natural consequence of the 1832 Reform Act; modern party politics can be said to date from that time. In spite of her early constitutional development, political democracy was a later addition; various reform acts (1867 to 1928) progressively extended the franchise, but complete adult suffrage was achieved no earlier than for many other countries.

The importance of the British pattern of development lay in the fact that (over a long period of time) basic social and political crises were resolved singly, each one dealt with before the next arose. Significantly, the shifts in power took place without the *status* of the former power-holders being undermined; the 'ascriptive' nature of British political culture aided stable evolution. In other European countries the non-resolution and accumulation of basic problems helped to multiply the points of social cleavage, and this was often accompanied by a failure to create mass parties of a non-extremist kind. The absence of multiple cleavage is shown by the nature of the British party system: for long periods only two major parties have been involved: the Conservative and Liberal parties until the First World War, Conservative and Labour thereafter. The decline of the Liberal Party from 1916 onwards was due in part to internal dissension, and probably related to this, in its failure to appeal to a sufficiently large social grouping. The Labour Party, founded in 1900, formed its first minority administration in 1924, and again from 1929 until 1931; it was able to rule for the first time as a majority party from 1945 until 1951. As a corollary to the long-term effects of Liberal decline, the Conservative Party has been in power for much of the last fifty years. It owed its strength to its pragmatic nature, its close association with the leading values of British society, and its ability to win the support of a large minority of the working-class vote. Its position was further enhanced by the unwillingness of the Labour Party to question the fundamental values with which the Conservative Party is identified; unlike most left-wing parties in Europe, the Labour Party has never passed through Marxist or anti-clerical phases. The result is an underlying consensus in British politics, epitomized in the concept of 'Opposition'. Although this tends to institutionalize political cleavage, it rests on the assumption that the party in power and the one in opposition are both geared to the smooth alternation of government; in practice, it further implies a high continuity of policy. The ready alternation of Labour and Conservative governments has been particularly marked in the post-war period; a Labour government (1945–51) was followed by Conservative governments (1951–1964), and the Labour government which then succeeded (1964–1970) in turn gave way to Conservative rule (1970–1974), Labour (1974–1979), and then to Conservative. This neat swing of the pendulum occurred through changes at general elections, not by government defeats in the House of Commons. Throughout the post-war period there has been a consolidation of policy; thus the fundamental changes initiated by Labour after 1945 (especially the measures of nationalization, provisions for social security, the process of decolonization) were all ultimately accepted by the Conservative Party.

However, the smooth pattern of the two-party system was suddenly upset in the course of the two elections held in 1974. The February 1974 election was called by Edward Heath in response to the growing trade union challenge to the Conservative Government's economic and wages policies. The election was widely seen in terms of the issue 'Who governs Britain?' and as a direct polarization between Conservative and Labour, but the electorate failed to respond in those terms—almost a quarter of the vote went to the minor parties.

The Labour Party formed a minority government under Harold Wilson, and at the following election in October 1974 Labour won a small majority in the Commons. Yet the results showed a continuing diffusion of the party system: the Labour Party had the support of only 28.6 per cent of the *electorate*, whilst the Conservatives recorded their lowest share in recent history. There was a large Liberal 'protest' vote—not translated into seats won—and the nationalist parties were very successful: the SNP took 30 per cent of the Scottish vote and the Ulster Unionists, formerly allied to the Conservatives, won 58 per cent in Northern Ireland.

Electoral disaffection with the existing party system was thus high, and the referendum on British membership of the European Community held in June 1975 (67.2 per cent in favour) also showed that voting alignments did not correspond with party lines—a feature that particularly applied to the Labour Party which, in moving substantially to the left, further estranged erstwhile supporters. The Labour Government faced additional difficulties in checking the runaway inflation which at one time posed a threat to parliamentary democracy. Forced to implement strict wage controls, the popularity of the Labour administration waned. However, under the leadership of James Callaghan (who succeeded Wilson in March 1976) a new governing style became evident. Mistrusting coalition government and not wishing to risk defeat at an early election, the Labour Government found itself forced into a minority position from April 1976 as a result of by-election losses. The period from 1976 until March 1979 can be described as one of 'stable minority government' since the Labour Party was able to survive with help from the minor parties and by means of the Lib-Lab Pact (in force from March 1977 until July 1978). Support from the nationalist parties was conditional upon the holding of referenda on the proposed Scottish and Welsh assemblies, but that alliance effectively ended when the referenda were unsuccessful. (In Scotland 32.5 per cent of the electorate was in favour and only 11.8 per cent in Wales, whereas the stipulation was that a majority consisting of at least 40 per cent of the electorate in both countries should vote for the devolution proposals.) In consequence, the Labour Government was defeated in March 1979 (by a single vote) on a no-confidence motion which made a general election inevitable.

The 1974 elections gave a multi-party look to the Commons, but the virtual annihilation of the nationalist parties and the Liberal decline restored the bi-polarity. The Conservatives, with a comfortable overall majority of seats, benefited, but Labour dropped to its lowest share of the vote in postwar years. An ideological thrust was also apparent: the Conservatives under Margaret Thatcher (who replaced Edward Heath in 1975) moved to the right whilst the Labour Party continued a leftwards drift.

Elections to the House of Commons, May 1979

| | 1979 | | 1974 Oct. | 1974 Feb. | 1970 |
	Seats	%	%	%	%
Conservatives	339	43.9	35.8	38.1	46.4
Labour	268	36.9	39.3	37.2	43.0
Liberals	11	13.8	18.3	19.3	7.4
SNP	2	1.6	2.7	2.0	1.1
Ulster Unionists	10	0.9	2.6	1.9	0.8
Plaid Cymru	2	0.4	0.6	0.6	0.5
Others	3	2.5	0.3	0.9	0.8

Notes: There was a poll of 76 per cent. The SNP is the Scottish National party; *Plaid Cymru* is the Welsh National Party. 'Ulster Unionists' includes a number of autonomous mini-parties. 'Others' includes the Speaker and one seat for the Northern Irish SDLP. The National Front won 0.6 per cent of the vote but no seats. There is little connection between a party's vote and the number of seats it wins.

Northern Ireland. The failure of the system of 'Home Rule' (introduced to Northern Ireland in 1922) to provide the means for a democratic integration for the Roman Catholic minority led to an escalation of political violence from 1968 onwards and finally to the imposition of direct rule by Britain in March 1972. A plebiscite held in March 1973 showed a high proportion of the voters (57.4 per cent) in favour of the continuing attachment to the United Kingdom. In the same month the British government put forward a number of constitutional proposals designed to overcome the bitterness between the two communities; a 'bill of rights' (itself a basic innovation) and a novel 'power-sharing' executive. The new assembly would be elected by proportional representation for a fixed four-year term and work through committees in parallel with government departments. The committee chairmen were together to form a collegial executive; the whole proposed structure was an amalgam of existing local government practice and the leading characteristics of the Swiss constitutional system.

However, the 1973 election to the new assembly gave one third of the seats to diehard 'Loyalists' bent on wrecking any parliamentary consensus. The old Ulster Unionist party fell completely under their influence and in consequence the majority Protestants effectively became identified with the loyalist intransigence. The constitutional proposals were incorporated into the Northern Ireland Constitution Act of 1973, and came into force in January 1974, Provision was also made for a 'Council of Ireland' which would bring representatives of the Republic and of Northern Ireland together to cooperate on matters of mutual concern. A meeting between representatives from the Irish Republic, Northern Ireland, and the British Government resulted in the 'Sunningdale Agreement' (December 1973) and a positive vote on the terms of this agreement by the Northern Ireland assembly in May 1974 led to direct action by the Protestants, and culminated in a general strike called by the Ulster Workers' Council. The renewed breakdown of civilian government led to the resignation of the Chief Minister (Brian Faulkner, Ulster Unionist) who anyway no longer represented the wishes of the loyalist Protestant majority. In consequence, the British Government had no alternative but once more to impose direct rule (May 1974). Previously when direct rule had been established, in 1972, political violence and terrorism emanated from the Roman Catholic IRA (Irish Republican Army) but armed Protestant groups ultimately redressed the balance of violence.

Later in 1974, a new Northern Ireland Act was passed which provided for the election of a Constitutional Convention (not a legislative body nor an assembly proper) which was supposed to work out the basis for a constitutional agreement between the various parties involved. However, the result of the election predictably gave the Loyalists a majority in the new Convention and their ingrained outlook was against *any* power-sharing solution. Indeed, the Loyalists simply wished to restore the *status quo*

ante, a reversion to Protestant dominance as in the old Stormont up to
1972. A major difference in the Northern Irish situation was that sectarian
murder had meanwhile become the normal pattern of political life. A
further important difference was that people and parties in Britain were increasingly concerned at the cost of maintaining this social catastrophe in
being: yet they could see no acceptable basis on which they could shed
their responsibility for the future of the province.

Reading

H. Berrington, 'Towards a Multi-Party Britain?', *West European Politics*, 2/1, January
1979.
A. H. Birch, *Political Integration and Disintegration in the British Isles*, Allen and
Unwin, 1977.
D. Butler and D. Kavanagh (eds.), *The British General Election of October 1974*,
Macmillan, 1976.
D. Butler and D. Stokes, *Political Change in Britain: Forces Shaping Electoral
Choice*, Macmillan, rev. ed., 1977.
C. Cook and J. Ramsden (eds.), *Trends in British Politics since 1945*, Macmillan, 1978.
H. Drucker (ed.), *Multi-Party Britain*, Macmillan, 1979.
T. Forester, *The Labour Party and the Working Class*, Heinemann, 1976.
J. Haines, *The Politics of Power*, Coronet Books, 1977.
Hansard Society, *Commission on Electoral Reform*, June 1976.
S. Haseler, *The Death of British Democracy*, Paul Elek, 1976.
V. Herman and E. Alt (eds.), *Cabinet Studies: A Reader*, Macmillan, 1975.
B. Hindess, *The Decline of Working Class Politics*, Paladin Books, 1973.
D. Howell, *British Social Democracy: A Study in Development and Decay*, Croom Helm,
1977.
N. Johnson, *In Search of the Constitution: Reflections on State and Society in Britain*,
Oxford: Pergamon, 1977.
A. King (ed.), *The British Prime Minister*, Macmillan, 1969.
A. King, *Why Britain is Becoming Harder to Govern*, BBC Publications, 1976.
R. King and N. Nugent (eds.), *The British Right*, Saxon House, 1977.
J. Mackintosh, *The British Cabinet*, Stevens, (3rd ed.), 1977.
J. Mackintosh, *The Government and Politics of Britain*, Hutchinson, (4th ed.), 1977.
C. Mellors, *The British MP: A Socio-Economic Study of the House of Commons*,
Saxon House, 1978.
P. G. Pulzer, *Political Representation and Elections in Britain*, George Allen and
Unwin, rev. ed., 1975.
R. M. Punnett, *British Government and Politics*, Heinemann, 1976 (bibliography).
R. Rose, *The Problem of Party Government*, Penguin Books, 1976.
R. Rose (ed.), *Studies in British Politics*, Macmillan, 1966 (article bibliography).
F. Stacey, *British Government, 1966–1974*, Oxford University Press, 1975.
R. Stankiewicz (ed.), *British Government in an Era of Reform*, Collier Macmillan,
1976.
P. Stanworth and A. Giddens (eds.), *Elites and Power in British Society*, Cambridge
University Press, 1974.
H. Wilson, *The Governance of Britain*, Sphere Books, 1977.
H. Wilson, *The Labour Government, 1964–1970*, Penguin Books, 1974.

NORTHERN IRELAND
D. P. Barritt and C. F. Carter, *The Northern Ireland Problem*, Oxford University
Press, 1972.

K. Boyle, T. Hadden and P. Hillgard, *Law and State: The Case of Northern Ireland*, Martin Robertson, 1975.

L. de Paor, *Divided Ulster*, Penguin Books, 1970.

R. Harris, *Prejudice and Tolerance in Ulster*, Manchester University Press, 1972.

R. J. Lawrence, *The Government of Northern Ireland*, Oxford University Press, 1965.

I. McAllister, *The Northern Ireland Social Democratic and Labour Party*, Macmillan, 1977.

C. C. O'Brien, *States of Ireland*, New York: Pantheon Books, 1973.

R. Rose, *Governing without Consensus: An Irish Perspective*, Faber and Faber, 1971.

R. Rose, *Northern Ireland: A Time of Choice*, Macmillan, 1976.

M. Wallace, *Northern Ireland: Fifty Years of Self-Government*, David and Charles, 1970.

The Sunday Times, *Ulster*, Deutsch/Penguin Books, 1972.

Parliamentary Representation in Western Europe since 1946

A Research note by Michael Smart

THE GRADUAL movement towards European integration since the Second World War has made the comparison of political trends between one country and another a subject of growing interest. For example, it is sometimes claimed that 'Europe' is moving to the left or right, or that a particular group of parties is getting stronger or weaker. The fact that such statements often contradict each other suggests a need for a measure which can show broad political movements over Europe as a whole and can also serve as a yardstick against which changes in individual countries can be assessed. This involves two main questions. Firstly, it is necessary to establish some classification of parties, however imprecise this may be because of the diversity of national conditions. Secondly, since the ratio of population to each parliamentary representative varies extremely widely between countries (from 3,000 in Iceland to over 120,000 in Western Germany), the strengths of parties represented in different national parliaments need to be weighted by population. The table below (p. 315 has been compiled on this basis so as to show the balance of political forces in Western European parliaments at a series of dates since 1946, making it possible to deduce broad trends of movement. The graph on pages 316–17 represents the data shown by the table in a somewhat simplified form.

Definition of the Area Covered

'Western Europe' comprises fifteen countries, namely, the original six EEC and the five Nordic countries, together with the UK, Ireland, Austria and Switzerland. The choice is justified by the geographical coherence of the resulting unit, and by the close political and economic relationships between most of the countries, which formed the main core of the OEEC and the Council of Europe. In addition, they all share competitive parliamentary systems in which two or more parties have always been strongly represented since the end of the war. There are also close family relationships between many of their parties, particularly on the left, facilitating a regular scheme of party classification.

Party Classification

This is based on eleven streams shown below. The streams have been defined empirically by grouping those parties which seem to have the closest resemblances. In the main, the streams represent the parties' self-images or overt historical traditions rather than any ostensibly objective criterion of support. The usefulness of such criteria in this particular context is limited both by their heterogeneity (for example, covering class, religion, economic interest and nationality) and by the difficulty of applying them to such cases as multi-class parties.[1] The resemblances tend to be closest between parties within broad geographical regions, especially the Scandinavian countries on one hand and the EEC countries on the other. Where these cannot obviously be grouped with parties outside the region (as in the case of the former agrarian parties of Scandinavia, with one exception), it seems right to leave them as a separate stream. The successive Gaullist parties offer another example of a political force in a restricted area which is sufficiently distinctive to constitute a stream on its own.

On this basis, the following streams have been identified, moving from conventional left to right:

(1) *Communist:* including such close allies as the French progressistes.

(2) *Independent Socialist:* including the French PSU, the Italian Socialist Party up to its merger with the Social Democrats (and the PSIUP subsequently), the Dutch Pacifist Socialists, and various Scandinavian groups.

(3) *Social Democratic:* in general, identical with parties affiliated to the Socialist International.

(4) *Radical:* including parties of radical, and sometimes anticlerical, tradition who commonly though not invariably ally themselves with parties on the left. The French Radicals, Italian Republicans, Dutch Democrats '66 and Danish Radical Left are in this stream.

(5) *Left Centre:* consisting of parties with a traditional largely agrarian base, which they are now attempting to broaden. These parties tend to be populist in outlook, and many find allies either on the right or the left. The stream includes the former Agrarian (now renamed Centre) parties of Norway, Sweden and Finland, the Danish Venstre, the Icelandic Progressives and also the Irish Fianna Fail.

(6) *Liberal:* traditional liberal parties often similar in outlook to conservative parties and allied with them, but sometimes finding allies on the left. These include the Italian, Belgian, Dutch, British, and Scandinavian Liberals, the German Free Democrats, and the Swiss Radical Democrats.

(7) *Centre:* including most parties with an explicitly Christian orientation. Although these are often allied with parties to the right, or effectively represent the bulk of right-wing opinion in their countries (notably in Germany, Belgium and Austria), they also often include significant left-centre elements (sometimes related to associated trade union movements), justifying a 'centre' classification separate from the Conservative stream. The French Reformists are included in this stream.

(8) *Conservative:* including the French Independents, the Dutch Anti-Revolutionary Party, the former Deutsche Partei, the Swiss Citizens' Party, the British and Scandinavian Conservatives, and the Irish Fine Gael.

(9) *Gaullist:* the UDR and its predecessors. Although generally conservative in outlook, the successive parties in this stream have pursued highly pragmatic policies, and have also included (moderately) left-wing elements, distinguishing them from the Conservative stream. However, their Centrist and Independent (Giscardien) allies are classified in the Centre and Conservative streams.

(10) *Extreme Right:* a variegated group of parties sharing a strong hostility to parties of the left and moderate right and a general refusal to co-operate with them. This stream includes the Italian Monarchists and MSI, the former Deutsche Reichspartei, the Austrian FDP (somewhat uncertainly), and also certain parties of a 'poujadist' character (in addition to the original Poujadists, the Dutch Farmers, the Finnish Rural Party and the Danish Progress Party).

(11) *Ethnic and Regional:* including the various French and Flemish parties in Belgium, the Südtiroler Volkspartei in Italy, the former Bavarian Party, the Swedish Party in Finland, and Nationalists of various types (Irish, Scottish and Welsh) in the UK Parliament.

There remain a few parties which do not clearly belong to any of the above streams, and which are put in a residual miscellaneous group. The most notable of these are the former German BHE (Refugee Party), Christian parties in Norway, Denmark and Finland, the Danish Retsforbund, and the Swiss Landesring, National Campaign, and Republican Movement.

Calculation of Party Strengths
This is based on a system of points which are awarded to each country according to its end-decade (i.e. 1950, 1960 and 1970) population as shown in the UN Demographic Yearbook. Metropolitan France has a constant weight of 200 points to which the weights of the other countries are related, subject to a minimum of three per country. For example, the faster population growth of West Germany compared with France during the 1950s raised its weight from 229 points in 1950 to 233 in 1960 and 239 in 1970. The points are distributed among the party streams represented in each country's lower house according to the number of members returned at the last general election, using the D'Hondt system (highest average). The main source of election returns is *Keesing's Archives,* except for France, where special calculations have been made of the members returned for Metropolitan France only.

Each point represents a notional unit of political strength. A party failing to win any points at all would be regarded as insignificant on the European political scene, while a party with 3 or 4 members in one of the major countries' parliaments (such as the ILP in the UK in 1945 or the

PSU in France in 1967) would win a single point and so be considered marginally significant. The minimum of three points for the smallest countries assures marginal significance in this sense for a party winning over a quarter of the seats in the Luxembourg or Iceland parliaments, and seems justified by common sense even if it slightly modifies the strict application of the population criterion.

The aggregation of the points shows the relative strength of the streams at any time throughout Western Europe. The relativity normally changes with each national election, indicating trends both in the distribution of political strength as a whole and in the relationship between particular streams. (For example, the relative strengths of Communist and Social Democratic parties may be of special interest). In the table the strengths of each party stream are shown as percentages of the total for Western Europe at the end of each year since 1965 and at certain other dates since 1946. It should be noted that the series is broken by the first post-war German elections in August 1949, the figures for 1946 representing the other fourteen countries.

For a very broad analysis of trends, it is convenient to group some of the streams together. The most appropriate groupings for this purpose seem to be: Non-Communist Left (2–4), Liberal/Left Centre (5–6) and Centre/Conservative (7–8), the remaining streams being left ungrouped. The strengths of these groupings are shown overleaf in the form of a cumulative graph, together with a note of the main national elections in each period. (For this purpose, 'main elections' are defined as those changing over 1 per cent of the total distribution of points between party streams, and so making a strong impact on the European political scene.)

Parliamentary Representation in Western Europe since 1946

Date		Com.	Ind. Soc.	Soc. Dem.	Rad.	Left Centre	Lib.	Centre	Cons.	Gaul.	Ext. Rt.	Eth. Reg.	Misc.
June	1946	13.0	5.2	31.0	2.7	2.8	4.0	23.3	14.5	—	2.0	0.5	0.8
July	1949	14.0	2.3	31.1	2.6	2.8	4.0	26.8	14.3	0.3	0.8	0.3	0.5
*Aug.	„	11.9	1.8	31.5	2.1	2.3	5.9	29.0	12.2	0.3	9.8	1.0	1.2
Dec.	1950	11.6	1.7	29.1	2.1	2.0	5.7	28.9	15.5	0.3	1.0	1.0	1.0
„	1955	8.6	2.4	27.6	2.6	1.9	4.8	27.1	17.6	3.4	2.5	0.2	1.2
„	1960	5.5	2.8	26.1	1.6	2.1	4.4	27.9	20.2	7.3	1.7	0.2	0.2
„	1965	7.4	2.8	29.9	1.9	2.1	6.0	24.8	14.3	8.9	1.2	0.4	0.2
„	1966	7.3	2.9	31.6	1.9	2.0	6.0	24.8	12.6	8.9	1.2	0.4	0.2
„	1967	8.5	3.0	31.9	2.1	2.0	6.1	24.5	12.5	7.4	1.3	0.4	0.2
„	1968	7.3	0.9	32.3	1.3	2.0	5.8	24.2	13.4	10.7	1.2	0.7	0.2
„	1969	7.3	0.9	33.2	1.3	2.1	5.0	24.1	13.4	10.7	1.2	0.7	0.2
„	1970	7.1	0.8	30.6	1.3	2.2	4.9	24.5	15.7	10.9	1.2	0.7	0.3
„	1971	7.3	0.8	31.1	1.5	2.1	4.5	24.1	15.7	10.9	1.0	1.0	0.3
„	1972	7.5	0.2	31.3	1.7	2.0	4.8	23.1	15.6	10.9	1.9	1.0	0.3
„	1973	9.0	0.3	32.8	1.5	2.1	4.5	24.0	15.4	6.8	2.2	1.0	0.7
„	1974	8.9	0.3	33.7	1.5	2.1	4.6	24.2	13.8	6.8	2.2	1.5	0.7
„	1975	9.0	0.3	33.9	1.4	2.2	4.6	24.2	13.7	6.8	2.1	1.5	0.5

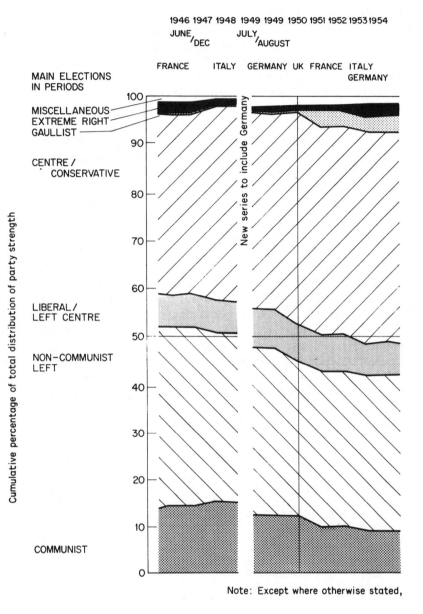

Cumulative percentage of total distribution of party strength

1946 1947 1948 1949 1949 1950 1951 1952 1953 1954
JUNE/DEC   JULY/AUGUST

FRANCE   ITALY   GERMANY   UK   FRANCE   ITALY
                                          GERMANY

MAIN ELECTIONS
IN PERIODS

MISCELLANEOUS
EXTREME RIGHT
GAULLIST

CENTRE /
    CONSERVATIVE

New series to include Germany

LIBERAL /
LEFT CENTRE

NON–COMMUNIST
LEFT

COMMUNIST

Note: Except where otherwise stated,

1955 1956 1957 1958 1959 1960 1961 1962 1963 1964 1965 1966 1967 1968 1969 1970 1971 1972 1973 1974 1975

GERMANY
FRANCE   FRANCE GERMANY FRANCE ITALY UK   UK FRANCE ITALY   UK   ITALY FRANCE
                                                            FRANCE   UK

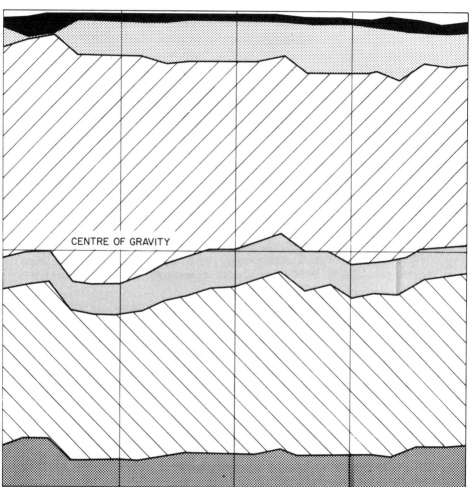

CENTRE OF GRAVITY

the dates refer to the situation at the end of the year

Commentary

The table shows that the Social Democratic and Centre streams have always been by far the largest, accounting between them for well over half the total distribution of party strength. The Social Democratic stream has usually been appreciably stronger, although it was overtaken between 1958 and 1961 by the Centre stream, reflecting the heavy Socialist defeat in the 1958 French elections. The Conservative stream has always come third, while the Communist and Gaullist streams have alternated in the fourth place. The only other stream to have won over 5 per cent of the total at any time since 1948 has been the Liberals, the other streams falling well below that level.

Fluctuations in the minor streams make it easiest to assess the long-term trends from the graph, where the groupings smooth out swings of support between (for example) the Centre and Conservative streams in France and Germany, or the effects of the changing patterns of the Italian Socialist parties. The graph also provides a more representative overall coverage, at some cost in precision, because of the many cases where an individual stream is not represented in a particular country (e.g. Conservatives in Germany, Italy and Belgium, Centre in the UK), whereas grouping permits broad comparability over Europe as a whole. On this basis, the main trends over the post-war years appear to be:

(1) A slight rise in Communist support up to 1948, followed by a declining trend until 1960; then a modest recovery, accelerating with the French elections of 1973.

(2) A fairly steady decline in the strength of the non-Communist Left until 1960. Successes in Britain, Germany and elsewhere produced a strong recovery up to 1967, which was reversed by defeats in France and Britain and then resumed more gradually after 1970.

(3) Liberal and Left Centre parties showed a gradual decline during the 1950s, recovering in the early 1960s and then declining again until 1971, since when they have held their ground.

(4) Centre and Conservative parties showed a strong rising trend of support up to 1960, when they accounted between them for nearly half the total distribution of party strength. Their support then fell sharply up to 1967, reflecting losses both to Gaullism and to parties on the left, and has since then been generally stable.

A notional centre of gravity can be traced by following the 50 per cent line on the graph. This shows the centre, initially located in the non-Communist Left, moving right to the Liberal parties with the German elections of 1949, and further right to the Centre-Conservative grouping with the German and Italian elections of 1953. The British election of 1964 moved the centre of gravity back to the Liberal parties, who lost it to the Centre/Conservative stream with the French elections of 1968, but regained it with the French elections of 1973.

Conclusion

The analysis supports the empirical observation that political movements in one European country are often mirrored in a number of others. Among the large number of elections during the period covered (averaging nine per country), very few show a movement strongly against the trend noted over the five-year cycle of elections in which they occur. Where a particular national election appears to be at variance with the preceding trend (e.g., the French elections of 1958 and 1968), it is likely to represent a turning point, and so to be followed by elections in other countries showing the same tendency. Many of the causal factors at work no doubt reflect specific conditions in particular countries, which are not (or only coincidentally) found in others. But some factors may be common to a number of countries, suggesting at least partial explanations of parallel political changes. For example, it may be suggested that the electoral fortunes of Communist Parties throughout Western Europe have been strongly affected by the policies of the Soviet Union and Western reactions to them; or that parties of the Extreme Right, and perhaps also ethnic and regional parties, have done best in conditions of political and economic instability; or that the successes and failures at different times of the movement towards European integration have affected support for the parties most committed to it. The analysis can provide a frame of reference within which these and other possible explanations of general political trends can be tested by more detailed research.

At the same time, it is necessary to emphasise the limitations of this, and perhaps of any, method of quantitative comparison between countries.[2] Apart from the approximate nature of the classification of political streams, the fact that many of them are represented in only a few countries precludes any precise comparison of the general movement with that in particular countries such as could normally be made in the regional analysis of a national election. (However, the rise of the Scottish and Welsh Nationalists has produced similar complications in the analysis of British elections). Moreover, variations in national electoral systems may give an exaggerated impression of the underlying movements of opinion in countries which do not have proportional representation, notably the UK and France since 1958. A complementary analysis based on votes cast in national elections could thus prove instructive, although methodological problems could arise on account of differences in the basis of the franchise and also in turn-out both between countries and within countries over time.[3] However, parliamentary representation has a more obviously direct effect on the composition of governments and the process of political decision making, and may therefore be regarded as a major political indicator deserving study and analysis in its own right.

Finally, the analysis illustrates the general durability of established political traditions, and the consequent pattern of overall stability, observed in pages 318–19. For this reason, the short term trends noted on page 319 may be seen largely as swings of the pendulum over the middle ground, altering the composition of governments to a disproportionate extent, but in large measure reversed on the next cycle of elections. (In any case, the largest shift recorded in any five-year period, between 1960 and 1965, affected only 9 per cent of the total distribution between groupings). The small amount of long term movement may be shown by comparing the present distribution of strength by main groupings with that which obtained in 1951, a suitable base year when the second wave of post-war elections had been completed:

Date	Comm.	Non-Comm Left	Lib/Left Centre	Centre/ Cons	Gaul	Ext. Right	Misc.
Dec 1951	9.4	33.1	7.5	43.4	3.4	1.0	2.1
Dec 1975	9.0	35.6	6.8	37.9	6.8	2.1	2.0
Change 1951–75	−0.4	+2.5	−0.7	−5.5	+3.4	+1.1	−0.1

The long term shift (represented by the sum of the positive changes) was only 7.0 per cent, representing advances by the Gaullist, Non-Communist Left and Extreme Right streams, mainly at the expense of the Centre/ Conservative grouping. Although this movement of course concealed much larger proportionate changes in a number of individual countries, it is remarkable that no main political tendency, except perhaps for the relatively volatile Gaullists, was decisively stronger or weaker in the whole European scene than it had been a generation earlier.

Notes.

1. The diversity of European party systems is discussed at length by S. M. Lipset and S. Rokkan in *Party Systems and Voter Alignments,* New York: Collier-Macmillan, 1967.

2. A review of the first edition of this book draws attention to these limitations, but does not in my view disprove the use of the analysis as one indicator, among many others, of the extent of political change (see Derek W Urwin and Kjell A Eliassen, 'In search of a continent: the quest of comparative European politics', *European Journal of Political Research,* March 1975).

3. Such an analysis was in fact published in *The Economist* on 29 November, 1975 (pp 16–19, 'Who will rule Europe in 1995 ?') The analysis, which is taken back to 1935, shows a pattern of movement over the post-war period broadly similar to that presented in this note.

Country Index

General Index

Adams, J. C., 63n, 226, 237n
Administrative Theory, administrative approach to politics, 189–90
administrative law, 115, 200–2
administrative specialization, 180
'*cabinet* system', 179
decentralization and deconcentration, 207–8
dual and fused hierarchies, 225 (diagram), 236n
'parallel hierarchies', 177
policy-agency separation, 179, 191
rational-legal authority, 102, 180
superimposed hierarchies, 178
See also, Bureaucracy, Territorial Aspects.
Allardt, E., 47, 210
Almond, G. A., 6, 38, 50, 51, 123n, 189, 203n
Anderson, M., 236n
Andreski, S., 191
Aron, R., 5
Assemblies, 109–114, 152–173
committee systems, 163–70
communications, 154, 171–3
controls on governments, 153–4, 197–200
decline in powers, 152–5
duration of terms, 155–7
elective functions, 154, 155–9
personnel functions, 154, 159–64
policing function, 197–200
and power of dissolution, 152, 155–6
Question Time, 198–9
rule functions, 154, 164–71
second chambers, 170–1
and socialization, 162–3
symbolic and legitimizing powers, 153, 172
techniques of control, 153–5, 197–9
See also, Opposition, Parliamentary Government.
Avril, P., 25, 203n

Barile, P., 63n, 226, 237n
Barrington Moore, J., 126, 148n
Barry, B., 7
Bendix, R., 102, 203n
Berlin, I., 7
Birnbaum, N., 30

Blondel, J., 12, 33, 37n, 74, 121, 172, 174n, 190, 195, 200, 204n, 236n
Board, J. B., 63n
Bottomore, T. B., 203n
Briggs, A., 188
Brzezinski, Z. K., 148n
Bureaucracy, 176–91
conditions for independent power, 190
constitutional bureaucracy, 176, 180–4
in the EEC, 243
'fallacy of aggregation', 190
historical contrasts, 180–3
and interest representation, 50, 51, 54, 59
and politics, 84, 163, 177–80, 182–4, 203n
public attitudes towards, 189
representative bureaucracy, 51, 191
and technocratic power, 190–1
in totalitarian states, 127, 177
Weber's ideal-type, 184, 203n
See also, Administrative Theory, Civil Service.
Buchan, A., 259n
Butler, D., 23, 36, 47n, 62n

Calleo, D., 241
Carey, J. P. and A. G., 149n
Carter, M., 123n
Castles, F. G., 62
Chapman, B., 180, 181, 186, 202n, 204n
Christian Democracy, 18, 24, 31, 46, 87
definition, 45
See also, individual country entries.
Civil Services,
centralization and decentralization, 184–5
conditions of service, 184
and educational systems, 185–9
entry and training, 184–9
and government membership, 163, 182
and parliamentary control, 197–9
social origins, 187–9
See also, Administrative Theory, Bureaucracy.
Communications, as assembly function, 154, 171–3
and European integration, 258
in local government, 222
nature of political communication, 258–9

339